The Origins of Major War

A volume in the series

CORNELL STUDIES IN SECURITY AFFAIRS

edited by Robert J. Art, Robert Jervis, and Stephen M. Walt

A list of titles in this series is available at
www.cornellpress.cornell.edu.

The Origins of Major War

DALE C. COPELAND

Cornell University Press

ITHACA AND LONDON

First published 2000 by Cornell University Press
First printing, Cornell Paperbacks, 2001

Library of Congress Cataloging-in-Publication Data

Copeland, Dale C.
  The origins of major war / Dale C. Copeland.
    p. cm. — (Cornell studies in security affairs)
  Includes bibliographical references and index.
  ISBN 978-0-8014-3750-2 (cloth : alk. paper)
  ISBN 978-0-8014-8757-6 (pbk. : alk. paper)
    1. World War, 1914–1918—Causes. 2. World War, 1939–1945—Causes. 3. Balance of power. 4. International relations. 5. Military history, Modern. I. Title. II. Series.

D511 .C626   2000
940.3'11—dc21
                                                                00-024040

Cornell University Press strives to use environmentally responsible suppliers and materials to the fullest extent possible in the publishing of its books. Such materials include vegetable-based, low-VOC inks and acid-free papers that are recycled, totally chlorine-free, or partly composed of nonwood fibers. For further information, visit our website at www.cornellpress.cornell.edu.

Cloth printing   10 9 8 7 6 5 4 3 2 1
Paperback printing   10 9 8 7 6 5

Contents

For my parents,
Barbara E. Copeland and Clare G. Copeland

Acknowledgments

The development of this book has a long history, and I am greatly indebted to many teachers, colleagues, and institutions. I am particularly grateful to three scholars at the University of Chicago: Stephen Walt, John Mearsheimer, and Charles Lipson. They offered penetrating insights at every turn and kept me focused on the goal. Their generous and constant support will always be appreciated. Robert Art at the Cornell Studies in Security Affairs was everything one could want in a reviewer and scholarly editor. His comprehensive comments had a significant impact on the final product. I also thank two reviewers for Cornell University Press for their detailed and useful comments. One of the reviewers, who revealed himself to be Stephen Van Evera, also provided much food for thought for future projects. I must also thank Charles Doran and George Liska of Johns Hopkins University for first inspiring me to investigate dynamic realist approaches to the origins of major war.

Colleagues provided trenchant criticisms and observations at crucial points in the book's development: Michael Barnett, Eric Budd, Michael Desch, John Duffield, Matthew Evangelista, James Fearon, Ben Frankel, Charles Glaser, Hein Goemans, Gary Herrigel, Ted Hopf, Alastair Iain Johnston, Chaim Kaufmann, Andrew Kydd, David Laitin, Melvyn Leffler, Jeffrey Legro, Jack Levy, Allen Lynch, Sean Lynn-Jones, Benjamin Miller, Andrew Moravcsik, Sharon Morris, Ido Oren, John Owen, Scott Sagan, Len Schoppa, Herman Schwartz, Randall Schweller, Jack Snyder, Michael Spirtas, Jennifer Sterling-Folker, Ashley Tellis, Marc Trachtenberg, Daniel Verdier, David Waldner, and Alexander Wendt. I also thank Spencer Bakich, Eric Cox, Kelly Erickson, Mark Haas, and Dennis Smith, graduate students at the University of Virginia, for comments that helped me to hone the final argument. Mario Feit and Scott Woodard assisted me in the translations of German documents.

Financial support from various institutions was instrumental in bringing this project to fruition. A postdoctoral fellowship at Harvard University's Center for Science and International Affairs offered a stimulating environment to do research on additional cases. I am also grateful to Samuel Huntington and Stephen Rosen of Harvard's Olin Institute for Strategic Studies at the Center for International Affairs for including me in the Institute's activities as a research associate. The writing of the manuscript was generously supported by the following institutions: the John D. and Catherine T. MacArthur Foundation; the Andrew W. Mellon Foundation; the Phoenix and Century Fellowships at the University of Chicago; the Social Sciences and Humanities Research Council of Canada; and the Sesquicentennial Fellowship at the University of Virginia.

Portions of chapters 1 and 8 appeared as "Neorealism and the Myth of Bipolar Stability: Toward a New Dynamic Realist Theory of Major War" in a special issue on realism of *Security Studies* 5, no. 3 (spring 1996). I thank Frank Cass Publishers for permission to use the material here. I also thank Roger Haydon of Cornell University Press for his unflagging support and valuable editorial suggestions.

Finally, I am deeply grateful to three individuals who made this book possible. Natasha E. Copeland kept up my confidence during the long months of writing, offered insightful comments, and ensured that I never lost sight of the world beyond my word processor. I dedicate this work to my parents, Barbara E. and Clare G. Copeland, who sparked my interest in politics at an early age and encouraged me to pursue my dreams. I cannot thank them enough.

D. C. C.

Charlottesville, Virginia

Abbreviations for Primary
Documents / Source Material

World War I

BD   *British Documents on the Origins of the War*, 11 vols. London: His Majesty's Stationary Office, 1926–38.

CDD   *Collected Diplomatic Documents Relating to the Outbreak of the European War*. London: Fischer Unwin, 1915.

DD   *Die Deutschen Dokumente zum Kriegsausbruch*, collected by Karl Kautsky, Max Montegalas, and Walther Schucking, eds. *The Outbreak of the World War*, trans. Carnegie Endowment for International Peace. New York: Oxford University Press, 1924.

DDF   *Documents Diplomatiques Français (1871–1914)*, Third Series, 11 vols. Paris: Imprimerie Nationale, 1929–36.

GP   *Die Grosse Politik der europäischen Kabinette, 1871–1914*, 39 vols. Berlin: Deutsche Verlagsgesellschaft für Politik und Geschichte, 1922–27.

ÖA   *Österreich-Ungarns Aussenpolitik von der Bosnischen Krise 1908 dis zum Kriegsausbruch 1914*, 8 vols. Vienna: Österreichischer Bundesverlag, 1930.

World War II

DGFP   *Documents on German Foreign Policy, 1918–1945*, Series C

[ix]

and D. Washington, D.C.: U.S. Department of State, 1933–37, 1937–45.

KTB   *Generaloberst Halder: Kriegstagebuch*, 3 vols., ed. Hans-Adolf Jacobsen. Stuttgart: Kohlhammer, 1962–64.

IMT   *Trial of the Major War Criminals before the International Military Tribunal*, 42 vols. Nuremberg, 1947–49.

NCA   *Nazi Conspiracy and Aggression*, 8 vols., supplementals A and B. Washington, D.C.: U.S. GPO, 1946.

NDR   *Nazism, 1919–1945: A Documentary Reader*, ed. J. Noakes and G. Pridham, 3 vols. Exeter: University of Exeter, 1983–88.

OKW KTB   *Kriegstagebuch des Oberkommandos der Wehrmacht*, ed. Hans-Adolf Jacobsen. Frankfurt: Bernard und Graefe, 1965.

Cold War

APWASU   *America's Plans for War against the Soviet Union, 1945–1950*, 15 vols. New York: Garland, 1989.

CIA (CC)   *CIA Documents on the Cuban Missile Crisis*. Washington, D.C.: CIA, 1992.

CWIHP   Cold War in International History Project. Washington, D.C.

CWIHPB   *Cold War in International History Project Bulletin*, Issues 1–11. Washington, D.C., 1992–1998.

DAPS   *Containment: Documents on American Policy and Strategy*, ed. Thomas Etzold and John Lewis Gaddis. New York: Columbia University Press, 1978.

FRUS   *Foreign Relations of the United States*. Washington, D.C.: U.S. GPO, various years.

ISR   *Nuclear Diplomacy and Crisis Management: An "International Security" Reader*, ed. Sean M. Lynn-Jones, Steven E. Miller, and Stephen Van Evera. Cambridge: MIT Press, 1990.

JFKL   John F. Kennedy Library.

JFKL NSF   John F. Kennedy Library, National Security Files.

KR   *Khrushchev Remembers,* trans. and ed. Strobe Talbott. New York: Little, Brown, 1971.

KR: GT   *Khrushchev Remembers: The Glasnost Tapes,* trans. and ed. Jerrold Schecter with Vyacheslav Luchkov. New York: Little, Brown, 1990.

KR: LT   *Khrushchev Remembers: The Last Testament,* trans. and ed. Strobe Talbott. Boston: Little, Brown, 1974.

KT   *The Kennedy Tapes: Inside the White House during the Cuban Missile Crisis,* ed. Ernest R. May and Philip D. Zelikow. Cambridge: Harvard University Press, 1997.

LC   Library of Congress.

NA   United States National Archives.

NSA (*BC*)   National Security Archive, *The Berlin Crisis, 1958–1962.* Alexandria: Chadwyck-Healey, 1991, microfiche.

NSA (*CC*)   National Security Archive, *The Cuban Missile Crisis, 1962.* Alexandria: Chadwyck-Healey, 1990, microfiche.

NSA (CMCR)   National Security Archive, Cuban Missile Crisis Releases (documents stored at National Security Archive, Washington, D.C., collected after 1990).

NSA (DOS CMCR)   National Security Archive, Department of State Cuban Missile Crisis Releases (documents stored at National Security Archive, Washington, D.C., collected after 1990).

NSA (*DR*)   *The Cuban Missile Crisis, 1962: A National Security Archive Documents Reader,* ed. Lawrence Chang and Peter Kornbluh. New York: New Press, 1992.

NSA (*SE*)   National Security Archive, *The Soviet Estimate: U.S. Analysis of the Soviet Union, 1947–1991.* Alexandria: Chadwyck-Healey, 1995, microfiche.

Introduction

Why do major wars occur? Why do international systems move from relative calm to the point where states either initiate system-wide wars or take actions that risk such wars? Since Thucydides, the puzzle of major war has been one of the most important but intractable questions in the study of international relations. Historians tend to view the causes of major war as unique to each case: Hannibal's need for revenge pushed him to attack Rome in 218 B.C.; religious differences between Protestant and Catholic states drove the Thirty Years War (1618–48); Napoleon's charges across Europe reflected his egomania and his lust for power; states stumbled into war in 1914 for fear that others would strike first; Nazi ideology and Hitler's personality caused the Second World War.

This book does not reject the unique aspects of such complicated cases. Instead, it poses this question: Is there a common cause of major wars across the millennia? Many international relations scholars will argue, along with historians, that cases across diverse historical periods must be treated as essentially unique. Cultures and ideas change over time, while the technological and social bases for polities shift. Thus, we should not expect the causes of the First World War or the Second World War to have any necessary relation to the causes of war in the ancient Greek and Roman systems or in early modern Europe. For many, perhaps the only thing common across these cases is "bad thinking": leaders acting from ignorant, misguided, or evil views about the way things are or the way they should be.[1]

The realist tradition approaches the question of major war from a different starting point. For realists, there is one factor that cuts across all these wars, one factor that drives states regardless of their particular characteristics: in a word, *power*. All great powers in history (apart from a few universal empires) have had to worry about their power positions relative to oth-

[1]

ers. This simple fact has allowed realists to construct general statements about the origins of major war that transcend time and space. Three main realist theories dominate the debate. For classical realism, since balances of power deter aggression, major wars are likely only when one state possesses a preponderance of power. Neorealism accepts this point, but emphasizes that bipolar systems are likely to be more stable than multipolar ones, mainly because bipolarity forces states to be more conscious about maintaining the balance of power. Hegemonic stability theory rejects the classical realist hypothesis. Equality between states is dangerous, since rising and near-equal states will attack to gain the status and rewards denied by the established order. Systems are stable, therefore, only when there is one very large state to keep the peace.

Each of these theories faces some important empirical anomalies. Classical realism cannot explain why war would break out in the three bipolar cases before the nuclear age—Sparta-Athens in 431 B.C., Carthage-Rome in 218 B.C., and France-Hapsburgs in 1521. In each case, there was a rough equality between the two great powers, not a preponderance on one side. War in 1914 is also a puzzle for classical realists because power was roughly balanced between the two alliance blocs. Neorealism not only falls short in explaining war in bipolar cases, but it provides an incomplete argument for war in multipolar situations. The First World War, as we will see, was not a war of miscalculation, as many neorealists assert. Instead, Germany wanted war and drove the system to it. Neorealists also have difficulty providing a primarily power-driven argument for conflicts such as the Second World War and the Napoleonic Wars, and thus often focus on the personal and ideological motives of key leaders.

Hegemonic stability theory is the most problematic of the three. Contrary to its predictions, in five of the six major wars that began in conditions of multipolarity from 1600 to 1945, war was brought on by a state with marked military superiority. Moreover, in every one of the thirteen major wars or major crises across the ten historical periods covered in this book, conflict was initiated by a state fearing decline. This challenges the hegemonic stability assertion that rising states are typically the instigators of conflict.

In this book I seek to overcome the weaknesses of the three main theories by synthesizing their strengths into an alternative, dynamic realist theory of major war. The existing theories are compelling but incomplete. Classical realism and neorealism rightly stress the importance of power differentials and polarity. Some versions of both theories also consider dynamic trends in relative power—in particular, the problem of declining power and the incentive it gives for preventive war. Yet the differing impact of relative decline in bipolar versus multipolar systems has not been adequately studied. Moreover, the more dynamic versions of classical realism and neorealism have not fully specified the conditions under which decline will lead states to war, to peace, or to something in between. Hegemonic stability theory captures the significance of power trends. By focusing on the rising state, however, the theory misses a basic logical point: rising states should want to avoid war while they are still rising, since by waiting they can fight later with more power.

The theory laid out in this book—what I call dynamic differentials theory—brings together power differentials, polarity, and declining power trends into one cohesive logic. It shows that major wars are typically initiated by dominant military powers that fear significant decline, although, as I explain shortly, polarity places important constraints on this rule. The theory also explains why states might take steps short of war—such as initiating crises or hard-line containment policies—that nonetheless greatly increase the risk of an inadvertent escalation to major war. Most theories treat states as having a dichotomous choice: they either initiate major wars, or they do not. This approach limits the theories' applicability to the modern age of costly warfare. In particular, when both sides have nuclear weapons, states are unlikely to launch premeditated major wars, given the likelihood that their own societies will be destroyed in the process. Yet, leaders understand that they might still fall into war owing to incentives to preempt in a crisis or to the commitment of their reputations. To make a theory of major war relevant to the nuclear era, as well as to the pre-nuclear era, we must explain why states would move from peaceful engagement to a destabilizing cold war rivalry, or from such a rivalry into crises with the type of risks witnessed in the Cuban missile crisis. This book offers such a theory.

THE SIGNIFICANCE OF THE ISSUE

Major wars are wars that are characterized by three attributes: all the great powers in a system are involved; the wars are all-out conflicts fought at the highest level of intensity (that is, full military mobilization); and they contain a strong possibility that one or more of the contending great powers could be eliminated as sovereign states. The centrality of the issue is clear: major wars are devastating, as well as system-changing. In the modern world of nuclear weapons, another major war between the great powers could be the last. Although many scholars are confident that major wars are a thing of the past, such optimism is premature. A similar and pervasive optimism continued for more than a decade after the First World War. After 1945, many were surprised that the horrors of the Second World War did not prevent the superpowers from falling into a dangerous cold war. As a new century begins, the rise of China under leaders opposed to U.S. hegemony entails the risk of a new cold war. Such a cold war could produce crises with the intensity of the Berlin crisis of 1961 or the Cuban missile crisis of October 1962. Recent revelations about the great risks of superpower war during these crises make avoidance of another cold war a critical policy issue. Underlying the theoretical and historical work in this book, therefore, is a highly practical objective. By understanding the conditions that push states into the rivalries and crises that can lead to major war, we can take steps to mitigate these conditions.

The study of major war also has a number of side benefits for international relations scholarship. Avoiding major war is a universal obsession of great powers, one that affects almost every aspect of their foreign policies. Properly specified theories of major war thus lead to predictions of why states participate in arms races or pursue arms control agreements, why they form alliances, and why they choose deterrence or reassurance strategies to deal with rivals. Accordingly, investigating the origins of major wars is a crucial point of departure in the development of stronger general theories of international politics.[2]

THE ARGUMENT

This book's argument starts with a basic point drawn from the literature on preventive war: states in decline fear the future. They worry that if they allow a rising state to grow, it will either attack them later with superior power or coerce them into concessions that compromise their security. Even if they are confident that the rising state is currently peaceful, they will be uncertain about its future intentions. After all, minds change, leaders are replaced, and states have revolutions that change their core values and goals. Consequently, states facing decline, if only out of a sense of far-sighted prudence, will contemplate war as one means to uphold their future security.

Decline, however, is a pervasive phenomenon in international relations. Yet major wars, or crises that risk major war, are quite rare. The mere fact of decline is clearly not enough; other systemic conditions must be added to explain these conflicts. The first and most obvious condition is power differentials. Declining states with little power will not risk major war. To paraphrase Bismarck, to provoke such a war would be to commit suicide for fear of death. Hence, we would expect only states at the top of the power hierarchy to contemplate actions that might cause a major war.

Yet polarity and the size of the differentials of power also matter. Decline in a multipolar system is likely to lead to major war only if one state is significantly superior in military power, such that it can take on the system. The declining state in multipolarity cannot expect to fight a war against the rising state alone; the other great powers will likely align against the de-

[4]

clining state's attack, since they fear being its next victim. Even when no coalition is expected, however, a declining state only equal to the others in military power must fear long and costly bilateral wars. Such wars, even if victorious, would so reduce the attacker's strength relative to states that remain on the sidelines that initiating war is inherently irrational. In bipolarity, however, the declining great power has to defeat only one other state. Moreover, it does not have to worry about third parties rising to the top by sitting on the sidelines. Hence it can think about fighting a major war even if only essentially equal to the rising state in relative military power. The conditions for the outbreak of major war in multipolarity are therefore less permissive than they are in bipolarity: major war in multipolarity requires a significantly superior state, whereas major war can occur in bipolarity if the declining state is either superior or only equal (indeed, it might even be somewhat inferior).

Combining declining trends, polarity, and power differentials is still not enough to explain the full range of cases. A declining state, even when militarily superior, will not jump into preventive war at the first sign of decline. After all, major wars are highly risky ventures, and the decline may be just a small "blip" in an otherwise stable situation. Two aspects of its decline will be of utmost importance to the declining state's calculus: the depth of decline—how far the state will fall before it bottoms out; and the inevitability of decline—the degree of certainty that the state will fall if it sticks with current policies.

The question of the depth and inevitability of decline forces leaders to examine three general forms of decline. The first is the one analyzed by hundreds of scholars, namely, decline caused by the deterioration of a state's economic, technological, and social base relative to other states. Many reasons for such decline have been identified. The techniques and tools that once sustained a state's superiority may be diffusing outward; the citizens may be increasingly complacent, focusing on consumption over investment in future production; the state may be facing diseconomies of scale as it grows past a certain size (the S-shaped growth curve); and so forth.[3] I refer to this ubiquitous form of decline as "entrenched relative stagnation." States facing such stagnation will, of course, struggle to overcome it through a variety of internal reform measures. Yet it may be difficult to reverse. The more difficult the task, the more the leaders will expect decline to be deep and inevitable, and thus the more likely they will be to consider preventive war or risky crisis policies. By 1618–19, for example, two decades of economic stagnation pushed Spain to take actions that escalated a local German conflict into the devastating Thirty Years War.

The second form of decline is much less studied, but typically even more problematic. This comes about when a state is strong in relative military power but is inferior in two other types of power: economic power and potential power. Economic power is simply a state's total relative economic activity (measured, say, by GNP). Potential power includes all the capital and resources, both physical and human, that could be eventually translated into measurable economic output, but have not yet been so translated for whatever reasons. Potential power would thus include such things as population size, raw materials reserves, technological levels, educational development, and unused fertile territory. A declining state superior in military power, but inferior in the other two forms of power will tend to be very concerned about the future. Simply put, the rising state has a huge long-term advantage: it possesses a far larger base for military growth, and to become preponderant, all it has to do is sit and wait. Increased arms spending by the declining state will not solve the problem. The rising state is better equipped for an arms race over the long haul; indeed, by trying to run such a race, the declining state will only further undermine its economy. In such a situation, then, the declining state is more likely to believe that decline will be deep and inevitable, and to see preventive war as perhaps its only hope. This, as we shall see, was Germany's dilemma vis-à-vis Russia twice in the past century.

The third form of decline is also underplayed by scholars. This is the problem of power oscillations: the military and geopolitical decline caused by the short-term relative success of the other state's arms-racing and alliance-building policies. Both great powers in a rivalry may be making every effort within their spheres to keep up with the other. Over the near term, however, one side's policies may simply prove more successful, or may be expected to be so. This creates the prospect of a loss in relative power, which, if left unchecked, will leave the declining state in a temporarily vulnerable position.[4] To avoid this situation, the declining state may begin to favor hard-line actions that risk major war. As we shall see, such power oscillations were particularly problematic during the early cold war, leading to crises over Berlin and Cuba.

As I noted, to make a theory of major war equally relevant to the nuclear age, we need to be able to explain not only when a state will deliberately initiate war, but also when it will take steps that greatly increase the risk of such a war through inadvertent means. To tackle this issue, this book builds a decision-making model that presumes leaders understand both the upsides and downsides of hard-line and soft-line policies. In particular, leaders are aware of three key risks: the risk of losing any war that their state starts; the risk of continued decline if they choose accommodative policies; and the risk that hard-line actions short of war, designed to overcome decline, can provoke an inadvertent escalation to major war. Because of the first risk, states in decline will see preventive major war as an option of last resort. If shifting to harder-line policies such as increased arms spending and crisis initiation can mitigate decline, these policies will gen-

[6]

erally be preferred. Yet leaders, in adopting such policies, must weigh the long-term benefits of averting decline against the near-term risk of causing an inadvertent slide into war. All things being equal, therefore, they will try to avoid more severe policies if less severe policies can be expected to maintain their state's power position.

This logic, elaborated in chapter 2, allows us to predict when declining states will shift to harder-line actions that risk an inadvertent slide into major war. They will do so when previous (softer-line) policies are insufficient to reverse decline, but when upping the ante holds out the promise of stabilizing the power trends. In 1945, for example, Washington moved from engagement to containment of the Soviet Union in order to restrict Soviet postwar growth. In doing so, Harry Truman understood that he would likely spark a dangerous cold war spiral; yet not acting would have greatly damaged America's long-term power position. In October 1962, John F. Kennedy initiated a crisis over Cuba to compel Nikita Khrushchev to remove Soviet missiles from the island. The risks of inadvertent war were clear, but Kennedy felt that if he did not act, U.S. security would be directly threatened.

The argument here builds on balance-of-power thinking integral to both classical realism and neorealism—states take actions to sustain their current position in the strategic power balance. I contribute to this thinking in the following way. As chapter 2 discusses, realist theorists remain divided: some focus on the importance of maintaining the power balance and avoiding decline; others emphasize the security dilemma and the risks of provoking spiraling by overly hostile actions.[5] My argument *combines* the risks of decline and the risks of inadvertent spiraling into one model. The model can thus show the rational trade-offs that states make when they have to decide on the relative severity of their foreign policies. This book, in short, does not introduce new causal variables. Rather, it synthesizes the various strands of current realist approaches into a more integrated realist argument that explains when major wars are likely to occur and when states will take steps that risk such wars.

THE EVIDENCE

This book covers ten periods of history that led either to major wars or to cold wars and crises that carried great risks of major war. Given the availability of documentary evidence, the main focus of the empirical analysis is on three twentieth-century periods: two multipolar (the periods before the First and Second World Wars), and one bipolar (the early cold war up to the Cuban missile crisis). Through an in-depth examination of the primary documents, I seek to provide a parsimonious explanation that challenges the standard interpretations of events. Notwithstanding some clear differences (to be addressed) between the First and Second World Wars, both conflicts were rooted in a common cause: the German fear of the rise of Russia, a state with three times Germany's population and forty times its land mass. This marked inferiority in potential power led German civilian and military leaders to one conclusion: unless strong action was taken, an industrializing Russia would inevitably overwhelm Europe, and Germany, on the front line, would be its first victim. Thus, twice in a generation German leaders prepared the state for preventive war and launched it soon after military superiority had been maximized.

American thinking after 1944 was driven by the same geopolitical concern—Russian growth. I show that the United States, not the Soviet Union, was most responsible for starting the cold war, since it was the first state to shift to hard-line policies after the war with Germany. As early as mid-1945, Harry Truman moved toward a strong containment policy, despite his awareness that this policy would likely lead to a destabilizing spiral of hostility. He took this action not because he saw Stalin as inherently hostile—in fact, Truman liked Stalin at this time. Rather, Truman recognized that if the United States did *not* act, Russia would grow significantly, and Soviet leaders down the road might not be so moderate. This does not mean that the U.S. leadership ignored the brutal nature of the Soviet dictatorship. Yet future uncertainty and the need for preventive action, rather than fear of present Soviet intentions, were the primary forces leading Washington to accept a marked jump in the probability of major war. The fact that the United States did not initiate preventive war against Russia as had Germany twice earlier reflected less the differences in regime-type or moral principles, and more America's superiority in economic and potential power. Given this superiority, arms racing was a more rational first step.

In the early cold war, there were three crises that led to further large increases in the probability of major war: the two crises over Berlin (1948 and 1961) and the Cuban missile crisis of 1962. I show that all three were driven primarily by negative power oscillations caused by the expected relative success of one or the other of the superpowers' policies. Lacking a viable means to mitigate the oscillation by actions within its own bloc, the superpower in decline initiated a crisis to overcome the anticipated downturn. In 1948, Stalin brought on a crisis over Berlin in order to compel Washington to reverse plans that would have unified western Germany and integrated it into the western bloc. In 1961, Khrushchev initiated another crisis over Berlin to stabilize the deterioration of his eastern European sphere. In 1962, in the face of missiles in Cuba that could not simply be countered by more arms racing, Kennedy accepted the risks of a crisis in order to force Khrushchev to withdraw the missiles.

To demonstrate that the argument applies to wars beyond the twentieth

[8]

century, the final empirical chapter briefly examines the seven best-known major wars prior to 1900. The three bipolar cases—Sparta-Athens (431–404 B.C.), Carthage-Rome (218–202 B.C.), and France-Hapsburgs (1521–56)—uphold the argument. Sparta, Carthage, and France respectively initiated major war only once they were in long-term decline, and even though they were only essentially equal in military power to the rising states of Athens, Rome, and the Hapsburgs. Moreover, in each case, but especially in those of Carthage-Rome and France-Hapsburgs, the decline was deep and inevitable because of the rising state's superiority in potential power. Three of the four multipolar cases before 1900—the Thirty Years War (1618–48), the wars of Louis XIV (1688–1713), and the Napoleonic Wars (1803–15)—also support the theory. War was initiated by a state (respectively, Spain, France, and France again) possessing significantly superior military power, but one that also faced long-term decline, due mostly to entrenched relative stagnation and inferiority in certain dimensions of potential power. The anomaly is the Seven Years War (1756–63). Although decline was critical to Austria's provoking of Prussia into a preemptive war, war broke out in this multipolar system even though the belligerents were essentially equal in military power. In chapter 8, I explore some of the reasons for this deviation from the general argument of the book.

THE STRUCTURE OF THE BOOK

The first two chapters constitute the theoretical core of the book. Chapter 1 critiques the existing realist theories (nonrealist theories are discussed in the empirical chapters).[6] It also outlines the basic logic of dynamic differentials theory when power is viewed by actors as exogenous—that is, as an external factor they must take as a given. Narrowing the focus in this way not only replicates the approach of most realist theorists; it also exposes the essential problem of decline that states face across bipolar and multipolar systems, especially when decline is seen as deep and inevitable. At the end of chapter 1, I examine issues of methodology. The methodological discussion is critical to the book's overall purpose, namely, the building of a better systemic realist theory of major war. Much confusion surrounds what a systemic theory can and cannot do, how it can be falsified, and even how it should be tested. My discussion seeks to clear up the confusion and, by doing so, to suggest ways in which systemic theories and more domestic- and individual-level ("unit-level") theories work together in explaining international phenomena.[7]

Chapter 2 adds flesh to the bare-bones structure of chapter 1 by relaxing the assumption that power is strictly exogenous. I build a decision-making model that allows leaders to overcome decline by shifting to more severe policies such as intensified arms racing and crisis initiation, but only as they recognize the risks of provoking war by an inadvertent escalation. The model thus helps to predict shifts in the probability of major war even when leaders are loath to fall into major war, as they are in the nuclear age.

The empirical tests of the book's argument are to be found in chapters 3 through 8. In chapter 9, I conclude by examining the theoretical and practical implications of the argument.[8]

[1]

Rethinking Realist Theories of Major War

The three most prominent realist explanations for major war among great powers, as I noted earlier, are classical realism, structural neorealism, and hegemonic stability theory.[1] Classical realism argues that major war is likely when one state is preponderant and unlikely when great powers are relatively equal. A balance of power keeps the peace by convincing potential aggressors that war will have both high costs and a low probability of success. An imbalance provides the key condition for major war, since the superior state is more likely to expand in the belief that war can pay.[2] As for this superior state's motives, classical realists would agree with Hans Morgenthau that the preponderant state initiates war for unit-level reasons—for greed, glory, or what Morgenthau saw as its "lust for power" manifested in "nationalistic universalism."[3]

Given the propensity of superior states to attack, classical realists argue that multipolarity should be relatively more stable than bipolarity. Since exact equality cannot always be ensured, alliance restructuring (external balancing) in multipolarity can create the requisite balance of power between blocs, even if individual states are unequal. As long as flexibility is maintained, such that great powers can easily shift alliance ties in response to a stronger power, preponderant states can be deterred from aggression. Conversely, bipolar systems are prone to be unstable since if any inequality between the two great powers opens up, no large alliance partners exist to forge an effective balance of power.[4]

Classical realism's strength is its emphasis on power differentials, which provides a fine-grained sense of the relative weights that go onto the scales of the balance of power.[5] It also highlights a flaw in theories that argue for the stability of bipolar systems: states in multipolarity have another mechanism—alliances—in addition to arms racing to help deter an aggressor when rough equality cannot be maintained. In bipolarity, great powers have no viable alliance option to fall back on when arms racing alone is not enough.

Classical realism confronts two main empirical problems, however. First, it cannot explain how multipolar systems with tight alliances against the potential hegemon, such as the one that existed before 1914, can still fall into major war. In such cases, the overall balance of power between the blocs fails to keep the peace.[6] Second, in the key bipolar cases in history—Sparta-Athens, Carthage-Rome, and France-Hapsburgs—war ensued when the two great powers were essentially equal. Here, the balance of power between the individual great powers did not deter war. The theoretical problem behind these empirical anomalies lies with the largely static nature of classical realism. The theory derives predictions primarily from snapshots of the international systems. The result is the familiar picture of great powers as billiard balls of varying sizes.[7] The importance of dynamic trends in the differentials of power is understated in such an analysis. Some classical realists such as Morgenthau recognize in passing that preventive wars—wars for fear of decline—are a significant problem in history. Yet the conditions under which preventive war motivations are invoked remain theoretically undeveloped.[8]

The second approach, neorealism, focuses on two enduring structural features of the international system, anarchy and polarity. Anarchy—the absence of a central authority to protect the great powers—produces the recurring pattern of conflict seen in international politics over the millennia.[9] Across anarchic realms, neorealists assert that bipolar systems are less likely to experience major war than multipolar systems. Three main reasons are given: in bipolarity, great powers avoid being chain-ganged into major war by crises over small powers; they also stand firm, however, to prevent losses on the periphery, thus enhancing deterrence; and finally, the great powers are less inclined to neglect internal military spending that might allow a superior military power to arise.[10]

Neorealism's strength is its isolation of the structural effects of anarchy and polarity. This leaves us with a profoundly tragic view of international relations: even when states only seek security, they may still fall into devastating wars that threaten their survival.[11] In its Waltzian form, however, neorealism suffers from the same deficiency as classical realism: it is not dynamic enough. With polarity as the key structural variable, there is nothing to vary within either a bipolar or multipolar system to explain why any system should move from peace to war.[12] As Waltz explains, "within a system, [systemic] theory explains recurrences and repetitions, not change." If changes in state behavior "occur within a system that endures, their causes are found at the unit level."[13] This is an unnecessarily limiting view of the explanatory power of a systemic theory. As I explore below, changes and

[12]

trends in the differentials of relative power between states—a systemic variable going beyond the mere number of great powers—can have marked effects on behavior without necessary consideration of unit-level changes.

Other neorealists have sought to go beyond Waltz by incorporating the classical realist point that power inequalities increase the likelihood of major war.[14] Still others emphasize that states face a security dilemma, whereby the actions one state takes to enhance its security end up reducing the security of its adversaries. As a result, states sometimes have preventive incentives to eliminate a growing adversary before it becomes too strong.[15] I build these additional elements into my synthetic argument. Since I examine the effects of power trends in bipolar versus multipolar systems, however, I reach conclusions different from those of neorealism on the conditions for war in the two system-types. Moreover, chapter 2 moves beyond existing structural arguments by fusing within a leader's decision-making logic both the risks of decline and the risks of an inadvertent spiral to major war. Finally, by considering different forms of decline, including power oscillations and decline driven by inferiority in economic and potential power, I provide additional conditions constraining the rational response to decline.

The third realist perspective on major war is the security variant of hegemonic stability theory,[16] represented most prominently by A. F. K. Organski and Robert Gilpin. Turning classical realism on its head, they argue that a hegemonic system with one powerful actor will be stable because of the hegemon's self-interest in maintaining the political-military order. When a second-ranked state rises to near equality with this now former hegemon, however, this ascending state is inclined to initiate war to receive the status and rewards denied by the traditional system.[17] Hence, contrary to the classical realist view that a balance of power keeps the peace, major war is the result of a growing equality of power between the two most powerful states in any system.

The strength of this approach lies in its dynamic nature. Hegemonic stability theory thus provides a more extended analysis of the impact of power changes on great power behavior than is offered in either classical realism or neorealism. Two main problems remain, however. First, hegemonic stability theory has no deductively consistent theory of war initiation. There is no logical reason why a state should attack while it is still rising, since by simply waiting, the state will be able to achieve its objectives more easily, and at less cost.[18] This argument holds even if rising states have goals other than security, such as status and prestige, as hegemonic stability theorists assume they do. Waiting until the state has maximized its power ensures the maximum return on its war investment. After all, even more status and rewards are obtained by fighting when one stands the best chance of winning quickly and at low cost.[19] Hegemonic stability theory thus cannot explain why German leaders in both World Wars did not initiate war until after they saw that Germany was declining. Moreover, it cannot account for the fact that in the seven other major wars prior to 1900, it was the declining great power that brought on the hostilities. A similar pattern is seen in each of the key crises of the early cold war: it was the state foreseeing decline that initiated the dangerous crisis period.

The second limitation is that hegemonic stability theory's core logic for major war is confined to the two most powerful states in any system—the leading state and the rising challenger. The theory thus minimizes the importance of third-, fourth-, and fifth-ranked great powers on the calculations of the other two.[20] This might make some sense in a bipolar system, as I show, but it makes little sense for the multipolar cases of European history from 1556 on. Empirically, for example, the theory has a hard time explaining how one state in each of the two major wars of this century—Germany—was able to take on a coalition of second-, third-, and fourth-ranked great powers, fight a long war, and nearly emerge victoriously, if indeed Germany was only equal to the formerly dominant state in military power.[21]

Interestingly, the evidence provided by hegemonic stability theorists confirms that Germany was in fact preponderant when it took on the system. Organski and Jacek Kugler conclude that by 1913, "Germany [had] clearly surpassed the United Kingdom," the formerly dominant state, while by 1939, Germany had a "significant advantage" over Britain.[22] Kugler and William Domke, to explain how Germany could have come so close to winning both wars, show that Germany in 1914 and 1939–40 was significantly superior in actualized military power. In 1914, Germany was almost as powerful as Britain, Russia, and France combined. In 1939–40, Germany was almost twice as strong as France and Britain combined; in 1941–42, it matched the Soviet Union on the eastern front even as it continued to wage war in the west.[23]

To accommodate these facts, hegemonic stability theorists adjust the theory: they argue that although equality between individual great powers may not be associated with major war, relative equality between their *alliance blocs* is. Organski and Kugler conclude: "it is clear that [the World Wars] occur after the intersection when the two nations fight alone (which is contrary to what the power-transition model leads us to expect), but before the coalition of the challenger overtakes the coalition of the dominant country."[24] Woosang Kim, in an important statistical reworking of Organski's argument, shows that major wars occur at points of essential equality only when power is adjusted to incorporate alliance partners.[25] This reformulation still allows hegemonic stability theorists to challenge classical realism: as noted, classical realists cannot explain why in cases like World War I war occurred despite the relative equality between two tight alliances.

Overall, however, the primary challenge of hegemonic stability theory has been dissipated. Classical realists and hegemonic stability theorists now essentially agree that in 1914 and 1939 one state—Germany—was significantly superior to any other individual state, even if Germany (along with minor partners) was opposed by a coalition of equal strength. Military historians, as I discuss in chapters 3 through 5, would agree.[26]

The agreement between classical realists and hegemonic stability realists on German military superiority in the twentieth century simplifies the task ahead. Yet we still lack a theory that can explain, without invoking ad hoc unit-level factors like "lusting for power" and "dissatisfaction with the status quo," why preponderant states in multipolarity attack the system in the face of the staggering risks and costs. Moreover, how the pressures to initiate major war change between multipolar and bipolar systems is still underspecified. Providing a comprehensive systemic theory of major war, one that synthesizes the strengths of current realist approaches, is the objective of the rest of this chapter.

DYNAMIC DIFFERENTIALS THEORY

The core causal or independent variable of the argument is the dynamic differential: the simultaneous interaction of the differentials of relative military power between great powers and the expected trend of those differentials, distinguishing between the effects of power changes in bipolarity versus multipolarity.[27] In addition, I break the notion of power into three types—military, economic, and potential—to show how decline in the latter two forms affects the behavior of states that may be superior in military power.

The theory makes three main assertions. First, in any system, assuming states are rational security-seeking actors which remain uncertain about others' future intentions,[28] it is the dominant but declining military great power that is most likely to begin a major war. Second, the constraints on the dominant state differ in bipolar versus multipolar systems. In multipolarity, major war is likely only if the declining state has a significant level of military superiority. In bipolarity, however, the declining state can attack even when only roughly equal, and sometimes even if it is second-ranked. Third, the probability of major war increases when decline is seen as both deep and inevitable. A consideration of overall economic power and potential power is thus necessary, since the levels and trends of these two other forms of power are crucial in determining the extent and inevitability of military decline.

The first proposition is relatively straightforward: because major wars are so costly, and because they risk the very survival of the state, the initiator of war is more likely to be the dominant military power; smaller military powers simply lack the capability to "take on the system." Moreover, it is irrational for any great power to begin a major war while still rising, since, as noted, waiting allows it to attack later with a higher probability of success, and at less cost. All major wars, if actors meet the requirement of rationality, therefore must be preventive wars.[29]

The second proposition requires more explication. To state it slightly differently, while near equality between individual great powers is likely to be stabilizing in multipolarity even when some states are declining, near equality in bipolarity can be very unstable when either of the great powers, but especially the dominant power, perceives itself to be declining. Thus, the conditions for major war in multipolarity are less permissive than those in bipolarity, meaning that for any given set of power differentials and trends, war is less likely in multipolar systems.[30]

The logic behind this assertion is as follows. In multipolar systems, if all states are relatively equal in military power, no state will make a bid for hegemony against the system, for four main reasons. First, even if a state expects the others to remain disunited—that is, even if it does not expect a counter-coalition to form against it—equality with its rivals will likely mean long and costly bilateral wars, wars that will sap the state's ability to continue the fight until hegemony is achieved. If complete hegemony is not achieved, those states sitting on the sidelines will emerge in a stronger position relative to the state that initiates war. Hence launching all-out war in the first place is irrational.[31]

Second, to the extent that a coalition does form against the challenger, there is even less probability that the initiator could emerge in a stronger and more secure position after the war. Coalitions in multipolarity, since they are made up of states with "great power," become formidable fighting forces as their unity increases.[32] The third reason follows from the other two. A declining but only equal great power in multipolarity has reason to think that a rising state, as long as it does not grow too preponderant, will also be restrained in its ambitions simply by the presence of so many other great powers. Therefore, a preventive war for security is less imperative.

Fourth, to the extent that an equal but declining power can form alliances against the state that is rising, it will have less concern about being overtaken. This restates classical realism's insight that states in multipolarity, compared to bipolarity, have recourse to an additional means to uphold their security besides internal balancing, namely, external balancing through alliances. Because of the collective action problem that may be present, however, my deductive logic as to why an equal but declining state does not initiate war in multipolarity does not depend on this state's ability to form a tight alliance for its security (although such alliances certainly reinforce the argument). Rather, the argument revolves around the

[16]

state's recognition that even if no alliances form against it if it begins a major war, it will not have enough power to win a victory against all the others; and even if no alliances form *with* this state if it chooses to "decline gracefully," the presence of many actors should help deter the rising state from attacking later. Consequently, in multipolarity, only when a given state is clearly superior to any other individual state in military power can it contemplate waging a war for hegemony.

In bipolar systems, however, these arguments push in the opposite direction, and therefore preventive war is likely even when states are near equals. First, a declining and near-equal state realizes that it has to face only one other great power, not many, and therefore even if the war is long and difficult, there are no additional opponents to defeat after the bilateral victory is achieved. A successful bid for hegemony is thus easier to achieve. Moreover, even if the declining state fears a stalemated and inconclusive war with the rising state, it does not have to worry about a relative loss to third party actors that sit on the sidelines to avoid the costs of war. Such actors, since small, are unlikely to gain enough to raise themselves to the top of the system.

Second, the declining state knows that even if a coalition forms against its attack, the small states joining the rising great power are unlikely to alter the expected outcome significantly. In comparison with multipolarity, individual coalitional partners simply have far less weight to throw against the initiator of major war.[33] Third, because the declining state realizes these two factors are in *its* favor when it is slightly superior, it knows that the rising state will not be terribly constrained after it achieves superiority. Fourth, the declining state knows that the other states in the system, even if some are willing to ally against the ascending state, are not substantial enough to shore up its waning security. Hence preventive war before the point of overtaking makes rational sense.

Note that because of the absence of significant third parties, even the second-ranked state in bipolarity can initiate major war when in steep decline. The core logic applies: it has to beat only one other great power, and there is little concern about stalemated wars that allow sideline-sitters to rise to the top.[34] Of course, the greater the second-ranked state's level of inferiority, the less confidence it will have in a hard-line policy.

The argument I have outlined is summarized visually in figures 1 and 2. These heuristic diagrams present the main systemic situations that might be faced in either multipolarity or bipolarity.[35] Note that at times t_1, t_4, and t_5, the probability of major war should be low for both system-types, since the trends in the military balance are stable; with no state experiencing decline, there is no imperative to go to war for security reasons.[36] At time t_2, however, the impending decline of the dominant state in the bipolar situation (fig. 2) means the likelihood of major war is high, while in the multipolar situation the likelihood is low because of the restraining presence of the

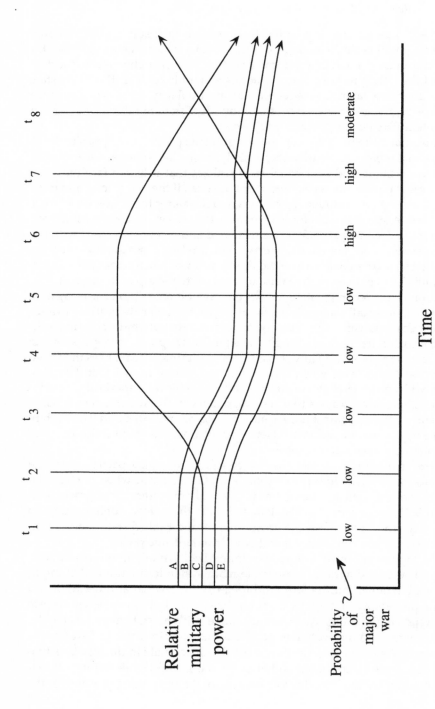

Fig. 1. Relative military power curves and the probability of major war: multipolarity

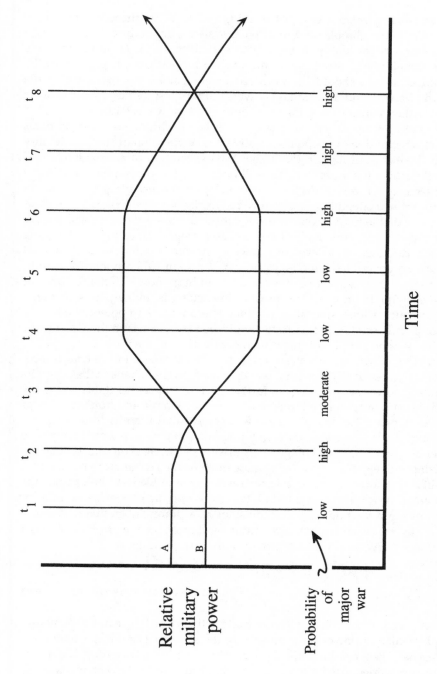

Fig. 2. Relative military power curves and the probability of major war: bipolarity

other equal great powers.[37] At times t_6 and t_7, when there is marked inequality in both bipolar and multipolar systems, impending decline should make major war highly likely in both system-types. At t_8, however, while the probability of war is again high in the bipolar case, instability in the multipolar case should be tempered somewhat by the existence of the third-, fourth-, and fifth-ranked powers (although since these latter powers are weaker than at time t_2, the probability of major war is still "moderate").[38]

In both multipolarity and bipolarity, it is a declining state that initiates war. When it does so depends greatly on its estimation of the inevitability and the extent of its fall: the higher the expectation of an inevitable and deep decline, the more the state will be inclined to preventive war simply for security reasons. If decline is caused by entrenched stagnation relative to the rising state, this will certainly be worrisome; the fewer internal measures available to overcome the stagnation, the more the state will see decline as deep and inevitable. Of even greater significance for the declining state's calculus is its level of economic power and its overall potential power compared to its military power.[39] A state in either bipolarity or multipolarity that is superior but declining in military power, but also superior and growing in the other two power dimensions, is unlikely to be that anxious about decline. After all, given that its economic and potential power is strong and ascending, this state should be able to reverse the downward military trend simply by spending more on arms in the future.

A state, however, that is superior in military power but *inferior* in economic and especially potential power is more likely to believe that, once its military power begins to wane, further decline will be inevitable and deep. This is especially so if the trends of relative economic and potential power are downward as well. The state will believe that there is little it can do through arms racing to halt its declining military power: it would simply be spending a greater percentage of an already declining economic base in the attempt to keep up with a rising state that has the resources to outspend it militarily. Moreover, economic restructuring is unlikely to help, since the potential power that is the foundation for economic power is also inferior and declining. Under these circumstances, a dominant military power is likely to be pessimistic about the future and more inclined to initiate major war as a "now-or-never" attempt to shore up its waning security.[40]

THE CONTRIBUTION OF THE ARGUMENT

As noted, this book's goal is to build a theory with greater explanatory and predictive power by synthesizing the strengths of current realist approaches. The resulting theory offers two new contributions. First, the theory provides a deductively consistent argument for how changes in relative power should have differing effects in bipolar versus multipolar systems. Classical realism and neorealism emphasize the importance of polarity and occasionally consider dynamic trends, but they do not analyze the effect of power trends across the system-types. Hegemonic stability theory and preventive war arguments are fundamentally dynamic, but they do not include polarity as a critical boundary condition.

Second, the book divides power, for theory-making purposes, into three categories—military, economic, and potential. By considering the differentials and trends in each realm, we can determine when declining military power will lead directly to war and when it will lead to measures short of war.[41] Even theories emphasizing the problem of relative decline, such as preventive war arguments, have trouble explaining why some situations of decline are more destabilizing than others. Polarity, of course, plays a significant role here, as I have emphasized. Decline is more likely to lead to major war in bipolarity, since the declining state does not have to possess marked military superiority and may even be somewhat inferior. Yet equally important is the declining state's military power in comparison to its economic and especially potential power. A dominant military state that is inferior in economic and potential power is much more likely to expect decline to be both deep and inevitable, inclining it to risky actions. Negative trends in the latter two forms of power will only make things worse.

The theory thus helps answer two long-standing questions: Is major war more likely when great powers are equal or unequal? And can major war occur between states seeking only security, or must there be actors with inherently aggressive motives?

The answer to the first question is clear: it depends on the polarity of the system. Major wars in multipolarity require a preponderant military power, but they can occur in bipolarity whether the two great powers are equal or unequal.[42] This helps explain why in the three bipolar cases before 1945 (Sparta-Athens, Carthage-Rome, and France-Hapsburgs), it was the declining and formerly dominant great power that initiated major war against the rising adversary, despite relative military equality between the states. In the early cold war, there was great instability whenever one of the superpowers feared serious decline, even though the United States remained militarily superior throughout. The multipolar systems before 1914 and 1939, on the other hand, were destabilized only after one state (Germany) came to possess significant military superiority over other states taken individually. In three of the four major wars before 1900—the Thirty Years War, the wars of Louis XIV, and the Napoleonic Wars—the conflict was initiated by the power with marked military superiority. Only in the Seven Years War was the declining state essentially equal, an anomaly I discuss in chapter 8.

The answer to the second question is equally clear: innately aggressive actors, even though they may exacerbate the likelihood of major war, are neither necessary nor sufficient conditions for such wars. Aggressive unit-level motives are not a sufficient condition, since even the most hostile leaders will be deterred from initiating major war unless power conditions make the bid for hegemony feasible. For the period of the last five hundred years, we might identify a number of European leaders who would have wanted hegemony purely for glory or greed-driven reasons. Yet there were only seven clear cases of major war during this time.[43] That so few major wars occurred is explained by a simple fact: few states ever achieved the military superiority needed to take on the system.[44] (And as I show in the empirical chapters, these wars were driven primarily by fears of decline, even when unit-level factors were also present.)

Aggressive motives are also not a necessary condition for major war. A purely security-seeking state may initiate war in either bipolarity or multipolarity solely because of its fear of inevitable and profound decline. Needless to say, a rising state showing signs of hostile intentions will make this declining state even more likely to attack.[45] But the *initiator's* attack is still a function of security motives, not unit-level aggressive designs. Perhaps the clearest case is Sparta's initiation of major war against Athens. The Spartans feared revolt at home if the soldiers were away fighting a large-scale war. Yet fear of the rise of Athens forced the Spartans into war, even as these domestic factors inclined them to peace.[46] As we shall see, Germany in 1914 faced a very similar situation: the key German leaders believed that war would only exacerbate domestic instability at home; yet it had to be chosen to prevent the rise of the Russian menace.

Even more to the point, the declining security-seeking state may initiate major war even if all other states in the system, including the rising state, are also only security-seekers. The declining state, given the anarchic environment, will be inclined to doubt the present intentions of other states, despite their best efforts to show their peaceful desires.[47] Indeed, rising states have every incentive to misrepresent their intentions as peaceful to reduce the possibility of preventive attack. The declining state will therefore have a hard time sorting out those states that are genuinely peaceful from those that are not.[48] Even today, for example, it is unclear whether or not Czar Nicholas II privately desired hegemony but was only postponing a bid until Russia grew stronger. Hence, German leaders, despite Nicholas's efforts to communicate his benign intentions, still felt compelled to initiate major war. Russia faced the same problem in 1939–41, when, despite his best efforts, Stalin could not convince Hitler of his good intentions.

Finally, the declining state may even know with certainty that the other has peaceful intentions, but still initiate war for security reasons. The problem is a profound one: the other's intentions might change in the future after it reaches a position of dominance, perhaps because of a change in government or leadership or simply because of its stronger power position.[49] Depending on the likelihood of this domestic change in the other, preventive war or preventive measures that knowingly increase the likelihood of major war through inadvertent means can become rational even against an adversary recognized to be peaceful. Truman acted in mid-1945 to contain the Soviet Union, raising the risk of an undesired war, even though he believed Stalin was a reasonable individual. Truman feared not Stalin's intentions per se, but rather the intentions of those who would take over after his death. In 1962, Kennedy initiated a crisis over missiles in Cuba, not because he thought Khrushchev wanted nuclear war, but because he could not be sure of Russian intentions down the road should the Soviets achieve a perceived measure of nuclear superiority.[50]

Questions Regarding the Theory's Logic

I now address three questions that arise about the logic of the argument presented in this chapter. First, does the preponderant state in multipolarity (state C in fig. 1) need to possess military power greater than all other great powers combined to make major war a rational option?[51] The answer: not necessarily. A state in multipolarity can make a potentially successful bid for hegemony with less than 50 percent of the system's military power by taking advantage of the difficulties coalitions have in coordinating their military actions. In short, there is good reason to expect that coalitional strength will be less than the sum of its parts.[52]

States that are considering whether to form a coalition against a preponderant power are faced with two contrary sets of incentives. On the one hand, no great power smaller than the preponderant state has an interest in seeing this state defeat the others, since it knows it could be next.[53] Accordingly, smaller great powers are pushed toward a coalition to prevent the elimination of their partners. On the other hand, owing to anarchy and the concern for relative power, great powers in multipolarity face an intense form of the collective action problem. Individual states in a coalition against a challenger have an incentive to sit on the sidelines or to contribute less than their fullest effort, so as to maximize their relative position after the war ends.[54] Hence, coalitional tightness is likely to vary between the extremes of concerted effort when the potential hegemon appears particularly strong, to coalitional disunity when the threat to the system appears minimal.[55] Challengers can take advantage of this disunity by trying to eliminate other great powers one at a time. This argument helps explain why states may make bids for hegemony in multipolarity when they are larger than any single state but smaller than the combined resources of all other powers.

Because of the incentive to "hang together or hang separately," however, challengers that take on the system cannot depend on complete allied disunity. Hence, coalitional unity and fighting power will likely be somewhere between strong and nonexistent. What we would expect is that the more evident the preponderant state's military superiority versus any other individual great power, the higher the others' incentive to band together against this threat. Conversely, the smaller the leading state's level of superiority, the greater the others' incentive to sit on the sidelines.

It may seem contradictory to argue that a declining preponderant state may make a bid for hegemony because the collective action problem keeps others disunited, and also to argue that a declining near-equal state in multipolarity avoids war for fear of provoking a coalition or from a belief that it can form alliances. It is not. In both cases, the leading state recognizes that others are torn between two contrary incentives: to unite for fear of defeat, or to sit on the sidelines to maximize power. Thus any state taking on the system will likely have to contend with some coalitional effort, but it can also expect some disunity. The key difference is that a near-equal state has no way of defeating every other power singlehandedly even if the coalition against it is nonexistent; costly bilateral wars will sap its strength. A preponderant state, however, stands a chance of defeating the system even with a coalition against it, and especially if the level of coalitional disunity is fairly high. Bilateral victories will be quicker, with lower costs, and thus will not deplete its strength for future attacks.

This discussion helps resolve a second major question: why does the rising and increasingly dominant state in multipolarity (state C in fig. 1 from t_2 to t_4) not fear a preventive attack by an offensive coalition of the other states, even though it represents an obvious and growing threat? The likelihood of such an attack is low precisely because of the intense collective action problem. Even if the coalition can be formed, each partner fears that its allies will deliberately hold back their full commitment to shift the costs of preventive war to others. When states are in a purely defensive alliance, the collective action problem is moderated by the fact that the alliance does not automatically mean war; thus, actors can be convinced to ally solely to deter the growing state from war. Coordinating an *offensive* coalitional strike is more difficult: attacking a rising dominant power guarantees war, thus instantly raising each state's fear that it will bear the brunt of the rising power's fury. A "you first" mentality will ensure disunity in any offensive coalition that is suggested.[56] Accordingly, the rising state in multipolarity will likely grow unmolested, with each declining state hoping either that the rising state will not achieve sufficient power to take on the system, or that their own internal and external measures can deter it from doing so.[57]

The third issue is the most complicated. Notwithstanding the earlier discussion, one may still wonder if the theory ultimately needs unit-level drives for major war, such as greed, glory-seeking, or ideological hostility, to be workable. The short answer is yes.[58] The *possibility* of such drives arising in the future is a necessary condition for the theory's causal argument. That is, the fact that human beings have the ability to use violence for nonsecurity objectives is required to make preventive war fully rational. Imagine a planet where the beings were hardwired by nature never to strike unless they were immediately about to be struck—that is, a planet where the actors were physically incapable of using violence for nonsecurity motives like greed and glory. The basis for the security dilemma would, at least over time, disappear. Leaders would understand that even if they allowed rising states to become preponderant, these states would never attack later at their peak for aggressive unit-level reasons. Nor would such states attack later for their own preventive reasons, since they as well would know that they had nothing to fear from rising states. In Rousseau's terms, all great powers would be permanent staghunt actors, preferring peace to all other outcomes.[59] Major wars could occur only through preemption. But since there would be no reason to threaten another, beliefs that the other was readying itself for immediate attack—a necessary condition for preemption between staghunt actors—would not arise.

This argument does not mean, however, that on planet earth major wars require actors that are presently driven by aggressive, nonsecurity motives. As discussed, a declining state seeking only security could attack a rising state which also pursued security, simply because it was uncertain that the other was currently a security-seeker or would still remain one later at its peak. Yet the dilemma for the declining state does not end there. Even if it knows for sure that the other will still be a security-seeker later, it has reason for preventive war now. It knows that the rising state, once it peaks in power, will be faced with the same problem of uncertain intentions that the declining state faces now. So if the rising state is likely to launch a defensive preventive war later, with much more power, for fear of decline, then preventive war now by the presently declining state makes sense.

Figure 3 shows this dilemma for the bipolar situation.[60] State A at time t_0 knows that after time t_1 state B will consider preventive war for purely security reasons, since B cannot trust A's future intentions at time t_2. The causal sequence is clear but tragic: because A may turn into an innately aggressive state by t_2, B has incentives for preventive war at t_1, but because it does, A has incentives for preventive war at t_0. And of course even if A knows that it will still be a security-seeker by t_2—and knows it can convince B of this fact—B still has preventive motives at t_1 because it cannot be sure A won't launch a preventive attack at t_2 for fear of B's motives at t_3.[61] This argument, while logically consistent, may seem too convoluted to be borne out in practice. Yet as will we see, U.S. leaders in the cold war feared that if

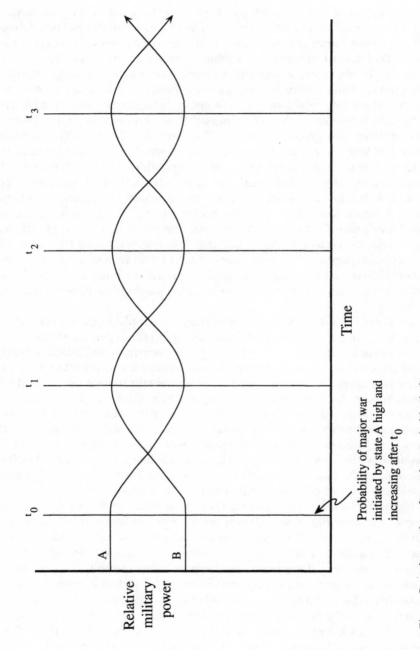

Fig. 3. Security motives for major war in bipolarity

the Soviets ever reached temporary superiority, they might attack preventively out of their own fears for future security.

For states to reason in this way in bipolarity and multipolarity, there must be the possibility that *eventually* one of the states will attack for nonsecurity, aggressive objectives. Yet we can see that major war can still occur even when there are no presently aggressive actors or even the likelihood of such actors on the horizon. Most tragically, the declining state may know these facts and still have an incentive for preventive war.

METHODOLOGY: THE DEFINITION OF MAJOR WAR

Major wars, as noted in the introduction, are wars that involve all the great powers, that are fought at the highest level of intensity, and where there is a strong possibility that great powers may be eliminated as sovereign states. As an ideal type, this definition is designed to establish boundaries for the analysis. Efforts to build universal theories of war are likely to be confounded by the diversity of wars through history. It is unlikely, for example, that civil wars, local conflicts like the Vietnam war, European imperialist wars of the nineteenth century, and major wars such as World Wars I and II will have a common cause.[62] By starting with the most profound conflicts—general wars that threaten the survival of the system's most powerful actors—I am seeking a more manageable theoretical goal. Yet since such wars, or the avoidance of them, so determine great power behavior, a strong theory of major war will often have much to say about the causes of smaller conflicts through history.

I purposefully do not define major wars according to their duration or number of casualties.[63] To do so would be to presuppose the type of war based on its outcome rather than its nature. By my definition, therefore, World War II would still have been a major war even if Germany had quickly dispatched France, Britain, and Russia, as seemed likely after France's defeat in June 1940; it was Germany's effort to destroy the other great powers that made it a major war. Not defining major wars in terms of duration or casualties has an important benefit. It allows one to measure the military balance between great powers in the most objective way possible, namely, by looking at how the war played itself out on the battlefield. As all military analysts recognize, overall military power, as a state's relative ability to fight and win in a war, reflects the combined influence of a whole host of quantitative and qualitative factors. Thus only in actual war do we see each side's true military strength (after adjusting for fortuitous factors such as weather).[64] But to use this technique to measure military power while defining major wars according to duration and battle deaths would introduce an important bias: measures for the dependent variable (major war) would also be factors influencing the measure of the independent variable (relative power). My definition thus requires only that the states fight at the highest level of intensity—that they are fully mobilized. Thus a state like France in 1940, which gets beaten easily despite complete mobilization, was still involved in a major war. Yet the details of the battle are useful in establishing the objective military balance between the two sides.

This definition establishes only the ideal-typical major war; no actual war will ever fit the criteria perfectly. The criteria provide a standard for separating wars of fundamentally different types, but they should not be held to religiously. Debating whether World War I was a major war until 1916 because the United States was not involved is hardly worthwhile: the war was so obviously close to the ideal-typical form as to require its inclusion. Nevertheless, lines do have to be drawn. To ensure a focus on system-wide wars, I exclude bilateral wars within multipolar systems. Thus while Organski and Kugler include the 1904–5 Russo-Japanese conflict as a major war, such a war must be excluded from my study since it involved only two of seven or eight major powers, had little possibility of escalation to systemic conflict, and was aimed not to eliminate either power but to control Korea.

RESEARCH METHOD

Six principal questions may be asked about the research that underlies the theory presented in this book. Should the theory be deductively or inductively driven? Under what conditions is the theory falsified? Should the evidence be evaluated primarily quantitatively, through statistical tests, or qualitatively, through intensive diplomatic-historical case studies? What are the best measures for the independent and dependent variables, relative power and the probability of major war? What criteria guide the selection of cases? How can one mitigate some common methodological obstacles, including selection bias and the omitted variable problem?

Dynamic differentials theory is a deductive systemic argument modeled on microeconomic theory. Microeconomics starts by assuming exogenously determined tastes for consumers and firms (as represented by fixed indifference curves), and it posits rational, self-regarding actors seeking the best means to their ends (the maximization of utility and profit). With this micro-foundation, variables such as prices and costs of inputs are introduced to predict deductively how behavior should change with changes in these external factors.[65] Similarly, I begin by assuming actors with singular goals—the maximization of their security rather than utility or profit—who calculate the rational steps to reach these ends. Then, by holding unit-level factors constant, I derive predictions as to how behavior should change in response to changes in a core systemic variable: the size of the differentials of power and the trend of those differentials.

Figure 4 provides a list of the theory's assumptions. Each assumption is a variable that is, for theory-making purposes, fixed at a particular point. This specification of boundary conditions permits one to conduct a controlled mental experiment isolating the expected causal impact of changes in the independent variable on the dependent variable.[66] In this book, some assumptions are particularly important. I assume, for example, that states are uncertain about the other's future intentions.[67] A declining state therefore does not know whether the rising state will attack it later, giving it reason to worry about its future security.[68] The assumptions that states are "neutral" in terms of their tolerance for costs and risks allows the theory to posit actors who do not shy away from war if it is the best means to security (nor do they embrace war as the only means). These assumptions help to reinforce a picture of highly rational actors who choose options that best maximize their long-term likelihood of survival.

Building a deductive structure in this way has important advantages. It allows one to build a stronger theory of the systemic pressures on actor behavior, even while recognizing that leaders will sometimes be influenced by domestic- and individual-level factors. Variations in such unit-level factors or in systemic factors like the offense-defense balance or geographic position act as "disturbing causes," pushing actor behavior away from what might be expected from looking at power differentials and their trends alone.[69] Theoretically, one can anticipate deviations from a theory's narrow predictions by simply relaxing the assumptions. That is, one allows assumptions to vary away from the fixed points, to determine deductively the impact on expected behavior. Thus when the theory is taken to the real world, where facts rarely conform perfectly to assumptions, behavior and outcomes can not only be predicted, but explained. I assume, for example, that states are the same distance from one another. Relaxing this assumption implies that distant rising states should be less frightening than rising states that are nearby (for any given rise). Thus, Britain's greater concern for Germany's rise after 1895 versus the rise of Japan or the United States can be explained within the theory's logic. In chapter 9, I relax the assumption that declining states are uncertain about the other's future character. This permits the theory to predict the likely effects of regime-type (e.g., rising democracies versus rising authoritarian states) on the declining state's behavior.

This discussion helps set the boundaries for falsifying the theory. A deductive systemic theory is not falsified simply by pointing to cases where unit-level factors drove actor behavior. These may simply be cases where unit-level factors, as disturbing causes, were so powerful that they over-

(Note: each assumption is a variable that could vary in practice, but that is, for theoretical purposes, fixed at a certain point, as indicated by the dotted line.)

Unit-level assumptions

1. Rationality: actor calculates best means to desired ends, given information available

2. Ends: actor seeks security above all else

3. Direction of ends: to self only

4. Nature of actor: unitary

5. Risk-tolerance: neutral

6. Cost-tolerance: neutral

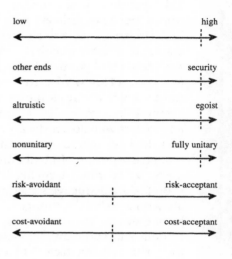

Systemic-level assumptions

1. Certainty regarding other's present intentions: largely uncertain

2. Certainty regarding other's future intentions: fully uncertain

3. Certainty regarding one's past and present power levels: largely certain

4. Offense-defense balance: neutral

5. Geographic positions of states: equidistant

6. Technological Costs of War: moderate

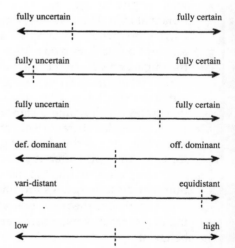

Fig. 4. The assumptions of the theory

rode the effects of the theory's systemic variable. Moreover, a good theory, as noted, will help predict deviations from narrow predictions as one relaxes core assumptions. The real standard for falsification must therefore be that the actors, in terms of the impact of systemic factors, did not act for the reasons the theory hypothesizes, but rather according to another systemically driven logic.[70] The theory in this book is thus not competing directly against unit-level theories, but only against other realist theories focusing on the role of power. Most evidently, if we find that leaders who believe their states are rising are initiating wars and crises, my systemic logic would be disconfirmed and the logic of hegemonic stability theory upheld. Likewise, if we see states in multipolarity taking on the system despite only essential military equality, then the theory would again be wrong and hegemonic stability theory correct.[71]

Unit-level factors do not falsify a systemic theory, nor do systemic factors falsify unit-level theories. There is, however, the separate issue of *salience*. If unit-level variables are almost always more dominant in historical cases, then we have reason to doubt the causal importance of systemic theories. Accordingly, in the empirical chapters, I test the theory not only against other systemic arguments, but also against domestic- and individual-level theories. The theory will gain in credibility if it can be shown that power differentials and trends often overrode unit-level factors. The clearest tests are examples where unit-level factors push toward peace, but the actors choose conflict anyway because of the systemic pressures. Yet the theory must be seen as less salient (even if logically sound) if actors evaluate power in the expected way but end up acting for primarily unit-level reasons.

The ideal evidence necessary either to falsify different theories or to establish their salience comes from internal documents. To determine causality, correlations between objective factors and actor behavior are insufficient. We must ultimately examine how the actors thought, that is, we have to see if they acted according to the logic of the theory. Many scholars wrongly assume that systemic theories must avoid examining actor perceptions, since this seems to require a descent to the unit level. Hence many systemic theories rest only on measures of objective factors, such as the number of tanks or troops. Yet social science is about human behavior, and human beings act only from their *beliefs* about phenomena.[72] In fact, what a scholar might establish as the objective balance in tanks fifty years after a war is largely irrelevant in testing any theory, since if decision-makers did not or could not observe such evidence, they could not have acted upon it. No one would develop of theory of fire-behavior by analyzing, after the fact, whether there really was a fire; what explains behavior is whether the actors believed a fire was in progress, and its perceived severity. Similarly, all theories of international relations, to establish causality and not just correlation, ultimately must be tested against the beliefs of the actors at the time.[73]

To test any social science theory, therefore, two questions must be asked. Did the actors act for the reasons the theory hypothesized? And if they did, were the beliefs underpinning their actions reasonable given the information available? Answering yes to the first question establishes the causal power of the argument. If leaders take their nations into major wars or dangerous crises because they perceive their states are in severe decline, and not for other reasons, then the book's theory explains why they acted the way they did. If they acted according to another power logic, the theory is falsified. If they acted as a result of the overwhelming influence of non-power variables, then the theory lacks salience.

The second question tests the "realistic-ness" of the rationality assumption. If, given the information available, leaders should have reasonably seen that the state was rising, not declining, then social and psychological pathologies might have to be brought in to explain why the leaders chose preventive war. Note, however, that even in this case dynamic differentials theory, not hegemonic stability theory, explains why the actors did what they did. Its causal logic is thus upheld, while hegemonic stability theory would be disconfirmed.

"Objective" evidence an investigator can collect might still have a role to play. It would help one answer the second question, by showing that the actors' beliefs were reasonable or unreasonable. But even here, to demonstrate irrationality, it must be shown that the actors had access to this information and chose to ignore it, or they could have had access but because of psychological barriers, performed an incomplete information search. In my case studies, I do make reference to objective evidence on the military, economic, and potential power levels of nations. As noted, the most objective measure of relative military power is what happens on the battlefield, where quantitative and qualitative factors come together as one. Yet to test causality, documented evidence of actor beliefs about the power balance is still the key measure.[74]

In sum, examining perceptions does not automatically mean that a theorist has dipped down to the unit level. If the perception is of a phenomenon external to the state and the phenomenon is evaluated rationally, then the primary cause of behavior is at the systemic level.[75] Causality is at the unit level only if the perceptions driving behavior are of a domestic-level phenomenon, such as internal instability or bureaucratic maneuvering. Note that examining perceptions also does not mean one is necessarily a "constructivist." Constructivism focuses on how state-to-state interaction can reshape identities and interests.[76] My focus is simply on leaders who learn about the other's material power. Such leaders are not changing core values and interests, only their beliefs about an external reality (indeed, my deductive logic assumes that actor ends are fixed). Moreover, no interaction between states is required: states can collect information by means of spying, satellites, published documents, and so forth.[77]

This leads to a discussion of why this book uses qualitative case studies rather than the quantitative approach of some realists.[78] Most important is the above point: that quantitative studies are a second-best approach to establishing causality when internal documents are available (although I do use statistics to reinforce that leader perceptions were for the most part reasonable). Moreover, quantitative studies lack a good way to measure my dependent variable, the *probability* of major war. Perhaps because of this, they almost invariably examine the dichotomous dependent variable, war/not-war. I estimate changes in the probability of major war by changes in the extent of the states' planning for major war, changing internal estimates of the likelihood of such a conflict, and fluctuations in the general level of hostility between states, shown most clearly by major crises like the Cuban missile crisis. This approach may not be fully satisfying, but it does capture our intuitive notion that even when major war is not occurring, some situations are relatively more stable than others.

Making the dependent variable continuous, both in theory-building and theory-testing, offers a number of advantages. It forces any theory to explain more than just the historical outbreak of actual major wars. This means that times of crisis and conflict, such as the Cuban missile crisis, can be brought within the purview of the theories (see chapter 2). In doing so, we greatly expand the size of the data set (the number of "observations").[79] Instead of examining just two data points in the twentieth century, 1914 and 1939, which are then compared to the many years of peace, the analyst can explore variations in the likelihood of major war over time. Periods of relative calm, such as the 1920s, can be compared to the 1930s, and the 1930s themselves can be studied for yearly shifts in the level of tension and crisis. Fluctuations in the level of crisis within the cold war can also be brought within the theory's purview.

The bulk of my empirical work focuses on three main periods: the run-up to World War I; the interwar years up to World War II; and the early cold war from 1945 to 1962. In chapter 8, I also briefly cover seven other key major wars in western history. Aside from their sheer historical importance, the twentieth-century cases satisfy the most important criterion for establishing causality: a huge number of declassified documents. Moreover, since Germany lost both wars, the German documents provide a relatively complete and unbiased view of internal decision-making.[80] The openness of the American declassification system also offers such a view into the logic of the cold war. The cut-off of 1962 was established for one main reason: given the "thirty-year rule" for U.S. declassification, documents released after this date are less numerous and more politically suspect.[81]

Despite the focus on these three periods, since I examine the changes in state behavior across time and space, the number of observations is far larger than three. This expansion of the realized "cases" helps to avoid the bias caused by selecting on the dependent variable, namely, looking only at the years when major wars broke out.[82] Analysis of the run-ups to major wars and crises provide us with variations on both independent and dependent variables.[83] In addition, the consideration of seven other major wars prior to 1900 provides a check against the possibility that the twentieth century is biased toward my argument. In this way, the generalizability of the argument across time and space can be tested.[84]

It is also worth noting that the twentieth-century cases are not easy ones for the theory. Almost every study of the origins of World War II emphasizes the unit-level causes of the war, most obviously the characteristics of the Nazi state and its leader. If I can show the salience of my argument in such a case, there is greater reason for confidence in the theory.[85] Arguments on the origins of the cold war and the crises of the 1945–62 period also tend to emphasize either the ideological roots of superpower conflict or the role of misperception regarding the other's intentions. Although arguments on the impact of shifting power may be more common here than for World War II, they still face strong competition from unit-level theories.[86] The run-up to World War I seems on the surface to be the easiest period to make my argument stick, since a number of scholars have documented German fears of a rising Russia. Yet this case is still, in a different way, a hard one for the theory. World War I seems to support practically every theory of major war out there, at both the systemic and unit levels. To show, as I seek to do, that only dynamic differentials theory provides a comprehensive explanation for the war is thus a difficult undertaking.

A problem for many studies is the problem of omitted variables—variables that are left out of an empirical test but have a strong causal relation to both the dependent and independent variables.[87] I deal with this problem in a straightforward way. For each of the twentieth-century cases, I include all the primary causal arguments that have been established to explain actor behavior. I then use the documentary evidence to test the explanatory power of these arguments against this book's theory. In this way, we can be sure that there is no hidden variable causing the result. Moreover, this method helps deal with the problem of overdetermination. If the documentary record supports dynamic differentials theory, but also calls alternative hypotheses into question, then there is greater confidence that shifting power differentials and not other variables are driving the observed behavior and outcomes. Thus, in cases like the First World War, I am not simply adding yet another hypothesis to the many that exist but rather seeking to show the limitations of competing arguments as I support the plausibility of my own account.[88]

[2]

Foreign Policy Choices and the Probability of Major War

To establish the basic causal logic, chapter 1 treated relative power as an exogenous force that states took as a given and to which they were compelled to respond. Leaders understand, however, that power is often not simply exogenous: it can be affected by their policies. An obvious example is the choice states make between guns and butter—between resources devoted to military power versus consumption and economic growth. Leaders also face a less examined but potentially more problematic dilemma. They know that by initiating hard-line actions, they might avert decline. Yet they realize that such moves may have high risks attached to them: they can bring on a major war through inadvertent means. In October 1962, for example, John F. Kennedy felt he had to blockade and possibly attack Cuba to prevent a significant shift in the balance of power. But he also knew that such moves would greatly increase the risks of superpower war either through preemption as the crisis escalated, or through the overcommitment of reputations that would prevent either side from backing down. More generally, leaders understand that during periods of peaceful engagement initiating hard-line policies to contain the other's growth can lead to a cold war, and thus to a greater chance of war through preemptive and reputation-driven mechanisms.

The question posed in this chapter is a simple one: why do leaders knowingly initiate hard-line policies that could lead to inadvertent major war via crises and cold wars? To express it differently, what explains why actors shift to stronger policies along the hard-line/soft-line spectrum, despite the fact that these policies increase the probability of major war? This chapter provides a dynamic realist model to answer these questions.

The core argument is straightforward. If a state is facing decline, all-out preventive war is not necessarily the most rational way to maximize security. If the state can moderate or avert decline by less severe options, such as firm deterrence or the initiation of a crisis, these options will generally be preferred. After all, they overcome the problem of decline without automatically plunging the state into the highly uncertain venture of major war. Hard-line strategies and crisis initiation, however, pose risks of their own: they can lead to an action-reaction spiral that brings on major war through inadvertent means. Thus the rational security-seeking state must constantly grapple with profound least-of-many-evils choices. In particular, it must balance the pursuit of hard-line policies to mitigate decline with the increased risk of inadvertent war such policies produce. By understanding the factors that shape these trade-offs, we can determine under what conditions actors in decline will adopt conciliation, move to more provocative policies like containment or crisis initiation, or simply turn to the ultimate option—preventive major war. In this way, we can build a model that explains not just war versus peace, but changes in the *probability* of major war over time. Intense crises or the onset of destabilizing cold wars can thus be brought within a theory's purview.

This argument finds its inspiration in three sets of literatures: theories of crisis initiation; security-dilemma arguments; and the theories of major war of chapter 1. My goal is to synthesize the insights of these literatures into an argument that explains variance in the severity (or "toughness") of state policy, and therefore the likelihood of major war, across time and space.

As they stand, these analyses remain disconnected. Crisis scholars observe a critical fact: states often accept high risks of inadvertent war when initiating crises in order to mitigate an otherwise exogenous decline in power.[1] Security-dilemma scholars—both liberal and realist—stress that hard-line policies have a significant downside, namely, they can provoke escalation. In a security dilemma, actions taken by one state for its security undermine the other side's security, leading to counteractions. An action-reaction spiral occurs which, by heightening fear and mistrust, increases leaders' willingness to initiate war either for preemptive or for preventive reasons.[2]

These insights have not been well integrated into existing theories of major war. Classical realism contends that peace is likely if states maintain a balance of power and credibly communicate resolve. The downside of such behavior—that balancing policies can spark inadvertent escalations to major war—is underplayed or ignored. Neorealists, especially defensive neorealists, highlight the tragic implications of the security dilemma, and their structural logic strongly influences my approach.[3] Still, the parameters and causal mechanisms that determine when and how power changes affect the severity of state policy have not been fully fleshed out. Moreover, a disjuncture remains between the two most developed neorealist theories of major war—those of Kenneth Waltz and John Mearsheimer—and defensive neorealism in general; neither Waltz nor Mearsheimer integrates the inadvertent spiraling aspects of the security dilemma into his deductive logic.[4] In this chapter I seek to fill these gaps.

The chapter's argument perhaps poses the strongest challenge for hegemonic stability theory. Given its concern for the rising state, hegemonic stability theory has little interest in the security dilemma. The rising state initiates major war not because of security fears in a spiraling arms race, but simply to grab the status and rewards denied it by the established system. Yet there is little reason for a state, while still rising, to initiate either a major war or a crisis that significantly risks such a war, since waiting allows it to achieve its objectives later and more easily.[5] In short, the hegemonic stability argument is logically flawed. We should thus expect only states that are anticipating decline to accept the risks of crisis initiation (and this is confirmed in the empirical studies).

After outlining the model's general logic, I assess its implications for two main types of risky policy: crisis initiation within an existing rivalry; and the choice to begin a cold war rivalry by moving from peaceful to hard-line policies.

OVERVIEW OF THE MODEL

I begin by developing a model to explain state policies across the hard-line/soft-line spectrum. Explaining changes in the severity of policies over time helps us explain changes in the probability of major war, since different policies have varying implications for the likelihood of such a war. Clearly if a state chooses to initiate major war against the system, the probability of major war is essentially 100 percent, since we can assume that great powers, when attacked, will fight to protect themselves. If the state selects less extreme policies, however, this does not mean the probability of major war is zero. As the crisis and security-dilemma literatures emphasize, hard-line policies like crisis initiation or general containment strategies raise the likelihood of major war through inadvertent spiraling. Below I integrate the risk of inadvertent spiraling into a broader dynamic realist logic stressing the risks of decline.

The model begins with a decision-theoretical framework. The declining state acts on the basis of its estimates of various external conditions. The rising state's current preferences and diplomatic actions are assumed to be largely irrelevant to its decision (even if the rising state's *future* intentions may be important). This assumption not only makes the analysis more tractable; it also reasonably approximates reality. A state in decline knows that rising states, regardless of whether they possess aggressive or simply security-seeking motives, have an incentive to send conciliatory signals to buy time for their growth. The declining state will therefore usually dismiss these signals as tangential to its main concern: its declining power and the possibility of future conflict.[6]

Figure 5 outlines the causal logic. The dependent variable to be explained is shifts in the probability of major war over time within any system-type (either bipolarity or multipolarity).[7] What drives this probability is the policy choice of the declining state. For sake of simplicity, I consider five main policy options along the soft-line/hard-line spectrum: reassurance (accommodation/conciliation); doing nothing; deterrence/containment (arms racing, alliance buildups, harsh rhetoric, etc.); crisis initiation; and the direct initiation of major war.[8]

Six causal factors work together to determine which option is most likely to maximize the state's security. Three are independent variables reflecting the dynamic differentials concept: the initial differential of relative military power; the depth of decline in the absence of strong action; and the inevitability of decline in the absence of strong action. Chapter 1 showed how these variables shaped the more dichotomous choice between preventive major war or staying at peace.

Three parameters must now be incorporated, however, to predict the exact severity of a state's policy and thus the probability of major war (as a continuous variable). The first is the extent to which hard-line policies such as crisis initiation or containment hold out the prospect of overcoming the state's decline. The more such policies are expected to mitigate or even reverse decline, the more attractive they will be versus the more extreme step of preventive war. The second parameter is the extent to which such hard-line actions will increase the probability of major war through inadvertent means (where inadvertent war is defined simply as a war that occurs even though *prior* to these actions, no state preferred war to continued peace).[9] The greater the likelihood that hard-line policies will cause an inadvertent spiral to major war, the less attractive such policies will be versus the alternatives, including doing nothing or accommodation. (How accommodation strategies affect both decline and the probability of inadvertent war is considered later.)

The final parameter is the probability of the other attacking later should it be allowed to rise.[10] This parameter allows for the effects of both diplomacy and domestic processes on the other's perceptions of threat and interests, and thus on its propensity to attack the declining state down the road. For the sake of building the systemic realist logic, we can start with the assumption that the declining state is fundamentally uncertain about the other's future type. That is, the probability that the other will attack later after it peaks is either as likely as not (a 50–50 chance), or a function of how far the other rises.[11] In chapter 9, I relax this assumption to show the value

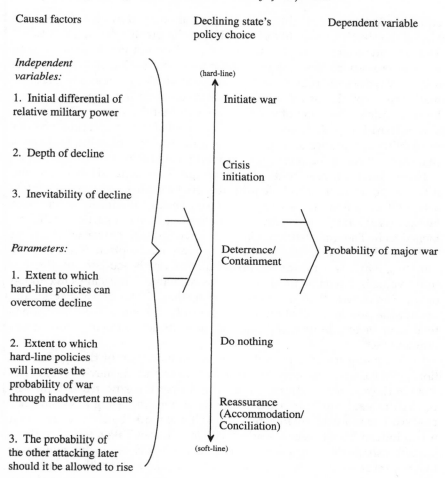

Fig. 5. Causal logic of the model

of integrating liberal and constructivist variables into a dynamic realist foundation.

In choosing among the five general types of policy, a rational security-seeking state will operate according to a simple rule: *pick the option that maximizes the state's security, that is, the option which, all things considered, leads to the highest expected probability of survival (EPS) over the foreseeable future.*[12] Stripped to its core, the EPS for any particular option is a function of two main factors: the probability that the option will lead to major war; and the probability of winning any major war that does occur. All things being equal, the lower the probability of a major war entailed by an option, or the higher the state's probability of winning it, the greater the option's EPS.[13] The dilemma confronting states, however, is clear: individual policies often work at cross-purposes regarding these two factors. Conciliatory reassurance may reduce the probability of major war breaking out as a result of an inadvertent spiral. But by sacrificing relative power in the process, it can lower a state's likelihood of winning any war that does occur. Conversely, a more hard-line policy may sustain a high level of power and thus a higher probability of winning in war, but only at the cost of increasing the chance that war will come about through inadvertent escalation.

Given such inherent trade-offs, how can a state decide between the different policy options? While formulas can be derived showing the interactive effects among the six variables/parameters,[14] the intuitive logic can be expressed straightforwardly. Each policy option has a particular EPS attached to it. The initial differential of relative military power will be most critical in determining the EPS for the "initiate war" option. Since directly initiating major war means the probability of war is 100 percent, this option's value is driven by the other dimension, namely, the state's likelihood of winning the war.[15] Thus we would expect that, all things being equal, the greater the present level of military superiority, the more likely the state is to achieve victory in war, and thus the more attractive the initiate-war option will be.[16]

In evaluating the EPS for either the accommodation or do-nothing options, two variables are key: the depth of decline and the inevitability of decline in the absence of strong action. The deeper the expected fall, the less power the state will have if war occurs later once the rising adversary has peaked. The more nearly inevitable the fall, the more the state realizes that it will indeed have to face the other with less power. Taken together, these variables shape the state's estimate of how likely it is to win any major war that occurs down the road after the other has peaked. Hence the deeper and more inevitable the decline in the absence of strong action, the more likely the state is to reject soft-line/do-nothing policies in favor of more hard-line ones.

The EPSs of the two hard-line options short of major war—deterrence/containment and crisis initiation—will be driven primarily by the first two parameters in figure 5. The more the state expects that it can avert decline through hard-line policies (the first parameter), the more attractive these policies will be. Containment strategies like restrictions on trade, arms racing, and alliance building help mitigate decline by reducing the other's potential growth. More severe policies like crisis initiation work somewhat differently: they are designed to ameliorate declining trends more directly by coercing the adversary into territorial and military concessions.[17]

Hard-line options cannot be implemented in a vacuum. In assessing their impact on the state's EPS, a leader must consider their possible downside—the likelihood that they will spark an escalation to inadvertent war (the second parameter). In short, once the spiral effect emphasized by crisis and security-dilemma theorists is acknowledged, a logical theory of major war cannot ignore the predicament confronting leaders: hard-line policies may improve the state's chances of winning any war that does occur (and reduce the other side's willingness to launch an aggressive war deliberately); but by heightening mistrust and by increasing concern for power trends, these policies make war more likely through inadvertent means. This leaves states with a tragic lesser-of-two-evils choice: do nothing or accommodate, at the risk of war later after the other has grown in strength; or adopt a hard-line stance, at the risk of a spiral to major war in the short term.[18]

By bringing together the problem of inadvertent spiraling and the problem of relative decline, we see how states grapple with the various options before them. For any given level of tension at any point in time, leaders will be reluctant to move to harder-line policies. They will do so only when current policies cannot be expected to avert decline. For example, in mid-1945, during a period of relative calm, Truman knew that shifting to containment would likely set off a destabilizing cold war. He did so only because he believed that not acting would allow Moscow to consolidate its sphere, thereby increasing its long-term threat. Once the cold war was underway, both sides were loath to initiate crises, given the obvious risks of escalation. They did so only when it was clear that continued arms racing and alliance building would not be enough to overcome decline.

This analysis suggests a prediction to guide the empirical case studies. All things being equal, *the more severe a state's decline will be in the absence of strong action, the more severe its actions are likely to be, that is, the more risks of inadvertent spiraling it will be willing to accept.* In the extreme, when decline is expected to be both deep and inevitable, and when even hard-line crisis or deterrent/containment policies are unlikely to overcome it, leaders may see preventive major war as the only option. As chapter 1 discussed, such a situation is most likely when the state is militarily preponderant but is inferior and declining in economic and potential power. This was the German problem before both World Wars.

When a hard-line strategy can mitigate or reverse decline, however, it will normally be adopted as the rational first step prior to a conscious decision to attack. Since the initiation of a crisis entails greater risks of inadvertent escalation than deterrence/containment, the former is rational only when the latter will not stem decline. Thus crises are relatively rare events in great power politics compared to deterrence policies like arms buildups and alliance restructuring. Yet such deterrence policies may not be enough, for three reasons. First is the problem just mentioned—the state is inferior and declining in economic and potential power. In such a situation, spending increasing amounts on military containment will likely fail over the long term, given the other's superior resources for such an extended competition. Second is the problem of entrenched stagnation relative to other states, which I outlined in the introductory chapter. The third problem, as I discuss below, is differential rates of success across geomilitary programs. States may simply not be able to keep up with their rivals—even though they are trying to—because the other's strategies are relatively more successful. In such situations, crisis initiation becomes an attractive option. This, as we will see, was the problem faced by the Soviet Union in 1948 and 1961 and by the Americans in 1962.

CRISIS INITIATION AND CONCILIATION

Let us look in more detail at why declining states, once in an enduring rivalry, might choose to initiate risky crises rather than simply opting for war. In considering various pathways to major war, I seek to underscore the critical connection between preventive actions short of war and inadvertent escalation, including escalation to preemptive war. I also analyze the conditions for moving away from confrontation, that is, for preferring conciliatory policies over continued hard-line containment.

Pathways to Major War

Figure 6 lays out five distinct pathways to major war. The first is simply the direct initiation of major war for preventive reasons. The attack could come as a surprise, or only after a crisis period. The key here, however, is that the initiator uses the crisis only to justify the war to its population or to a foreign audience.[19] The crisis itself has little independent role in bringing on the war, since the actor's preferences are firmly "deadlock"; that is, it strongly prefers major war to the continuation of the status quo.[20] As I show in chapters 3 through 5, given their views on the inevitable rise of Russia, German leaders in 1914 and 1939 preferred general war to a continued status quo (even if they preferred to eliminate opponents one-by-one).[21]

The second pathway is also one where the actor is either initiating major war directly or employing a crisis simply to justify its attack. The attack in this case, however, is driven by aggressive unit-level motives rather than national security.[22] Such motives could include: greed (material gain); domestic cohesion (diversionary motives); glory and the lust for power; the spreading of one's ideology; and so forth. Genghis Khan's attack on the system in the thirteenth century seems to epitomize such an aggressive war—although his Mongol forces did have some reason to fear neighbors,

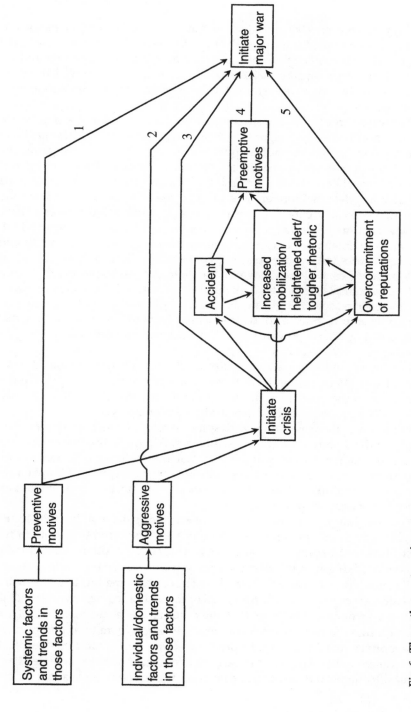

Fig. 6. The pathways to major war

his actions seem largely driven by greed and glory. Glory and ideology also shaped Hitler's calculus in 1939. My argument does not claim to explain the origins of such unit-level factors, and they may play an important and independent role in causing major war. The issue for the empirical chapters, however, is their relative historical salience versus my theory's more systemic factors.

Pathways three to five are situations where a state initiates a crisis without necessarily desiring major war; that is, the crisis is not a mere justification for war, but serves another purpose. In each of these three paths, the foundational motives can be either preventive (security-driven) or aggressive (unit-level based). My concern is with the former. In the third path, the initiator has deadlock preferences prior to the crisis because of steep decline that makes the continued status quo unacceptable. It provokes a crisis, however, in the hope that it can coerce sufficient concessions from its adversaries to ameliorate decline and make major war unnecessary. Should the adversaries fail to offer adequate concessions, the state, given its deadlock preferences, will then move to initiate major war as per the first pathway. For example, before the Peloponnesian War, Sparta, a state reluctant for domestic reasons to fight a major war, sought to coerce Athens into giving up its empire. Such a concession would have reversed the decline that was pushing Sparta toward war. Yet once Athens refused to comply, Sparta was forced to attack.

The fourth and fifth pathways capture the two primary means of inadvertent war. As noted, inadvertent war is a war that occurs despite the fact that prior to the crisis period, no state preferred major war to continued peace.[23] The processes of the crisis itself, therefore, play a significant role in causing one state to initiate war despite these pre-crisis preferences. And war is indeed chosen; it is a conscious act. Although the literature often refers to accidental war,[24] implying that neither side made a decision for war, in practice major war is too significant to "just happen." Figure 6 thus reexpresses within a cohesive framework the various elements of inadvertence in the crisis literature.

Pathway four is war through preemption. Each side, or at least the initiator, has "staghunt" preferences, where peace is preferred to getting in the first blow. But because of first-move advantages (an offensive-dominant system), striking first is better than an outcome where both attack essentially simultaneously and is certainly preferred to being hit first.[25] In such a situation, since peace is preferred to all of the war outcomes, a state will initiate a war only if it believes that the other is preparing to strike.[26] Thus even though the two are often conflated, preemptive motives and preventive motives remain distinct. In preventive war, the initiator has deadlock preferences (preferring war to peace) not because it fears immediate attack against its homeland, but because its declining situation means that the rising state will be able to attack later with more power (independent of whether there are first-move advantages). In preemptive war, the actors still prefer peace to war. But since they believe that the other is preparing to attack, they cannot afford to be caught unaware, given the offense-dominance of the system.[27]

Crisis periods thus have a significant impact on the motives for preemptive major war. Most important, crises typically involve the increased mobilization of each side's military forces, the placing of these forces on alert, and hostile rhetoric (demands and threats). These measures ensure that the state will not be caught unprepared, while also serving as signals of a state's resolve. Yet they can also produce a mutual fear of surprise attack, since each side is uncertain as to what the other will do with its mobilized forces. As figure 6 indicates, accidents within the crisis will greatly heighten this fear. In the Cuban missile crisis, for example, as both sides moved to higher states of alert, each side feared that accidents like the U2 downing over Cuba might reinforce perceptions that the other was readying itself for attack.[28]

Preemptive wars in general, not to mention preemptive *major* wars, are rare events in history.[29] The Seven Years War resulted from Prussia's preemption of Austria and Russia's impending preventive attack, but this is the only clear preemptive major war of which I am aware. A plausible story about preemption and World War I can be told (indeed, it remains the standard account). As I discuss in chapters 3 and 4, however, preemptive motives drove only Russian behavior, and German leaders exploited these Russian fears to bring on the preventive major war that only they wanted. Yet the rarity of preemptive major wars in practice is not surprising, given leaders' awareness of the dangers of things getting out of hand.[30] The risks of preemption, therefore, cannot be dismissed; indeed, the very act of downplaying these risks would make such wars more likely. Moreover, the Seven Years War and the fact that preemptive wars on a lesser scale do occur—the clearest examples being the U.S.-Chinese war in Korea in 1950 and the 1967 Arab-Israeli war[31]—show that preemption at the level of major war is always a real possibility. In the modern era, in fact, nuclear weapons so fundamentally alter the costs of war that preemption is one of the few pathways to major war which can still be seen as "rational."[32] Any theory of major war hoping to be applicable to the post-1945 period must therefore explain why states would ever initiate crises that significantly increase the risk of a preemptive total war.

If the fourth pathway shows how a crisis can reshape beliefs, the fifth pathway shows the effect of crises on preferences. Crises force states to put their reputations on the line. Actions such as crisis mobilization, harsh rhetoric, and military moves against third parties often have high audience costs: should a state take such actions and then back down, domestic and international audiences may perceive it as weak.[33] As work on incomplete-information games shows, actions with high audience costs send "costly signals" revealing a state's true resolve. Since weak actors are less likely to take such actions, challengers can update their beliefs about a defender's toughness, and thus back away before things go too far.[34] There is a downside to this, however: actions with large audience costs make it harder for states to make concessions within a crisis, thus narrowing the bargaining space of negotiated solutions both prefer to war. In short, reputations may get over-committed. The crisis then transforms actors who had chicken or staghunt preferences before the crisis into deadlock actors, who prefer war not only to the old status quo but also to any negotiated deal within the crisis.[35]

Reputational commitments help explain Russian behavior in 1914 and British/French behavior in 1939. In the July crisis, Russian leaders did not want major war and thus sought a negotiated solution. Yet as the crisis unfolded, the reputation loss entailed in abandoning Serbia shifted Russian preferences toward conflict. Likewise, in August to September 1939, the reputational costs of backing away from promises to defend Poland meant that war for London and Paris was preferred to any negotiated deal. World Wars I and II were not inadvertent, since, as chapters 3 through 5 show, Germany brought on war despite knowing that its adversaries would have to respond. Still, these situations do show how the commitment of one's reputation can pull states into major war. Although there are few cases where overcommitted reputations were the sole cause of major war, such a pathway is clearly a profound risk, especially in the nuclear era. In the Cuban missile crisis, for example, U.S. leaders understood that a strike on Cuba would force Moscow, for reputational reasons, to attack Berlin or the U.S. missiles in Turkey. Yet as Robert McNamara noted on 27 October, this would then require U.S. retaliation, perhaps against Russia's Black Sea fleet. Each round of tit-for-tat would have made it increasingly difficult to retreat from general war.

Crisis Initiation versus Accommodation / Conciliation

The discussion of pathways to major war clarifies the logic of the decision-making model. In maximizing security, declining states will not jump into preventive war if crisis initiation can reverse the decline. Still, leaders know that crises put both sides on a slippery slope to major war through either preemption or reputation-driven escalation. Indeed, it is precisely the risk of things getting out of hand that permits leaders to believe they can coerce concessions from the other and thus mitigate decline.[36]

Leaders understand the risks of inadvertent war. In thirteen of the sixteen crises examined by Glenn Snyder and Paul Diesing, policy-makers feared that the crisis might spin out of control.[37] This result should not be surprising: it is intuitively evident that great power crises like the Cuban missile crisis involve a higher risk of all-out war.[38] In fact, the rarity of crises in history is easily explained by states' fears of provoking their adversaries, knowing that inadvertent escalation to war might occur.[39]

Critical to explaining why a state might choose crisis initiation over more moderate options is understanding the specific source of the state's decline: where is the decline coming from, and how "fixable" is it by crisis measures? For the initiation of crisis to be rational, given the escalatory risks, a leader must expect that a crisis can coerce geopolitical concessions of the kind that will address the root of decline.

If decline is rooted in a state's inferiority in economic power and potential power, there is a problem. It is generally difficult to compel large concessions on such things as GNP and population/territorial mass through crisis initiation. This was part of the German predicament before 1914 and 1939. It was highly unlikely that Russian leaders could have been coerced by a crisis into relinquishing huge amounts of territory and population or into forgoing industrialization. Yet barring such concessions, Russia was destined to overwhelm Germany over the long term. Exploiting short-term military superiority, German leaders plunged into two devastating wars.

Even when states have more equitable distributions of territory, population, and raw materials, entrenched relative stagnation can still set in. Depending on the cause of stagnation, crisis initiation may or may not overcome it. Spain's steep decline after 1600, for example, was driven by deep structural problems within the Spanish economy. Initiating crises against France, Spain's primary adversary, would not have solved these problems; preventive war to buy breathing space for reforms seemed the only way (chapter 8). Likewise in the case of Soviet stagnation in the 1980s, as I discuss shortly, crises would not have resolved Russia's need for modern technology. Fortunately, accommodation held out the possibility of securing this technology, while the preventive war option was very unappealing.

When neither inferiority in economic/potential power nor entrenched stagnation is the main problem, the situation is less dire, and states should be reluctant to accept the risks of crisis initiation. They may still do so, however, because of the third form of decline: power oscillations. In an ongoing rivalry, deterrence/containment measures like arms racing and alliance building are usually preferred to crisis initiation. Deterrence actions are certainly provocative. Yet since they are steps largely internal to a bloc, they usually entail lower risks of inadvertent escalation than crises. Crises are more escalatory because they typically involve a direct challenge to the politico-territorial status quo and thus to the other's position and reputation. But deterrence policies are often not enough. Sometimes a state, despite its best efforts, cannot keep up with another in the short term.

Relative geostrategic strength is a matter of the *relative* success of a state's armament and alliance programs. Both sides may be trying vigorously to match the other side's actions. Yet one side may be far more successful, at least for a while, in building actualized military-geopolitical power. For the state less able to keep up in the short term, this creates a dual dilemma. On the one hand, the state fears that the adversary's growing strength may give it the confidence to attack later for nonsecurity reasons. On the other hand, a time lag in the effectiveness of the declining state's deterrence/containment programs means that its very capability to reverse the trends later may give the other a strong security-driven reason for war. In short, the state knows that its very attempt (and its ability) to reverse the short-term trends—to catch up after falling behind—can push the other into preventive war. Thus oscillations in the relative geopolitical balance caused by differing success rates for deterrence policies can push states to more extreme options.[40] In the short term, decline will be seen as exogenous in the absence of stronger action. More dangerous policies like crisis initiation will therefore be seen as necessary to mitigate the decline that arms racing and alliance building alone cannot address.

As we will see in chapter 7, power oscillations were behind the three key crises of the early cold war. Stalin pressed on Berlin in 1948 in order to compel Washington to reverse its plan to unite the three sectors of western Germany and integrate the result into the western bloc. In 1961, Khrushchev initiated another crisis over Berlin to force an agreement that would stabilize the economic situation of East Germany. In 1962, Kennedy brought on a crisis over missiles in Cuba to avert a significant short-term shift in the balance of power. In each case, two conditions for crisis initiation were present. First, greater arms and alliance activity alone would not have stopped the negative power oscillation in the near term. Second, the leaders in question could reasonably believe that initiating a crisis might compel concessions that would address the cause of decline, albeit at a heightened risk of inadvertent war.

In some situations, neither crisis initiation nor hard-line deterrence policies hold out the prospect of averting decline. If the state does not have the military power necessary for a successful war, then accommodation with the rising state(s) may be the rational option.[41] This option can be expected to be effective, however, only under certain strategic circumstances. In multipolarity, if one is declining in relation to two or more states, boundary conditions such as geography and technology can play important roles in determining which state one accommodates, and which state one opposes. That England after 1890 decided to align with the rising United States and Japan rather than fighting a preventive war against either is not surprising. Geography meant that America and Japan were much lower threats to Britain's existence than a rising Germany. The technology of the day reinforced this tendency. With the emergence of the airplane, the British splendid isolation policy was becoming increasingly outdated. Yet since U.S. and Japanese planes could not reach British shores, these states posed little threat from the skies.[42]

In more bipolar situations, accommodation may be the smart strategy, but only if such a policy stands a good chance of reversing decline. For sound strategic reasons, we are unlikely to find many declining states accommodating just to buy the rising state's goodwill—that is, to buy a promise that it will not attack later when it has become preponderant.[43] The problem, as James Fearon notes, is one of trust under anarchy. The rising state may genuinely wish to commit now to not attacking later, but the commitment is not enforceable; there is little to stop it from changing its mind after preponderance has been achieved, particularly if current leaders are no longer around.[44] If the accommodation involves concessions that only cause the state to decline even further, accommodation is even less likely to be adopted simply for the sake of security promises.

There are those rare circumstances where accommodation in bipolarity holds out the prospect of mitigating one's decline. In the mid-1980s, for example, Gorbachev and the Politburo moved away from a hard-line policy that was only exacerbating Russia's entrenched economic stagnation. By shifting to détente, the Soviets had a clear goal: to secure trade and technology concessions that would revitalize the Soviet economy.[45] Without these concessions, Soviet economic and potential power was expected to continue to fall behind the west. For this accommodation strategy to be the rational choice depended on a number of conditions. Preventive nuclear war would hardly have furthered Soviet security, given each side's ten thousand strategic warheads. Initiating a crisis, such as another move on Berlin, would have been fruitless. It would not have dealt with the root problem: the inferiority of Soviet technology as the world moved into the information age. The Soviets also could rest behind their huge strategic arsenal as they made the concessions on eastern Europe, Euromissiles, and the like necessary to secure U.S. promises on trade and technology. In most bipolar situations, accommodation is less likely to be effective. In the Sparta-Athens, Carthage-Rome, and France-Hapsburgs cases, the declining states had no powerful nuclear second-strike to lean upon; preventive war thus emerged as the rational strategy.

This discussion reinforces the importance of understanding the source of a state's decline, and to what extent a particular policy will address it. One factor in both bipolar and multipolar systems is the specific foundation for potential power. In the nuclear era, technology and education are critical components of potential power. They are not only the basis for economic growth but are essential to the ongoing modernization of nuclear weapons and their supporting logistical and communications structures. The Soviets in the 1980s, therefore, had reason to fear the widening technological gap.

In particular, the deployment of such innovations as the Strategic Defense Initiative ("Star Wars") system might have undermined the Soviet second-strike capability. It is thus not surprising that a critical objective in Gorbachev's bargaining posture, in addition to loosening trade constraints, was obtaining restrictions on Star Wars research and deployments.

Before 1945, however, territorial size and population were typically the key components of potential power. Superiority in land mass implied the diversity of raw materials and food production needed for a growing economy, which in turn ensured that a large population could be shaped into an effective fighting force. Inferiority implied the opposite. As noted, Germany's core problem in this century was precisely its severe inferiority vis-à-vis Russia in territory and population. The same was the case in the pre-1945 bipolar cases. Sparta tried to demand Athenian concessions on its empire, the basis for Athens's potential power, but it seems clear that Sparta had little hope Athens would comply. Carthage by the 220s B.C. was dealing with a Rome that controlled the Italian peninsula, Sicily, Sardinia, and the coast of southern France. Having won these territories through costly wars, the Romans were unlikely to give them up just to allay Carthaginian fears of decline. In the French case, the Hapsburgs by 1520 controlled twice as much territory in Europe and had just conquered large parts of Latin America. In each case, preventive war against the rising colossus before it had consolidated its strength thus appeared to be the only rational strategy.

The choice between war, crisis, deterrence, and accommodation is a difficult one. Preventive major wars, given their high risks, are options of last resort. Crisis initiation is also a risky option, and will usually be chosen only when less provocative hard-line policies like arms racing and alliance consolidation prove ineffective in sustaining the power balance. But the crisis must hold out the hope of coercing the kind of concessions that can address the source of the state's decline. Hence, when decline is rooted in technological change and certain types of economic stagnation, and when preventive war is infeasible, accommodation to the rising state may be the only feasible strategy. This is especially the case when accommodation is the only way to secure the trade needed to revive one's economic-technological base.

THE BEGINNING OF COLD WAR RIVALRIES

We have seen why, within an existing rivalry, a state might shift from ongoing deterrence policies to the more risky strategy of initiating a crisis. But why might states in a period of peaceful relations shift from a policy of calm engagement to one of hard-line deterrence/containment? The dilemma is clear. Moving to a hard-line policy to contain the other is likely to undermine any trust between the relevant great powers. Yet it may be the only way to prevent the other's steady rise.

In this sense, cold wars (or "enduring rivalries") do not just happen.[46] They are initiated, in the same way crises are initiated. And like crises, cold wars are recognized to be events that raise the probability of an inadvertent slide into major war (thus our collective sigh of relief in 1989–91).[47] Cold wars may not have the immediate salience of events like the Munich crisis or the Cuban missile crisis. But by raising levels of suspicion, provoking arms races, and encouraging states to put forces on higher levels of alert, they not only make such crises more likely, they also increase the risks that one side will see preventive and preemptive major war to be in its interest.

In this section I reiterate the logic of the model as it applies to the beginning of cold wars and compare it to the relevant alternative theories. The argument represents a synthesis of spiral-model reasoning on the risks of cold war escalation and deterrence-model reasoning on the importance of maintaining power. I thus seek to bring the two models together within one common causal framework.[48]

A rising great power in a situation of peaceful relations has little problem deciding on its policy: it has no reason to disturb the current situation as long as engagement continues to facilitate its growth.[49] The declining state is in a more uncomfortable position, since it faces trade-offs similar to those confronting a state having to decide whether to initiate a crisis. In choosing between staying with a peaceful, soft-line posture or moving to hard-line deterrence, a state will have its behavior shaped by the six variables/parameters outlined in figure 5. The greater the depth and inevitability of long-term decline in the absence of stronger action, and the more such action is expected to mitigate or reverse this decline, the more likely the state is to switch to a harder-line policy. Yet the state must also take into account the extent to which a hard-line policy will increase the probability of major war through inadvertent escalation. As the spiral model would emphasize, hard-line deterrence cannot be implemented in a vacuum. Given the security dilemma, such policies tend to be misintepreted as preparations for possible expansion.[50] They therefore provoke a destabilizing action-reaction cycle.[51]

In making a rational decision, therefore, a security-maximizing state must recognize the upsides and the downsides of both soft-line reassurance and hard-line deterrence. We can therefore anticipate that when decline is not expected to be deep or inevitable great powers will choose peaceful engagement over containment. In the 1990s, for example, the United States pursued engagement toward China, and, as chapter 9 discusses, this was the logical and predictable policy. Yet, when profound decline can be anticipated should the state fail to switch to containment, then such a switch is likely. Truman's move to containment in mid-1945, even at a time when he felt that Stalin had relatively moderate intentions, shows the profound impact of such dynamic power trends.

Critical to a state's determination of the prospects for long-term decline are the initial differentials and trends of economic power and especially potential power. In general, we can predict that the stronger the state is in economic and potential power, the more sanguine it will be about the future, and thus the less willing it will be to accept the risks of inadvertent escalation inherent in a cold war rivalry. The United States in the 1990s, for example, possessed advantages over China in technology, raw materials, and education. Thus, despite China's economic growth, there was no immediate reason to believe that it could overtake the United States in overall power. This situation was quite a bit different from the U.S. position versus Russia in 1945. America certainly was not in the dire position of Germany earlier in the century (when Germany had about one-third of Russia's population and one-fortieth of its land mass). The Soviet Union in 1945, however, already possessed a strong educational/technological base and a high level of industrialization. Hence there was good reason to worry that this state might overtake the United States if nothing was done to restrain its growth. In short, the degree of a state's superiority or inferiority in economic and potential power has much to do with its willingness to accept the risks inherent in hard-line policies.

This analysis builds on the insights of both the deterrence and spiral models. It is important to note, however, that when realists of different stripes (and liberals) debate the strengths and weaknesses of these models, they tend to focus on the actors' military policies, not on the differentials and trends of economic and potential power. For defensive realists and liberals who emphasize the value of the spiral model, the security dilemma is fundamentally a function of each side's arms and alliance policies; it is one state's efforts to improve its security through such military means that is so frightening to the other side.[52] My argument supplements this view by considering how states deal with actors who are not currently developing the kind of military power needed to attack but who might be able to build this power later, should their growth in economic and potential power be allowed to continue. In the traditional security dilemma underpinning the spiral model, if state B is not building its military strength, state A should be relatively sanguine. In my model, even this situation can provoke state A to move to containment if the trends of economic and potential power are against it. The United States shifted to containment in 1945 even though it was known that the Soviet Union was drastically demilitarizing; the fear of Soviet growth in economic and potential power drove the hard-line policy.

The argument I have outlined shows why spiral modelers and deterrence modelers need not be at odds with one another.[53] Both sides, I believe, can accept the variables/parameters outlined in this chapter and the basic causal logic linking them. Both could agree, for example, that if a state is declining deeply, can do little about it through either hard- or soft-line policies, and will almost certainly be attacked later, preventive war, however unpalatable, is the option that will probably maximize the state's expected probability of survival. If decline is not at all inevitable, the other's intention to attack later not clear, and a hard-line policy would pose a fair risk of inadvertent war, then soft-line engagement is typically the best option. Alternatively, if decline would be deep and inevitable in the absence of stronger action but could be reversed by a hard-line posture, such a posture will likely be preferred so long as the risks of inadvertent war are not abnormally high and there is a fair chance the other might attack later if allowed to rise. The more severe the decline and the fewer the lower-level options, the more likely the state is to accept significant risks of inadvertent escalation.

The disagreement between deterrence and spiral modelers theoretically—and between hawks and doves in the real world—is therefore less about causal logic, and more about the exact *values* of the variables and parameters.[54] Consider U.S. policy versus China at the turn of the new millennium, for example. Hawks and doves could agree that if it could be known for sure that China would become clearly preponderant in twenty years and would be aggressive at that time, then preventive containment would be advisable now, notwithstanding the risk of sparking a new cold war. Yet doves reject both premises. They would thus conclude that peaceful engagement is preferred, at least until such time as China's long-term growth and future aggressiveness seem inevitable.

In sum, both the deterrence model and the spiral model have part of the puzzle right. Yet the models remain disconnected and incomplete. The deterrence model correctly notes that hard-line policies can avert decline, but it ignores the spiral-model point that these policies can increase the probability of war through inadvertent escalation. The spiral model captures this risk. Yet it minimizes the potential downside to reassurance policies, namely, that they may permit exogenous decline to continue, thereby leaving the state less able to defend itself later. By integrating the risk of inadvertent spiraling into a primarily power-driven model, this book specifies more clearly under what conditions states will remain peacefully engaged, and under what conditions they will fall into cold war.

This chapter has sought to show how incorporating the insights of the crisis and security-dilemma literatures can help build a more powerful dynamic realist approach to major war. Leaders are not ignorant of escalation effects. Most obviously, they know that if they provoke a crisis by challenging another's vital interests, things may get out of hand. Crises are therefore likely only when less risky options will not achieve the state's ends. Leaders also know that if they adopt hard-line policies during periods of relative calm, the other may interpret these acts as hostile, leading the actors into a cold war rivalry. U.S. leaders today are aware of the risks of trying to contain China, just as Truman was in 1945.

Dynamic differentials theory helps answer the question of why leaders, knowing the risks of hard-line policies, would ever choose them over more accommodative strategies. Hence, one need not fall back on domestic-level forces or leader misperception to see why states sometimes take such gambles. Rational security-seeking actors pursue the option that maximizes the state's expected probability of survival. When a state is not in decline, or is in fact rising, peaceful engagement is usually the best strategy. Declining states, however, face different constraints and therefore have different induced preferences. The more severe the state's deteriorating position, the more likely it is, all things being equal, to adopt severe policies with a high risk of inadvertent escalation in order to avert further decline. This analysis thus allows us to predict changes in the probability of major war over time through a power-driven systemic logic.

SUMMARY OF THE COMPETING HYPOTHESES

In the following six chapters, I test the hypotheses about major war from dynamic differentials theory both against current realist theories and against other explanations in the literature. But first it will be useful to summarize the main competing realist hypotheses. Evidence that would falsify a theory or reduce its salience is specified in parentheses.[55]

Dynamic Differentials Theory

1. Leaders perceiving their states to be in decline will be the initiators of major wars or of crises/cold wars that increase the risk of inadvertent major war. The more severe a state's decline will be in the absence of strong actions, the more likely the state is to initiate such actions. In general, therefore, the greater the declining state's inferiority in economic power and potential power, the more likely it is to pursue highly risky policies. (Falsified if rising states are the initiators of major wars and crises/cold wars. Falsified if the greater a state's rise, the more it is willing to take such risks. Falsified if steeply declining states with the requisite military power [points 2 and 3 below] do not initiate war or crisis/cold war, even when such policies can avert decline. Salience reduced if states begin major wars or crises/cold wars for unit-level reasons.)

2. In multipolarity, the declining state will be more likely to initiate ma-

jor wars or crises/cold wars that increase the risk of inadvertent major war when it possesses marked military superiority versus the other great powers taken individually. The more marked its military superiority, the more likely it is to initiate such actions. (Falsified if the state initiates major war or highly risky policies with only military equality or less.)

3. In bipolarity, the declining state will be more likely to initiate major wars or crises/cold wars that increase the risk of inadvertent major war if it is either preponderant *or* near-equal in military power. The second-ranked great power may also initiate such policies if it is declining, but the greater its level of inferiority, the less likely it is to do so. (Falsified if the second-ranked state attacks even though significantly inferior and when decline is not that severe.)

Classical Realism

1. Major wars and crises/cold wars raising the risk of inadvertent major wars are most likely to occur when one state has a preponderance of power. Such events should not occur when there is a balance of power between individual states or between alliance blocs. (Falsified if these events occur when individual great powers are in relative balance or their alliance blocs are in balance.)

2. Major wars and crises/cold wars are started by a state with aggressive unit-level motives for expansion. (Salience is reduced if the initiator is only or primarily seeking security.)

Structural Neorealism

1. Major wars and crises/cold wars raising the risk of inadvertent major war are more likely to occur in multipolar systems than bipolar systems. (Falsified if such events are as common or more common in bipolar systems.)[56]

Hegemonic Stability Theory

1. Major wars and crises/cold wars raising the risk of inadvertent major war are most likely to occur when the two most powerful states in the system are roughly equal and one state is overtaking the other.[57] (Falsified if such events occur when one state is preponderant.)

2. The initiator of major wars and intense crises/cold wars should be the rising state. It will initiate only when, because of unit-level factors, it is dissatisfied with the status and rewards provided by the system. (Falsified if such events are initiated by the declining state. Salience is reduced if initiator is solely or primarily seeking security.)

[3]

German Security and the Preparation for World War I

World War I is probably the most analyzed and contested case in international relations scholarship. Given its complexities, practically any theory—whether at the individual, domestic, or system level—seems to find some empirical support. To avoid adding yet another interpretation to what seems like an already highly overdetermined case, I first examine the many empirical puzzles left unexplained in current theories. I then show how dynamic differentials theory covers these anomalies. In doing so, I seek to demonstrate that only this argument provides a consistent explanation for all the diverse evidence.

This chapter covers the lead-up to the July crisis of 1914 in two main parts: the growing sense in Germany of the necessity for preventive war; and the significant differences between German policy during the four Balkans crises in 1912–13 and policy in July 1914. I also discuss the problems with domestic-level arguments for the war. As will be evident, I focus almost exclusively on German decision-making. The reason becomes clearer in the following chapter as the July crisis is analyzed in depth: since only Germany can be considered responsible for wanting and bringing on major war, its changing view on the desirability of war is of utmost interest.

This book predicts that major war in multipolarity is likely only when one state is significantly superior in military power. Moreover, this state will initiate war only when it sees itself to be declining deeply and inevitably. I also predict that as this state begins to peak in relative military power it should be more likely to engage in risky crisis behavior to ameliorate anticipated decline. To support the argument, I need to show that German preventive-war thinking became increasingly entrenched up to July 1914, and that Germany, for long-run security reasons, manipulated the July crisis to bring on general war at a moment seen as most favorable. We should also see an increasing number of crises preceding the outbreak of war, as German leaders become more confident of their superiority but also worried about their long-term position. At the same time, German leaders should be expected to debate the actual moment when German power is peaking and calibrate the risks of inadvertent escalation against the benefits of provoking crises. When risks are high and benefits minimal, these leaders should seek to moderate the extent of these crises. This will ensure that major war breaks out only when German military power is maximized relative to German adversaries.

The documentary evidence bears out these predictions. German leaders after 1904 began to see Germany as the militarily preponderant state in the system. Yet the long-standing fear remained the growth of Russia, a state with far superior potential power (land mass and population) and a rapidly industrializing economy. A number of crises were thus provoked or fueled to help shore up Germany's position. In 1912, however, as both civilian and military leaders moved toward a consensus that Germany could not avert decline merely by crisis diplomacy, they accepted that major war must be implemented. They thus acted to maximize Germany's military preponderance and at the same time to avoid bringing on general war too soon. Knowing that any attack by Austria-Hungary on Serbia would force Russia to respond, they restrained Vienna's enthusiasm for war in the Balkans whenever it seemed Russia might be drawn in.[1] By June 1914, however, with relative military power now at its height, German leaders switched policy: in the face of the latest Balkans incident, they pushed Austria to invade Serbia. This was designed to force Russia to act, allowing Germany to blame Russia for the major war only Berlin wanted.

This view draws from evidence revealed by historians that German officials up to August 1914 were increasingly obsessed with the rising Russian threat.[2] As will become clear, my argument differs from that of these historians in two ways. First, scholars such as Fritz Fischer contend that military decline from a position of superiority only provided Berlin with the opportunity for a war actually driven by domestic goals. I show that security was the only key objective motivating those leaders responsible for the critical decisions; in fact, domestic factors inclined these individuals to peace.[3] Second, I reject the position of historians such as Egmont Zechlin and Karl Dietrich Erdmann, who contend that while German leaders were driven by security concerns, their primary goal was not continental or world war, but a localized conflict in the Balkans to support an ailing Austrian ally.[4] While this "calculated risk" thesis would not be inconsistent with the argument made in chapter 2, in that fears of decline were pushing Berlin to accept the risks of inadvertent war, the thesis is historically incorrect. The German chancellor and his associates preferred major war to even a localized war or

[57]

a negotiated solution—they had firm "deadlock" preferences. They thus used the crisis to manipulate the other states, including Austria, into war.

Overall, my perspective competes with three types of explanations for World War I. The first, drawn from the spiral model, would see the war as inadvertent: no state wanted major war, yet the pre-1914 arms race put the great powers on a hair trigger. Hence, when the crisis began in the Balkans in July 1914, all states mobilized and then acted for preemptive reasons.[5]

Analyses of misperceptions, cults of the offensive, and military time-tables supplement this basic spiral view. Richard Ned Lebow argues that decision-making pathologies led Berlin to expect others to back down so that German objectives could be achieved without war. By late July, when it was clear that all states including Britain would oppose Germany, German leaders were so incapacitated by the shock of the new information that they could not avert catastrophe.[6] Stephen Van Evera argues that the pervasive belief among European leaders that the offensive was dominant led states to rush to preemptive war for fear their adversaries would strike first.[7] This view is underpinned by the argument that military leaders, particularly in Germany, seized the reins of power, putting states on mobilization schedules that made preemptive war inevitable.[8]

The second category of explanations rejects the idea that no one wanted war. Some states, most importantly Germany, were indeed aggressive, not as a result of misperceptions and security fears, but because of domestic pathologies. One such argument is that hypernationalism, fed through a rapacious press, pressured leaders to adopt aggressive, expansionary postures.[9] Others argue that as Germany after 1890 moved to a policy of belligerent self-assertion to achieve its "place in the sun," it could not help but act aggressively in the European theater.[10] Jack Snyder, building on Eckart Kehr, contends that Germany's tendency to overexpansion reflects the strategic ideology shaped by a cartelized political system: the sharing of power between interest groups led to expansion through domestic logrolling.[11]

The most influential domestic-level explanation is Fischer's argument that German leaders initiated war to solve their internal crisis. Emphasizing the "primacy of domestic policy," Fischer asserts that Berlin sought "to consolidate the position of the ruling classes with a successful imperialist foreign policy."[12] Germany's declining military power affected only the timing of German actions; the core objectives were still social imperialist.[13]

The third category of explanations operates at the systemic level. For neorealists, the war was one of miscalculation caused by multipolarity. Since states could not abandon their allies without endangering their security, once Russia moved to support Serbia, Germany was forced to defend Austria and France to defend Russia. A small Balkans crisis thus dragged all great powers into major war.[14] Hegemonic stability theorists like Gilpin and Organski contend that Germany's rise to near equality with Britain led to war, with rising Germany initiating war.[15] Finally, as noted, a number of scholars have emphasized that fears of decline drove German leaders either to take a calculated risk in July 1914, or actually to seek major war.

EMPIRICAL PUZZLES AT ODDS WITH CURRENT THEORIES

All these theories face some significant empirical problems. For the spiral model to argue that war was caused by incentives to preempt, it must show that German leaders thought Russian mobilization meant that Petersburg had a possible desire for war. Yet German leaders knew with certainty that the czar and Russian officials were desperate to avoid war in 1914, if only because Russia had not completed its rearmament.[16] The argument that Berlin reacted with preemptive strikes because of a belief in offense dominance is also suspect. If true, why did Germany threaten Russia with war on 29 July in response only to initial Russian preparations against Austria, when in the winter of 1912–13 it had done nothing after a much more extensive Russian mobilization against Austria? More broadly, preemptive arguments must explain why in four previous crises in the Balkans from 1912 to 1913 spirals did not break out. In particular, the shift from German restraint of Austria in previous crises to German pressure in July 1914 must be explained.

Furthermore, why was Russian mobilization, even general mobilization, so frightening when German leaders knew that Russia could not reach full strength for months? One might respond that Germany had to act because the Schlieffen Plan required destroying France first. But this only begs the question: Why the Schlieffen Plan, and why was the plan for attacking only Russia set aside in April 1913? Moreover, why would German leaders fear French attack in the critical period of early August 1914 when they knew Paris had moved its troops ten kilometers back from the border, precisely to avoid suspicion that France wanted to strike?

Integral to the issue of preemption is whether Germany truly could not stop its war machine once it got rolling, either because the military seized the reins of power or because logistical schedules produced some sort of technical determinism. Yet if this were so, why on 2 August would Chancellor Theobald von Bethmann Hollweg tell the kaiser that he was delaying a declaration of war and an attack on France "in the hope that the French will attack us," and then proceed to war only when the French would not oblige?[17] If the military controlled the situation, why did the chancellor's opinion on 29 July that Germany should delay general mobilization win the day? Why was the crucial decision to declare war on Russia, made on 31 July and implemented on 1 August, kept secret from all military leaders except Helmuth von Moltke, the army's chief of the General Staff? More generally, why did the military have no control over German diplomatic maneuvering from 28 June to the day the war began?

The view, propounded by many, that the war was caused by Berlin's misperception that Britain would remain neutral,[18] is also suspect. The evidence shows that all German leaders, including Bethmann, knew that the possibility of British neutrality was very small from at least 1911 onward because of traditional British balance-of-power policy. Moreover, if they pinned their hopes on Britain staying out, why would they delay fighting a major war in December 1912 precisely to prepare for a war that included Britain?

The Fischer thesis that Germany initiated war to solve its domestic crisis is also problematic. It is clear that Bethmann and the other key officials believed both before and during the July crisis that major war would only *increase* the possibility of social revolution in Germany. And if the generals sought to maintain the traditional class structure, why would they greatly expand the army after 1911, a move that not only undermined the army's aristocratic core, but one that put more weapons into the hands of the working class? The Waltzian and hegemonic stability theory argument that European states were roughly equal before the war is undermined, as noted in chapter 1, by the evidence that Germany was indeed military preponderant in 1914. This explains how Germany could fight almost singlehandedly (with only minimal help from Austria and Turkey) against France, Britain, Russia, and later the United States for four years, and come very close to winning. Moreover, the hegemonic stability thesis that rising states initiate major war is at odds with the fact that German leaders believed that their state was inevitably and profoundly declining versus Russia.

Probably the greatest puzzle for all current theories, and one that has gone virtually unnoticed, is why Germany declared war on Russia on 1 August. The declaration served no diplomatic or domestic purpose (indeed, it hurt Germany's efforts to blame Russia for the war). Nor did it serve a military purpose, since it only provoked both the Russians and French to speed up their mobilizations. If German civilian leaders were truly seeking a way out, knowing that the only choice was world war or a negotiated peace (including one giving Austria almost everything it wanted), why would they cut off all possible last-minute negotiations, making war truly inevitable? Furthermore, why would they set up both Petersburg and their own military to have no inkling that a declaration of war was coming? This puzzle is crucial, since almost every argument, including even Fischer's, ultimately accepts that things got out of control in the last days of the crisis (why else would Berlin not have chosen a favorable negotiated settlement instead of world war?).

In this chapter and the next, I show how the dynamic differentials logic provides a parsimonious and complete explanation to these outstanding puzzles. German leaders were so convinced of the necessity of preventive war by 1914 that once they had secured the support of the German masses and Austria by blaming Russia, they deliberately undermined all chances for peace.

The Growth of a Preventive War Imperative in Germany

The argument that preventive war was essential to long-term security was increasingly accepted within Germany after 1900. Leaders within the army were the first to promote the view. Yet as evidence grew that Germany was peaking in relative power, the civilian leadership also accepted the need for general war. Russia would overwhelm Germany once it completed its industrialization. Moreover, Russia's rapid military buildup and expanding railway system meant that after 1917 Germany would no longer have the military superiority needed to win a total war. If the nation were to survive, German leaders believed, war would have to be fought sooner rather than later, and this required Germany to bring it on.

This preventive war logic was not simply a product of an aggressive political culture after 1890, as Wilhelm II sought to enhance Germany's global status.[19] On at least two occasions during Bismarck's time—1875 and 1877—the preventive war option was actively discussed.[20] Although major war did not occur, it can hardly be argued that this reflected Bismarck's love of peace; after all, Bismarck had picked the optimal time to fight three limited wars between 1864 and 1870 to build the German Empire. He was restrained by the fact that Germany was still undergoing a massive industrialization program.[21] Moreover, France, Russia, and Britain clearly signaled that they would work together to oppose any further German expansion on the continent.[22] In short, Bismarck realized that Germany did not yet have the military superiority to take on the system, nor was it necessary to do so since Germany was still growing economically.[23]

Still, the fact that Russia was a long-term threat was recognized at an early date. In December 1887, at a time when preventive war was again being contemplated, future chancellor Bernard von Bülow, then Secretary of the German embassy in Petersburg, indicated that "if we fight the Russians we must not make peace until we have made them incapable of attacking us for at least a generation."[24] In 1890, General Friedrich von Bernhardi argued that Germany had to build its strength, and then "methodically to bring about war [against Russia] and not to wait until we have again been outstripped."[25]

The Schlieffen Plan, whose logic was first outlined by General Alfred von Schlieffen in 1892,[26] focused on eliminating France first, so that Germany's full weight could be turned against Russia. The plan was revised in early 1905, at a time when Russia was bogged down in a disastrous war with Japan. Schlieffen saw the opportunity of using the Moroccan crisis as a pretext to destroy at least France, if not also Russia. In the summer of 1905, he argued that Germany was "surrounded by an enormous coalition . . . [but now] we can escape from the noose."[27] By September, the German military still considered war against France and Britain a real possibility. London's support for France, however, greatly worried the chief of Germany's naval staff, Admiral Alfred von Tirpitz, who knew that the German navy was not yet ready for war against Britain. This, plus the fact that civilian leaders did not see domestic and military conditions as optimal, helped deflect Berlin from war.[28] Still, the probability that Germany would move to major war was clearly growing as military arguments for preventive war were set against additional evidence of decline.

In the next crisis—the 1908–9 tension sparked by Austria's annexation of Bosnia Herzegovina—arguments for preventive war reemerged, again coming mostly from the military. In January 1909, with war between Austria and Russia still a possibility, political leaders in Berlin and Vienna asked their military commanders to coordinate war plans against France and Russia. The chiefs of the general staffs, General Moltke and General Franz Conrad von Hötzendorf, began a correspondence lasting until August 1914.[29] In March 1909, after Russia capitulated, Moltke expressed to Conrad his disappointment that they had lost an opportunity for war "which is unlikely to reappear under such favorable conditions." Still, the two countries should "look confidently to the future." As long as Austria and Germany stood together "we shall be strong enough to break any circle."[30] Given Berlin's recognition of increasing Austrian military weakness up to 1914,[31] Moltke's words indicate his belief that Germany, as the dominant ally, stood at least a fair chance of defeating any coalition against it. The growing pervasiveness of this belief within Germany is shown by the fact that other capitals were aware of it. In 1909, the former Russian ambassador to Berlin wrote that the German military was "moving towards the conviction that the superiority of the army at the present moment promises the greatest prospects of success." With Russia rebuilding after the Russo-Japanese war and France paralyzed by domestic conflict, Germany might be tempted to destroy both states "with one big blow."[32]

Russia's humiliation in the Bosnian crisis led to large-scale Russian military reorganization. In late 1910, the Russian war minister, V. A. Sukhomlinov, instituted a new defense plan that increased the number and effectiveness of the reserves. David Hermann notes that "foreign observers all thought these changes would make the Russian army much more effective," although the full impact would only be felt over a number of years.[33] The Prussian General Staff's assessment in late 1910 indicated that the

Russian reorganization meant a "significant increase in readiness" and thus a "stronger threat." The British military attaché reported in 1911 that Russia by late 1912 would have an efficient, well-equipped force of front-line troops. This reinforced a forecast from 1909 that given Russia's "almost unlimited" resources and its military resurgence, "for offense she will soon be most formidable."[34]

Postponing the Great War: German War Planning, 1911–1913

The next crisis began on 1 July 1911 when the German warship *Panther* moved into the Moroccan port of Agadir, despite the 1906 agreement placing Morocco firmly under French control. Berlin hoped such a move would split the Entente or at least achieve concessions in Africa. As in the first Moroccan crisis, however, Britain firmly supported France. On 17 August, the kaiser and his political and military advisers decided against war, with Tirpitz's arguments again being critical. The navy was not yet ready to fight Britain, Tirpitz argued, but with each passing year "we shall be in a much more favorable position." He was supported by Admiral George Alexander von Müller, chief of the German Naval Cabinet, who advised Bethmann and Wilhelm "to postpone this war which was probably unavoidable in the long run until after the completion of the [Kiel] canal." German leaders were also aware that Austria did not see the dispute in Morocco as the *casus foederis* needed to invoke alliance obligations.[35]

British resolve and Austrian caution in 1911 helped shape later events. It was becoming increasingly apparent that Britain would not remain neutral in any continental war; by 1914, Bethmann knew that the hope was slim at best. Regarding Austria, Berlin needed its army, as weak as it was, to ensure a successful bid for hegemony; Austrian forces had to divert Russia in the first stage of war to allow Germany to destroy France in six weeks. Berlin thus had to create a situation where Austria would be compelled to act, so that Germany could have its war by appearing to come to Austria's aid, rather than the other way around. As Bethmann told the kaiser in September 1910, "let us hope that if there is a war the attack will be aimed against Austria which will then need our assistance and not against us so that it is not left to Austria to decide whether to be loyal to the alliance or not."[36]

Through 1912, fear of Russian growth began to pervade the civilian leadership. Bethmann was greatly sobered by his visit to Russia in July 1912. A meeting with Czar Nicholas reinforced his belief that the Russians had no desire for war, at least while they were rebuilding: "Russia needs peace to consolidate itself. For this reason . . . its present rulers want to be on good terms [with Germany]." Yet he worried about Russia's "wealth of mineral resources and solid physical manpower," noting "Russia's rising industrial power, which will grow to overwhelming proportions."[37] His pessimism would only deepen over time: overlooking his estate before the war, he told his son that there was little reason to plant new trees, since "in a few years the Russians would be here anyway."[38]

It was Bethmann's growing recognition that general war would have to be fought sooner rather than later that pushed him to support the army's call for a massive increase in war readiness. The chancellor supported the 1912 and 1913 military laws that would increase standing land forces by 25 percent. As Hermann shows, the originators of the new policy were well aware that it would spark a competition with Germany's neighbors. Indeed, the war ministry had always warned Bethmann's office that steps to markedly increase Germany's land power should only be taken if war was seen as inevitable.[39] By late 1911, the ministry made its case that this time had come. On 19 November, Prussian Minister of War General Josias von Heeringen wrote to Bethmann that despite recent setbacks, he and Moltke were convinced that Germany's army was still equal to the combined strength of its opponents in the near term. Yet since the adversaries' growing strength was making deterrence more difficult, Germany must "reckon with war . . . if any particular provocation to it is given."[40]

Ten days later, on 29 November, General Franz von Wandel, the individual responsible for drafting the new army bill, produced a memorandum providing more details on the army's logic. The situation was not very favorable. Italy would not help Germany, while England would support France "under all circumstances" with both land and sea power. Moreover, "Russia is working with gigantic financial resources on the reconstruction of its army," and having solved its problems with Japan, it could now intervene in a European war. Still, Germany was militarily strong, with its adversaries having not yet completed their rearmament programs.[41]

Moltke reiterated these arguments in a report to Bethmann on 2 December. He also noted that Russia had made substantial improvements in its reserve and railway systems, its artillery, and the number of front-line troops, while cutting mobilization time in half compared to five years earlier. Overall, the Schlieffen Plan could still work, but time was running out: "For a number of years, the [power balance] has shifted substantially to the detriment of the allied Monarchies."[42]

With general war looming, the chancellor initiated discussion through Richard Haldane, the British war minister, to see if any hope of British neutrality remained. When Haldane arrived in February 1912, it was soon apparent that Berlin sought Britain's promise of unconditional neutrality: even if Germany were the aggressor, Britain had to agree to stay out of a continental conflict. Needless to say, if Berlin had no intention of initiating major war, it would not have had to insist on unconditional neutrality, something which the British quickly recognized. London responded that it could agree never to join an offensive attack on Germany, but this was rejected. Combined with Berlin's inability in 1905 and 1911 to split Britain from France, the failure of the Haldane Mission confirmed the need to prepare for a world war that included Britain.[43] This conclusion was bolstered on 3 December 1912, when Berlin received a telegram from Prince Karl Max von Lichnowsky, German ambassador in London, relaying a message from Haldane. Referring to the Balkans crisis that had begun in October, Haldane told Lichnowsky that Britain would not remain a bystander should Austria invade Serbia. British policy was based, according to Haldane, on the conviction that the balance of power must be preserved. Britain would not allow a situation in which it faced "a united continental bloc under the leadership of a single power."[44]

On 8 December, the kaiser called his military leaders to a secret meeting to discuss the dilemma of almost certain British intervention in a continental war. This infamous War Council (so named by Bethmann) and the events that immediately followed are highly significant. They show that German leaders, both military and civilian, began actively preparing for a preventive war to be initiated within one to two years.[45]

Admiral Müller, who attended the meeting, recorded its proceedings in his diary. The kaiser began by arguing that Austria, to survive, must deal energetically with the Serbian problem. Yet "if Russia supports the Serbs, which she evidently does . . . then war would be unavoidable for us too." From Haldane's statements it was clear that war could not be confined to the continent. Hence, "the fleet must naturally prepare itself for the war against England." Moltke, who had sought preventive war since 1909, readily agreed, arguing: "I believe a war is unavoidable and the sooner the better."[46] The stumbling block was once again the navy. Tirpitz, as in 1909 and 1911, argued that the navy was still not quite ready, and hence "would prefer to see the postponement of the great fight for one and a half years," by which time the Kiel canal and the Heligoland U-boat harbor would be complete. Moltke responded that "the navy would not be ready even then and the army would get into an increasingly unfavorable position."[47] Since Britain's involvement was now seen as a given, however, Tirpitz's argument for postponing war won the day.

Three important points emerge from this meeting. First, no one disagreed with the thrust of Moltke's argument, namely that preventive war for hegemony had to be fought, and soon. Rather, the decision was only postponed, owing mainly to Tirpitz's insistence that the German fleet was not ready. Not coincidentally, naval preparations of the kind Tirpitz emphasized were indeed completed by July 1914, eighteen months later. Reinforcing the decision to postpone was Prussian War Minister Heeringen's argument that Germany's land forces still needed more time to prepare.

When asked by the kaiser to prepare a new army bill for 1913, on top of the one in 1912, Heeringen demanded the postponement of its introduction until autumn because the army "could not digest yet more big increases; all troop exercising areas were overfilled, the armaments industry could not keep pace."[48] The kaiser accepted the need to wait. Two days after the War Council, he confidentially told the Swiss ambassador that the "racial war . . . of Slavdom against Germandom" could be postponed but not avoided and "will probably take place in one or two years."[49]

Second, all participants understood that Britain would oppose a German attack on France. Not even the chancellor, the individual usually seen to have the greatest faith in British neutrality,[50] put much hope in it. On 20 December 1912, the chancellor wrote privately to a colleague regarding the kaiser's fears about Britain: "Haldane's disclosure to Lichnowsky was not all that serious. It merely reflected what we have long known: that Britain continues to uphold the policy of the balance of power and that it will therefore stand up for France if in a war the latter runs the risk of being destroyed by us."[51] Bethmann's beliefs did not mean he would abandon all efforts to achieve British neutrality; even late in the July crisis he would make offers to secure it. Yet the evidence from December 1912 on shows that he did not *count* on British neutrality when he pushed for war in July 1914; it would be an added bonus, but general war would have to be chosen even if Britain fought.

Third, every key leader seemed to agree on the necessity of motivating Germany's population for a war directed against Russia. Moltke had argued in the meeting that "we ought to do more through the press to prepare the popularity of a war against Russia." Müller's diary notes speak of the need to provoke Germany's enemies into war, a technique used so effectively in July 1914: "The Chief of the Great General Staff says: War the sooner the better, but he does not draw the logical conclusion from this, which is to present Russia or France or both with an ultimatum which would unleash the war with right on our side."[52] That afternoon, Müller informed Bethmann of the "military-political situation" discussed at the meeting. The government must now enlighten the people about Germany's interests should war erupt over the Austrian-Serbian conflict: "The people must not be placed in a position of wondering only at the outbreak of a great European war, what the interests are that Germany must fight for in this war. Instead [they] should be accustomed to the idea of such a war beforehand."[53]

This evidence calls into question the argument that World War I resulted from popular pressure, fed by distorted ideas about war as a glorious enterprise. The causality is the reverse: the German government started to whip up war sentiment only after agreement that general war had to be fought. Far from leaders responding to the public's aggressive passions, they deliberately created those passions to fight the war more effectively.

After the War Council meeting, the chancellor "now impressed upon the Emperor the need to prepare for a great war."[54] On 4 December, four days before the meeting, he had called for a new army bill; this bill was approved by the kaiser on 1 January for submission to the Reichstag. The diplomatic ground for war at the most favorable moment also had to be prepared. Austria, as I discuss shortly, had to be restrained from taking any action in the Balkans that would precipitate war with Russia before the completion of German army and navy preparations. Germany's other, less trustworthy ally—Italy—would also have to be readied for war.[55]

Until 1913, the German military had two military plans which had been updated annually—one for attacking both France and Russia (the Schlieffen Plan), and one for attacking just Russia. In April 1913, because the military leaders recognized that Russia could not be attacked without French intervention, the plan for attacking only in the east was put aside.[56] German planners were becoming obsessed with Russia's military buildup, in particular the growth of strategic railways financed by France. By the spring of 1912, they had calculated that the railways would be completed by 1916–17, and by that point the Russian army's overall strength would have grown by 40 percent.[57] Germany could not compete quantitatively with the Russian masses. Still, its army had distinct qualitative advantages over both France and Russia in the short term, providing a small window of opportunity for a successful general war.

The most exhaustive analysis of the relative military strengths of the continental armies—that of Hermann—concludes that Germany "enjoyed a period of appreciable military superiority" in the years immediately prior to the war. German corps had more artillery overall and were significantly stronger in modern heavy field artillery. In general, the German army was rich in technical equipment, while the thoroughness of its training made it superior in fighting mass warfare.[58] This qualitative superiority explains why Germany was able to fight largely single-handedly against three, and then four, major powers over four years and come dangerously close to victory.[59]

Leaders were aware of this short-term superiority and the need to use it. In his influential book *Germany and the Next War*, published in 1912, General Friedrich von Bernhardi wrote that in the face of large empires like Britain and Russia, Germany must strive not only for colonial expansion, but, more important, for expansion within Europe. Germany was outnumbered, but it possessed a special advantage given its better equipment, superior training, and brilliant leadership. Thus, while victory would not be easy, German leaders still had the moral duty to "begin the struggle while the prospects of success and the political circumstances are still tolerably favorable."[60]

The Germans knew that they needed marked overall superiority, given the weak commitment of Italy and Austria's deteriorating strength. In November 1912, Moltke's office drafted a memorandum arguing that the army had to be further strengthened, since "we will fight together with allies but nevertheless largely with our own forces." Moltke clarified his position in a note to Heeringen in December. Germany currently could face a war with confidence, but within two or three years things would be different as Russia grew and France solved its diplomatic problems. By that point, "Germany must be strong enough to rely on its own power." It therefore had to maximize its military strength immediately.[61] When Heeringen met privately with Reichstag leaders in April 1913, he expanded on Moltke's logic. Russia was developing surprisingly fast, as it poured vast sums into improving equipment and adding new corps. At the moment, the excellence of German troops meant Germany's situation was still tenable, but in the future Russia's growing qualitative and quantitative strength would overwhelm Germany.[62]

In short, both Moltke and Heeringen were convinced by 1912–13 that Germany had enough short-term superiority to take on the system without substantial help from any ally. This belief was not unique to Germany. Norman Stone's research indicates that across Europe "there were widespread ideas that the German army was the most powerful in Europe, a vast warmachine of unconquerable strength."[63] The Russian ambassador to Berlin wrote shortly before the war that "the mood of [German] military circles draws strength from the conviction that the present temporal superiority of the army promises Germany the greatest chances of success."[64] Moreover, as William Fuller shows, even though the Russians took every opportunity to mock the strength of Austria, they had a palpable sense of inferiority when it came to Germany: "Stress was placed on the superiority of German training, German technology, and German mobilization."[65] The implications for system stability were clear. In February 1913, the Russian war minister, Sukhomlinov, told the French that Germany "is in a very critical position. It is encircled by enemy forces: to the west France, to the east Russia—and it fears them." Moreover, Britain was against it and Austrian strength was deteriorating. "It is therefore up to Germany to play a large role on its own."[66]

The German military's belief in its short-term qualitative superiority was maintained right up until the start of the war. On 31 July 1914, G. H. Lerchenfeld, minister in Berlin to the president of the Bavarian Ministerial Council, reported that the military's confidence was strong. "Months ago, even, [Moltke had] made the statement that, from a military point of view, times were more favorable than they might be for an extremely long period to come." Moltke had given three reasons for his view: superiority of the German artillery; superiority of the German infantry rifle; and the wholly insufficient training of the French army.[67]

The above evidence demonstrates that critical to the German decision for preventive war was the belief—quite accurate as the war revealed—that Germany did indeed have enough military power to take on the system.[68] Yet as Russia translated its huge potential power into real economic and military strength, Germany would have to act sooner rather than later if it were to guarantee its long-term security.

THE FINAL TOUCHES: PREPARING GERMANY FOR TOTAL WAR, 1913–1914

The years 1913–14 were spent readying the German people, particularly the workers and their leaders in the Social Democratic Party, for the war to come. The main concern was the populace's will to fight a general war, a concern that remained until late July 1914, as I show in the next chapter. Hence, a propaganda campaign was initiated to bring the classes together.[69] After the 8 December War Council, newspapers quickly moved toward a new, more alarmist view of the German geopolitical predicament. On 1 January 1913 in an article titled "End of the Year—Turn of Fate," the government-funded *Jungdeutschland-Post* stated that if war was required "then the German people will demonstrate that today as in the past it can defy a world of enemies."[70] Over the next eighteen months, the case was built that the war to come would be one against the rising Russian colossus. Since the leaders knew that Russia, at least until its preparations were complete, had no desire for war, propaganda painted the struggle as a racial conflict between the virtuous German race and the innately aggressive Slavs.[71]

The economy of Germany also had to be prepared: financial plans were developed estimating the costs of war; war reserves in the form of gold, silver, and treasury bills were increased; concerns about long-term food supplies were addressed.[72] In addition, a Permanent Commission for Mobilization Affairs was set up at the end of December 1912, composed of representatives of all key ministries and the military. From that time on until May 1914, the commission, as Fischer summarizes, "met regularly and although it concentrated on the food supply situation, it dealt also with the labor market, the provision of industry with coal and other raw materials and the upkeep of goods traffic in wartime."[73] In the end the commission did not argue for active intervention to gear up the economy for war, but this does not support the argument that German leaders fell into war believing it would be short and relatively costless.[74] Rather, the commission and the responsible ministries concluded that Germany was already economically ready for war, and there was little more to do. Clemens von Del-brück, the minister of the interior, told Bethmann on 28 December 1912, that commission deliberations "have shown that it is impossible to take major steps in peacetime to organize the German economy for war. To the extent that it is possible to step in at various points all available means will be examined."[75]

Probably the most conclusive fact indicating that German leaders accepted the possibility of a long war, even if they hoped for a short one, is that violation of Dutch territory, called for in the 1905 Schlieffen Plan, was dropped in the plan's final version. Leaders recognized that this would limit the plan's effectiveness to some degree. They agreed, however, that the Netherlands's benevolent neutrality would be needed in a long war as a lifeline to food and raw materials should Germany be blockaded by the British navy.[76] Army Chief Moltke knew that the nature of war had changed. Germany now had to fight whole nations in arms, he argued in a pessimistic prewar evaluation: it would be "a war between peoples," a "long, exhausting struggle . . . that will push our own people, even if we are the victors, to the brink of exhaustion."[77]

The sense of inevitable decline continued to grow through 1913–14. In the spring of 1913, the chancellor warned the Reichstag of Russian growth, as his personal secretary Kurt Riezler relates: "A huge, ever lengthening wave grows steadily. Once the mass of the Russian people becomes aware of its nationalism the world will see the greatest movement ever as regards extent and unused intensity."[78] By 1914, the sense that Russia was translating its massive potential power into overwhelming economic and military power began to crystallize into a tangible fear. In late 1913, the czar had approved what was called the Big Program, a plan to increase the Russian army by 470,000 men, or approximately 40 percent, by 1917.[79] In early 1914, the German military attaché in Petersburg passed on a report on Russian growth. This became the basis for an important memorandum from Moltke to the Foreign Office in March 1914, emphasizing Russia's growing preparedness for war since its 1905 defeat by Japan.[80] On 24 February 1914, the lead article in the *Post*—a newspaper with ties to the military—openly advocated preventive war. Should Germany wait until its opponents were better prepared, it asked, "or shall we seize a propitious moment to bring about a decision?" If a conflict of interest should arise, Germany must be willing to "risk a war which we should start with a determined offensive . . . the pretext is unimportant because what matters is not this, but that our whole future is at stake." The article concludes: "The question arises whether our opponents' numerical superiority makes victory impossible. The answer is: *not yet!*"[81]

This was not just propaganda. The internal documents overwhelmingly show that such phrases mirrored the thinking of German leaders. As the

Russian ambassador in Berlin wrote to Foreign Minister S. D. Sazonov in March: "According to confidential information (which I have from various sources) Russia's growing strength is causing great apprehension in Berlin. Government circles here are of the opinion that our siege artillery will be ready by 1916 and at that moment Russia will be the dreaded rival for whom Germany will allegedly be no match." The ambassador also noted that "Germany spares neither means nor energy to bring its military preparedness to the pitch of perfection."[82] Thus even foreign capitals were aware of German efforts to maximize their short-term power for the coming preventive war.[83]

The early part of 1914 was used to solidify alliance arrangements with Austria, so it could play its proper role in the coming conflict. Yet Berlin knew that the others did not want war. Moltke wrote Conrad on 13 March that the news from Russia "suggests that at present they have no intention of adopting an aggressive attitude." France, he observed, would likely be even less desirous of war, considering its even less favorable military situation.[84]

By late spring, there was little question that both German political and military leaders were in agreement as to the necessity of preventive war. On 29 May, after a private discussion with Moltke, Foreign Secretary Gottlieb von Jagow wrote:

> The prospects for the future weighed heavily upon him. In two to three years Russia would have finished arming. Our enemies' military power would then be so great that he did not know how he could deal with it. Now we were still more or less of a match for it. In his view there was no alternative but to fight a preventive war so as to beat the enemy while we could still emerge fairly well from the struggle. The Chief of Staff therefore put it to me that our policy should be geared to bringing about an early war.[85]

This passage neatly sums up much of the argumentation made by German leaders over the past year. Moltke's comments on the chances for victory also suggest the military's assessment of Germany's relative power position. Moltke was known to have little faith in the real strength of Austria's military. Moreover, since December 1912, he had been under the assumption that the war would be against France, Russia, *and* Britain. Hence, even if the "we" and "our" in the quoted passage refers to both Germany and Austria (which is unlikely), they indicate that Moltke believed that Germany was superior enough to any other single state to take on the second-, third-, and fourth-ranked powers in the system largely singlehandedly. He was also realistic on the chances for success: he did not say Germany would win for sure, only that it was more or less of a match.

The army chief's comments are also significant regarding his advice that Germany policy should be geared to bringing about an early war. This was not a call for a bolt from the blue, but rather for the active manipulation of the diplomatic environment so as to make war appear justified. In July 1914, as will be seen, Moltke was very much in favor of the chancellor's policy of attempting to blame Russia for the war. As he had said to Conrad in early 1913, "Russia must appear to be the aggressor" if Germany was to have an "effective slogan" for the war at home.[86]

THE BALKANS CRISES OF 1912–1913: AVOIDING INADVERTENT WAR

A good theory should not only explain why war broke out in August 1914, but also why it did *not* break out earlier under apparently similar circumstances. The German leadership, this section shows, was aware that any Austrian move against Serbia posed a high risk of reputation-driven escalation to major war. Russia, because of commitments to its Serbian ally and previous humiliations, would have to respond to uphold its image among allies. Yet if Russian and Austrian armies directly clashed, France would feel compelled to act should Germany support Austria, dragging all states into war. The conditions for inadvertent spiraling, as per the story often told about July 1914, were indeed present. What is significant, however, is that Berlin recognized these risks. It thus deliberately restrained Vienna through four Balkan crises in 1912–13 whenever events threatened to draw Russia in. Yet in July 1914, German policy dramatically switched to pushing Vienna to attack Serbia as soon as possible.

There is a straightforward reason for German leaders' moderate Balkans policy up until 1914: they did not believe that conditions were yet ripe for preventive war. So while they did want to help Austria mitigate decline by shoring up its regional position, Vienna was permitted to make aggressive moves only when it was clear that Russia would not intervene. With German military superiority now evident, Austria was allowed to pursue a riskier course in the Balkans—explaining the higher frequency of Austrian-Russian crises in 1912–13. But the risks had to be kept within bounds. By July 1914, however, Germany had maximized its relative military preponderance and would have only declined thereafter. Hence, Berlin's Balkans policy shifted to a hard-line stance which would force Russia to mobilize, thus thrusting the blame for major war on to Russian shoulders.

The First Balkan War, which began in October 1912, had its roots in an earlier offensive alliance formed by Greece, Montenegro, Serbia, and Bulgaria against Turkey. Austria's worry through 1912 was that Russia and Serbia would exploit Turkey's declining position to increase their power. In mid-August, Austrian Foreign Minister Count Leopold von Berchtold encouraged the Balkan states not to fight Turkey, at least in the short term.[87] Russia and France were also against war. Nevertheless, Montenegro de-

clared war on Turkey on 8 October with Bulgaria, Serbia, and Greece joining soon after. By early December, Turkey was close to being pushed out of
Europe. An armistice, brokered by the great powers, that required the
states to hold their positions was signed on 3 December, with a peace conference opening in London on 16 December. Negotiations and intermittent
fighting continued for another six months, however, and only on 30 May
1913 was a peace treaty signed. This treaty was immediately undermined
by the start of the Second Balkan War in June.

The First Balkan War witnessed three periods of marked tension, when
great power war was at least a possibility: from October to the peace conference in December; from January to March, when Austria and Russia stood
eye-to-eye in states of partial mobilization; and from April to May when
Austria resisted Montenegro's claims on Scutari, a small city in Albania.

In each crisis, German policy was to support Austria, but never to the
point where Austrian actions might bring in Russia and thus provoke a
general war. Bethmann and Berchtold met on 7–8 September to discuss the
growing Balkan tension. Alfred von Kiderlen-Wächter, Germany's foreign
minister, irritated by Vienna's willingness to make diplomatic moves without consulting Berlin, advised Bethmann to tell Berchtold that he must inform Berlin of his intentions and not just present it with a fait accompli.
Germany had no obligation "to support Austria-Hungary in her Near Eastern plans, let alone adventures, all the less so as Austria-Hungary has not
promised outright her support against France."[88] In November, however,
two cornerstones of Austria's Balkan policy—an independent Albania as a
check on Serbia and the prevention of Serbian access to the sea—were
threatened by the successes of the Balkan League. Austria mobilized while
Russia, in support of Serbia, responded by deploying 220,000 troops along
the Galician border. In late November, Vienna increased its troop strength
in Galicia by 50 percent, called up more reserves, and told the fleet to prepare for mobilization.[89] The armistice on 3 December between the Balkan
states and Turkey did not reduce Austrian-Russian tension. In fact, Austria
feared that Serbia, since it was no longer fighting against Turkey, would
now turn against Austria. On 5 December, Vienna activated 27,000 more
troops in the south.

Recognizing the risks of escalation, German leaders were cautious. Three
days after the 8 December War Council in Berlin, where it had been decided to postpone major war, Berchtold met with the heir-apparent, Franz
Ferdinand, and advised him against war. As Samuel Williamson summarizes, Berchtold's central point "was his well-founded belief that Berlin
would never agree to a unilateral move by Vienna." Later that day, the
civilian ministers made the same argument to Emperor Franz-Joseph.[90] The
monarch apparently agreed, and by the end of December a fragile peace
was still holding.

From January to March, however, Austria and Russia remained in states of partial mobilization across their borders. This fact alone led to the second great power crisis of the First Balkan War. Austria had decided against attacking Serbia, but the Russians did not know this. Hence both sides maintained a state of high military readiness until March. Yet an uncontrolled escalation to war was again avoided. Why was the German military machine not mobilized in response to Russian mobilization, as in 1914?[91]

The answer is clear: given the War Council decision, Germany still needed more time to maximize its superiority. In January, Berchtold sent Count Friedrich von Szápáry on a secret mission to Berlin to clarify the German perspective. Szápáry was told that the Germans had no desire for war.[92] Just to make sure Vienna got the message, however, both Bethmann and Moltke sent letters to their respective Austrian counterparts. The chancellor's letter on 10 February reminded Berchtold that "for Russia, with her traditional relationship to the Balkan states, it is almost impossible without an immense loss of prestige to be an inactive spectator of a military action on the part of Austria-Hungary against Serbia." Moreover, in any war, Germany "would have to bear the full brunt of the French and English offensive." Hence, "to bring about a forcible solution—even if many interests of the Austro-Hungarian Monarchy were to urge it—at a moment when a prospect, even if only a distant one, opens up of settling the conflict in conditions essentially more favorable to us, would in my opinion be an error of incalculable magnitude."[93] Moltke's letter to Conrad on 10 February, like the chancellor's, did not advise the Austrians to abandon thoughts of war, but only to hold off for now, so it could be fought later under better circumstances. Significantly, Moltke's main concern was that Russia be blamed for any war so as to find an "effective watchword" for the propaganda campaign back in Germany. "[A] European war must come sooner or later in which ultimately the struggle will be one between Germanism and Slavism," he wrote Conrad. "But the aggression must come from the Slavs."[94]

Thus the crisis which, in terms of mobilization, bore the closest parallel to July 1914 was resolved without war by mid-March 1913. During April and May, a third crisis erupted over whether the city of Scutari, in Albania, belonged to Albania or Montenegro. Serbia supported Montenegro's claim, and Austria prepared to move against the Montenegrans. This time Berlin gave its support for Austrian action. Berlin supported Austria, however, only once it became clear that Russia would not react. Petersburg had already convinced the Serbs to withdraw from Scutari. Moreover, Sazonov had stated from the beginning of the Scutari crisis, as Luigi Albertini relates, that "he would not protest against separate action by Austria provided it were limited to Scutari and did not threaten Serbia." The crisis was finally resolved thorough Montenegro's agreement in May to give Scutari to Albania in return for economic aid from the great powers.[95]

A fourth crisis arose as a complication of the Second Balkan War, started by Bulgaria in late June, when it attacked Serbian and Greek forces. Berchtold felt that Austria needed to attack Serbia in support of Bulgaria, and this was communicated to Berlin in early July.[96] For Berlin, this situation was far more dangerous than the Scutari crisis. This time the threatened Austrian attack was directed not against tiny Montenegro, a nation that Russia had said it would not support, but against Serbia itself, a nation firmly within Russia's sphere. German officials reacted quickly, going straight to Austrian ambassador Ladislas von Szögyény to inform him that they "saw no reason for Austria-Hungary to give up the waiting attitude she has till now maintained." Alfred Zimmermann, Germany's undersecretary of state for foreign affairs, also advised the kaiser that Vienna should be "dissuaded from precipitat[ing] action," and be persuaded "to take no decision without German advice."[97] The kaiser agreed.

Bethmann, out of town during the first few days of the crisis, returned to Berlin on 5 July and was soon informed of Austria's hard-line position. Clearly concerned, he told Szögyény that Austria should be satisfied that its two southern Slav neighbors were destroying themselves in war. But if Austria attempted to use force, then "it would mean a European war. This would most seriously affect the vital interests of Germany and I must therefore expect that before Count Berchtold makes any such resolve, he will inform us of it."[98] We see once again the common theme in the 1912–13 Balkan crises. When there was little possibility of Russian intervention, Berlin allowed Austria to act forcefully; but whenever it seemed that Russia might be obliged, for the sake of its reputation, to oppose Austrian actions, Berlin withheld support and advised Vienna to maintain its "waiting attitude." By July 1914, this policy would be reversed.

Why World War I Was Not the Result of Domestic Conflict

Having discussed why World War I did not start inadvertently, I now show that the other most accepted explanation for its beginning—that German leaders used war to solve a domestic crisis—is also suspect. This social-imperialist explanation, which traces back to Eckart Kehr, has been forwarded by notable historians such Fischer, Hans-Ulrich Wehler, and Volker Berghahn.[99] Despite some differences, these scholars agree on certain key points. Germany pursued a *Sonderweg* or "special path" after 1850: it experienced neither the revolution nor the reform needed to reduce the traditional landed aristocracy in favor of the bourgeoisie. As

Germany industrialized, the bourgeoisie thus aligned with the landed elite to forestall the rise of their common enemy, the working class. To maintain control, these two dominant classes sought an aggressive external policy to divert the masses' attention from the lack of domestic change.

Weltpolitik of the 1890s is seen as the first expression of this objective: in creating a colonial empire and a powerful navy, the dominant classes hoped that the population would rally around the flag and support the established order. Over time, however, they began to see war in Europe as the only viable response to growing working-class discontent. Victory would cause the masses to recognize the validity of the traditional class structure, abandoning thoughts of revolution. Internal strife thus led to an "escape forward," the elites' reactionary plunge into war to forestall the loss of their domestic primacy.[100]

This argument has fundamental problems. As an explanation for *Weltpolitik*, it has some merit: although the drive for colonies and sea power after 1895 had a strong security component,[101] there is evidence that German leaders in the 1890s also expected *Weltpolitik* to dampen domestic conflict.[102] Yet proponents of the social-imperialist thesis fail to recognize that the logic for imperialism against weak preindustrial societies has no necessary connection to the motives for general war. Leaders might expect military moves against small states to yield low-cost victories promoting national unity (as U.S. victories in Grenada 1983 and Panama 1989 demonstrated). General war against other great powers, however, can be foreseen to have the opposite consequences: since such wars involve tremendous costs in blood and treasure, they are much more likely to undermine domestic order than to stabilize it—even when the state is victorious.

The evidence shows that German leaders understood these points. As chapter 4 discusses, Bethmann Hollweg in particular saw that general war would only increase the risk of social revolution. Yet he nevertheless felt compelled to initiate it before Russia rose any further. In this view he was not alone. Advocates of the social-imperialist argument not only produce little evidence showing that German leaders sought general war to solve a domestic crisis; their evidence shows that all key leaders after 1905 were petrified by the domestic consequences of even a victorious war.

Events within Russia after the 1904–5 Russo-Japanese war taught German elites their first big lesson: great power wars mean revolution. For the kaiser, such wars meant that the army could not remain at home to keep the peace. He wrote in 1905 that sending a single man abroad would, because of the socialists, create an "extreme danger to the life and the property of the citizens."[103] Prince Bernhard von Bülow, Bethmann's predecessor as chancellor, stated in 1907 that even if an arms buildup helped relieve domestic conflict, war itself "would have the most depressing consequences politically, economically and socially."[104] A year later he told the crown prince that history shows that even in victory, "every great war is followed by a period of liberalism, since a people demands compensation for the sacrifices and effort war had entailed." Should war end in defeat, "it might entail the fall of the dynasty."[105] During the Moroccan crisis of 1911, Kiderlen, the German foreign minister, likewise argued: "All great victories are the work of the people and the people must be paid for it. . . . Another victory will bring us a parliamentary regime."[106]

Germany's military leaders were no believers in diversionary war. In February 1905, the Admiralty Staff reported that if war with Britain broke out, it would lead to a blockade and thus "a financial and social crisis with incalculable consequences." In the winter of 1905–6, Tirpitz sought to counter "radicals" in society who advocated war with England or a military crack-down as means to maintain the domestic order. He feared that such policies would only cause chaos at home.[107] Army Chief of Staff Moltke would assert as late as 29 July 1914, even as he was helping bring on total war, that war "would destroy the culture of nearly all of Europe for decades to come."[108]

It is telling that while the quotations cited are taken largely from scholars seeking to uphold the social-imperialist thesis, these authors offer no quotations from key leaders showing they believed major war would improve the domestic situation. Instead, the evidence garnered is indirect: analyses of German domestic tension prior to the war combined with a few statements that war might unify the nation from far-right leaders not actually in power. With direct evidence lacking, social-imperialist scholars fall back on a more circuitous route to war, whereby reluctant officials are pushed into war by powerful interests *outside* the government. This argument also has significant problems.

First, even if we accept that the dominant classes had influence, Germany was hardly unique in terms of the landed elite's strength and the struggle between modernizing and reactionary factions. Arno Mayer shows that the landed aristocracy was a powerful class not only in Russia, but also in Britain and France.[109] David Blackbourn and Geoffrey Eley also question the uniqueness of Germany's political structure: Britain was hardly a model bourgeois democracy without domestic strife, while the German bourgeoisie was not particularly unified as a class.[110] Yet if Germany's domestic structure and level of class conflict were not so different from other European states, it is hard to explain why Germany would be aggressive and others peaceful.

Second, there is reason to doubt that the dominant classes in Germany had much influence over decisions on major war. Social-imperialist proponents present no evidence showing that government leaders felt compelled by far-right demands into initiating war. Bethmann and his associates were aware of the far right's arguments, but they rejected them as foolhardy and irrelevant in comparison to the real problem: the rise of Russia.[111] Moreover, the social-imperialist thesis assumes that Germany's landed elites and bourgeoisie were tightly aligned, enough to cooperate in pressuring the government to pursue an aggressive foreign policy. This assumption may hold up for the initial *Weltpolitik* period (1897–1907). After this period, however, the partners in the "marriage of iron and rye" became separated and then divorced. As Berghahn himself shows, the two blocs could not agree on how to handle the Social Democrats—whether by reform or reaction— and thus "a broadly-based *Sammlung* [coalition] had no chance of success." Indeed, the blocs themselves fragmented. The National Liberals, representatives for the bourgeoisie, split into a more imperialist right wing (one that still did not generally support the landed elites) and a more moderate reform branch.[112] The landed parties maintained some cohesion, but they were increasingly marginalized by Bethmann's government. Bethmann had decided early on to pursue a "policy of the diagonal," encouraging internal reforms to gain lower-class support without relinquishing elite power. He became increasingly intolerant of the far right's opposition to any changes threatening its position, especially his plans to tax landed wealth. In 1912–14, Bethmann found support for reforms and for tax increases to pay for the military buildup more from center and moderate left parties than from the right.[113]

The above evidence undermines the social-imperialist argument. Its advocates cannot show either that German government or military leaders were convinced by the diversionary war argument, or that they felt the need to respond to elite pressure from outside.[114] Moreover, the dominant classes could not have exerted decisive pressure even if they had wanted to: they were too busy dealing with the intra-elite struggle.

This chapter has sought to build the case for a purely systemic explanation for the First World War. There is a great deal of evidence showing that concerns for the long-term growth of the Russian colossus pushed German leaders to prepare to wage war as soon as Germany's armed forces were ready. Significantly, in postponing war on at least two occasions because of the state of the German navy, these leaders were recognizing that Germany needed to be able to fight not just France and Russia but also Britain. The chapter has also called into question the two most established alternative arguments for the war, the inadvertent war thesis and the social-imperialist argument. The next chapter will add further evidence against these explanations.

[4]

The July Crisis and the Outbreak of World War I

In this chapter I argue that Germany actively sought war in July 1914 and that German leaders by the end of July preferred world war to a negotiated peace, even to one that gave Austria most of what it wanted. Berlin thus took all steps necessary to prevent any kind of negotiated solution, while at the same time ensuring that Russia was blamed for the war. This argument goes a few steps beyond Fritz Fischer, whose view that Germany preferred continental war over a return to the status quo sparked a heated controversy that is still with us.[1] Fischer contends that Bethmann Hollweg, the German chancellor, expected Britain to remain neutral, and would not have pushed Austria against Serbia had he known that Britain would intervene. Moreover, Fischer is vague as to whether Germany preferred a localized war giving Austria a victory over Serbia to a continental war.[2]

Chapter 3 demonstrated that German leaders, including Bethmann, saw the chance of Britain remaining neutral as very low given Britain's balance-of-power tradition. Hence, while they certainly preferred continental war to world war, and while diplomacy in a crisis might help keep Britain out—at least in the early stages of war—it is clear that no leader in Berlin counted on British neutrality in pursuing a hard-line strategy. In this regard, I seek to explode one of the most persistent myths surrounding the First World War, namely, that Bethmann and his associates got cold feet on 29 July when they realized that Britain would fight for France. Even Fischer accepts this view of 29 July, and thus like Luigi Albertini falls back on the notion that things got out of hand after that date. As I show, however, Bethmann knew two days earlier that little hope remained that London would stay out of the war. In the face of this knowledge, he simply continued forward. In short, given a choice between world war and a negotiated peace, the German leadership preferred the former and did nothing to achieve the latter.

Yet even more striking is the fact that, in the last days of the crisis as Russia sought a face-saving measure giving Austria almost as much as the latter would have gained from a localized war against Serbia, German leaders cut off all negotiations between Austria and Russia. They then sealed the war's inevitability by an unexpected declaration of war on Russia on 1 August. There was no diplomatic or military reason for this declaration. And since Germany did not expect to be at war with Russia for weeks, if a solution had been sought there was still plenty of time to reach one. I argue that Berlin deliberately brought on a world war by declaring war to avert a last-minute capitulation by Russia to Austrian demands. Since Bethmann's diplomatic efforts had set up a war under circumstances as favorable as could ever be expected, the last thing Germany wanted was a peaceful solution, even one desired by Austria.

Negative power trends drove this decision-making. Given the rise of the Russian colossus, German leaders believed that continental or world war had to be fought in 1914, since by 1917 as Russia completed its military reforms and strategic railways, Germany could no longer expect to take on the system. After that, Russian growth would overwhelm Germany. These facts provoked Bethmann and the German command to establish the best possible conditions for major war. Two conditions were critical. First and most important, the German populace had to be behind the war effort. In particular, German leaders were fearful that the Social Democratic Party and the workers would be against any war seen as aggressive. Second, Germany needed Austrian help in at least the early stages of the conflict to maximize the success of the Schlieffen Plan. A third condition was also desired, but not necessary, namely, the delaying of British entry into the war long enough to complete the conquest of France.

These three conditions could be achieved simultaneously with one overall strategy: blaming Russia for the war. If the Russians could be provoked into mobilization so that it appeared that Germany was only reacting in self-defense, this would create a groundswell of domestic support. It would also draw Austria into the war for fear of a Russian attack. Finally, with Russia as aggressor, British support for Russia and France might be more tentative.

In what follows, I show that German leaders systematically sought to draw Russia into the war and then to preclude any possibility of Russia escaping the trap by capitulating to Austrian demands. Berlin pushed Vienna to make its demands so harsh as to be unacceptable to the Russian leaders searching for a face-saving exit from the crisis. Austria itself was alternatively cajoled, pushed, and threatened into taking a hard-line stance versus

Serbia and therefore Russia, and into mobilizing and declaring war against Russia to suit German strategic goals, not Austrian.[3]

Bethmann Hollweg and the German Foreign Office thus had two main fears during July: that Austria would lose the will to pursue a hard-line stance; and, more important, that Russia in the end would back out of its mobilization efforts, making it impossible to blame Russia for a war. These two fears collapsed into one possibility: that in the final stages of the crisis, Austria and Russia would reach an agreement to avoid the major war that only Germany really wanted. Hence, Bethmann manipulated the diplomatic messages on 31 July and then went immediately to a declaration of war on 1 August to prevent any last-minute diplomatic solution giving either Austria and Russia a way out of war.

This chapter reexamines the events of the July crisis in some detail. Given the complexity of the German strategy, and the fact that the July crisis is probably the most misunderstood event in diplomatic history, only in-depth analysis will reveal the truly Machiavellian nature of German actions.

PREFERENCE ORDERINGS FOR THE KEY ACTORS

Each interpretation of the cause(s) of World War I depends heavily on an author's implicit or explicit views regarding the preferences of the actors for four main outcomes: localized war between Austria and Serbia; continental war of the great powers excluding Britain; world war which would include Britain; and a negotiated peace between the actors representing a maintenance to some degree of the status quo.[4] The inadvertent war thesis has to assume that German leaders, while they might have desired a localized war above all else, certainly preferred a negotiated peace to either a continental war or world war. Otherwise, major war would have been something Germany sought, instead of something it did not want but was unable to prevent. The "Fischer Controversy" was sparked exactly by Fischer's assertion that Berlin preferred continental war to a return to the status quo; Germany, Fischer asserts, wanted war, although not a world war with Britain included.

The problem with this debate, as will become clearer, is that it too narrowly circumscribes the nature of the possible outcomes seen by leaders in Germany. The four options listed above had subtle variants that were crucial to ultimate decision-making. Attached to the outcomes of continental war or world war were two possibilities: either the German public supports the war or it does not; and either Austria supports Germany militarily on the eastern front, or it does not.[5] Attached to the outcome of world war was the question of whether Britain might delay its involvement long enough to help Germany defeat France, or whether Britain would enter immediately. The negotiated peace outcome was also far more subtle than is commonly believed: there were at least eight different diplomatic solutions discussed at the critical stages of the crisis, ranging from one extreme—giving Austria essentially what it wanted, namely, the destruction of Serbia—to the other, where Russia would secure a return to the status quo.[6]

The essence of my argument is that German leaders, as Fischer suggests, saw continental war with domestic and Austrian support as their best option, and certainly preferred that option to a return to the status quo. More important, however, they saw a world war that had domestic and Austrian support as better not only than the status quo, but also than a negotiated peace that gave Austria a diplomatic victory almost equal to victory in a localized war (that is, one where Serbia would be effectively destroyed). If, however, domestic and Austrian support could not be secured, then Berlin preferred a negotiated peace.[7] As I show, Bethmann's strategy throughout July was thus to achieve the domestic and Austrian support required to fight either a continental or a world war and, once that was achieved, to cut off all possibility of a negotiated settlement.

EARLY JULY: SETTING THE STAGE FOR PREVENTIVE WORLD WAR

Archduke Ferdinand, heir to the Austrian throne, was assassinated on Sunday, 28 June. On 4 July Count Alexander Hoyos, the Foreign Ministry's chief of cabinet, was sent to Berlin to inform the Austrian ambassador, Szögyény, of Vienna's desire for action against Serbia. Szögyény met with Kaiser Wilhelm at Potsdam the next day. In the first meeting, about midday, the kaiser told Szögyény that he could not give a definite answer until he had consulted the chancellor, noting the risk of grave complications in Europe.[8] In the afternoon, however, the kaiser, after talks with Bethmann, assured Szögyény of Germany's full support in whatever strong measures Austria chose to pursue. Austria had its "blank check."

Why did Germany press Austria to take such a hard-line stance, when in previous Balkan crises it had restrained its ally whenever Serbia was involved? There are three possible explanations: Berlin falsely assumed that Russia would not intervene (consistent with the inadvertent war thesis); Berlin expected and hoped that the conflict would remain localized but accepted the possibility of continental war (the notion of "calculated risk"); Berlin, seeking preventive war, expected and hoped that Russia *would* intervene so it could blame Russia for the general war to follow. The evidence supports the third interpretation.

Recall that Bethmann, in February 1913, had noted that it was impossible for Russia to be an inactive spectator should Austria attack Serbia. To uphold the inadvertent war or calculated risk theses, one has to argue that Bethmann and his associates had somehow forgotten the chancellor's own counsel a year and a half later. They had not. Foreign Office Undersecretary Zimmermann had let slip in conversations with Hoyos that an Austrian attack on Serbia would lead "with a probability of 90 percent to a European war."[9]

On 2 July, the Saxon minister in Berlin reported to his capital that should an Austro-Serbian war occur, the top officials in the Foreign Office believed that "Russia would mobilize and world war could no longer be prevented." He added that the military favored "allowing [this] thing to drift to war while Russia is still unprepared," although the kaiser might prevent this.[10] The Saxon plenipotentiary the next day communicated that Count Georg Waldersee, quarter-master general in the German General Staff, felt that everything depended on Russia's reaction: "I had the impression that they would regard it with favour [in Supreme Headquarters] if war were to come about now. Conditions and prospects would never become better for us."[11] Thus we see that of the key participants, only the kaiser was worried about the prospects of general war. The chancellor, his Foreign Office, and the military all viewed general war as a necessary evil to deal with the rise of Russia.

Perhaps the most telling evidence on the preference for general war comes in the diaries of Kurt Riezler, Bethmann's personal secretary and confidant. The diaries show that Bethmann, faced with the choice between German decline or fighting while Germany still had a chance, reluctantly put Germany on the path to war. On 6 July, the day after the blank check, the chancellor had a long talk with Riezler. Bethmann's secret news, Riezler recorded, "gives me an unnerving picture." Anglo-Russian naval negotiations were the last link in the chain.

Russia's military power [is] growing rapidly; with the strategic extension [of Russian railways] into Poland the situation is intolerable. Austria increasingly weaker and immobile. . . .

. . . An action against Serbia can lead to a world war [*Weltkrieg*]. From a war, regardless of the outcome, the chancellor expects a revolution of everything that exists. . . . Heydebrand said a war would lead to a strengthening of the patriarchal order. . . . The chancellor is furious about such nonsense. Generally, delusion all around, a thick fog over the people. . . . The future belongs to Russia, which grows and grows, and thrusts on us a heavier and heavier nightmare.[12]

This passage highlights three points. First and most important is the clear statement that general war is critical owing to Russia's growth. Second, Bethmann is not pushing Germany toward war to solve a domestic crisis.

Instead, he expects that war, regardless of whether Germany wins or loses, will only increase the likelihood of social revolution at home. Third, Bethmann is aware even by 6 July that any great power war will likely be a world war, not a continental war; that is, Britain will be involved.

These revelations align with his thinking up to July. Bethmann had written to Lichnowsky in June that "not only the extremists, but even level-headed politicians are worried at the increase in Russian strength."[13] On 20 July, three days before Austria's ultimatum to Serbia, Riezler writes of another talk with Bethmann. The feeling was that Russia, with its "tremendous dynamic power" could "no longer be contained within a few years, especially if the present European constellation continues."[14] Bethmann's subordinates thought similarly. On 25 July, Foreign Minister Jagow smiled as he confidentially told Theodore Wolff, editor of the *Berlin Tageblatt*, that war would certainly occur soon if things continued on as they were, "and in two years' time Russia would be stronger than it is now." Wolff heard this logic reiterated later that day in conversations with Wilhelm von Stumm, political director of the Foreign Office.[15]

Three years later, Bethmann acknowledged to Wolff that preventive war had dominated his thinking. Since the visit of Russian Foreign Minister Sazonov and Russian Finance Minister K. N. Kokovtsov to Berlin in January 1914, "I had the fear that war was becoming inevitable." The Russians had just received 500 million francs from Paris "under the familiar conditions," namely, that the money would go to building strategic railways in Poland. Kokovstov "did not want [war]." But "I sensed from him that he himself feared that this would set a war in motion." To Wolff's statement that a diplomatic arrangement with Russia might have been possible, the chancellor shot back: "Who can say? But if war had come about later, Russia would have been in a better position. Where would we have been then?"[16]

Bethmann's deep concern that war would lead to revolution is shown by his comments in June to Lerchenfeld, the Bavarian minister to Berlin. Some still thought that war might improve internal conditions, he noted. But he thought "that the effects would be the exact opposite; a world war, with its incalculable consequences, would greatly increase the power of Social Democracy, because it had preached peace, and would bring down many a throne."[17] While this quotation is Fischer's, it and the Riezler passage put the final nail in the coffin of the argument that war was driven by domestic politics. Given Bethmann's recognition that war only increased the chances of revolution, Germany's internal tensions should have inclined him toward peace. Yet systemic trends pushed him to war.

Bethmann's point to Riezler that the war would be a "world war" is consistent with his view in 1912 that Britain would act to uphold the balance of power. He never relinquished this view. On 5 June 1914, Bethmann told the leader of the National Liberal Party that "if there is a war with France, every last Englishman will march against us."[18] The day before, the chancellor noted to Lerchenfeld that through history, "British power had stood against the strongest power on the continent," and now would oppose Germany.[19] That the chancellor knew that world war, not continental war, was very likely should Russia react has great significance: it helps explode the myth that he scrambled to avoid war on 29 July.

Reinforcing the argument that Bethmann sought general war is a revealing entry in Riezler's diaries from 8 July:

> Message delivered by Hoyos to Franz Joseph. . . . The chancellor thinks that perhaps the old kaiser [i.e., Franz Joseph] will in the end decide against it. If the war comes from the East, so that we go to war for Austria and not Austria for us, then we have the prospect of winning it. If the war does not come because the czar does not want it or because an alarmed France counsels peace, then we still have the prospect [*so haben wir doch noch Aussicht*] of maneuvering the Entente apart over this matter.[20]

This passage not only expresses the expectation that general war is more likely than a localized war, but it strongly implies that the former is *preferable* to the latter. If war "comes from the East"—that is, if Russia is seen to be the initiator—then the Austrians will likely fall into line, and victory is possible. Yet if war is averted, Germany will "still" have the prospect of splitting the Entente. The "still" is critical since it indicates that localized war is seen as the second-best outcome (as in: "if we can't get A, then we can still get B"). Moreover, note that general war might be avoided not because Germany did not desire it, but because Russia, possibly restrained by France, might decide against intervention.

This discussion makes clear that by early July Berlin was seeking to bring on a preventive war, even a preventive world war, before it was too late.

EXECUTING THE PLAN FOR GENERAL WAR

Between 8 and 23 July, there was what Imanuel Geiss calls the "lull before the storm."[21] Yet Bethmann and his associates were hardly relaxing. Although they had convinced Wilhelm and military leaders to go ahead with the planned holidays so as not to create suspicion abroad, behind the scenes they were actively preparing for the coming war. German public opinion had to be shaped to accept Russia as the aggressor; an Austrian ultimatum to Serbia had to be designed to preclude a negotiated settlement; Italy had to be convinced to join the German side through whatever means, including territorial concessions from Vienna; and as many secret military measures as possible had to be taken to facilitate immediate mobilization once it was announced.

A key concern was keeping Austria on the course to war against Serbia, so as to draw Russia in. The fear was that Vienna would get cold feet once Russia intervened. On 5 July, Minister of War Erich von Falkenhayn wrote to Moltke that Bethmann had "as little faith as I do that [Vienna] is really earnest," even if its language seemed resolute.[22] On July 9, Zimmermann told H. von Schoen, the Bavarian chargé d'affaires in Berlin, that he doubted that Vienna would really move against Serbia. These feelings were apparently shared by all German leaders.[23]

Berlin had the means to influence Vienna's behavior. Heinrich von Tschirschky, German ambassador in Vienna, was in constant contact with Austrian leaders and even attended many of their most important conferences. Berlin also wielded the ultimate weapon: the implied threat that Germany would abandon Austria to its enemies. On 8 July, Berchtold remarked to Hungarian Prime Minister Stephan von Tisza, after Tschirschky told him "most emphatically" that Berlin expected action, that it would see any Austrian-Serbian deal as a sign of weakness, "which must have repercussions on our position in the Triple Alliance and on Germany's future policy."[24]

The Austrian ultimatum to Serbia, delivered on 23 July, was designed to avoid any diplomatic solution, and Germany complicity here is beyond doubt. On 8 July, Tschirschky informed Berlin that Berchtold would make the demands impossible to accept.[25] Vienna, aware that Berlin was expecting such a stand, had Tschirschky relay Austria's position that "the note is being composed so that the possibility of its acceptance is *practically excluded*."[26] The essential contents of the ultimatum were known by Berlin as early as 12 July, with the full text communicated 22 July, the evening before the ultimatum was to be delivered.[27] This gave German leaders almost a full day to reject the harshness of the demands if indeed they wanted to avoid a confrontation. They did not do this, and for good reason, since they were pressing Austria to be as harsh as possible.

Integral to the plan was the creation of the facade that Germany had no responsibility for the events that were to follow. From Riezler's diary on 14 July:

> Yesterday and today, [we] worked a little on an old web of lies [*Gespinsten*]. The countryside is wrapped up in it. . . . If war should come and the veil [*Schleier*] then should fall, the whole nation will follow, driven by need and danger. Victory is liberation. The chancellor thinks that I am too young not to succumb to the lure of the unknown, the new, the great movement. For him this action is a leap in the dark and a most serious duty. Kiderlen [foreign minister until 1912] had always said we must fight.[28]

Italy wanted as a price for its participation the Austrian-occupied territory of Trentino, Riezler continued. However, "one cannot talk to them beforehand; it would give away everything in Petersburg." If war came, "England [will] immediately march." Italy, however, would join in only if Germany's victory seemed assured.[29]

The chancellor was evidently setting the stage , however reluctantly, for a successful general war. This is also shown by the secret military measures taken even before the ultimatum was delivered. On 6 July, the navy had been quietly mobilized.[30] On 18 July, important preparations for mobilization were initiated in the key ministries in Berlin.[31] By the next morning, General Waldersee, who was in charge as Moltke remained on holiday, could tell Jagow that he was "ready to jump"; the General Staff was "all prepared."[32]

In conferences between 18 and 20 July, Bethmann met with Interior Ministry officials to discuss actions to ensure popular support for the war. The chancellor worried that all-out mobilization, despite its military benefits, "would not compensate for the damage which it would do in the political and ideological spheres."[33] Of particular concern was the reaction of the workers. On 23 July, Riezler records that if war came, Bethmann would "ensure himself [of the Social Democrats' support] by personally negotiating with them," and by offering guarantees against "red-baiters" in the military. Reflecting preparations taken, Riezler notes: "mobilization of transportation; secret war-defenses emphasized."[34] Two days later, and still before any word on Russian military measures, Riezler writes that Bethmann was constantly on the phone with the military. "Merchant marine has been warned. Havenstein [prepares] financial mobilization." Still, "at present, nothing may be done out in the open."[35]

The Austrian ultimatum was delivered at 6:00 P.M. on Thursday, 23 July. Only forty-eight hours were given for the Serbian reply. On 24 July, the Russians held a top level meeting to discuss the ultimatum. Given Russia's slow mobilization schedules, it was decided to start military preparations as a first step to either partial or general mobilization.[36]

To avert a diplomatic solution, Berlin meanwhile was pushing Austria to declare war on Serbia as soon as possible after the ultimatum deadline at 6:00 P.M., 25 July. Vienna, however, wanted to declare war only after mobilization was complete, and this was communicated to Berlin on 24 July. Since the Austrians required sixteen days to mobilize properly, Berlin immediately rejected this timetable. Austrian ambassador Szögyény telegraphed from Berlin on 25 July that Germany's position was that once Serbia rejected the demands, Austria's declaration of war should follow immediately. Any delay in war operations "is regarded as signifying the danger . . . that foreign powers might interfere."[37] Yet the German fear was not that powers like Russia might intervene militarily; as we have seen, war with Russia was desired. Rather, Berlin was concerned that Russia might pressure Serbia to concede to avert general war. In addition, German leaders worried that without a declaration of war, another state might find a diplomatic way out: *Austria*. These dual fears are revealed in Schoen's report on 18 July of a conversation with Zimmermann. German leaders wanted Austria to act, he wrote, but Jagow and Zimmermann were doubtful. Vienna

> [did] not seem to have expected such an unconditional support . . . and Mr. Zimmermann has the impression that it is almost embarrassing to the always timid and undecided authorities at Vienna not to be admonished by Germany to caution and self-restraint. . . . So it would have been liked even better here if [the Austrians] had not waited so long with their action against Serbia, and the Serbian Government had not been given time to make an offer of satisfaction on its own account, perhaps acting under Russo-French pressure.[38]

Ironically, it was the head of the Austrian army, Conrad, the man in Austria who had most supported preventive war over the previous five years, who now resisted German pressure to declare war immediately. Berlin wanted the declaration by 28 July at the latest; Conrad argued internally for 12 August. On Monday afternoon, 27 July, Berchtold overruled Conrad and agreed to the German request. At 3:20 P.M., Tschirschky relayed to Berlin, "They have decided here to send out the declaration of war tomorrow, or the day after tomorrow at the latest, chiefly to frustrate any attempt at intervention."[39] Berchtold's report to Franz Joseph that evening shows his understanding of Berlin's logic: the Triple Entente "might make another attempt to achieve a peaceful settlement of the conflict unless a clear situation is created by the declaration of war."[40]

The reasons for German maneuvering here help to make sense of that great mystery on 1 August: Germany's surprise declaration of war on Russia. As we will see, the only plausible explanation for this action is the same as that for the declaration of war on 28 July, namely, Berlin's desire to forestall any last-minute diplomatic solution.

This takes us to the most critical seven days of the crisis, Sunday, 26 July to Saturday, 1 August. Interpretations of this week have been driven by the universally accepted belief that German civilian leaders—specifically Bethmann Hollweg—got cold feet on the night of 29–30 July and then tried but failed to keep Austria from pulling the system into war. This notion—critical to almost every explanation of the war[41]—grows out of two crucial telegrams, sent at 2:55 A.M. and 3:00 A.M. on July 30. The telegrams seem to show a German chancellor, worried that world war is about to occur, pleading with Austria to reach an agreement with Russia to keep the peace.[42]

Yet if one puts these telegrams within the context of everything happening that night, the previous two nights, and the next day, a very different picture emerges. As I discuss, these telegrams represent only one thing: Bethmann's effort to get the Austrians to moderate their position as it appears to the world, so that Russia would still be blamed for the general war to follow. Pinning responsibility on Russia, as noted, was essential to build domestic support, to ensure that Austria fought, and, it was hoped, to delay British intervention. Yet to achieve this, Russia had to be perceived as being poised to attack the German homeland. Austria also had to be convinced not to back out through a negotiated solution with Russia. Finally, the world, and the German people in particular, had to believe that Russia mobilized while Germany and Austria were still seeking a peaceful outcome to the dispute. If any of these elements failed, the preventive war could not be successfully waged.

The German plan for achieving these ends consisted of seven carefully coordinated steps. First, Russia had to be provoked into at least partial mobilization against Austria—that is, a mobilization similar to the one in 1912–13. This was achieved not only by having Austria declare war on and then immediately attack Serbia, but also by falsely promising Petersburg that partial mobilization would not lead to general war. Second, Germany had to position itself as the honest broker, appearing to know little about Austria's tough stand, but desiring the localization of conflict. Third, Germany had to scare Russia into proceeding to a general mobilization that would direct Russian forces against Germany. At the same time, the public had to believe that fixed mobilization schedules meant that Germany was not to blame if, for security reasons, it felt it must preempt the enemy's attack.

Fourth, once Russian general mobilization was a given, Berlin had to ensure that the Russians did not get cold feet. This required softening German diplomatic rhetoric, to convince Petersburg that mobilization on both sides could proceed without automatically bringing on war. Fifth, the world had to believe that German and Austrian leaders were pursuing a negotiated solution until the end, but that Russian general mobilization had precluded a diplomatic solution. To this end, Austria had to appear to be negotiating seriously with Russia, and Germany had to appear to be actively mediating on behalf of peace. Sixth, Austrian leaders had to be prevented from negotiating a last-minute agreement with Russia. These last two steps worked against each other, since the more Vienna appeared to be negotiating by actually making concrete offers, the greater the chance that either Austria or Russia would find an acceptable negotiated solution. Austria thus would

[89]

have to be pressed to present the appearance of negotiating, while actually keeping its demands extreme enough that Russia could not agree to them.

The seventh step was the most ingenious. Berlin would send Petersburg an ultimatum, stating that Germany would have to go to mobilization in twelve hours, but giving no indication that mobilization would mean war. Then, as soon as the twelve-hour limit was up, German would surprise Russia with a declaration of war. As with the declaration of war on Serbia, this would preclude any last-minute negotiated solution. Germany thus would have its major war under the "favorable conditions" being sought for the previous two years.

Although this view seems to attribute supreme Machiavellian dexterity to German officials more often disparaged as incompetent bumblers, the following shows that it is the only consistent explanation for the events of the last week of the crisis. In fact, convincing the world that they were not in control of events was all part of the German plan. They were so successful that even eighty years later, the conflict is still seen as the archetype of a major war that no state wanted.

THE FATEFUL WEEK: JULY 26 TO AUGUST 1

In drawing Russia into a war, German leaders faced a possible dilemma: while they knew that Russia would not remain an inactive spectator should Austria attack Serbia, they also knew Petersburg had no desire for war, if only because Russia was still rearming. Hence, even though a hard-line Austrian stance would probably push Russia to mobilize against Austria, as it had in 1912–13, the Russians might back down in the crunch if they knew the war would be general.

The evidence that Berlin knew that the Russians had status-quo intentions is overwhelming. On 16 June, Bethmann wrote Lichnowsky that while Russia now had more resolve to defend its interests in the Balkans, "I do not believe that Russia is planning an early war against us."[43] A month later, on 18 July, Jagow wrote Lichnowsky that "Russia is not ready to strike at present. . . . According to all competent observation, Russia will be prepared to fight in a few years. Then she will crush us by the number of her soldiers. . . . In Russia this is well known, and they are therefore determined to have peace for a few years yet."[44] A week later, Jagow confirmed to Wolff that "neither Russia, nor France, nor England wanted war."[45]

Even *after* word that Russia had started military preparations, Berlin knew that the Russians sought peace. On 30 July, in a session of the Prussian Ministry of State in which Bethmann said that "it was of the greatest importance to put Russia in the position of the guilty party," he also acknowledged: "Although Russia had proclaimed mobilization its mobilization measures could not be compared with those of the West European [powers]. Russian troops could remain standing in the state of mobilization for many weeks. Russia did not want a war, it had been forced by Austria to take this step."[46]

This evidence calls into question a critical element of the inadvertent war explanation, namely, that the Germans launched a preemptive war on the assumption that Russian mobilization signaled aggressive Russian intentions. Indeed, Bethmann's statement confirms that he knew that Russian mobilization did not in any way mean Russia had to attack Germany, and that many weeks for negotiations remained.

German leaders knew Petersburg did not want war, but they also knew that it would resist any Austrian attack on Serbia. On 25 July, Friedrich von Pourtalès, German ambassador in Petersburg, sent a telegram recording Sazonov's stern warning: "If Austria-Hungary devours Serbia, we will go to war with her."[47] The next day, Pourtalès relayed word that "Grand Headquarters are in the throes of great excitement over Austria's procedure. I have the impression that all preparations are being made for mobilization against Austria."[48] So by Sunday, 26 July, three days before the Russian partial mobilization, Berlin was perfectly aware of Russian resolve. Nor should this have been a surprise, since the Russians had done the same thing in 1912–13.[49]

The key now was to provoke Russia into partial mobilization without scaring it into capitulation. In the afternoon on 26 July, Bethmann received word that Russia had implemented preparatory measures, a stage below partial mobilization. At 7:15 P.M. that evening, he wired Pourtalès that he should tell Sazonov that such measures would force Germany to mobilize its army, and "mobilization . . . would mean war" against both Russia and France. Yet if at the same time Russia took a "waiting attitude" toward the Austria-Serbian dispute, Berlin would act to preserve Serbia's integrity, with agreement still possible "at a further stage of the affair."[50] The phrase that mobilization would mean war—used here for the first time—is one with great significance. As we shall see, the chancellor used it selectively during the next week whenever he wanted to goad an adversary into *speeding up* its mobilization effort, as he did with the French on 31 July.

The even more Machiavellian element of this telegram is its suggestion that Germany would accept Russian partial mobilization as long as Russia took a "waiting attitude." This was designed to assure Russia that, as in 1912–13, it could mobilize against Austria without bringing on general war. The next day, Jagow bolstered this belief by letting it be widely known that Germany would not respond to a Russian partial mobilization. This was pure deception: Bethmann and Jagow were already planning to use Russian partial mobilization as the *casus foederis* needed to unleash war—if indeed they could not get Russia to go all the way to general mobilization.[51]

I now turn to evidence showing that German leaders did nothing in the last week of the crisis to help achieve a negotiated peace, even though it was clear that a world war was almost certain. Many diplomatic solutions were offered up from 26 July to 31 July; none was seriously pursued. Moreover, as it became clear that Petersburg was desperately seeking a way out, Berlin sought to forestall any agreement, while still giving the appearance that it desired peace.

In the early morning of Monday, 27 July, three telegrams arrived. At 12:07 A.M., a note from Lichnowsky arrived noting London's view that Foreign Secretary Edward Grey's proposal to hold a European-wide ("*à quatre*") conference was "the only possibility of avoiding a general war." The tone was very serious. The English position was that Austria must not cross into Serbia, or "everything would be at an end, as no Russian Government would be able to tolerate this." Then, "world war would be inevitable."[52]

At 12:45 A.M., a message arrived from Petersburg stating that Sazonov was "looking for a way out" of the crisis. Pourtalès had taken the unauthorized step of proposing direct talks between Russia and Austria with a third party (implying Germany) acting as mediator, a step which pleased Sazonov.[53] Also at 12:45 A.M., information was received that Italy "would not dare to intervene actively."[54] Three more telegrams were received between 4:37 and 8:40 P.M., reinforcing that London saw it in Berlin's hands to stop the war, and that if Berlin did not, Britain would actively oppose Germany.[55]

By Monday evening, then, it was apparent that an Austro-Serbian conflict could not be contained to even a continental war, and that Italy would not support Germany. Some scholars argue that German leaders discounted this evidence, since they were convinced that war would remain localized. This view is critical to sustaining the idea that it was only on Wednesday night that they woke up to the reality and then tried to avert a general war.[56] Riezler's diary for Monday, however, shows that Berlin was perfectly aware of Britain's new stand: "The reports all point to war. . . . England's language has changed. Obviously London has suddenly realized that a rift will develop in the Entente if it is too lukewarm [in its support] of Russia."[57] Since Riezler, given his position, could only have gathered this information through the chancellor, Bethmann was clearly aware by Monday that if things continued as they were, a world war would result.

That night Bethmann wrote to Tschirschky, stating that since Berlin had already rejected Grey's proposal for a European conference, it could not now ignore the new English suggestion that Germany act as mediator. He went on: "By refusing every proposition for mediation, we should be held responsible for the conflagration by the whole world, and be set forth as the original instigators of the war. That would also make our position impossible in our own country, where we must appear as having been forced into the war."[58] This passage is revealing. Bethmann is not only seeking to shift the blame; he is assuming war as a given, despite the fact that Austria had not yet declared war on Serbia, nor had Russia moved to even partial mobilization. Moreover, the issue of blame is critical not because of any need for British neutrality, but simply to ensure domestic support for the war.[59]

Back in Berlin, the German Foreign Office and the chancellor were playing an elaborate game to prevent the kaiser from wrecking the plan for war. The text of the Serbian reply arrived in the afternoon of 27 July. Wilhelm, against Bethmann's advice, had returned from his cruise that same afternoon. This created the possibility that Wilhelm, after seeing Serbia's conciliatory position, would try to get Austria to cancel the declaration of war set for 28 July. The Serbian reply was thus delivered to him only the next morning. Yet, as feared, the mercurial kaiser got cold feet. He wrote to Jagow that the reply was a "capitulation of the most humiliating kind, and as a result, every cause for war falls to the ground." Although Austria should still act, it could be "so arranged that Austria would receive a hostage (Belgrade), as a guaranty for the enforcement and carrying out of the promises."[60]

This is the kaiser's famous "Halt in Belgrade" proposal. It was actually an ingenious diplomatic measure, since it would allow Austria to ensure Serbian compliance, while giving Russia a face-saving way out, since Serbia would not be completely destroyed.[61] Yet Bethmann and the Foreign Office immediately acted to subvert its potential value, even while appearing to be upholding its spirit.

Wilhelm ends his note by instructing Jagow to "submit a proposal to me along the lines sketched out, which shall be communicated to Vienna." Although these instructions were received at 10:00 A.M. on 28 July, Bethmann and Jagow waited until 10:15 that evening to send a message to Vienna, that is, until after word was received confirming the Austrian declaration of war. This ensured that a reluctant Vienna was given no excuse to delay the declaration.

More important, the proposal was significantly altered. Wilhelm's formula consisted of a halt in Belgrade alone; negotiations were to follow, implying European-wide negotiations. In a telegram Tuesday night, Bethmann instructed Tschirschky to tell the Austrians to consider halting in Belgrade *plus* "other places." Moreover, there was no hint of negotiations, let alone the European conference desired by England. This telegram is perhaps the single most revealing document of the crisis, and deserves to be quoted at length.

The telegram begins by emphasizing the need for more information on Austria's military and diplomatic plans. Serbia's conciliatory reply to the ultimatum was a problem, since "in case of a completely uncompromising attitude on the part of [Vienna], it will be come necessary to reckon upon the gradual defection from its cause of public opinion throughout all Europe."

The next paragraph focuses on the need to blame Russia for the war to come. As with the telegram the previous night, this had nothing to do with keeping Britain neutral; war with Britain is assumed as a given.

> According to the statements of the Austrian General Staff, an active military movement against Serbia will not be possible before the 12th of August. As a result, [Germany] is placed in the extraordinarily difficult position of being exposed in the meantime to the mediation and conference proposals of the other Cabinets, and if it continues to maintain its previous aloofness in the face of such proposals, it will incur the odium of having been responsible for a world war [*Weltkrieg*], even, finally, among the German people themselves. A successful war on three fronts cannot be commenced and carried on on any such basis. It is imperative that the responsibility for the eventual extension of the war among those nations not originally immediately concerned should, under all circumstances, fall on Russia.

Having established the importance of blaming Russia, the chancellor turned to the problem at hand: how Austria is perceived by others. Since Sazonov had conceded that Serbia would have to be punished, Vienna should tell Petersburg that it had no territorial aims, and that

> her military preparations are solely for the purpose of a temporary occupation of Belgrade and certain other localities on Serbian territory in order to force the Serbian Government to the complete fulfillment of her demands. . . .
> An occupation like the German occupation of French territory after the Peace of Frankfort, for the purpose of securing compliance with the demands for war indemnity, is suggested.

Here is the chancellor's Halt proposal. Far from recommending Wilhelm's "Halt plus negotiations," Bethmann is suggesting a peace equivalent to that imposed on France after the Franco-Prussian war! He could hardly have believed Russia would accept such a proposal. It seems clear that Bethmann's only goal was to so alter the original Halt formula as to placate Wilhelm while shifting world and German public opinion against Russia. As he notes, should Petersburg fail to see the justice of this position, "it would have against it the public opinion of all Europe, which is now in the process of turning away from Austria. As a result, the general diplomatic, and probably the military, situation would undergo material alteration in favor of Austria-Hungary and her allies [i.e., Germany]."[62]

Thus by Tuesday night, the groundwork in the campaign to blame Russia was being laid. Much more was to come. At 1:45 A.M. the next day, the kaiser sent a letter to the czar, written by the Foreign Office, providing a moral justification for Austria's tough stance. The letter indicated that Wilhelm had already started mediation efforts, which was false, since he had had no contact with Vienna, nor was he ever to have.[63] This first of the kaiser's telegrams to the czar seems to suggest that Berlin now sought a peaceful solution. Yet the message went out more than two days after word was received that the Russians felt that a telegram from Wilhelm to Nicholas "would prove the surest means of maintaining peace."[64] Had Bethmann really wanted peace, why wait so long to open such a dialogue? As will become clear, Bethmann encouraged the "Willy-Nicky" correspondence only to provide evidence of Russia's responsibility for the war.

At 6:15 A.M. on 29 July, Berlin was informed that Sazonov was again earnestly seeking German mediation to avoid war.[65] For Bethmann, this message, plus the fact that Russian partial mobilization had not yet been confirmed,[66] posed a problem: if Russia did not go to at least partial mobilization, it could not be blamed for the war. Hence, Bethmann sent out two telegrams that, when contrasted with his actions on 31 July, provide a key piece of evidence that Germany sought war. On 29 July, Bethmann was very threatening with the Russians, yet reassuring with the French. On 31 July, he was the exact opposite: reassuring to Russia but threatening to France.

The best explanation for this bizarre behavior is the following (see also the discussion below for 31 July). On 29 July, Russia had not mobilized and Bethmann needed them to, so he was deliberately provocative. Yet since the French were faster mobilizers, he needed them to postpone mobilization until Germany had a reason to mobilize, that is, until after Russia had done so. By 31 July, Russia had gone to general mobilization, and thus Germany could act. But because Bethmann feared that the Russians would get cold feet, he needed to assure them that negotiations could continue while both sides mobilized. With the French, he now needed a justification for attacking them first. Thus he wanted to provoke them into mobilization.

Bethmann's one-sentence telegram to Pourtalès at 12:50 P.M. on 29 July stated:

> Kindly call Mr. Sazonov's serious attention to the fact that further continuation of Russian mobilization measures [*Massnahmen*] would force us to mobilize, and in that case a European war could scarcely be prevented.

His telegram to Paris, sent at exactly the same time, read as follows:

> Reports of French preparations for war are becoming more frequent. Kindly take up the matter with the French Government and call its attention to the fact that such measures [*Massnahmen*] would force us to take actions for our self-protection. We should have to proclaim a state of "risk of war" which, although it would not yet mean mobilization or the calling in of any reserves to

the colors, would nevertheless increase the tension. We continue to hope for the preservation of peace.[67]

Note that these telegrams are in response to military "preparations"/ "measures" by both France and Russia, steps much less serious than mobilization, as all governments understood (and as indeed the second telegram reiterates). Yet while Russia is told that its measures will force Germany to mobilize, such that war could not be prevented, France is told that its measures would not even lead to German mobilization, let alone war. If Bethmann had been truly seeking peace, and perhaps thought that threats would deter Germany's adversaries from going further, the tone of the telegrams should have been the opposite. France, as the much faster mobilizer, should have been the one to receive the strong threat; Russia, since its forces would not be up to full strength for many weeks, should have been sent the much weaker and more hopeful telegram.

Given that the German threat to mobilize in response to mere Russian preparations was so disproportional—and the opposite behavior from 1912–13—Berlin evidently expected that Petersburg would view this telegram as a sign that Germany was looking for a pretext for war. This is exactly how the Russians saw it. Coupled with Vienna's refusal to engage in direct talks and the bombardment of Belgrade on the morning of 29 July, Sazonov could only conclude that Germany wanted war. General mobilization by Russia would have to be called.[68]

Two hours after the dispatch of these two telegrams, the first confirmation that Russia had ordered partial mobilization was received.[69] Although part of Bethmann's objective had been achieved, this was still not the optimal scenario: Germany could go to war over partial mobilization, but to truly blame Russia, Berlin needed a Russian general mobilization. In a conference later that afternoon, Bethmann was able to convince the military to delay even public "risk of war" preparations until word of Russian general mobilization. Without this Russian action, he argued, "we would not have public opinion on our side."[70] Moltke supported Bethmann, which is not surprising considering his point in February 1913 that the aggression must be seen to come from Russia. They knew that they did not have long to wait. Signs were growing that the Russians would soon go to general mobilization. In Petersburg, the necessity of general mobilization had been discussed on the night of 28 July; the next morning, the czar signed two orders, one for partial and one for general mobilization, the latter to be implemented only on his command.

The night of 29–30 July, most historians would agree, is probably the most pivotal of the crisis. It is generally interpreted as the night German civilian leaders confirmed British opposition, got cold feet, and hurriedly scrambled to find a last-minute solution. This interpretation is based on two key telegrams sent to Vienna in the early morning of Thursday, July 30 that seem to show Bethmann desperately seeking to rein in Austria to prevent world war. Nothing could be further from the truth. As with Bethmann's policy over the two previous nights, he was only attempting in the face of Austrian intransigence to push Germany's ally to appear more conciliatory. Thrusting blame onto Russia remained his prime objective.

A 5:07 P.M. telegram from London noted Grey's agreement that direct talks between Russia and Austria were the most likely way to peace. Yet the British were "firmly convinced" that "unless Austria is willing to enter upon a discussion of the Serbian question, a world war is inevitable."[71] The term "world war" (*Weltkrieg*) reinforced what had been known since Monday—that the British would opposed Germany. Thus twelve hours before the world-on-fire telegrams, it was evident that the only choices left were negotiated peace or all-out world war. Berlin still did nothing.

At 8:29 P.M., a telegram was received from Petersburg. Sazonov had been notified that Vienna had refused direct Austro-Russian talks, and had replied that there was now nothing left but to return to British proposal for conversations *à quatre*. Sazonov made clear that he was not expecting Austria "to submit to a sort of European court of arbitration," but that "he was only looking for a way out of the present difficulties, and that in doing so he was grasping at every straw."[72] Bethmann now had to be careful. He had heard nothing from Vienna regarding his instructions the previous night, and he needed Austria to appear to be negotiating with Russia. But in Sazonov's desperate state of mind, he might accept an Austrian offer if it allowed him to save face. Thus, at 10:18 and then again at 10:30 P.M., Bethmann sent two one-sentence messages to Vienna. The first asked if the 28 July instructions—the long telegram detailing his version of the Halt proposal—had arrived; the second said simply that he "expect[ed] immediate carrying out" of these instructions. His urgency is shown by the fact that the first message went out uncoded, to speed up transmission.[73]

Four telegrams arrived between 8:29 P.M. and 10:14 P.M. strongly suggesting that Russia would soon move from partial to general mobilization.[74] Bethmann had provoked Russia into a total military response. It was now time to shift to a softer position to lead Petersburg to believe that, as in 1912–13, Germany would tolerate Russian mobilization as long as Austria was not attacked. At 11:05 P.M., Bethmann sent a telegram to Petersburg containing none of the previous threats. Instead, he stated that although things were starting to get out of hand, Berlin was still seeking a negotiated solution.[75]

I now turn to the two world-on-fire telegrams sent to Vienna at 2:50 and 3:00 A.M. It is typically argued that they reflect the chancellor's realization that Britain would indeed fight, based on a Lichnowsky telegram arriving at 9:12 P.M. and on a meeting with the English ambassador at 10:00 P.M. Yet this view cannot explain why Bethmann's telegrams to Vienna for the six hours between 9:00 P.M. and 3:00 A.M. show no signs of nervousness about Germany's situation. Instead, they show Berlin pressing Austria to appear to be negotiating with Petersburg in order to blame Russia for war. At the same time, they are carefully manipulated to mislead Vienna as to Russian resolve, and thus the real possibility of world war. In behavior perfectly consistent with the previous two nights, Bethmann sought to avoid the appearance of responsibility while simultaneously ensuring that Austria did not back out for fear of general war.

Bethmann sent a message to Tschirschky at 12:10 A.M. providing information on the kaiser-czar correspondence. The full texts of the kaiser's two letters to the czar are included, emphasizing that Russia could remain a spectator of any Austro-Serbian conflict and that an understanding between Petersburg and Vienna was desirable.[76] Significantly, however, Bethmann does not give the text of the czar's letter, but says of it only that the czar "made an appeal for the mediation of His Majesty [the kaiser]." Nicholas had indeed made such an appeal. But the czar's missing text is conspicuous in its absence:

> The *indignation* in Russia [regarding the Austrian declaration of war], *shared fully by me*, is *enormous*. I foresee that very soon I shall be *overwhelmed* by the *pressure* brought upon me, and be *forced* to take extreme measures which will *lead to war*. To try and avoid such a calamity as a European war, I beg you in the name of our old friendship to do what you can *to stop* your *allies* from *going too far*.[77]

That this was a deliberate effort on Bethmann's part to downplay the likelihood of war is clear: in an almost identical telegram to the ambassador in Petersburg less than an hour later, he reproduces the kaiser's letters and then provides the complete text of the czar's response.[78]

At 12:30 A.M., the chancellor sent another message to Vienna. Instead of communicating the text of Lichnowsky's telegram from 9:12 P.M.—the clearest statement that England would fight with France—Bethmann sent only selective parts of the Lichnowsky telegram that had arrived at 5:07 P.M. Since he had been completely informed of the 9:12 P.M. telegram, this move was again designed to avoid scaring Vienna unless it was absolutely necessary. Of the 5:07 P.M. telegram, Bethmann relayed only two small parts: that Russia was aware that Vienna had refused direct talks; and that Grey was forwarding a proposal suggesting Serbia might accept the harsher demands if Austria agreed to it.[79] Conveniently, Bethmann left out the part where Grey warned that Russia "could not and would not stand by quietly" while Serbia was destroyed.[80] The chancellor instructed

Tschirschky to inform the Austrian leaders that Berlin considered compliance to the proposal "an appropriate basis for negotiations, if founded on an occupation of a portion of Serbian territory as a hostage."[81] Bethmann had still heard no word on whether Vienna would agreed to appear to negotiate with Russia. He thus reiterated his watered-down Halt proposal.

At the same moment, 12:30 A.M., Bethmann sent another message to Vienna relaying Pourtalès's message that Russia had gone to partial mobilization. This telegram nicely demonstrates Bethmann's technique of relaying the text from other ambassadors either word-for-word or with his own paraphrasing, depending on the desired impact. Here, instead of quoting Pourtalès's text, he simply states that "Russian mobilization, however, is far from meaning war, as in western Europe; the Russian army might be a long time under arms without crossing a frontier; relations with Vienna not broken off, and Russia wants to avoid war, if in any way possible."[82] These lines are actually Sazonov's, but Bethmann presents them as *Berlin's* opinion of the situation! The chancellor was obviously trying to convince Vienna not to be too worried by Russian partial mobilization.[83] The chancellor ends the telegram saying that "Russia complains that . . . the conferences [have not] made any headway. Hence we must urgently request, in order to prevent a general catastrophe, or at least to put Russia in the wrong, that Vienna inaugurate and continue with the conference according to telegram 174."[84]

Telegram 174 was the one that went out the previous night with the modified Halt proposal (*DD*: doc. 323). So here we have the German chancellor, more than three hours after final confirmation of British opposition, telling Tschirschky to carry out instructions that he knew had little chance of success, in order to "at least put Russia in the wrong."[85] Where are the cold feet that Bethmann should have had at this time? Is it at all conceivable, since the world-on-fire telegrams did not go out until 3:00 A.M., that the information from Britain somehow had a delayed psychological effect on him, enough to then prompt a change of mind? Of course not. If it had not hit him by 12:30 A.M. that his policy was leading to world war, there is no reason why it would hit him two and a half hours later, especially since no new troubling information was received during that time. Indeed, the very fact that Bethmann would stay up until the small hours of the morning indicates that he was waiting for some other piece of crucial information.

So what information did arrive that led to the world-on-fire telegrams? Finally, at 1:30 A.M., after sending three telegrams that evening seeking information on Vienna's response to the Halt proposal,[86] Bethmann received the following message from Tschirschky:

Count Berchtold's thanks for the suggestion. Minister is ready to repeat declaration concerning territorial disinterestedness which he has already made at Petersburg. . . . So far as the further declaration with reference to military measures is concerned, Count Berchtold says that he is not in a position to give me a reply at once.

In spite of my representations as to the urgency of the matter, I have up to this evening received no further communication.[87]

This telegram could not have pleased the chancellor. That Austria continued to show resolve was heartening. But Vienna had not implemented his modified Halt proposal. As Bethmann had stated on Tuesday night, such an uncompromising attitude from Austria would make it impossible to carry out a successful war on three fronts.

The chancellor was thus in a bind: now that he had pushed Vienna into a hard-line posture, Austria was so convinced it could destroy Serbia—or that Berlin would accept nothing less—that it would not even go through the motions of appearing willing to compromise. To shift responsibility, Berlin had to be seen to favor the English proposals for a mediated solution. This was especially so now that Russia, after Austria's intransigence, had turned to England and its idea of European-wide conversations.[88]

Yet here was the dilemma. If Bethmann suggested that Austria accept the idea of European-wide mediation, as had occurred in December 1912, Austria would likely refuse, and the odium for world war would fall on Germany's shoulders. Even worse, Austria, fearing general war, might *accept* the idea. Russia would then agree, and preventive war would have to be postponed. Berlin therefore needed something to satisfy the British request, make Austria appear to want peace, and at the same time ensure that no diplomatic solution could ever be achieved. The solution: direct Austrian-Russia talks around an unacceptable Halt proposal, with Germany playing the role of mediator.

It is this objective that led to the two world-on-fire telegrams, sent to Vienna at 2:55 and 3:00 A.M. The first began by providing the first three paragraphs of the Lichnowsky telegram that had arrived at 9:12 P.M. on Wednesday (the last two paragraphs being studiously left off). The first two paragraphs concerned Sazonov's request that Grey again take up mediation efforts. Grey saw two possibilities: mediation either *à quatre* (European-wide) or by Bethmann himself. It would be a suitable basis for mediation, Grey said, if Austria, after occupying Belgrade or other places, should announce its conditions. The third paragraph contained Grey's warning that if Germany and France were to become involved, Britain could not stand aside, and the resulting war would be the greatest catastrophe ever experienced.[89] After the presentation of Lichnowsky's message, Bethmann writes that if Austria continued to refuse all mediation, Austria and Germany would stand alone against all other great powers including England. Austria could satisfy its honor and claims against Serbia by the occupation of Belgrade or of other places.

Under these circumstances we must urgently and impressively suggest to the consideration of the Vienna Cabinet the acceptance of mediation on the above-mentioned honorable conditions. The responsibility for the consequences that would otherwise follow would be an uncommonly heavy one both for Austria and for us.[90]

This grim picture of an impending world war, with a suggestion for a diplomatic way out, seems to demonstrate a sudden desire for peace on the part of the chancellor. Yet note that Vienna is not asked to accept a Halt, but only "*mediation* on the above-mentioned conditions," that is, negotiations with the Halt as a potential point of discussion. The beginning of such negotiations would deflect blame from Germany while ensuring that no solution was quickly found.[91] And what kind of mediation is Berlin pushing for here? This message is vague as to whether Vienna should accept mediation *à quatre* or only through Germany. The second telegram to Tschirchsky at 3:00 A.M. resolves this ambiguity: Austria should choose the second.

This telegram starts off by reproducing most of the Pourtalès telegram that had arrived in Berlin at 8:29 P.M. on 29 July. Sazonov had told Pourtalès of Vienna's categorical refusal to enter into direct negotiations, and that therefore it seemed necessary to return to British proposals for conversations *à quatre*.[92] Bethmann told Tschirschky that this did not agree with Tschirschky's previous reports indicating that Count Berchtold and the Russian ambassador in Vienna had begun discussions (i.e., bilaterally, not *à quatre*).

[Vienna's] refusal to hold any exchange of opinions with Petersburg . . . [is] a serious error, as it would be [a] direct provocation of Russia's armed interference, which Austria-Hungary is beyond all else interested to prevent.

We are, of course, ready to fulfill the obligations of our alliance, but must decline to be drawn wantonly into a world conflagration by Vienna, without having any regard paid to our counsel.[93]

Berlin was clearly pushing Austria to accept direct Russian-Austrian talks with German mediation, as opposed to European-wide intervention. Yet this proposal did not represent any real change from what Berlin had been suggesting since Monday evening. By controlling the mediation process, Germany could not only appear as the honest broker; it could also ensure that any Austrian offer to "halt" remained harsh enough to preclude Russian agreement.

If any doubt remains that the chancellor and the Foreign Office conspired to unleash general war under favorable conditions, it is dispelled by their other actions from 29 July to 1 August. The trick was to maneuver Germany and German public opinion into position so that as soon as Russian general mobilization was announced, war could be instantly initiated. As Admiral Müller nicely summarized on 27 July, the "tendency of our policy [is] to keep quiet, letting Russia put itself in the wrong, but then not shying away from war."[94]

On 29 July, as noted, Bethmann had secured the military's agreement to delay even the announcement of "risk of war" preparations until after Russian general mobilization. That same day, in meetings with the top officials of the Social Democratic Party, he secured their support for a general war against the Slavic threat.[95] By the next day, Bethmann could tell his colleagues that the "general public feeling was good in Germany," with "[nothing] particular to fear from Social Democracy or from the leadership of the Social Democratic Party."[96] Riezler had noted on 27 July that the chancellor was going to "work the Social Democrats from all sides."[97] The strategy was evidently paying off.

One potential obstacle remained: the kaiser. Since his signature was needed to wage war, he had to be convinced that Russian actions would necessitate German mobilization without scaring him into a compromise. At 11:15 A.M. on 30 July, the chancellor sent two telegrams to Wilhelm. In the first, Bethmann confirmed England's determination to fight and then noted that while he had carried out Wilhelm's instructions regarding mediation, he had heard no word yet from Vienna. Needless to say, Bethmann did not explain that he had altered the kaiser's instructions without authorization. His next lines are revealing as to his intentions:

I instructed [Tschirschky] . . . to demand an immediate explanation from Count Berchtold, in order that this episode may be closed in one way or another. I also called his attention to the fact that every declaration by Vienna to Petersburg concerning the purpose and extent of Austria's action against Serbia would only emphasize and openly label Russia's responsibility before the entire world.[98]

This language is hard to reconcile with the view that the chancellor sought peace when he sent the world-on-fire telegrams. Here he is, a mere eight hours later, talking again about thrusting blame onto Russia.

In the second 11:15 message, we see the chancellor using the kaiser to advance his plan. Bethmann suggests that Wilhelm send a message to the czar stating that if Russia continues with partial mobilization, "then the role of mediator which I [the kaiser] took upon myself at your request will be endangered, if not made impossible. Yours alone is for the moment the responsibility of deciding." Bethmann ends his telegram with the following:

As this telegram will be a particularly important document historically, I would most humbly advise that Your Majesty do not—as long as Vienna's decision is still outstanding—express in it the fact that Your Majesty's role as mediator is ended.[99]

Why would Bethmann say such an odd thing just when he should have been seeking a negotiated solution? The answer, of course, is that he wanted no such solution. Hence, he was already planning ahead to the time when the German people would be given documented evidence on Russian aggression. It is no coincidence that the German White Book—titled "Germany's Reasons for War with Russia"—was published just three days later on 2 August[100] and then presented to the Reichstag the next day (before hostilities with France began). Considering simple publishing logistics, the book must have been in preparation all through the previous week, when Berlin was supposedly seeking a mediated solution. It is also not by accident that Exhibit 23 of the White Book is Wilhelm's very telegram to the czar that Bethmann notes will be a "particularly important document historically."

The machinations do not end there. In the White Book, the telegram's time of sending is given as 1 A.M., 30 July. But it was actually sent at 3:30 P.M. Berlin time that day, and only arrived in St. Petersburg at 5:30 P.M. The final version of the telegram, and the one appearing in the White Book, ends: "the whole weight of the decision lies solely on your [the czar's] shoulders now, who have to bear the responsibility for peace or war."[101] Given that Russian general mobilization was not ordered until 5:00 P.M., an earlier dispatch time had to be put on the published document to make it appear that the Russians, despite being given plenty of forewarning, had still aggressively moved to mobilization against Germany. A "particularly important document historically" indeed![102]

During the day on 30 July, reports showed that Russia was gearing up for general mobilization.[103] The night before, it had been ordered by the czar at around 8:00 Moscow time. Just after 10:00, however, Nicholas received a letter from Wilhelm which frightened him enough that he canceled the order. On the morning of 30 July, Sazonov and the military, distressed by this change, agreed on the need to reinstate general mobilization. At around 3:00 P.M. Petersburg time, Nicholas and Sazonov met, and after about an hour, the reluctant czar agreed to move once again to general mobilization. By 5:00, the order was sent out, with a starting date of 31 July.[104]

The need to sustain Russian mobilization gave Bethmann and his colleagues still one more scheme to execute. The chancellor had already secured the military's agreement to delay public military moves until after Russian general mobilization. The next part of the plan went as follows. As soon as word was received from Petersburg confirming this mobilization, Berlin would send Russia an ultimatum giving it only twelve hours to recall it or face German general mobilization. Meanwhile, all energy would be directed to averting any last-minute diplomatic solution. This required a coordinated three-pronged effort.

First, Russia would be told that rejecting the ultimatum would lead only to German mobilization, with any hint that mobilization meant war now removed. Petersburg would thus believe that mobilization could continue while both sides negotiated an agreement. Yet upon the Russian rejection, Berlin would surprise Russia by declaring war. This move, as with the declaration of war on Serbia, would prevent all possible diplomatic settlements. Second, Austria would be instructed to cease all negotiations and move immediately to war against Russia. If the Austrian leaders were getting cold feet, this tactic would forestall an Austrian-Russian agreement. Moreover, it would ensure that Austria redirected the bulk of its troops against Russia rather than concentrating on its main goal, the destruction of Serbia.

Third, Britain, the power most able to play the honest broker, had to be prevented from convincing Russia to capitulate. London therefore had to be told that Russian-Austrian talks had begun and that Berlin was actively mediating. It was also important that London not know that Germany was preparing to jump immediately to war, since it might then press the czar to accept Austrian terms, and war would be off. With France, Berlin had an ironic and self-caused dilemma: France had not proceeded far enough in its mobilization to allow Berlin to blame France for the blow to come. Hence, on 31 July, the same technique previously used to provoke Russia was now to be employed against the French: Paris would be told that its military measures inevitably meant war. In short, German diplomacy toward Russia and France would be reversed from just two days before. On 29 July, Russia had been provoked and France assuaged; now, Russia would be assured that negotiations could continue, while France was told that nothing more could be done.[105]

Up until Russian general mobilization was confirmed, Berlin still needed Austrian agreement to open talks with Petersburg along the instructed lines. Hence, all through Thursday, 30 July, Bethmann continued to press for word from Vienna. At 5:20 P.M., a report from Tschirschky arrived stating that Austria had instructed its ambassador in Russia to begin conversations with Sazonov. This, although overdue, was encouraging. Yet the telegram also indicated that Austria was unwilling to halt on Serbian territory, and would pull back only after peace was concluded to "compel [Serbia] to the complete fulfillment of [Austrian] demands." Of equal concern was word that despite Vienna's partial mobilization against Serbia, the Austrians were uncertain as to whether general mobilization was necessary.[106] In short, it seemed by late Thursday that Austria might not only fail to appear conciliatory, but also that it would not fight Russia in the critical first days of war.

As they had done in February 1913, Bethmann and Moltke worked together to whip Austria into line. At 9:00 on Thursday night, Bethmann wrote to Tschirschky, noting that should Vienna decline to make concessions, "it [would] hardly be possible any longer to place the guilt of the outbreak of a European conflagration on Russia's shoulders." Austria's stand in the face of English diplomacy "would place us, in the eyes of our own people, in an untenable situation. Thus we can only urgently advise that Austria accept the [British] proposal."[107] Once again, Bethmann's goal was not to save the peace, but to shift blame to Russia. That afternoon, Moltke spoke with Austria's military attaché, who reported to Vienna at 5:30 P.M. that Berlin desired Austria's immediate mobilization against Russia. Moltke also promised that this move would invoke German alliance obligations, a promise Vienna had been anxious to hear.[108]

Late in the evening, Bethmann met with Moltke and Falkenhayn to discuss the military situation. The military now revealed that Russian general mobilization was truly impending.[109] The significance was clear: Germany could now blame Russia for the war. Yet Bethmann now had to *stop* Austria from acting on Berlin's demand that it offer Russia a halt in Serbia (a demand Bethmann had reiterated just two hours before). At 11:20 P.M., Bethmann sent uncoded (to speed transmission) the one-line message "Please do not carry out instructions number 200 [the 9:00 P.M. telegram] for the present." The reason for this sudden cancellation was written up but never sent, probably because it revealed too well Berlin's plan to await Russian mobilization and then compel Austria to fight:

> I [Bethmann] cancelled the order of instruction in No. 200, as the General Staff just informs me that the military preparations of our neighbors, especially in the east, will force us to a speedy decision, unless we do not wish to expose ourselves to the danger of surprise. General Staff earnestly desires to be informed definitely and immediately as to Vienna's decisions, particularly those of a military nature.

Instead, at 2:45 A.M. on 31 July Berlin forwarded a spurious explanation stating that the cancellation was a result of a letter from the king of England.[110]

The situation was now primed for war. On the morning of Friday, 31 July, the chancellor and the military gathered to wait for word of Russian general mobilization. At 11:40 A.M., confirmation was received.[111] General Karl von Wenninger recorded the reaction at the German War Ministry: "Everywhere beaming faces, people shaking hands in the corridors, congratulating one another on having cleared the hurdle."[112] The hurdle here is obviously the risk that Russia would *not* go to general mobilization, thus preventing Germany from blaming Russia for the war.

Now Bethmann could execute the final diplomatic instruments to ensure

Russian responsibility. An ultimatum with a twelve-hour deadline was prepared for dispatch to Petersburg, telling the Russians to back down or face German mobilization. The wording of this ultimatum, and the way other embassies were informed, constitute perhaps Bethmann's most subtle manipulation in the crisis, so subtle that it been missed by almost every historical account.[113] Between 1:45 P.M. and 3:30 P.M. on 31 July, five telegrams were sent to the five key capitals. All but the one to Vienna paint a similar picture: that Berlin was being forced by circumstances to present an ultimatum to Russia. The telegram to Russia containing the ultimatum was written by the chancellor himself. The other four were written by Jagow but carefully altered by Bethmann before being forwarded.[114] This allowed Bethmann to tell each capital a slightly different story, tailored to his objectives for each situation.

The ultimatum to Petersburg, sent at 3:30 P.M., stated:

> In spite of the still pending negotiations for mediation and although we ourselves have up to the present hour taken no mobilization measures of any kind, Russia has mobilized her entire army and navy, thus against us also. For the security of the Empire, we have been compelled by these Russian measures to declare a state of threatening danger of war, which does not yet mean mobilization. Mobilization must follow, however, in case Russia does not suspend every war measure against Austria-Hungary and ourselves within twelve hours and make us a distinct declaration to that effect.[115]

The first sentence is deliberately deceptive. Negotiations were not "still pending"; Berlin had asked Tschirschky to cease pursuing them the previous night. And while Germany had not yet gone to mobilization, it had secretly taken all measures needed to achieve it within days (indeed it was able to cross into Luxembourg on 2 August).

The critical aspect of this telegram, however, lies in what it does not say. There is no mention that Berlin was preparing to follow a Russian rejection of the ultimatum with a declaration of war, as was already planned as the ultimatum was being drawn up. Moreover, even though on 26 and 29 July Berlin had threatened war in response to mere preparations, there was now not even a hint that German mobilization would lead to war.

This was no oversight. The telegram to Paris, sent at the same time, begins with the same line about "still pending negotiations" and Russian mobilization. But it continues:

> As a result we have declared a state of threatening danger of war, which must be followed by mobilization in case Russia does not suspend every war measure against Austria and ourselves within twelve hours. *Mobilization will inevitably mean war.* Please ask the French Government if it intends to remain

neutral in a Russo-German war. Answer must be given within eighteen hours.[116]

"Mobilization will inevitably mean war"?! If Berlin had truly wanted to warn the Russians, it should have included this line in the Russian draft. Yet this line, absent from Jagow's original draft, was added by Bethmann just before it went out.[117] Since Berlin had been telling Paris that a negotiated peace was still possible, the reason for the switch is clear: having used the "mobilization means war" phrase to provoke Russia, it was now time to push France into mobilization to blame the French for Germany's attack in the west.[118]

Thus while the ultimatum to Petersburg was designed to prevent Russia from capitulating, the note to Paris was designed to force the French to go instantly to general mobilization (as they did). The telegrams to Britain and Italy were equally manipulative. Each begins by protesting Russia's mobilization. The dispatch to Rome notes that Germany would move to mobilization if Russia did not "suspend every war measure against Austria and ourselves within twelve hours." It continues:

> Mobilization will mean war. We have put the question to France whether she will remain neutral. . . . If France's reply should be in the negative, as we certainly expect, war between France and ourselves will also have to be declared at once.
>
> We are counting with assurance upon the fact that Italy will live up to the obligations she has assumed.[119]

Drawing Italy into war was clearly the goal. Since the Triple Alliance invoked support only if an ally was attacked, Bethmann moderated the blunt tone of Jagow's original draft. Jagow had used the phrase: "mobilization will inevitably mean war." Bethmann, clearly realizing that the word "inevitably" might signal that Germany was seeking a pretext for war, deleted it from the final draft, and added the phrase suggesting that Russia could prevent war by canceling its war measures.[120]

With London, the objective was to keep the British off the scent long enough to prevent them from intervening at Petersburg. Hence, Bethmann had to minimize suspicions that Germany wanted war, and instead convince London that a diplomatic solution was still possible. In the opening line about "still pending negotiations" common to all four telegrams, it is only in the message to Britain that the words "and apparently not hopeless mediation" are included, words that would have helped buoy British hopes. The phrase in both French and Italian telegrams—that Germany would mobilize if Russia did not cancel its war measures—is also in the British. Yet there is no subsequent line that "mobilization will mean war," as the Italians were told, or that it will "inevitably mean war," as the French were informed. In Jagow's draft, we see that he thought Bethmann would want at least to hint at the possibility of war, since after stating that Russian rejection of the demand would be followed by German mobilization, Jagow wrote: "it looks as if war with Russia were hardly to be avoided." The chancellor in the final draft crossed out this line.[121] As restrained as Jagow's draft is, Bethmann's final version communicates a very different message: it eliminates any linkage between mobilization and war, while implying that Germany is willing, for the sake of peace, to give Russia more time. Read independently, this telegram is only a low-key warning that tensions are rising. The reality—that Berlin planned to declare war on Russia within a day, and then invade Luxembourg hours after that—is nicely hidden.

These four telegrams clearly confound the argument that Bethmann lost control over the process after 30 July. Yet where is the telegram to Austria? In fact, no parallel message ever went out to inform Austria of the ultimatum to Russia and the twelve-hour limit. Instead, about two hours before, at 1:45 P.M., Bethmann sent a short dispatch to Vienna:

> Since the Russian mobilization we have declared threatening danger of war, which will presumably be followed within forty-eight hours by mobilization. This inevitably means war. We expect from Austria immediate ACTIVE participation in the war with Russia.[122]

The incredible nature of this telegram, from a state supposedly seeking peace or at least the localization of conflict, might not be evident at first glance. Not only is Vienna the only capital not informed of the ultimatum, but Bethmann tells the Austrians that the declaration of threatening danger of war will *presumably be followed within forty-eight hours by mobilization.* It was not "presumably," it was for certain; it was not "forty-eight hours," but something less than twenty-four (considering transmission time of the ultimatum and the twelve-hour limit); it was not to be mobilization, but a declaration of war ending all negotiations. One might think that if any state should have been told the truth of the matter, it should have been Germany's last true ally.

Combined with the telegram the night before canceling the instruction that Austria offer Russia a halt in Serbia, there seems only one explanation for this deception: Berlin wanted Vienna to know that the time for diplomacy had ended, and that it must move immediately to a war footing against Russia, not Serbia. To have told the Austrians of the ultimatum, let alone of the real plan, would have alerted them to the urgency of concluding an agreement with Russia, something Berlin did not want.

All this is shown by the chancellor's words "This inevitably means war. We expect from Austria immediate ACTIVE participation in the war with

Russia." The phrase "inevitably means war" suspiciously arises again. The reason is evident: if war is a given, then diplomacy, by definition, is at an end. There is also a simple explanation for the phrase that Berlin "expects" from Austria immediate and active participation in the war against Russia. That Vienna's goal was to destroy Serbia, not to fight the superior Russians, was well known. Moreover, for the previous few days, Conrad had been hinting that even if Germany pulled Austria into general war, the bulk of the Austrian forces would still be deployed south against Serbia. Moltke had tried to persuade Conrad that it was in Austria's own interest to fight a general war, but Conrad remained unconvinced.[123] Hence, Berlin was now not "requesting" or "suggesting" that Austria "consider" waging war against Russia—the kind of language used on previous nights with regard to the Halt proposals; rather, it was "expecting" it. In diplomatic terms, given Germany's preponderant position in the alliance, this was essentially a demand.

Moreover, the expectation was for "immediate ACTIVE" participation, with Bethmann's emphasis on the active. To make the Schlieffen Plan work, Berlin needed Austria not only to concentrate troops against Russia, but also to go on the offensive to divert Russian forces away from Germany. For obvious reasons, Austria was reluctant to sacrifice its troops just so Germany could dispose of France. Berlin had already employed the implicit threat of leaving Austria to the full onslaught of the Russians, the Austrians' single greatest fear.[124] This short telegram thus could have had only one meaning to the Austrians: do not presume that you can focus on Serbia or use diplomacy to keep the Russians out; general war is a given, so all effort must go against Russia.

Only one possible hitch remained: Russia might back out by capitulating to Austrian demands. There was one sure way to prevent this, namely, a declaration of war on Russia. Germany's premature declaration of war on 1 August provides the final proof that by the end of July, world war was preferred over all possible negotiated solutions, even one giving Austria everything it wanted. Through Bethmann's diplomacy, German workers were ready to fight a war of self-defense against the Slavic aggressors, and with Austrian help. Such favorable conditions, with Germany at the peak of its military power, would be hard ever to recreate.

Thus we have the puzzle that confounds other theories: Why would German civilian leaders plan for a declaration of war on Russia as soon as the twelve-hour ultimatum was up, and yet not warn anyone, including the Russians? Military strategy would argue against declaring war until one's forces were ready to attack. Recognizing this, the civilian leaders kept the decision to declare war secret from all the top military leaders (except one) until after it was a fait accompli. It also makes no sense to argue, as Bethmann tried with his outraged military, that Germany was compelled to follow international law, which required declarations of war before an attack commenced. Considering Germany's unannounced plunge into neutral Belgium three days later, this argument is clearly absurd. Moreover, Berlin deliberately held back the declaration of war against France, even though France was to be attacked weeks before Russia. Nor can it be argued that the declaration of war had a diplomatic or political value. If anything, the declaration hurt Bethmann's own efforts to blame Russia for the war.

The argument that the leaders acted irrationally, without thinking through the implications, also cannot stand. Against this view, we have the careful planning that went into the declaration and the moves to keep it secret from the military. We also have the evidence that Germany pushed Austria to declare war on 28 July solely to preclude a diplomatic solution. One has to wonder how German leaders could have put less thought into a declaration guaranteeing general war than one merely ensuring an Austro-Serbian war. Moreover, it seems odd that the reasoning behind the premature declaration on 28 July could have been forgotten less than a week later.

Finally, we have two important pieces of direct evidence. A senior official in the German Foreign Office made a slip on 31 July. He admitted to a representative of a neutral power who then told George Buchanan, British ambassador in Petersburg, that "the only thing which [the German] Government fears was that Russia would, at the eleventh hour, climb down and accept [the ultimatum]."[125] Even more damaging is a comment by Army Chief of Staff Moltke, the only individual in the military informed of the plan to declare war on Russia. On 1 August, just after the kaiser had signed the mobilization order, Moltke was recalled and told of an English promise to keep France neutral. Wilhelm, overjoyed with the idea that France would stay out of the war, called for an immediate halt to deployment in the west. Admiral Müller's diary records Moltke's emotional response:

> This we cannot do; the whole army would fall into disarray and we would end all chances of winning. Besides, our patrols have already invaded Luxembourg and the division from Trier is immediately following up. All we need now is for Russia to back off as well [*Jetzt fehlte nur noch, dass auch Russland abschnappt*].[126]

Far from fearing Russian attack, Moltke is worried that Russia might also want peace! The fact that Moltke could say this in the presence of Germany's most important civilian and military leaders, and that Müller records no reaction, suggests either that his opinion was already well known or that they agreed with it. Either way, combined with the evidence presented below, it is clear that the biggest fear in Berlin in the last days of peace was not that war might occur, but that it might not.

We have seen that the German ultimatum to Russia mentioned only that mobilization would follow its rejection, not war. One might suppose that on the afternoon of 31 July when the ultimatum was sent, Berlin still sought peace, and therefore worried that stronger threats might make Russia hostile to negotiation. Yet the very same day the ultimatum was sent, a telegram that would be used to instruct Pourtalès to hand over a declaration of war rather than the promised word of German mobilization was being drafted in the Foreign Office.[127] In short, it was not as though on 1 August, due to the emotions of the moment, the civilian leaders panicked and declared war. They had already decided *the day before* to surprise Russia with the declaration of war immediately after the deadline.

Berlin also made sure that the peace-inclined Pourtalès would not hint to Sazonov that refusing the ultimatum would lead to a surprise declaration, thus providing Sazonov a last-second chance to back down. Pourtalès was instructed not to hand over the declaration of war until Sazonov gave him official word that Russia was rejecting the German demands.[128] As it was, Pourtalès, when he met with Sazonov at 7:00 P.M. on 1 August, asked him three times whether he could accept the ultimatum; following the negative reply, he reluctantly handed over the declaration of war. Thus every diplomatic detail was organized to guarantee Russia's refusal of the ultimatum.

The telegram with the declaration of war went out at 12:52 P.M. on 1 August. It again pinned all blame on Russia, stating that Germany would have to declare war for purely defensive reasons. So that Russia did not try to prolong negotiations by simply not responding to the ultimatum (as opposed to an outright refusal), the declaration of war had written into it both possibilities, neither of which could change the outcome.[129] Bethmann and his cohorts also carefully planned the timing of its hand-over to prevent any intervention by Wilhelm and the German military, both of whom were kept in the dark regarding the impending declaration. Hence, while the original telegram said that Pourtalès should present the declaration "immediately upon the expiration of the respite, at the latest, however, this afternoon at five o'clock," Jagow and Bethmann crossed this out and substituted the much more precise statement: "at 5 o'clock this afternoon, according to Central European time,"[130] or five hours after the actual deadline. It is surely not coincidental that this was the exact time military and civilian leaders were to meet with Wilhelm to get his signature on the order for general mobilization. The civilians were making it physically impossible for either the kaiser or the military to stop the declaration of war from being presented, even if they somehow got wind of it at this meeting.

The meeting at 5:00 P.M. is also of interest because of the news presented to Wilhelm of an apparent British offer, received by the Foreign Office at 4:23 P.M., that "in case [Germany] did not attack France, England would remain neutral and would guarantee France's neutrality."[131] Sometime after the meeting started, just after Wilhelm had signed the mobilization order,

Jagow announced that a "very important dispatch" had arrived and would be brought in shortly. Despite this news, Moltke and Falkenhayn left the meeting to send the order to the troops. As Albertini suggests, they almost certainly did this to avoid the chance that the dispatch might avert war.[132]

As noted, the kaiser, delighted by the English offer, recalled Moltke to tell him that Germany could now focus on the east. Bethmann and Jagow expressed joy over the English message, but it seems certain that this was just an act to placate Wilhelm's fears. Behind the scenes, they did everything to ensure war proceeded. Jagow's announcement of this "very important dispatch" ten minutes before it was brought into the meeting is suspicious. How could he have known it was very important unless he had already read at least parts of it? Yet he provided the group with no details, nor did he try to restrain Moltke and Falkenhayn before they ran off to implement mobilization.[133] It thus seems likely that his announcement was simply a cue to the military to leave as soon as possible.

The evening of 1 August was a nerve-racking one for Moltke, as the kaiser had put the Schlieffen Plan on hold as Berlin awaited the English response. Around 11:00 P.M., word was received that the English proposals were a misunderstanding.[134] Wilhelm recalled Moltke, telling him, "now you can do as you will."[135] The Schlieffen Plan was thus back on, with the invasion of Luxembourg to take place early the next morning.

The view that after 30 July the civilians gave up control to the military and their mobilization schedules—a myth Bethmann helped foster, and one accepted not only by inadvertent war scholars, but even by Albertini and Fischer—has been severely shaken by the above evidence. It is now time to put it in its final resting place. Far from the military's controlling the process, only one military leader—Army Chief of Staff Moltke—knew of the plan that would have a much greater effect on military actions than on civilian operations: the surprise declaration of war on Russia. When Tirpitz found out in the late evening of 1 August, he was outraged. Aside from the obvious military reasons for not declaring war until Germany was ready to attack Russia, Tirpitz felt that the move would undermine efforts to blame German adversaries for the war.[136] Minister of War Falkenhayn was also up in arms. To smooth ruffled feathers, at 2:30 A.M. on 2 August Bethmann met with Tirpitz and the generals to discuss the issue, as well as the timing of the declaration of war on France.

From records of the meeting, it is clear that many in the military were still wondering whether the declaration of war on Russia had actually been served. Bethmann admitted that the telegram containing the declaration had already been sent. But by failing to mention that it was to be delivered to Sazonov at 5:00 P.M. the previous day, he evidently sought to keep them confused on this point. In yet another example of Bethmann and Moltke's insidious collaboration, Moltke informed the group that Russia had fired shots across the border. Tirpitz then records Bethmann's response: "then, of course, the case is clear, that means the Russians have been the first to start and I shall have the declaration of war handed over the frontier by the nearest General." The military left the meeting still believing that the declaration of war was in the *process* of being delivered, even though the Russians had received it more than eight hours before. Thus Falkenhayn grabbed Jagow just after the meeting, pleading with him "to prevent the foolish and premature declaration of war on Russia." Jagow's reply: it was now too late.[137]

It is surely revealing that Moltke knew the whole time of the plan to declare war, yet said nothing to his colleagues. As with the chancellor, Moltke's key objective over the previous two days was to ensure that Austria kept on the road to war with Russia. On 30 July, Moltke had sent messages to Conrad instructing him to turn his forces against Russia. By the evening of 31 July–1 August, however, Berlin had received no confirmation of Austrian military plans, and the signs were unfavorable. On the afternoon of 31 July, Conrad hinted to Moltke that Austria would focus on Serbia and would stay on the defensive against Russia. Moltke immediately replied that Germany would soon be at war with Russia, but like Bethmann's message to Vienna that same afternoon, he said nothing about an ultimatum to Russia, nor of an impending declaration of war. Instead, he asked pointedly: "will Austria leave [us] in the lurch?"[138]

At 9:30 that evening, Conrad wrote back to say that Austria had already proved its willingness to wage war, and that it was only holding back to shift the blame by letting Russia declare war first, as per Berlin's "desire." He then said the words Moltke did not want to hear: that he thought he could "count on finishing off [the] war against Serbia before [the] move against Russia [is] necessary." Conrad asked for clarification on German intentions, pleading that only on 31 July had he received information "mak[ing] known Germany's intention to begin war against France and Russia."[139] Bethmann and Moltke's communications to Vienna had gotten them into a bind. Since neither could admit how quickly war was to come without scaring Austria off, they had said nothing to their Austrian counterparts about the twelve-hour ultimatum to Russia, let alone the plan to declare war. Conrad was thus under the impression he still had time to destroy Serbia.

For Berlin, this was worrisome. Despite Bethmann's 1:35 P.M. dispatch demanding Austria's immediate participation in the war with Russia, it now seemed that Austria was concentrating its troops in the south, not the east. This fear was reinforced by another telegram received from Conrad at 10:30 P.M. on 31 July:

> I beg His Excellency von Moltke for a definite statement whether it is now necessary to reckon with waging a major war against Russia immediately

and unconditionally, that, in other words, there is no likelihood of our desist-
ing from the war against Serbia without coming to grips with Russia. This
definite statement is indispensable and urgent for our own decision.[140]

A moment of decision had arrived. If Berlin now revealed the plan against
Russia, it would not only show that Bethmann had withheld information; it
might push Austria into a peace with Russia, the very fear that had led to
the withholding of information. But the revelation of Berlin's plan now
seemed necessary if Austria was to play its designated role in the Schlieffen
Plan. Hence, at 11:20 P.M., Moltke revealed that indeed there was an ultimatum.[141] Then at 2:20 A.M. on 1 August, knowing that Conrad had to decide
that day whether to concentrate troops against Serbia or Russia, Moltke finally let him know the truth. Germany had demanded Russia's suspension
of all military measures.

> If Russia rejects this demand, German declaration of war follows immedi-
> ately. Russian reply demanded with twelve-hour time limit. Thus decision
> must be taken tomorrow. I regard acceptance of German demands by Russia
> as impossible.[142]

Conrad now knew that localized war against Serbia was out, and that he
had to concentrate forces against the Russian masses.

This interchange reveals much about Moltke's role in the last days of the
crisis. With Moltke the only military leader privy to the plan to declare war
on Russia, there is little doubt that he conspired with the civilian leaders—
Bethmann, Jagow, and the others in the Foreign Office—to bring on war
while minimizing last-minute interference from either the kaiser *or* the German military. The declaration of war on Russia was a brilliant stroke, as
Moltke surely understood: as with the Austrian declaration of war against
Serbia, it would end any possibility of diplomatic intervention. Preventive
war could then proceed. It is not surprising therefore that Moltke would
confide to a friend a year later, just after being dismissed: "It is dreadful to
be condemned to inactivity in this war which I prepared and initiated."[143]

The final piece of evidence showing the German leadership's guilt is its
efforts to blame the French for the German attack on Belgium and France.
By telling Paris on 31 July that Germany would mobilize after Russian rejection of the ultimatum, and that mobilization inevitably means war, Germany had successful provoked France into mobilization. This mobilization
was confirmed on the evening of 1 August. After heated discussions the
next morning, it was agreed that the declaration of war against France
should be delayed until Monday night at 7:00 P.M.

Why the delay, when the military now knew of the declaration of war on

Russia and also understood that France had to be attacked first? Bethmann Hollweg provides the answer. At 9:00 A.M. on 2 August, just a few hours after meeting with the military, the chancellor sent a telegram to the kaiser. He informed Wilhelm of reports of Russian border crossings, as well as his requests to Vienna that it fulfill its alliance obligations. He continued: "In accordance with understanding with Ministry of War and General Staff, presentation of declaration of war to France not necessary today for any MILITARY reasons. Consequently it will not be done, in the hope that the French will attack us."[144] Berlin was holding off a declaration of war in the hope that the French would attack? Perhaps no single line better demolishes the argument, critical to the preemptive-war thesis, that Germany went to war because it feared it would be attacked first, given the supposed advantage of the offensive. Here, instead of a French invasion feared, that invasion is actually desired. Undoubtedly Bethmann was hoping, as he had with the Russians, to thrust the blame for war onto French shoulders.

The argument that Germany was forced by mobilization schedules into war collapses completely when one sees that the real fear was not that France would get the jump on Germany, but that the French would not mobilize *enough*. Despite confirmation of French mobilization, by 2 August there was still worry that France had not mobilized extensively enough to give Germany the pretext to launch the Schlieffen Plan. Moltke's memo to the Foreign Office on the military situation, delivered that afternoon, noted: "I do not consider it necessary yet to deliver the declaration of war to France; [rather] I am counting on the likelihood that, if it is held back for the present, France, on her part, will be forced by public opinion to organize warlike measures against Germany." Moltke expressed the hope that France would move into Belgium once it heard of the harsh German ultimatum to Brussels (written by Moltke). Thus a crossing into France would be avoided "until activities on the part of France render it necessary."[145] It would be hard to find a clearer statement of the coordinated machinations of Moltke and Bethmann's Foreign Office in the final days of peace. By delaying the move against France, German leaders hoped France would increase its military readiness and even enter Belgium. Germany could then justify its full-scale attack.

For the next two days, until the declaration of war against France was delivered at 7:00 P.M. on 3 August, Berlin did its utmost to convince the world—especially Britain, which still might delay its involvement—that Germany was only responding to French provocations. French violations and atrocities were fabricated and communicated to London as truths.[146] French leaders, however, refused to fall into the German trap. They wisely mobilized, but the troops were ordered to move back ten kilometers from the border to prevent even an accidental clash that could be interpreted as

French aggression. By Monday it was evident that France would not go into Belgium first. Although France took these precautionary measures to ensure British support, the measures made it difficult for Berlin to blame the French for the war.

By Monday afternoon, German leaders could wait no longer for evidence of French hostility. Hence, they simply pretended that it existed, and proceeded anyway. Paris was told that even though German troops had obeyed orders to respect the French frontier, French troops, in spite of the assurance of the ten-kilometer zone, had already crossed over the German frontier. Accordingly, "France has forced us into a state of war."[147]

On 4 August, as German troops crossed into Belgium, London sent an ultimatum to abstain or face a British declaration of war. It was ignored. The intricate maneuverings of the chancellor, the Foreign Office, and Moltke had delivered a war under favorable conditions: with Russia taking the blame, the German public supported a war for the survival of the fatherland; and Vienna had been cornered not only into fulfilling its alliance obligations, but into concentrating its troops on the Russian, rather than Serbian, border. English neutrality was not secured, but no one including Bethmann had ever thought it was likely in the first place. Yet by stringing London along, Berlin had at least delayed by a few days the deployment of the British Expeditionary Forces.[148] It is no wonder that Admiral Müller would write in his diary on 1 August: "The morning papers carry the speeches of the Emperor and of the Reich Chancellor to the enthusiastic crowd assembled outside the Palace and the Chancellor's Palais respectively. The mood is brilliant. The government has managed brilliantly to make us appear the attacked."[149] Bethmann and his cohorts had indeed succeeded in the difficult task of making others seem responsible for a war only Germany wanted. Their activities were so effective that eighty years later we still debate who or what caused the First World War.

This chapter has presented evidence demonstrating that the German leadership deliberately initiated a crisis in July 1914 in order to bring on war before Russia grew any stronger. At the same time, I have shown why none of the other explanations for the war, either realist or nonrealist, can be accepted. One can always find some evidence within this complex case to support some aspects of a particular theory. Yet only this book's argument, I believe, is consistent with all the evidence. The other explanations simply face too many contradictions to remain plausible.

The implications of this are significant: the case of major war in which multiple causality was apparently most at work turns out to be one of the most mono-causally driven major wars in history. As with Sparta before the Peloponnesian War, domestic factors were pushing German leaders in the opposite direction: toward peace to avoid revolution at home. Yet the systemic pressures of relative decline were so strong that war was chosen anyway.[150] Moreover, there is little evidence that Bethmann Hollweg or his closest associates ever acted irrationally because of the pressures of the crisis; rather, they manipulated others into war with the greatest of dexterity. Although the other states did face conditions that could draw them into war through alliance commitments or incentives to preempt, German leaders knew this. They thus restrained Austria until Germany was ready to take on the system, and then exploited these conditions to the maximum.

Finally, it is hard to argue that German fear of Russia's rise was a paranoid and unreasonable one. With its huge population and land mass, Russia's future superpower status on the Eurasian continent seemed assured. To build a case for why Germany should not have been worried, one would have to explain why Russia would not have moved into western Europe after achieving preponderance, or why Germany's decline versus Russia should not have been seen as deep or inevitable. Yet Nicholas ruled the same state that had expanded in 450 years from the tiny Duchy of Muscovy to become the world's largest land empire. It was also a state undergoing intense industrialization, technological development, and concomitant military modernization. It did not take a genius to foresee that the chances of Russia moving westward at a later date (with Germany as its first victim) were more than negligible.

This case, perhaps more than any other, illustrates the tragic dimension of world politics. Bethmann Hollweg, the "philosopher from Hohenfinow," can hardly be characterized as an individual who liked war for its own sake. The Riezler diaries, moreover, reveal a man accepting the burden of what he was about to unleash with the utmost reluctance. And yet it had to be done, even if it led to a "revolution of everything that exists." Bethmann was trapped in a lesser-of-two-evils choice. He thus made what he knew to be a leap in the dark, a decision likely to undermine the dominance of his class and possibly lead to Germany's defeat, all to avoid an even worse fate: a Germany faced with a Russia of overwhelming size and unpredictable intentions.

[5]

The Rise of Russia and the Outbreak of World War II

The Second World War in Europe is one of the most studied cases of major war in history, and its social, political, and moral aspects are so complex that to capture it in a short space risks oversimplifying one's argument. The sheer horror of what Nazi Germany wrought in Europe is so overwhelming that to emphasize the security side of German policy, as I do below, seems to temper our conviction that this was one of the most evil regimes in history.

Such tempering is not my objective. Rather, I seek to show that responsibility for the evil must also be put squarely on the shoulders of German military leaders. These leaders not only accepted Hitler's long-term geopolitical objectives, but worked untiringly to bring about their realization. Yet by posing as unwilling participants in a Nazi Party conspiracy, the German military have managed for the most part to escape the ire of the western world.[1] They have presented their occasional resistance to Hitler's plans as evidence that they tried to stop the steamroller. As this chapter shows, however, almost all military resistance to Hitler's plans in 1938–40 was driven by expedient, not moral, reasons: the generals felt Hitler was bringing on major war *too soon*, and so recommended delays or tactical adjustments to his strategic goals. After surprisingly easy victories from September 1939 to June 1940, all military "resistance" to Hitler mysteriously dried up. The generals were not coerced into submission; they merely now believed in Hitler's strategic genius. Thus from July 1940 to June 1941 they fell with great enthusiasm into the most arduous task of all—the destruction of the Soviet Union.

While literature on the origins of the European war overwhelmingly emphasizes Germany's nonsecurity objectives, this chapter shows that fear of the rise of Russia was a primary and probably dominant force pushing Hitler and his generals to war. The causes of war in 1939 thus parallel those in 1914. German leaders continued to face a state with three times Germany's population and forty times its land mass. Once Russia completed its industrialization and translated economic power into military power, they worried that Germany would be its first victim.[2] To prevent this, Germany had to take on the system while it still stood a chance of European hegemony. Such hegemony would provide the base of potential power needed to compete over the long term with other world powers. Not to act, they believed, would mean almost certain destruction as the Russian menace grew to overwhelming proportions.

This lesser-of-two-evils view of German decision-making before both world wars omits the most obvious difference between the cases, namely, the racist ideology of Nazism. Hitler's far-reaching racial objectives unquestionably shaped his view on the necessity for war and how it must be waged. In particular, his entrenched belief in an insidious Jewish conspiracy bent on destroying a superior German culture is evident in so many documents, going back to *Mein Kampf*, that its significance in defining the uniqueness of the Second World War cannot be ignored.

What is critical to understand, however, is exactly how Nazi racism affected the nature of the war, that is, how and why it was fought. Specifically, how important was racism to the decision to *initiate* major war versus its importance in shaping the *complexion* of the war, once underway? I suggest that Hitler was driven to major war by both a rational fear of a rapidly industrializing Russia and an irrational obsession with a nonexistent Jewish conspiracy—a conspiracy allegedly hiding behind the facade of global Bolshevism and therefore headquartered in Moscow. The two fears combined, convincing Hitler that he must destroy the growing Soviet threat before it was too late. The rational geopolitical side of his fear was analogous to that of German leaders before the First World War. That war, of course, had failed to eliminate the Russian colossus and only temporarily retarded its industrialization. The second fear cannot be considered rational by any definition of the term. Jews within Germany posed no threat to the German state, and even in the Soviet Union they remained a persecuted minority. Hitler's deep hatred of Judaism took root in his youth, and can only be described as pathological.[3]

Hitler's racist world view leaves us morally repelled, and has been studied extensively. We need here to examine another issue: the geopolitical basis for his military actions. Hitler's fear of Russian growth was not original in any way. It grew out of discussions with such geopoliticians as Karl Haushofer in the early 1920s,[4] which in turn reflected entrenched arguments from the pre-1914 period. Moreover, while the pre-1914 fear was of a czarist Russia, after 1920 the Russian state was guided by an ideology with the declared goal of destroying capitalism. For the traditional upper class, which included German military leaders, Russia had become doubly dangerous.[5]

It is thus not surprising that German military leaders followed Hitler willingly into war. The generals went to war for a long-established geopolitical objective—the Wilhemine goal of destroying the rising Russian colossus and establishing a territorial basis for long-term security. As we shall see, Hitler was well aware of the security focus of the German military. From 1933 to early 1941, he rarely motivated them with talk of plans for racial purity in the new Europe. His arguments were geopolitical; ideology, when brought in, was anti-Bolshevik rather than anti-Semitic. Hitler understood that his military leaders were motivated by fear of Communism, not of Judaism.

Were geopolitical fears or Nazi racism necessary or sufficient conditions for German aggression in 1939? If one accepts that without German military support Hitler could not have brought about the war, then the geopolitical logic was at least a necessary condition. Yet if one imagines a Germany in 1939 with superior but declining military power, but led by military leaders lacking the racist ideology of Nazism, would these leaders still have gone to war? Given that to a man, senior generals were holdovers from the First World War, and given that the military pushed for war in 1914 because of a rising Russia, it is hard not to argue that German geopolitical insecurity alone would have led to Germany's military expansion across Europe.[6]

Racism clearly drove the social phenomenon of Hitler and Nazism[7] and is the only explanation for the *manner* in which major war was conducted (the most horrendous example being the death camps).[8] Yet to explain why Germany initiated world war for a second time in a generation, racism appears to be neither a sufficient nor even a necessary condition. It is best thought of as an accentuating condition, one that turned the Second World War into the most devastating and chilling war the world has ever seen. Still, German geopolitical vulnerability and the desire to eliminate the Russian threat would have existed with or without Nazi ideology.

All accounts of the origins of World War II emphasize the impact of the Versailles humiliation and the devastation of the Depression in bringing Hitler to power. They disagree fundamentally as to why the German leadership finally initiated major war. There are two main camps in the literature. The "intentionalists" such as Klaus Hildebrand, Eberhard Jäckel, and

Andreas Hillgruber build on the traditional historical account of the war that emerged in the first decade after the war's end. These authors argue that Hitler and his followers assumed power in 1933 with the intention of waging a new European war for German hegemony. They then manipulated the diplomatic and military environment to bring about this war as soon as possible and under the best possible circumstances.[9]

The "structuralist" counterargument, led most prominently by Hans Mommsen, Martin Broszat, and Tim Mason, is a revisionist effort to show that Hitler had no set program for German hegemony, as the intentionalists contend. Hitler, structuralists contend, lacked clear long-range goals. He reacted to the domestic forces unleashed as he sought both to rebuild the German economy and to grapple with struggles within a divided German polity.[10] Internal policies created an unexpected economic crisis in 1938–39, which pushed Hitler to conclude that war might forestall economic dislocation and divert the populace's attention. The controversial aspect of the structuralist argument is obvious: it suggests that Hitler was nothing but a improvising opportunist, gradually "radicalizing" his goals to deal with the latest domestic crisis.[11]

As structuralists indicate, the intentionalist view ignores the social dimension of German history, wrongly assuming that Hitler led a centralized totalitarian regime which blindly implemented his long-range plans. Nazi Germany, as is now widely accepted, was quite divided.[12] Not only did bureaucracies compete over the share of resources, but the army and the civil service struggled incessantly with the party apparatus for power and money. Nevertheless, it is also widely accepted that in foreign policy, as opposed to domestic policy, Hitler was firmly in control.[13]

There are three main problems with the structuralist argument. First, overwhelming documentary evidence (summarized below) shows that Hitler desired major war as soon as he assumed power in 1933, and that he made this intention perfectly clear to the military. Second, although it is true that Hitler did adjust tactically to changes in the general environment from 1935 to 1939, such as moving to absorb Czechoslovakia earlier than envisioned in the infamous war council of November 1937, this does not demonstrate that he lacked an overall strategy for major war. Hitler's geopolitical plan, designed to isolate the other great powers to maximize the chance for hegemony, was clearly in place by the 1937 meeting.[14]

Third, the notion that Hitler went to war in response to an internal economic crisis—that World War II was a diversionary or social-imperialist war—mixes up the causal sequence. It ignores the fact that it was Hitler's urgent directives from 1933 to 1936 to rearm, to become capable of launching what he called an "offensive war," that led to economic crisis. In short, the crisis was the result of his plan for major war, not the cause of it. So while economic crisis may have sped up Hitler's timetable, there is no persuasive way to argue that Hitler went to war out of a sudden fear of domestic turmoil.[15]

Structuralist arguments are severely deficient in explaining the origins of war in 1939. This does not leave the other camp victorious, however. The intentionalists are right to say that Hitler planned for major war, but they are less than clear as to why. Some (Hillgruber, Hildebrand) focus on Hitler's geostrategic objectives: the desire to destroy France and Russia and eventually the British empire and the United States. Yet their analyses obscure Hitler's ultimate objectives—whether he sought national security, or wealth, or the spread of Nazi ideology. Most intentionalists would probably accept Alan Bullock's classical realist line that Hitler had a pathological lust for power.[16] Yet such a conclusion is not only unilluminating (do not all leaders thirst for power?), it is essentially tautological: in the very act of seeking geopolitical hegemony, leaders who initiate major wars show they "want" to dominate others.

Realist interpretations are also lacking. Neorealists blame the war on the Allies: by failing to rearm sufficiently or to form a tight alliance, Britain, France, and Russia could not deter Germany.[17] Neorealists rightly note Germany's military preponderance in 1939–41, but they have trouble providing a systemically driven explanation for its behavior. Germany's insecure position in the heart of Europe is noted. But since this, like polarity, is a constant factor, it cannot explain changes in German willingness to initiate war over time. Neorealists thus fall back on unit-level variables (the hypernationalism embedded in Hitler's Nazism) to explain the specific motive for war in 1939.[18]

Classical realism correctly identifies Germany as a militarily superior state that almost succeeded in its bid for hegemony.[19] Yet, like neorealism, it misses the German fear of Russia's potential power. Hence, classical realists tend to follow the intentionalist account, arguing that Hitler's lust for power and his "nationalistic universalism" provide a sufficient account of German ends.[20] Aside from suffering from the problems inherent in the intentionalist argument, classical realism leaves unexplored why the German military followed Hitler into war.

Finally, the hegemonic stability argument emphasizes Germany as a rising power that had been denied the status and rewards commensurate with its new power.[21] As I show, however, Hitler drew Germany into war only after he saw Germany's relative military power starting to decline. Those in the military who disagreed with his actions accepted that Germany should attack once declining; they simply believed that Germany in 1939 was still rising and war therefore should be postponed. In short, the key decision-makers followed dynamic differentials logic, not hegemonic stability logic. Moreover, Hitler and the generals saw Germany as militarily superior to any other individual great power, given its qualitative advantages in weaponry, training, and strategic acumen. The evidence thus undermines the hegemonic stability thesis that major wars occur only when the top two states believe they are at parity.

Current explanations for the outbreak of the Second World War are inadequate. To go beyond them, we need to reexamine Hitler and his generals' strategic military logic, a logic rooted in German geopolitical thinking for the previous half-century.

The Coming of World War II

German fear of Russia had deep historical roots. As early as 1769, Friedrich II was warning his brother that "in a half-century [the Russians] will make all of Europe tremble."[22] As we saw, this anxiety crystallized in the years before 1914 as Russia transformed itself from a backward feudal state into a future superpower. It is tempting to believe that with the Weimar Republic, German geopolitical thinking changed. If only the German leaders of the 1920s, in particular Gustav Stresemann, had stayed in power, the tragedy of world war might have been avoided. A democracy led by Stresemann (winner of the Nobel Peace prize) would not have attacked other democracies; only an authoritarian state could have wanted another horrific war. So the popular liberal logic would go.[23]

We can never know how Stresemann would have acted in 1939 leading a German state possessing superior but declining military power. Still, we do know something about the private objectives of Stresemann himself, objectives that should make us reconsider the simple equation of democracy with peace, fascism with war. During World War I, Stresemann and his National Liberal Party were rabidly annexationist. A report of the party's May 1915 Executive Committee meeting noted that to improve German security, territory was needed in both the east and west. A month later, Stresemann argued at an internal party meeting that "we must weaken our opponent so ruthlessly, that no enemy will ever again dare attack us. For this, frontier alterations in east and west are absolutely necessary." Even in September 1918, with hope of victory in the west gone, he was still arguing that Germany had to "maintain [its] eastern position" set by the treaty of Brest-Litovsk, adding prophetically: "Perhaps in the future Germany's whole face will turn rather more to the east."[24]

Stresemann appeared to be a changed man by the mid-1920s, a man seeking a stable peace for future generations. His private memoranda reveal otherwise. In 1923, as chancellor, he argued that once Germany rebuilt its internal strength, it could again form alliances and challenge its enemies.[25] Just before signing the Locarno Treaty—committing Germany to existing borders in the west, but, by design, not in the east—the now–foreign minister wrote to the crown prince. Germany's foreign policy had three objectives: first, the assurance of peace, to allow Germany to regain its strength; second, the protection of twelve million Germans living under foreign yoke; and third, "the rectification of our eastern frontiers" and later the absorption of Austria. And these were the German objectives "for the short-term."[26]

The desire for fundamental territorial changes in the east never left him. To the ambassador in Washington Stresemann wrote that Locarno would not only protect the Rhineland and split the Entente, but would "open new possibilities in the East."[27] To the crown prince he wrote that Germany had to choose between allying with Russia or becoming a "continental spearhead for England," a phrase indicating a future military move east. For Stresemann, the latter course was clearly preferable, for he went on to warn against cozying up to a Moscow that sought only to Bolshevize eastern Germany.[28]

These writings advance no specific plan to recapture territory won at Brest-Litovsk. Yet when they are placed beside his earlier calls for eastern annexations, it is hard not to conclude that this "man of peace," had he commanded the military power of Germany in 1939, would have reignited the heroic *Drang nach Osten* ("drive to the east"). Germany's peaceful behavior in the 1920s reflected not its regime-type, but its inferior power position.[29]

Against this backdrop, Hitler's own obsession with Russia is a straightforward extension of traditional German geopolitical thinking.[30] In his 1925 *Mein Kampf*, Hitler reserved his penultimate chapter for Germany's relation to Russia, the key question in foreign affairs. Germany exists in a world of "giant states" which far surpass it in population, and whose territories are "the chief support of their political power. Never has the relation of the German Reich to other existing world states been as unfavorable. . . . Today we find ourselves in a world of great power states in [the] process of formation, with our own Reich sinking more and more into insignificance." To solve the problem of living space, Germany must first destroy France to provide cover for the core goal: the destruction of Russia and its vassal border states. With the Soviet Union preparing to overwhelm Germany, one political testament should govern Germany's foreign policy, namely

Never suffer the rise of two continental powers in Europe. Regard any attempt to organize a second military power on the German frontiers, even if only in the form of creating a state capable of military strength, as an attack on Germany, and in it see not only the right, but also the duty, to employ all means up to armed force to prevent the rise of such a state, or, if one has already arisen, to smash it again.[31]

Hitler held to this political testament as the guiding force in his life.[32] Just before coming to power, he spoke of his fear of Russia in private conversations with Otto Wagener, his economic adviser. Russian industrialization was inevitable, since Russia could not afford to remain backward amid other industrial powers. Wagener's argument about growing Russian armament "serves only to make us realize that the sooner we can make up our minds to shatter the universal danger of Russian Bolshevism at its center of power, the easier it will be to be got rid of."[33]

THE INITIAL BUILDUP: 1933 TO 1936

Three days after assuming power, Hitler outlined his foreign policy program to the military. On 3 February 1933, he called his top generals together and explained that the most important short-term task was the rebuilding of German military power. Its most likely end: "the conquest of new living space in the east and its ruthless Germanization."[34] Later that month, Hitler promised the army a massive rearmament and conscription, as well as the militarist indoctrination of the nation.[35] Thus, in the first month of his regime, his generals were made perfectly aware of his rearmament plans and their intended purpose. Far from resisting Hitler's program, they embraced it. Colonel Walther von Reichenau, head of the Armed Forces Office, wrote in February that the orientation of the Wehrmacht had "never before" been "so identical with the State."[36] Only after the war would the generals pretend they had rejected Hitler's plans.[37]

The new rearmament program built upon a 1932 plan calling for a 21–division army by 1938. In December 1933, the generals agreed to triple this schedule through conscription. General Ludwig von Beck, often painted as a leader in the resistance, was a key framer of this program.[38] As we shall see, Beck's disagreement with Hitler in 1938–39 was merely tactical: he promoted the idea of smashing the rising Russian threat. Here it is sufficient to note that Beck worked hand-in-hand with Werner von Blomberg, the minister of defense, to develop an army that would, according to a December memorandum, enable Germany to fight a war on several fronts as soon as possible.[39]

A primary army concern was the SA, Hitler's brownshirts, which the generals feared might become the nation's military instrument. In January 1934, Hitler reassured the generals that the Wehrmacht was the Reich's sole armed power.[40] In February, he addressed the military again. According to Field Marshal Maximilian von Weichs's record, he reaffirmed his resolution to build a people's army out of the traditional armed forces; the SA would be confined strictly to internal tasks. Hitler's behavior shows that he understood that the military's allegiance was a necessary condition for war against the system; such a war could not be won with the same ruffians that had helped him to power.[41]

At the February meeting, Hitler expanded on his plans. The economic recovery could last for only eight years. Economic decline could thereafter be remedied only by creating living space: a short, decisive attack on the west and then a move east. The army thus had to be ready "for any defense purposes after five years, and after eight years suitable for attacking." Weichs's record notes that after Hitler's address, "the feeling of contentment reigned amongst the military audience."[42]

With alacrity, the military threw themselves into their tasks. On 23 January 1934, a meeting of the Working Committee of the Reichs Defense Council (a body coordinating various bureaucracies) was chaired by none other than Ludwig Beck. Given the military-political situation, Beck noted, the Council's work permitted no delay. Discussion focused not on building an economy to support better deterrence, but on the financial and social measures required for a war economy. As a counselor for the Reich Economy Ministry stated bluntly, at issue was "whether to pick up where the war economy of 1918 left off or to start from scratch."[43] It is thus not surprising that from 1934 on, Beck ignored warnings that rapid rearmament would hurt the economy if war did not occur.[44] He knew that Germany was preparing for offensive war. The long-term effects of rearmament on a *peace*time economy were of little importance.[45]

Thus we see that despite the generals' later efforts to minimize their responsibility, few had any illusions as to Hitler's long-term plans. A foremost expert on the military during this period, Wilhelm Deist, concludes, "there is no evidence whatever of military . . . opposition to Hitler's rearmament goals," even though the army was being built for offense, not deterrence.[46] And as we will see, the generals' resistance in 1938–39 amounted only to disagreement about how and when the plan for hegemony was to be implemented, not whether it was the right course. From 1933 to 1942, the military worked closely with Hitler for one simple reason: his geopolitical goals matched their own.

In fact, Deist shows that the generals were often one step ahead of Hitler. In early March 1935, Beck argued that increased rearmament was the only way to guarantee German security. Germany needed an army greater than the 21 peacetime and 63 wartime divisions laid down in December 1933. His superior, Commander-in-Chief of the Army General Werner von Fritsch, approved these conclusions and advocated an increase to 30 to 36 divisions.[47] Soon after this, on 16 March 1935, Hitler announced that Germany would build a peacetime army of 36 divisions using general conscription. Hitler thus not only followed the military's numbers, but accepted conscription measures that Beck had been pushing since December

1933. As Deist summarizes, "Hitler's proclamation was therefore the expression of a consensus on military objectives between the German generals and the political leadership."[48]

On the political side, the task from 1933 to 1936 was to get through the transitional period of rearmament without provoking preventive war from either France or Poland.[49] Hitler sought to assuage enemy fears by projecting peaceful intentions; in the case of Poland, he went so far as to sign a nonaggression treaty in January 1934.[50] By 1935–36, however, rearmament was in full swing. The army could now anticipate a shift from defense to offense. A June 1935 meeting of the Working Committee of the Reich Defense Council, chaired by Reichenau, agreed that the key foundations for the restoration of military preparedness and "the direction of the nation in war" had been laid. Pointing to the buildup's purpose, Reichenau argued that securing supply bases and preparing Germany's economic resources "are just as important prerequisites for the defense of the German living space [*Lebensraum*] as are the military preparations proper." Since no one saw Germany's living space as adequate, "the defense of German living space" could only have meant a future offensive war.[51]

The generals did have one small disagreement with Hitler during 1935–36: they worried that too rapid a buildup would reduce the percentage of officers in the army, hurting quality. Yet this did not stop them from discussing in summer 1935 what they termed ways of "Increasing the Army's Offensive Capacity." The key issue was how to achieve the greatest military effect at the lowest possible cost. The solution was found in superior mobility. After impressive exercises in July 1935, Panzer Commander Heinz Guderian's idea for independent tank forces within armored divisions was accepted.[52] Also in July the general staff supported faster rearmament to ensure completion of the overall program by autumn 1939. Beck argued that the German army had to be "fully ready for war" by April 1940.[53] As Michael Geyer summarizes, "now the general staff became the main proponent of accelerated armament. They wanted more than a simple acceleration, they wanted the premature completion of offensive armament."[54]

Soon after, Army Commander-in-Chief Fritsch began to talk of "offensively conducted defense" founded on mobility.[55] In general, the army's military plans grew in direct proportion to its anticipated or already-realized military power. A general staff memorandum in mid-November 1935 noted that given current constraints, the army could only stay on the defensive. In the short term, therefore, "other intentions had to stand aside," including improved offensive capabilities and mobility "as prerequisites for an army which is ultimately capable of fighting a decision-seeking offensive war [*entscheidungssuchender Angriffskrieg*]."[56]

Systemic conditions were changing fast enough, however, to permit a shift to a more aggressive posture. In December, Beck, now army chief of the General Staff (number two behind Fritsch), wrote a report titled "Considerations on Increasing the Offensive Capacity of the Army." It went beyond his point in December 1933 that the army had to be able to wage war on several fronts. Now the army could think "on a larger scale." In particular, the defense of the realm would be successful only "if it were able to be carried out in the form of an attack." Beck's arguments were soon accepted within the army. In February 1936, general staff officers were briefed that "the goal of the future build-up of the army [is the] creation of a mobilized army with the highest possible mobility and offensive potential."[57]

Beck's 1935 report showed his adherence to Guderian's ideas: Beck advocated that every army corps should contain at least one armored brigade, effectively doubling the number of such brigades. Armored divisions should not only support infantry, but have independent use in association with armored divisions. These points led to radical restructuring[58] and would have great significance: it was the superior mobility of German panzer units, coupled with air superiority, that made Germany such a formidable military opponent.

ENTERING THE CRISIS PERIOD: 1936 TO 1937

The phenomenal growth of Germany's army by 1936 emboldened Hitler to begin pressing, albeit with caution, for territorial changes. The series of crises from 1936 to 1939 support the contention that as a great power in multipolarity begins to reach military preponderance, but anticipates a peaking in relative strength, it will take greater risks.[59] In this case, gains through crises could sustain temporary growth but could not alter Germany's inferiority in potential power. Thus Hitler's strategy, under the guise of self-determination, was to position Germany for total war, with Russia's destruction still his core objective. Reabsorbing the Rhineland in March 1936 was his first victory in this delicate game of brinkmanship.

If Hitler's generals and economic advisers needed reminding of the reason for rearmament, Hitler's August 1936 memorandum on the Four-Year Plan provided it. This plan directed both groups to ready Germany for offensive war within four years. Concerned about Germany's trade problems in the face of global protectionism,[60] Hitler used the memorandum to restate his world view. He began by noting that even ideological conflicts were ultimately about the struggle of nations for survival. In recent years, with Marxism controlling one of the world's largest empires, this struggle had intensified. Soviet military resources were "rapidly increasing."

One has only to compare the Red Army as it actually exists today with the assumptions of military men of ten or fifteen years ago to realize the menacing

[128]

extent of this development. Only consider the results of a further development over ten, fifteen, or twenty years and think what conditions will be like then.

All efforts must focus on destroying the Russian threat, he argued. Germany could not wait; "otherwise, time will be lost, and the hour of peril will take us all by surprise." Should German industry not grasp the new challenges, "it will [be] incapable of surviving any longer in this modern age in which a Soviet State is setting up a gigantic plan."[61]

The plan was accepted with enthusiasm by the Wehrmacht, including War Minister Blomberg. As the war-economy staff observed on 1 October 1936, the Four-Year Plan was "an enterprise of great boldness and determination in the economic field," and could be accomplished on time.[62]

Such memoranda were not simply justifications for a war driven by other concerns. Joseph Goebbels's diaries detail private conversations with Hitler about his fear of the rising Russian-Bolshevik menace. Goebbels records a talk with the Führer in November 1936: "He is very content with the situation. Rearmament is proceeding. . . . In 1938 we'll be completely ready. The showdown with Bolshevism is coming. Then we want to be prepared." During 1936–37, Hitler was still uncertain as to the exact timing of the war against Bolshevism, since much would depend on the pace of foreign rearmament. In February 1937, he told Goebbels that he expected a showdown with Russia in five or six years. The month before, Hitler had said that he hoped for six years, but would act earlier if necessary.[63]

On 5 November 1937, his thoughts on timing clarified, Hitler held a war council with War Minister Blomberg, Foreign Minister Konstantin von Neurath, and the Commanders-in-Chief of the Army (Fritsch), Navy (Erich Raeder), and Air Force (Hermann Göring). Hitler used the meeting, called to resolve growing internal struggles over resources, to expound on his overall strategy. Without more land it would be impossible to "arrest the decline of Germanism." Regarding short-term policy, Hitler foresaw three contingencies. The first involved Germany's predicament should France not be weakened by internal conflicts or war:

Contingency I: Period 1943–45
    After this date only a change for the worse, from our point of view, could be expected. . . . Our relative strength would decrease in relation to the rearmament which would by then have been carried out by the rest of the world. . . . It was while the rest of the world was [rebuilding] that we were obliged to take the offensive.

The second and third contingencies outlined how Germany would react if France suffered internal strife or became involved in a war with another state. In both cases, Germany would act before 1943–45. Specifically, Germany would move against Czechoslovakia and Austria to improve its geopolitical position for subsequent attacks on the great powers.[64]

There is strong evidence that military commanders shared Hitler's view that German military strength would soon peak and then decline. From 1934 on, Beck was being warned that the very speed and extent of the buildup would hurt Germany's economy over the long term. Fritsch reported to Blomberg in October 1936 that a powerful army was being formed in the shortest possible time and would be ready as early as 1 October 1939. The same fall, Fritsch was informed by the general army office that the Wehrmacht had to be "used in combat very soon, or the situation must be alleviated by reducing the required level of war-readiness."[65] By 1936 raw material shortfalls were becoming evident; Blomberg, Fritsch, and Beck, rather than reining in rearmament, accelerated it.

One might surmise that the generals simply did not understand economics and how it affected their program.[66] Such a view assumes, however, that they did not realize the real purpose of the buildup. Yet they had known of Hitler's plan since 1933 and saw that Germany had only a short time to achieve superiority. If the rush to superiority destabilized the peacetime economy, it was unimportant; Germany would have initiated major war by then. Thus their concern through 1937–38 was simply that the army would not be ready fast enough. Severe raw material shortages by early 1937, for example, led army commanders to conclude that the October 1939 deadline had to be pushed back to April 1941.[67] This conclusion shaped their "resistance" to Hitler in the summer of 1938. In short, although they accepted Hitler's view that Germany should strike after peaking in power, they came to disagree on exactly *when* that peak would be reached.

The Year of Crisis and "Resistance": January to December 1938

In multipolarity, the militarily dominant but declining power cannot invade only the rising state: since other powers will fear being the next victim, they will generally support the attacked state. The declining state will thus be worried about threats at its rear even as it prepares to eliminate its main adversary. In 1914, Germany was forced to take on both France and Britain in order to destroy Russia. In 1938, Hitler faced a similar calculus. He knew that to crush Russia, France would have to be eliminated, and that despite efforts to neutralize Britain, London would support Paris.[68] In January, later Foreign Minister Joachim von Ribbentrop, at the time ambassador in London, summarized the situation when he wrote to Hitler: "An alteration of the status quo in the East . . . can only be carried out by force. So long as France knows that, England . . . will support her, then France is likely to march in defence of its Eastern allies [which included

Czechoslovakia and Russia] . . . and that will mean an Anglo-German war."[69]

With English, French, and Soviet rearmament increasing, time was working against Hitler earlier than anticipated. He thus accelerated his plans. On 30 May, he issued a directive stating his decision to attack Czechoslovakia in the near future. That he would risk war with Britain and France is shown by the directive's title: "War on Two Fronts with Main Effort in Southeast."[70] Two days before, he told his military of his reasoning: France and Britain were still completing their buildups; Czech fortifications were improvised. Overall then, the "favorable moment must be seized."[71]

A study by the Supreme Headquarters of the Wehrmacht (OKW) in June assumed France's active intervention, while "Great Britain's entry into the war . . . *must be reckoned with*."[72] So by mid-summer, as Hitler confirmed 1 October as the start of the invasion of Czechoslovakia, he was ready to risk major war with two great powers (even if he preferred to pick Czechoslovakia off without interference). Consistent with the theory, Hitler's willingness to take risks increased as he began to see Germany peaking in military superiority.

During the summer a few generals challenged Hitler, most notably Army Chief of the General Staff Beck. On 7 May Beck wrote to his boss, Commander-in-Chief Walther von Brauchitsch, that the armed forces would not be ready for a few more years. In mid-June, Beck submitted another analysis stressing concern not with Hitler's geopolitical objectives but with the risks of acting too soon. He argued that Germany "needs greater living space" and such space "can only be captured through a war." Moreover, the Czech problem should be solved quickly, given increasing Czech strength and "advancing [French-British] rearmament." Nevertheless, Germany was still not ready to face both Britain and France in what would become a European or world war.[73]

In June and July, Beck presented two other memoranda to Brauchitsch reinforcing the need to postpone action. In early August, Brauchitsch told Hitler that a Beck memorandum had been read at a meeting of senior generals, suggesting military agreement that the time was not right for war. Hitler was furious. He argued that the generals were overestimating the risk of British-French intervention, but they were not persuaded. On 15 August, he met again with the generals, arguing that the moment was favorable and that Britain would not respond.[74] This time, he got no objections. Evidence from army exercises now indicated that France could not win easily on the western front. Military opinion thus shifted away from Beck's view.[75] Recognizing his lack of support, Beck resigned.

This confrontation between Hitler and the military has generated much discussion. Little evidence exists, however, showing that the generals opposed Hitler's overall goal of German hegemony. The disagreement was purely tactical: Hitler was risking major war too soon, especially given his argument the previous November that Germany would not peak until 1943. The generals had no moral qualms about initiating war.[76] And once evidence in August showed that Germany could overrun Czechoslovakia quickly, they abandoned Beck, the main advocate of delay. Perhaps most surprising, given Beck's reputation as the "good" general who tried to pull Germany back from war, is his complete agreement with the need to destroy the rising Russian threat (discussed later).

One might argue that by mid-1938 Hitler had removed generals opposing his views, the rest being coerced into silence.[77] The main piece of evidence here is Hitler's dismissal in early 1938 of Blomberg and Fritsch on charges of moral indiscretion (Blomberg for marrying a former prostitute, Fritsch on trumped-up charges of homosexuality). This argument cannot be sustained. Blomberg and Fritsch, as shown, had been active supporters of Hitler's program for major war since 1933. Even their "opposition" in the November 1937 war council—the generally cited reason for their dismissal—was highly muted, focusing only on tactics and timing, as the Hossbach memorandum shows.[78] Indeed, after the meeting Blomberg supported the preparation of the plan for Czechoslovakia's elimination.[79] Moreover, Blomberg was one of Hitler's closest associates, and Hitler was shocked by the revelations of his marriage (which Hitler had actually attended).[80]

As for Fritsch, his ouster was driven not by Hitler, but by Göring and Heinrich Himmler for reasons of personal ambition. That Brauchitsch, Fritsch's successor, was the generals' (not Hitler's) choice shows the still powerful position of the military. Moreover, the generals supported the dismissals, recognizing that such moral indiscretions, even if only rumors, would undermine army morale.[81] Finally, the reconstituted army hierarchy still challenged Hitler on key issues in summer 1938 and fall 1939, and yet Hitler demanded no resignations. Thus even after the dismissals, military leaders still felt free to express concerns without threat of demotion. Not until the disasters of 1941–42 did Hitler fire generals for opposing his plans. As Blomberg himself later wrote, through the prewar years "we soldiers had no cause to complain to Hitler. He fulfilled hopes which were dear to all of us. If the generals no longer choose to remember this, it is obviously a case of deliberate forgetfulness."[82]

To turn briefly to the crisis of September 1938,[83] it is clear that Hitler, despite reservations, was keen to invade Czechoslovakia by 1 October. The crisis was resolved at Munich on 29 September with the agreement to transfer the Sudetenland (about one-quarter of Czech territory) to the Third Reich. The significance of this resolution is that it was unexpected by late September. After Prime Minister Neville Chamberlain's second meeting with Hitler at Godesberg, Hitler rejected Britain's acceptance of his Godesberg demands; now only immediate military occupation of the Sudetenland was acceptable. The British cabinet, however, believed that the form of the Sudeten transfer was critical to Britain's reputation. Hence, the British rejected Hitler's new demands, signaled they would support France militarily, and waited for war.[84] It was Hitler, through Mussolini, who backed down and requested the Munich meeting.

There is no indication that Hitler's Godesberg demands were mere bluff to secure a better deal, and every indication that Hitler preferred an invasion of Czechoslovakia to its peaceful occupation.[85] He feverishly prepared the army for attack through September. Major-General Alfred Jodl noted in his diary on 8 September that "it gradually seems as if the Führer would stick to his decision even though he may no longer be of [the] opinion" that Britain and France would stay neutral.[86] Hence, Hitler clearly decided to back away from war at the eleventh hour. This seems to reflect his awareness that after Chamberlain's diplomatic efforts, the German population, far from viewing war as a justified act of self-preservation, preferred peace.[87]

Hitler's retreat probably also reflected his late acknowledgment that perhaps Germany had not yet peaked. In early September, Finance Minister Lutz Schwerin von Krosigk sent him a report warning that England might indeed enter the war given expected U.S. participation. Germany had a head start militarily and others were racing to catch up, but it was still not at maximum strength. "*Time works in our favor*," Krosigk stressed. "The increase in power which we gain each month . . . through the completion of our military and primarily our economic preparations, is considerably greater than the added strength which the Western powers gain from their own re-armaments." Hence, Germany could only gain by waiting.[88] This argument could explain Hitler's ultimate reluctance to accept too large a risk of total war in 1938. By waiting a bit longer, Germany would be that much more able to take on the system. His subsequent arguments in early 1939 suggest that he had moved back to his 1937 view that Germany needed more time to maximize its military superiority, especially since Britain's participation was a given. The parallel to Berlin's postponing of war in 1912, in order to better prepare for war with France and Britain, should be evident.

TOWARD THE ABYSS: JANUARY TO SEPTEMBER 1939

After Munich, Hitler and his military organized for the next stage, the absorption of the rest of Czechoslovakia and the invasion of Poland. Rump Czechoslovakia was occupied in March 1939. On 5 April, Hitler issued a directive requiring that preparations allow for operations against Poland any time after 1 September 1939.[89] Yet Hitler was not necessarily convinced that the fall was the optimal time for general war. In late March, he told Rome that since Britain would almost certainly assist France, delaying for eighteen months or two years might be advisable to help maximize German land and especially naval strength.[90] Mussolini understood. He told Göring on 16 April that since general war was unavoidable, the issue was merely "when would be the most favorable time for the Axis powers."[91]

By late May 1939, however, Hitler shifted to the belief that major war should be launched as soon as possible. Two factors were apparently critical in changing his mind. The first was growing evidence that Britain and France were strengthening their deterrence stances. After Rump Czechoslovakia was occupied, London extended security guarantees to Poland. In April it announced a formal alliance with France, introduced general conscription, and made an initial proposal to Moscow for security guarantees to eastern Europe and possibly an alliance.[92] As the German chargé d'affaires in Paris telegraphed on 13 April, the new moves meant the end of appeasement and an increased effort to encircle Germany.[93]

The second factor was news that the main enemy, Russia, was growing at an accelerating rate. In early May, Hitler brought in Gustav Hilger, commercial counselor at the Moscow embassy, to assess Stalin's dismissal of M. M. Litvinov as foreign minister in favor of V. M. Molotov. There were few Germans with greater knowledge of Russia; Hilger had been born there and had worked at the embassy since the early 1920s. Hilger informed Hitler of Stalin's increased efforts to build up Russia and of the growing success of Soviet industrialization. Later, Hitler told Ribbentrop that if Hilger was right, "then we have no time to lose in taking measures to prevent any further consolidation of Soviet power."[94]

By late May, Hitler decided to align temporarily with Moscow to allow him first to eliminate the western powers.[95] Hitler's conference with senior commanders on 23 May shows how impending encirclement and others' accelerating rearmament had convinced him to speed up plans to invade Poland, regardless of the consequences. Despite his assurance to the military in April that Poland would be attacked only if it would not spark war with the west,[96] Hitler's view had changed. The conference's purpose, he said, was to determine the military tasks arising from recent developments. Although Germany's situation had improved, it was now being surrounded by a hostile balance of power. It was therefore time to solve the problem of Germany's territorial space: "The alternatives are rise or decline. In fifteen or twenty years' time the solution will be forced upon us," and Germany could not shirk the problem any longer. Poland provided only a weak barrier against Russia and had to be attacked at the earliest opportunity. Yet another bloodless victory could not be expected; there would be war. Isolating Poland was preferred, he argued, but if that proved impossible, Germany would have to attack Britain and France even as it finished off Poland. Moreover, while the government should strive for a short war, it must also "prepare for a war of from ten to fifteen years' duration."[97]

This was sobering news for the generals, to say the least. The task they had been preparing for since 1933 was fast approaching. Yet once again they showed not a trace of moral outrage at the mission assigned.

June and July were spent preparing the diplomatic ground for war. By mid-August Hitler had reason to believe he would beat out British and French suitors for the hand of Stalin. That his ultimate objective remained Russia's destruction, however, is clear. On 11 August, frustrated that London would not stay neutral, Hitler made a prophetic revelation to the League of Nations commissioner in Danzig: "Everything I undertake is directed against the Russians; if the West is too stupid and blind to grasp this, then I shall be compelled to come to an agreement with the Russians, beat the West, and then after their defeat turn against the Soviet Union with all my forces."[98]

On 22 August, Hitler addressed his military commanders to tell them that the time for war had come. The opposing powers were still militarily weak. Hence, "the present moment is more favorable than in two or three year's time." Germany must "take the risk with ruthless determination. . . . We are faced with the harsh alternatives of striking or of certain annihilation sooner or later." Britain and France might still decide against intervention. Still, "Everyone must hold the view that we have been determined to fight the Western Powers right from the start."[99] There was no time to lose in dealing with Russia, Hitler argued. The pact with Stalin was designed only to buy time, and "to Russia will happen just what I have practiced with Poland—we will crush [it]."[100]

The final days of peace were hectic. Any hope of isolating Poland was dashed by two developments on 25 August. The first was London's announcement, reaching Hitler around 5:30 P.M., that guarantees to Poland had been formalized into an English-Polish alliance. Combined with a 23 August letter from Chamberlain warning against the 1914 assumption that Britain would stay neutral,[101] it made clear that attacking Poland meant total war.[102] Then at 6:00 P.M., a letter arrived from Mussolini: Italy could not participate in the war, given the state of Italian preparations.[103] Germany would fight alone.[104]

After discussion with Foreign Minister Ribbentrop, Brauchitsch, and General Wilhelm Keitel, Chief of the OKW,[105] Hitler recalled the order for the attack on Poland, set for 4:30 A.M. the next day. Over the next week of negotiation, London and Paris would not back down; as a result, the Polish government decided to take a hard line.[106] With attack on an isolated Poland now out, Hitler proceeded to his next best option, an invasion that would automatically lead to war with the western powers. On 1 September, German forces crossed into Poland. Two days later, Britain and France responded with a declaration of war. The second world war in a generation had begun.

This was no war of miscalculation. Hitler hoped that Britain and France would swerve so he could maximize his strength for later attacks,[107] but he recognized that if his first preference was impossible, general war was preferable to a return to the status quo. Contrary to deterrence theory's view that Hitler invaded Poland believing the British and French lacked resolve, he acted *despite* expecting their response.[108] Ironically, it was the western powers' shift to a hard line after March that convinced Hitler that Germany's relative power had peaked, and that he could wait no longer.[109] Britain and France entered the war because their reputations were overcommitted. Yet since Hitler knew they would act, his action was a choice for major war—just as Bethmann Hollweg chose major war in 1914 knowing that Russia, for reputational reasons, would have to respond to an attack on Serbia.

FIGHTING WITH MAXIMUM SUPERIORITY: SEPTEMBER 1939 TO MAY 1940

Until May 1940, Germany, France, and Britain fought no major battles. Through the fall of 1939, however, Hitler pressed his military to attack France at the earliest date possible. The generals opposed such an attack in the short term. Their objections were again tactical. Hitler felt Germany had maximized its relative strength and must act; the generals believed Germany needed more time to complete preparations and to develop a viable plan to exploit its superiority in the air and in armored mobile warfare.[110] They understood that without a decisive defeat in the west, Germany would not have the residual strength for the real goal: destroying Russia. Both sides thus followed dynamic differentials logic. Their disagreement remained simply about whether Germany was still rising or had passed its peak.

Hitler told the military on 27 September that time was working against Germany and that an attack must begin as soon as possible. "As in 1914, we *now* have superiority, experience, aggressiveness."[111] On 9 October, a Hitler directive reinforced the fact that German military equipment was even stronger in quantity and quality than in 1914. Yet Germany's buildup had been so complete that little unused capacity remained. Over time the western powers, particularly Britain, would catch up.[112]

Through the fall, the generals, divided over war plans, resisted Hitler's designs. Some sought a Schlieffen-type plan. Others proposed a more radical solution—a bold thrust through the Ardennes forest to split Allied forces in two.[113] On 23 November, Hitler spoke to his supreme commanders of the parallel between the present situation and the pre-1914 dilemma. The elder von Moltke had rightly favored "preventive war" to exploit Russia's slow mobilization; "Today, the second act of this drama is being written." Stalin would buy time by downplaying Communist internationalism. Yet the Russians had far-reaching goals, he noted, and even if internationalism was renounced, they would revert to Pan-Slavism. In the short term, Germany had better soldiers and a superior airforce and artillery. This favorable situation, however, would last only for one or two years, and Germany could only oppose Russia when it was free in the west.[114]

The generals focused not on the question of superiority, but on whether Germany could win quickly enough in the west to have the strength for future battles. They knew that Germany was significantly superior to Britain and France taken individually. In June 1939, Army Chief Brauchitsch argued that Germany could likely beat the combined forces of Britain, France, and Poland.[115] General Georg Thomas, head of the OKW economics branch and one hardly known for overly optimistic assessments, told the Foreign Ministry in May that Germany's modern weaponry gave it significant qualitative superiority. The real issue was whether the advantage over the other powers could be maintained as the war proceeded.[116]

Hitler and his generals' perception of Germany's military superiority supports the theory's causal logic. That this was a reasonable assessment of the balance is shown first by Germany's performance in the first two years of the war. In the ultimate test of objective military power—the field of battle—Germany showed itself to be clearly superior. Indeed, among military analysts it is "conventional wisdom" that Germany had marked military preponderance.[117]

Interestingly, even the most noted critics of this conclusion, such as John Mearsheimer and Matthew Cooper, end up supporting it. Mearsheimer states that German military strength in early 1940 was equal to the *combined* strength of France and Britain, meaning that Germany was significantly superior to these two states taken individually.[118] Cooper accepts that the German army had superior leadership, and that its early successes "demonstrate[d] to the world an unequaled degree of military proficiency on the field of battle." He argues, however, that Germany was not fully prepared in 1939 and should have waited four years to complete its rearmament.[119] This parallels arguments made by many generals through 1938–39. Yet what Cooper misses is the difference between peaking in absolute versus relative power.[120] As Hitler stated at the 27 September meeting, German rearmament was not totally complete, yet "[its] relative strength will not improve in our favor," especially given others' aggregate economic superiority.[121]

The German military also understood that Russia's army was temporarily weak. It was a well-known fact that Stalin had decimated his officer corps in 1937–38.[122] Russian weakness was reinforced by the inability in fall 1939 to defeat Finland. A German General Staff study at the end of 1939 concluded that while the Red Army was huge, it was weak in organization, equipment, troop quality, and leadership. It was thus no match for Germany's modern army.[123]

Yet this did not mean that German generals discounted Russia's *future* potential. After visiting the Soviet Union in 1933, General Thomas came away "deeply impressed" with Russia's size, the vitality of its people, and its agricultural and industrial potential.[124] General Beck, far from resisting Hitler as is so often presumed, actually shared Hitler's obsession with the rising Russian colossus. In the fall of 1939, he circulated an anonymous series of analyses on the Russian threat. In two reports in September and October, he warned of Russia's return to European great power politics.[125] Later in the fall, Beck offered a more extended analysis. Russia's drive to the west was eternal, compelled by its geopolitical situation. It was the biggest empire on earth, but was hemmed in by a ice-bound northern coastline. History shows that such a power "naturally drives toward the sea," a drive that has "only grown stronger" in recent times.

Before the Russo-Japanese war of 1904–5, Russia had been pushing east. After its failure there, Russia shifted back toward Europe again. This move, Beck noted, was a key reason for the outbreak of the First World War. This war had helped push Russia back, and for a while Russia had again turned its attention to Asia. Yet with the English-French-Russian discussions in 1939 and the end of its conflict with Japan, Russia "had again appeared in Europe with its entire weight." The consequences "could be incredibly far-reaching": "The whole Russian problem from 1914 had arisen again."[126]

This pessimistic view was widely shared. In October, the army's Foreign Office liaison officer, Hasso von Etzdorf, wrote that Russia would "build up a front against us which we in the long run cannot be a match for, either in war material . . . or war economy." The result would be a collapse on the military and home fronts.[127] Etzdorf's comments are significant, for along with Lieutenant-Colonel Helmuth Groscurth he formed a group in October to avert an early attack on France, even if it required overthrowing Hitler. On 19 October, Etzdorf and another officer wrote an essay summarizing the group's views. Hitler's policies had only strengthened Bolshevism. Instead of turning west, Germany should join forces against Russia with France and Britain. This document was apparently warmly received by both General Franz Halder, Beck's replacement as chief of the General Staff, and his boss, General Brauchitsch.[128]

In sum, the military after 1918 never relinquished the view that Russia was Germany's primary geopolitical threat. That it was now the home of Bolshevism only made things worse.[129] These facts suggest that even if Hitler had been deposed, the generals would have pursued total war until Russia lay prostrate at their feet. Objections to Hitler in fall 1939 were solely tactical. Those in opposition simply felt that fewer concessions should have been given to Stalin and more done to secure the west's help in destroying Russia. This view was of course naïve given British-French interests in preventing German hegemony. Yet this does not diminish the key point that the military's geopolitical ends and Hitler's were the one and the same.

THE ULTIMATE TASK: PREPARING FOR BARBAROSSA, MAY 1940 TO JUNE 1941

By January/February 1940, the generals finally had a plan that promised quick victory at low cost: General Erich von Manstein's bold strategy for a blitzkrieg through the Ardennes.[130] The May attack succeeded brilliantly. Yet even as Germany was decimating France, Hitler's thoughts were on Russia. He preferred that Britain concede peacefully. On 20 May, upon hearing that his tanks had reached the Channel, he told Jodl that London could secure a separate peace at any time. With British forces trapped at Dunkirk, Hitler excitedly explained to General Gerd von Rundstedt that Britain would now seek peace, so that he could focus on "his real major task, the conflict with Bolshevism."[131] So while Hitler over the next year sometimes argued that defeating Russia would make London comes to terms, Britain for him was clearly an undesirable sideshow.[132]

After victory over France in June, the generals abandoned former doubts and embraced Jodl's view that Hitler was both a political and military genius. Hence, when it became apparent that Hitler was preparing to turn on Russia, the generals fell eagerly to their task. Even before Hitler directed the military to formulate invasion plans, the generals were developing their own plans. Army Chief of Staff Halder knew in late June that Hitler's focus was shifting to the east. On his own initiative, Halder began to prepare for action against Russia.[133] On 3 July, he explained to a colonel in Operations that Germany had to launch "a military blow at Russia which will force her to recognize Germany's dominant role in Europe."[134] In June, the army had already started to transfer units from the west to the east. On 4 July, Halder instructed subordinates to continue this movement, but to ensure that these forces did not reveal a hostile attitude. Although a two-front war was to be avoided if possible, military planning in early July took into account the likelihood of fighting Britain and Russia simultaneously.[135]

Brauchitsch was also enthusiastic about the eastern mission. When he and Halder met with Hitler on 21 July, they gave the Führer their initial report. Probably to Hitler's surprise, given the military's previous cautiousness, they told him that Germany could be ready to invade Russia as early as *the autumn of 1940*. Since Russia had only 50 to 75 good divisions, the generals argued, Germany would require only 80 to 100 to do the job, which would take four to six weeks. The goal was to "crush [the] Russian army" and "to penetrate far enough to enable our air force to smash Russia's strategic areas." The generals specified political aims similar to those achieved by the treaty of Brest-Litovsk: the takeover of White Russia–Finland, a Ukrainian state, and a federation of Baltic states.[136]

To see the significance of this, remember that Hitler had not yet officially directed the generals to plan the invasion; they were formulating these plans on their own, knowing that Russia's destruction was also the Führer's ultimate aim. Moreover, their confidence knew no bounds. Although subsequent analysis would reveal that invasion should be delayed until 1941, at this time Halder and Brauchitsch were pushing for an attack as soon as possible. Once again, far from being unwilling puppets, the generals were one step ahead of Hitler in the planning for hegemony.

A few days after the 21 July conference, word was received that Russia was stronger than previously estimated. Hitler, apparently more pessimistic than his military about an early eastern campaign, requested a separate assessment from his OKW. In late July, a report signed by Keitel and likely written by Jodl (the OKW's two top generals) informed him that owing to time and weather, an attack on Russia in the fall was not practicable.[137] Hitler now accepted the ideal date as spring 1941. But his determination had not waned. On 29 July, Jodl told his four key subordinates that Hitler had decided to destroy the Soviet danger once and for all by a surprise attack in May 1941. The collision with Bolshevism, Jodl noted, was bound to come and therefore "it was better . . . to have this campaign now, when we were at the height of our military power."[138]

Hitler met with the military on 31 July and announced his decision. Russia's elimination must be planned for spring 1941, and *"the sooner Russia is crushed the better."* The objective of the invasion: "the destruction of Russia's vital power [*Lebenskraft*]."[139] From late July until November, the army and Hitler's staff worked on war plans. The Marcks plan of 1 August, initiated by Halder, envisioned two main thrusts: one toward Moscow, and one toward Kiev. The capture of Moscow, consistent with blitzkrieg thinking, was critical since it would destroy Soviet internal coordination. Estimates of Russia's army had increased since July; both sides were now seen as quantitatively equal. Russian inferiority at the command level, however, would cause problems once their extended line was broken. Fighting in isolated groups, the Russian army would "soon succumb to the superiority of the German troops and leadership."[140] Confidence remained high as Army Headquarters spent the fall of 1940 revising the plan. A 5 December meeting of Hitler and the generals affirmed that the Russians were inferior in equipment and tanks and lacked proper leadership.[141]

One belief united Hitler and his generals through the winter of 1940–41: even though the Soviet Union was a huge future threat, Germany could beat it if action was taken soon. In November, Hitler reiterated that Russia "remains the great problem of Europe." The 5 December meeting noted that the battle with Russia would decide the issue of hegemony in Europe and that by the spring German power would be at a temporary peak.[142] On 18 December Hitler directed that Germany must crush Russia in a quick campaign even before concluding the war against England.[143]

Some contend that since Russia was at a low point militarily, and thus had no desire for war, Germany's attack could not have been a preventive one.[144] This argument mistakenly requires the adversary to be an immediate threat to classify the war as preventive. The German problem was always the prospect of Russia's long-term growth from its enormous base of potential power. Hitler and the military believed that although Russia was temporarily weak, and therefore could be beaten, it would be an overwhelming long-term threat. In the fall of 1940, Hitler told General Lieutenant-Colonel Bernhard von Lossberg that the present moment was his best and probably only chance of destroying Russia and the Communist system. The Soviets were getting stronger each day, but they would collapse within six weeks if he acted soon enough.[145] Hitler was not blind to the difficulty of the task. In a meeting on 9 January 1941, he told the military that despite Stalin's purges of his officer corps, the Russians should not be underestimated. Thus the strongest possible attack was required to prevent the Red Army from falling back into the Russian hinterland.

Hitler understood that rising states do not seek war. Stalin, he noted, was a clever leader who would not take an open stand against Germany. In the long term, however, as Russia's power grew, "his demands [would] become bigger and bigger." Russia had therefore to be destroyed while Germany still had the chance. Through victory, Germany would acquire a huge territory containing vast resources; then "nobody will then be able to defeat her anymore."[146]

These arguments aligned with the military's thinking. Halder told his senior officers in mid-December 1940 that Russia would use every opportunity to weaken Germany's position. He later acknowledged that Germany's invasion was a response to a "long but steadily rising political danger."[147] Yet while Halder saw Russia as a future threat, he, like the rest of the military, also believed it could be beaten in the short term. On 3 February, Halder and Brauchitsch took Hitler through the details of the upcoming operations. After the war Halder claimed that in this meeting he had cautioned Hitler against the campaign by noting Soviet strength. Contemporary records show otherwise. Halder did tell Hitler that the Soviets now had 155 divisions, including 30 mechanized divisions. Yet "our own strength [is] about the same [in quantity], [and] far superior in quality," especially in tanks, weapons, and artillery.[148]

At the Nuremberg trials, Brauchitsch also claimed that at this meeting he told Hitler of his misgivings: Russia's geography, large population, and "high armament potential" would make victory difficult.[149] Yet the OKW war diary shows Brauchitsch expressed no such misgivings.[150] If he did indeed entertain them, we can suspect that, like Halder, they were more related to Russia's *long-term* potential. Brauchitsch admitted at Nuremberg that German leaders were concerned "that if a war [against Russia] were to break out . . . it was to be a preventive war."[151]

In the last two months before the 22 June invasion, Stalin, accepting Russia's military inferiority, sought to buy time by projecting his good intentions. On 5 May, the acting military attaché in Moscow notified Berlin that Russia would do everything possible to avoid a war.[152] Yet the problem was still Russia's future intentions. As Halder noted in April, if one could free oneself "from the accepted belief that Russia desires peace and will not attack of its own accord, then one must admit that the Russian organization would very easily permit a quick change-over to the offensive, which could be very troublesome for us."[153]

This understanding of Stalin's calculus was not far off. On 5 May, Stalin held a private conference with his officers. Russia, he said, had to be prepared for a German attack, but the Red Army was not yet strong enough: "it is still suffering from a serious shortage of modern tanks, modern planes, and much else," while the training of soldiers was still far from complete. Russia must try to delay a German attack during 1941. If this worked, "then, almost inevitably, the war with Nazi Germany will be fought in 1942—in much more favorable conditions, since the Red Army will have been better trained, and will have far more up-to-date equipment." As for Soviet future intentions: "Depending on the international situation, the Red Army will either wait for a German attack, or it may have to take the initiative, since the perpetuation of Nazi Germany as the dominant power in Europe is 'not normal.' "[154] These arguments align closely with beliefs in Berlin. Like the Germans, Stalin knew that Russia was temporarily weak but would be much stronger within a year. And while short-term Soviet intentions were peaceful, they might change once rearmament was completed.

On 14 June, Hitler held his last big prewar meeting with the military. Commanders from all services were assembled to take him through invasion plans. After lunch, Hitler reiterated the reasons for war against Russia. According to the Navy High Command's record, he "explained . . . in [an] all-inclusive, convincing explanation, that the eastern campaign was inevitable, and that we therefore must conduct it in a preventive and offensive manner to avoid [the possibility] that the Russians could overrun us at a later time after longer appropriate preparations."[155] General Walter Warlimont, who attended the conference, noted that all commanders present came away in a confident mood.[156] The period when the military might disagree with even the tactical execution of Hitler's plans was past. The greatest and most brutal military undertaking in history would be undertaken without one German military leader showing any sign of dissent.

This analysis has shown the preventive logic behind German thinking. One might still argue that while Hitler and the generals did act according to the theory's logic, their attack on Russia was irrational, insofar as wishful thinking and other psychological pathologies led them to misperceive Russia's true strength. The documents indicate, however, that German leaders did conduct an objective evaluation of the information available. In the twelve months up to June 1941, estimates of Russian strength were continually updated, given new information from spies and reconnaissance. The report in early July 1940 of 50–75 Russian divisions was adjusted to 147 within a month. By February 1941, the estimate was raised to 177, and by June to 216.[157] After December 1940, the generals increasingly worried about Germany's ability to achieve a decisive victory. Yet they agreed that such an attack was still necessary.

Indeed, for Hitler and the generals, evidence of increasing Russian strength simply reinforced the need to act quickly to destroy the rising colossus. In February 1941, Hitler was stunned by news of large increases in the Russian air force, stating that conflict was now inevitable.[158] In April, the German air attaché in Moscow sent word that the Soviets were not as inferior in aircraft quality as previously believed. Hitler responded: "Well, there you see how far these people are already. We must begin immediately." By May/June, Hitler was not necessarily confident about the chance of success. Just a day before the invasion, Himmler told Reinhard Heydrich that the Führer was actually less optimistic than his military advisers.[159]

A postwar Soviet internal history confirms that Russia was weak in the short term but growing quickly. Despite efforts to double aircraft production, it notes, the vast majority of the new planes were obsolete. Even though Russia had a huge number of tanks by June 1941—Berlin estimated 10,000—less than 1,900 were either KVs or T-34s (the modern tanks that later proved superior to German models). Of the thousands of older models, only 27 percent were in working order. Moreover, Russian tank forces often lacked wireless communication or trained officers, while many tank operators had only two hours of driving experience. Compared to German forces with their significant battle experience in Poland and France, the Red Army was clearly inferior in quality. Indeed, not until 1943 did Russian military leaders see their soldiers and officers as being as competent as their German counterparts.[160]

In sum, German leaders went through a fairly rational information search: they sought out information through reconnaissance; and they updated estimates of Russian strength according to the data received.[161] Given what eventually transpired, their expectation of a quick victory might still seem irrational. Yet other capitals at the time also believed Russia was significantly inferior in technology, training, and leadership.[162] Moreover, in the final test of relative military strength—the battlefield—Germany showed itself as superior in 1941. It not only did very well in the first six months of the war, but came very close to winning it. If not for Hitler's error in failing to push on to Moscow in September before winter hit, Germany might well have won the eastern war.

Considering all this, it is not surprising that Hitler and his generals would expect Russia to collapse quickly when invasion began on 22 June. Given Russia's headlong retreat and its need to fight for four years to defeat Hitler, it is hard not to conclude that had the Russians lacked the advantage of geography, they would have suffered as devastating a defeat as the French in 1940.

This chapter has shown that, in addition to Hitler's horrific racial goals, the Führer and his military initiated World War II to complete the task left unfinished in 1918—the elimination of the rising Russian colossus. The urgency with which the German leadership undertook this second more narrowly geopolitical dimension of its project reflects the systemic situation of the post–World War I period. Having failed to stop Russia's growth, but still facing a multipolar system, Germany had only a very short timeframe to build the kind of military superiority needed to take on the system. Thus, the German leadership plunged into the construction of a war economy needed for massive rearmament. With a three-year head start on the western powers and Russia, Germany won the first stage of its risky game: temporary military superiority was reached by 1939–40. Yet precisely because they were knowingly overheating the economy to reach this objective, Hitler and the generals knew that this superiority would have to be used quickly if hegemony was to be won. To wait until after the peak would allow others to catch up as their rearmament programs were completed and as the German peace-time economy fell into crisis.

Driving the whole process, however, was Germany's marked inferiority in potential power versus Russia. As Stalin completed his massive industrialization program, this potential would be translated into overwhelming economic and military strength. Time was therefore of the essence. Destroying Russia would not only end the long-term threat, it would also give Germany the territory ("living space") needed to compete with other growing global powers, primarily the United States.[163] That is, if Russia's potential power made German leaders fear it, *taking over* that power would give Germany the base for future security. As in 1914, Britain and France were undesired obstacles in this strategic plan. France had to be eliminated since it would always support Russia; Britain, in Hitler's view, simply refused to see how its own interests mirrored those of Germany.

The Allies made one critical error in all of this. In the period from 1933 to 1936, downplaying the speed of German rearmament, they allowed themselves to fall behind. In multipolarity, maintaining rough military equality between states is essential to deterrence. Had this requirement been met, even Hitler would likely have held back from war. He would have recognized that costly bilateral wars would have so sapped German strength as to make the state even more vulnerable to powers like Russia. Thus the real Allied mistake was not the failure to take a hard-line stance in 1937–38— appeasement can make sense when one is inferior and needs to buy time for rearmament—but the failure to start rearming immediately four to five years earlier.[164]

Of existing realist theories, hegemonic stability theory is the one most at odds with the evidence. Not only was Germany significantly superior in military power by 1939–40, but Hitler initiated all-out war only once he believed that Germany was declining. Classical realist and neorealist explanations are incomplete: they rightly emphasize Germany's military preponderance, but they fall back on Hitler's ideology and German hypernationalism as primary driving forces for war. By emphasizing the disjuncture between Germany's military superiority and its inferiority in potential power, this chapter provides the necessary and sufficient conditions for German behavior (without denying that unit-level factors exacerbated the intensity and brutality of the conflict). This dynamic, systemic explanation can thus account for the remarkable agreement between Hitler and the traditional military on the requirements of German security.

[6]

Bipolarity, Shifting Power, and the Origins of the Cold War, 1945–1950

The puzzle that animates the following two chapters is a simple one: What explains the changes in the likelihood of major war between the United States and the Soviet Union from 1944 to 1963? This question has two parts. In this chapter I examine the first big jump in the probability of superpower war, namely, the move from wartime alliance to cold war. Given ideological differences, some disagreements between America and Russia were inevitable after 1945 (just as they are today with China). Yet the relationship could have stayed in the realm of a moderate spheres-of-influence détente, rather than escalating into a dangerous cold war. Why did it not? I argue that the United States was most responsible for the shift to cold war, since it was the first to adopt provocative hard-line policies. As early as mid-1945, American concern for the long-term rise of the Soviet state drove U.S. leaders to implement a vigorous and destabilizing containment strategy. The next chapter analyzes the second element of the puzzle: the movement from the sustained tension of normal cold war interaction to the intense crisis periods of the early cold war era. Here I show that crises over Berlin in 1948 and 1961 and over Cuba in 1962 were driven more by fears of relative decline during marked power oscillations than by domestic- or individual-level factors. These fears led leaders on both sides to take steps that put their nations on the slippery slope to nuclear war.

THE COLD WAR DEBATE

Three perspectives on the origins of the cold war have dominated the debate. For traditionalists, the cold war was caused by Soviet aggression, which forced the United States into a containment posture it would have otherwise avoided. The Kremlin sought to expand its sphere by promoting Communist revolution abroad and through direct occupation of neighboring lands. Consistent with deterrence theory and classical realism, proponents of this view argue that had it not been for hostile Soviet intentions—rooted in ideology, the need to justify internal repression, or a paranoid view of Soviet security needs—both superpowers could have cooperated.[1]

Revisionists turn the traditionalist view on its head, laying most of the blame on the United States. Washington initiated hostile actions from 1945 to 1947 as Soviet leaders sought to rebuild after a devastating war. Reasons for U.S. aggression vary across scholars. For neomarxist revisionists, American leaders strove to promote global capitalism in order to avoid depression. Others view U.S. behavior as more complex, reflecting a mix of factors which include economic motives, but also a paranoid view of security and distorted beliefs about the likelihood of Communist revolution in western Europe.[2]

The third argument, postrevisionism, offers a moderate and highly eclectic position incorporating domestic, individual, and systemic factors. Above all, however, the origins of the cold war are found in the tragedy of the security dilemma. Both superpowers sought security, yet each saw the other as aggressive. Each side's hard-line actions simply reinforced the perception that its rival desired its destruction. As a result, a spiral of hostility was created which persisted into the 1980s.[3]

This chapter breaks ranks with all three perspectives. Contrary to traditionalists, I argue that the cold war was sparked by actions taken by Washington, beginning in 1945, to contain Russia. I thus reject a core premise of traditionalism: that U.S. leaders were initially naïve, and only switched to containment once Moscow's hostile intentions could no longer be ignored. Traditionalists contend that containment began only in 1947 with the Truman Doctrine, within signs of a shift appearing in 1946. Containment as a policy certainly became more intense after 1947, but the core elements were in place by July–August 1945. Yet my argument rejects the revisionist view that American efforts to uphold capitalism, or paranoia about global communism, drove U.S. policy. Containment in 1945 reflected rational geopolitics: U.S. leaders recognized that if Russia was allowed to grow, it could eventually overwhelm the American sphere. Prudent security calculations, not elite paranoia and greed, were determinative.

This chapter's argument is closest to postrevisionism, in that U.S. security concerns led to hard-line policies which provoked Soviet suspicions, thus creating an intensifying spiral of tension. Three differences are evident, however. First, I argue that in mid-1945 Harry Truman moved to containment not because he perceived Stalin as innately hostile—in fact, he liked and even respected Stalin at this time. Rather, Truman recognized that if America did *not* act, Russia would grow significantly, and Soviet leaders—namely, those *replacing* Stalin—might not be so moderate down the road. The postrevisionist argument, like the spiral model, posits that the actor initiating the spiral believes the other is presently aggressive, even if it is not.[4] My argument operates from an even more tragic foundation. The actor which begins the spiral (in this case, the United States) is fairly sure that, currently, the other's intentions are relatively restrained. But in an environment of dynamic change, it remains uncertain about the other's future intentions should the latter reach a position of preponderance. Hence, the actor reluctantly initiates a hard-line policy—not because the other is seen as necessarily hostile but to avoid decline.[5] This argument does not mean that Truman had no concerns with Soviet behavior in eastern Europe/the Near East or with the brutal nature of Stalin's regime. He did. Yet these concerns, the evidence indicates, were less salient than fears of Soviet growth and future intentions.

Second, I demonstrate that U.S. decision-makers anticipated spiral effects, but chose a hard-line posture anyway. In postrevisionism, as in the spiral model, each side acts believing that the other will see its moves as defensive, not aggressive.[6] I show, however, that Truman and his advisers were quite aware that their policies would heighten Soviet suspicions and thus foster a cold war standoff, with all the attendant risks of inadvertent war. Yet they also felt such risks must be accepted in order to avoid a greater evil, namely, the unabated growth of Soviet power.

Third, and finally, by breaking power into three forms, the chapter provides a more complete systemic explanation for the cold war than other theories have offered. It was Truman's fear of Soviet growth in economic and potential power that led him to adopt hard-line policies. He recognized that should Moscow successfully consolidate its new larger realm, it could translate these gains into superior military power. Truman thus moved to restrict Russia's development through military, economic, and political means. Postrevisionists, by downplaying exogenous trends in economic and potential power, end up treating power as solely a function of state behavior. That is, the spiral gets going only when one state stupidly starts the ball rolling by increasing military power. I argue that leaders, knowing that decline may occur in the absence of strong action, may be forced into escalatory policies to avert a loss in power.

For political scientists schooled in established cold war debates, my perspective may seem too extreme to be fully plausible. Yet it aligns nicely with the most comprehensive documentary analysis of the Truman era, namely, the seminal work of the historian Melvyn Leffler.[7] Leffler shows that U.S. leaders sought to thwart Soviet growth to ensure America's preponderance and therefore long-term security. Thus beginning in 1945, Washington undertook forceful actions to avoid decline. My argument is strongly influenced by Leffler's, but it goes a few steps further. I seek to show that the U.S. containment strategy in mid-1945 was even more comprehensive than Leffler observes, despite Truman's relatively moderate view of Stalin.

Before turning to the evidence, I should discuss one evident aspect of the cold war period: major war never occurred. Neorealists use this outcome to argue that bipolar systems are more stable. This conclusion cannot be sustained.[8] The post-1945 period did experience strong jumps in the probability of major war, especially during the Cuban missile crisis. The fact that we often got close to major war despite the prudence inspired by nuclear weapons underscores the inherent instability of the bipolar cold war era. Moreover, as I discuss in chapter 8, three examples of bipolarity prior to 1945—Sparta versus Athens, Carthage versus Rome, and France versus the Hapsburgs—each gave rise to devastating major wars, and for the reasons anticipated by the theory. In each case a declining state with at best slight military superiority attacked the rising superpower before it became overwhelming. Moreover, the declining state was inferior in potential power and thus had reason to believe that decline would be both deep and inevitable. These cases provide strong additional support for my argument regarding the dynamics of bipolar systems.

The strong U.S. position after 1944 helps explain why Washington did not simply copy the pattern of previous bipolar conflicts and initiate war before it lost its nuclear monopoly. As I later discuss, U.S. leaders and officials actively considered preventive war in the late 1940s. Yet because America possessed the superiority in potential and economic power needed for long-term military preponderance, it was not necessary to turn immediately to this ultimate sanction. All-out preventive war, given its costs and risks, is rational only when there are no other means of reversing decline. Since Washington still had these other options, the better first steps were the ones taken: arms racing and containment to preserve superiority and thus security.

THE ORIGINS OF PREVENTIVE CONTAINMENT, 1945

Standard accounts of the cold war usually designate 1947 as the year when the American containment strategy was set in place. Yet the core elements of containment were actually laid down by August 1945. The full extent of this policy can be seen in the eight interlocking actions taken in 1945 to restrict Soviet growth in military, economic, and potential power:

1. The surrounding of Russia with air and naval bases, in order to project offensive power against the Soviet heartland.
2. The rebuilding of western Europe, which required the revitalization of western Germany, a nation that had just killed over twenty-five million Russians.

[149]

3. The ending of aid to Russia, even as it was extended to China. This included resisting Soviet claims to badly needed reparations from Germany.
4. The demonstration of the atomic bomb, which—in addition to ending the Pacific war quickly—was designed to restrict Soviet penetration of Manchuria and to convince Moscow to accept U.S. terms for the postwar peace.
5. The rushing of U.S. and Allied troops into Korea, China, and Manchuria to prevent Communist consolidation of areas already conceded to Moscow by prior agreements.
6. The exclusion of any role for the Soviet Union in the occupation and revitalization of Japan.
7. The denial of atomic secrets and materials to Russia.
8. The restricting of Soviet naval access to the Mediterranean and North Sea, despite recognition of Soviet legal rights.

In implementing this policy, Truman did not believe he was abandoning all chances for cooperation with the Soviet Union. But any cooperative arrangement would be on U.S. terms. In short, the United States would follow a two-track policy. Washington would do everything necessary to maintain a preponderant position. Simultaneously, it would try to work out a great power modus vivendi. If the Soviets went along, so much the better. If they did not, Truman preferred a cold war—with all its attending risks of inadvertent war—to a situation where the United States cooperated, but at the expense of long-term power. Allowing the Soviets to grow to a dominant position would threaten U.S. security, should their intentions prove more aggressive down the road.[9]

Truman and Secretary of State James F. Byrnes acted despite believing Stalin's intentions were relatively moderate. They also acted knowing that their policies could spark a cold war rivalry that would increase the likelihood of inadvertent war. The evidence thus supports the argument that in the face of decline, leaders will take their states into risky rivalries when hard-line postures offer a better means to security than either soft-line cooperation or preventive war.

U.S. Strategic Thinking up to June 1945

U.S. geopolitical concerns were already shifting before the end of the war. In spring 1944, Admiral William Leahy, Roosevelt's chief of staff, wrote to Secretary of State Cordell Hull that the outstanding fact about the new global situation was "the recent phenomenal development of the heretofore latent Russian military and economic strength—a development which seems certain to prove epochal in its bearing on future politico-military international relationship, and which has yet to reach the full scope attainable with Russian resources."[10] In December 1944, George Kennan, Averell Harriman's next-in-command at the Moscow embassy, expanded on this view. In a report to Harriman that foreshadowed his February 1946 Long Telegram,[11] he warned that by occupying eastern Europe, Russia had shifted the overall balance of population. Given Russia's industrial strength, this new larger realm "constitute[d] a single force far greater than any other that will be left on the European continent . . . and it would be folly to underestimate [its] potential—for good or for evil."[12]

Harriman thought enough of Kennan's analysis to forward it to the State Department, and it undoubtedly shaped his campaign in early 1945 to expose the growing Russian threat.[13] Yet Harriman was hardly a lone voice. On 2 April 1945, a top secret report from the Office of Strategic Services (the forerunner of the CIA) was sent to Roosevelt and subsequently to Truman. It summarized the dilemma:

> Russia will emerge from the present conflict as by far the strongest nation in Europe and Asia—strong enough, if the United States should stand aside, to dominate Europe and at the same time to establish her hegemony over Asia. Russia's natural resources and manpower are so great that within relatively few years she can be much more powerful than either Germany or Japan has ever been. In the easily foreseeable future Russia may well outrank even the United States in military potential.[14]

Two weeks later, the Joint Chiefs distributed a paper titled "Revision of Policy with Relation to Russia." Lend-lease to Russia, it argued, had ironically succeeded too well, leading to a "new and serious situation"—a much stronger Russia. The report not only recommended ending military aid, but also stressed the importance of maintaining a firm stand against Moscow.[15] An OSS report to Truman on 5 May stressed that if a hands-off policy were adopted, the Soviets might unite the resources of Europe and Asia and then within a generation outbuild the United States in military production.[16] Yet another OSS report on 11 May noted that despite Russia's wartime devastation

> her recovery and further [industrial] development promise to be rapid, and the sharp upward trend of her population is another favorable long-term factor of the greatest consequence. . . . Thus, Russia has every mark and characteristic of a rising power, destined to stand with America as one of the two strongest states in the world.[17]

These concerns were well understood. Acting Secretary of State Joseph C. Grew wrote to Harriman in May of his fears of steadily increasing Soviet power. A June paper by Secretary of War Henry L. Stimson underscored that Russia's control of a sphere of 200 million people would give it the capability to project influence into China and Japan. Army Chief of Staff

George C. Marshall told Stimson that the paper captured the U.S. dilemma, namely, that by helping Russia in the war, "we have made [it] . . . the unquestionably dominant power in Europe," a view reiterated by Byrnes in July, not long after he became secretary of state.[18] The potential power of technology was also worrisome. In a May cabinet meeting, Truman emphasized that America must not only keep up with the Russians in scientific research, but also stay "ten years ahead of them."[19]

Given these fears, a policy to hold onto U.S. preponderance naturally followed. A 2 April memorandum from the War Department to the Joint Chiefs of Staff bluntly argued that the United States could not wait until Soviet intentions were revealed before taking preparatory actions in anticipation of another world war. Washington should therefore build a "West-European-American power system as a counterweight to Russia."[20] Efforts toward a modus vivendi would not end. But the two-track strategy begun under Roosevelt would be maintained.[21] Marshall on 31 May told a meeting of the Interim Committee, the committee established to study the policy implications of the atomic bomb, that since Russia was driven primarily by security, some cooperation on atomic energy might be acceptable. Yet he still favored forming an alliance to force Russia to conform to U.S. wishes. Byrnes, who opposed atomic sharing, put the two-track approach in a form more acceptable to the group: he "expressed the view, *which was generally agreed to by all present*, that the most desirable program would be to push ahead as fast as possible in production and research to make certain that we stay ahead and at the same time make every effort to better our political relations with Russia."[22]

The Quest for Bases

The first pillar of the eight-pronged containment strategy was bases to project power against Eurasia. Already by December 1942, Roosevelt was asking the Joint Chiefs to consider postwar air base requirements.[23] A March 1943 report of the Joint Strategic Survey Committee noted that since international organizations might not keep the postwar peace, overseas bases were essential to U.S. security, "and their acquisition . . . must be considered as among our primary war aims."[24] Although Roosevelt hoped the bases would help implement his Four Policemen concept, it seems clear he hedged his bets to prepare for possible containment. On 22 August 1943, a Joint JCS/OSS committee issued a memorandum titled "Strategy and Policy: Can America and Russia Cooperate?" The United States and Britain, it argued, must immediately concentrate forces on the continent to make a policy of hostility unattractive to Moscow. This stance was necessary even though "the major Soviet war aim is the security of the Soviet Union."[25]

In November, the president approved JCS 570, which emphasized the need, in an era of strategic bombing, to keep any future enemy as far from U.S. shores as possible. To this end, the document envisioned bases in the western Pacific, west Africa, Iceland, Japan, and the east Asian mainland, including Korea and northern China.[26] In mid-January 1944, Roosevelt approved the idea of a system of U.S. air bases, and on 5 February he wrote to Hull to emphasize that the State, War, and Navy departments and the Joint Chiefs should study the issue of bases for naval and ground forces as well.[27]

By March 1945, Roosevelt had to reconcile his plan for island bases in the western Pacific with the principles of self-determination to be enshrined in the UN charter. The solution was to define "trusteeships" so as to provide a facade for U.S. control. As Stimson noted, the president knew he was constrained by his own declared principles. Yet "he is just as keen as anybody else to take the full power of arming [the islands] and using them to protect the peace and ourselves during any war that may come, and for that reason his people [at the first UN conference] will by trying to form a definition of trusteeships or mandates which will permit that to be done."[28]

Through spring and summer 1945, the military updated its list of required bases.[29] In late August, the value of such bases in an atomic era in which Russia would be the primary adversary was made clear. A Joint War Plans Committee paper argued that given the emergence of long-range aircraft and missiles, devastating attacks could now be launched from great distances. The enemy must therefore be destroyed "at the source," and the best means was "overwhelming force combined with surprise." In short, "in the event of a breakdown in relations between the U.S. and U.S.S.R. . . . U.S. dominated bases on the European and Asiatic continents will be required for full projection of our offensive power."[30]

The Rebuilding of Western Europe and the Rehabilitation of Germany

As the war entered its last year, there were many, led most prominently by Treasury Secretary Henry Morgenthau, who sought the destruction of Germany as a nation-state. Given the devastation Germany had caused twice in the century, in 1944 Roosevelt himself supported this position. It is thus significant that by spring 1945, majority opinion had swung to the opposite view, namely, that Germany's rehabilitation was critical to U.S. long-term security. The reason for the shift was simple: western Europe was devastated, and without Germany's integration into its economy, the region might fall prey to Communist revolutions. Such revolutions, even if Moscow did not actively promote them, would nonetheless increase the potential power of the Communist sphere.

By September 1944, Roosevelt, under Morgenthau's urging, had accepted the division of Germany into harmless independent provinces. Morgenthau's plan, in a watered-down form, was embedded in the September draft of JCS 1067. This document gave control of occupied Germany to the Allied military, and required the Allies to take no steps toward Germany's economic rehabilitation.[31] Through the winter of 1945, the State Department resisted this plan, arguing it would create economic chaos in Germany and thus in western Europe. On 10 March, Secretary of State Edward R. Stettinius convinced Roosevelt to rescind the order, but this was soon reversed. With Truman's approval in early May, JCS 1067 was apparently established as American policy in occupied Germany.[32]

Morgenthau's victory was more apparent than real, however. As U.S. forces marched deeper into Germany in March, the nation's total devastation became increasingly evident. Concerns that Europe might fall to Communist revolution now had more salience. On 14 March, a White House counsel informed Roosevelt of the dire food shortage in northwestern Europe.[33] Three days later, Stimson noted that the situation in Germany was approaching a crisis, leading him to write three memoranda to Roosevelt challenging the "economic fallacies" in Morgenthau's plan.[34] These views were reinforced by Assistant Secretary of War John J. McCloy upon his return from Germany. McCloy informed Truman on 26 April that the "complete economic, social, and political collapse going on in Central Europe" was almost "unparalleled in history."[35] On 16 May, Stimson told Truman that all members of the War Council agreed that famine in Europe was very probable. "This is likely to be followed by political revolution and Communistic infiltration. Our defense against this situation are the western [European] governments. . . . It is vital to keep these countries from being driven to revolution or Communism by famine."[36] Truman acted quickly. On 22 May, he sent a letter to the various agencies stressing that future peace required the restoration of western European economies.[37]

Germany was the key. In a letter to Stimson on 8 June, Acting Secretary of State Grew agreed that drastic steps had to be taken to supply German coal to what were already being called "our Western European Allies."[38] On 24 June, Truman told Churchill that military authorities in Germany had to exert every effort to increase German coal production for export to western Europe. Otherwise, "we will have turmoil and unrest in the very areas of Western Europe on which the whole stability of the continent depends."[39]

The need to resuscitate Germany for Europe's sake had much to do with the strong U.S. stand at Potsdam over reparations, as I discuss later. By minimizing reparations to Russia from Germany's western zone, Truman sought to strengthen western Europe at the Soviets' expense. As for U.S. policy in occupied Germany, Military Governor Lucius Clay was allowed to ignore the harsh dictates of JCS 1067. Clay understood that without German coal, revolution would engulf the western sphere.[40] Also critical was the Ruhr valley's integration, notwithstanding French objections, back into the west German zone. Both state department and JCS briefing papers for

Truman emphasized the Ruhr's importance to German recovery and thus to western European stability.[41]

Thus we see that by the start of Potsdam, Truman favored German revitalization. In a meeting on 3 July, Stimson argued that Germany should be rehabilitated and any desire for vengeance discarded. Truman said that "that was just the way he thought it should be exactly."[42] Considering the twenty-seven million lives they had just lost to Germany, Soviet leaders could not have viewed this development with equanimity.[43]

Economic Containment: Denying Lend-Lease and Reparations to Russia

The containment policy that emerged after February 1945 had an important economic dimension. Harriman made policy-makers aware of Russia's need for capital to rebuild a ravaged country. In January 1945, the Soviets had asked for a low-interest loan of six billion dollars, and at Yalta they had made twenty billion dollars the figure for discussions on reparations from Germany. Harriman's refrain through April was that loans should be used as leverage to exact concessions, while lend-lease should be limited only to material that would help the Soviets fight Japan.[44]

His arguments had an impact. On 9 May, Secretary of State Edward R. Stettinius wrote Grew that programs to assist "western Allies" should have priority over assistance to Russia, and that America should immediately curtail lend-lease shipments to Russia. U.S. policy on this "and similar matters" (presumably meaning reparation issues) should be one of "firm[ness] while avoiding any implication of a threat." Two days later, Stimson told Truman of the need for a more forceful policy regarding Russia and lend-lease.[45] Grew also spoke with Truman that day, arguing that lend-lease supplies designated for Russia not related to war against Japan should be cut off immediately and that such goods should be diverted to western Europe.[46] Truman approved this policy on 11 May. Bureaucratic overzealousness, however, led to the cancellation of *all* lend-lease to Russia. Although the order was quickly rescinded to permit aid for the Asian front, for Stalin this was a sign of things to come.[47]

Moscow soon became aware of the rediversion of lend-lease to western Europe and protested. Through June and July, Harriman, upon instruction, offered a number of excuses.[48] On 18 August, the contradiction of giving lend-lease to states such as France, which had played no role in defeating the Nazis, and denying it to Russia, became too great. Truman approved a directive ending all lend-lease aid (except for the secret aid that would be sent to China, as we will see). The actual cutoff of Russia had occurred on 17 August, even though lend-lease continued to others until 2 September. When the assistant chief of the Division of Lend-Lease inquired about this discrepancy, he was informed that the decision was deliberate and was "part of a general squeeze now being put on the U.S.S.R."[49]

As for reparations, Truman's get-tough strategy took the form of appointing Edwin Pauley to head the U.S. reparations negotiating team. In early July, Pauley, under direction from Byrnes and Truman, took a new tougher stand in the ongoing talks with Soviet Foreign Minister Molotov. From now on, Germany would have to pay for imports out of exports before any reparations would be allowed. This would ensure that western Germany could feed itself and revive its industry before having to pay heavy reparations. Even more significantly, Pauley told Molotov that no fixed sum of reparations from the western zone would go to Russia. The Yalta figure of twenty billion, of which ten billion was to come from western Germany, was discarded, despite Russian protests. In its place, Russia was offered only a certain *percent* of what the western zone could afford to pay, after paying for imports.[50] As the Soviets understood, this meant Russia would receive few if any goods from the western zone, since it could always be claimed that there was little surplus above and beyond German imports.

At Potsdam, Truman stuck to his guns, fortified by the recently successful test of the atomic bomb. After much discussion, the Russians were forced to concede to Pauley's position. Despite Molotov's willingness to reduce the ten billion dollar figure down to two billion—but as a guaranteed amount—the final agreement specified only a figure of 10–15 percent of western Germany's surplus industrial production. The agreement ensured there would be little coordination between western and eastern zones. The Soviets could take what they wanted from eastern Germany—a policy that of course would only hurt their sphere's overall strength. But they would receive little from the west. Since the west held most of Germany's industrial strength, this was a major blow to Soviet leaders' efforts to rebuild their industrial infrastructure.[51]

As Carolyn Woods Eisenberg notes, the American stand on reparations constituted a clear breach of the spirit of Yalta.[52] The twenty billion figure had been a symbolic recognition of the sacrifice made by Russia in defeating Nazi Germany. Now, just three months after Hitler's defeat, Washington was helping to build up the western part of Germany as well as America's "Western Allies." The huge influx of funds for western Europe would await the Marshall Plan of 1947. But it was already clear to Moscow by late summer 1945 that U.S. leaders would work actively to constrain Soviet economic development.

The Atomic Bomb and Containment through Preponderance

To control Moscow, it was soon recognized that America held what Secretary of War Stimson called the master card: the atomic bomb. Much has been written on whether the United States practiced atomic diplomacy in

1945, thus helping make a cold war inevitable. I argue that Truman and Byrnes did indeed see the bomb as an additional means to restrict Soviet growth, even if they still hoped, at least initially, for a great power modus vivendi.

Revisionists and traditionalists have been strongly divided on why America dropped the atomic bomb. Revisionists argue that Washington wanted to send a signal to Russia,[53] while traditionalists maintain that the goal was to end the war with Japan.[54] There is no need to choose between these perspectives. Truman and Byrnes saw the bomb as a best means to the simultaneous achievement of both ends. Overall, the bomb would help Washington shape the postwar peace on its terms by demonstrating U.S. military superiority and the resolve to use it. In particular, it would limit Soviet penetration into key areas of the Far East such as Manchuria and Korea—areas that had already been conceded to Moscow by prior agreement in order to draw Russia into the Pacific war. The bomb would also end the war quickly, saving lives, while minimizing any relative loss to Russia caused by continued U.S.-Japanese fighting.

In early May, Truman approved the formation of the Interim Committee. In a committee meeting on 10 May, the group "very confidentially" discussed the bomb's connection to the Russian question.[55] Stimson's view was that the bomb's diplomatic potential should be exploited to the fullest. He told Assistant Secretary of War McCloy on 14 May that it was time to "let our actions speak for words." America had to "regain the lead and perhaps do it in a pretty rough and realist way." Toward this end, the atomic bomb was a "royal straight flush, and we mustn't be a fool about the way we play it."[56]

On 15 May, in a meeting with Harriman and Secretary of the Navy James Forrestal Stimson noted that "it may be necessary to have it out with Russia on her relations to Manchuria . . . and various other parts of North China. . . . Over any such tangled wave of problems the S-1 secret [the A-bomb] would be dominant." The Big-Three meeting should be postponed, he felt, until after the bomb was tested, since it "seems a terrible thing to gamble with such big stakes in diplomacy without having your master card in your hand."[57] In late May, Truman agreed to delay the Potsdam meeting until after 15 July (the A-bomb test was 16 July).[58]

Until October, the most forceful advocate of using the bomb for diplomatic leverage was James Byrnes, Truman's representative on the Interim Committee, and Secretary of State after 2 July. In late May, Byrnes bluntly told Leo Szilard, a scientist on the Manhattan project, that "the demonstration of the bomb might impress Russia with America's military might," perhaps making it more manageable in Europe.[59] By late July, Byrnes's belief in the bomb's diplomatic efficacy would only be strengthened by word of its true power, as we will see.

In using the bomb to deal with Russia, the goal was not to deny Moscow its gains in eastern Europe. Truman, like Roosevelt, understood that he could not alter the division of Europe. Truman's willingness to write off eastern Europe is shown by the Hopkins mission to Moscow in late May. In late April, Truman had scolded Molotov, demanding that Moscow live up to the Yalta agreements. Yet, as with Roosevelt, Truman's main concern was that Stalin provide the *facade* of democracy in eastern Europe to satisfy U.S. public opinion. Harry Hopkins's objective was to bring back this figleaf for Poland. Truman instructed Hopkins that he wanted "fair understanding" with Stalin, and that Hopkins should make Stalin aware that what transpired in eastern Europe "made no difference to U.S. interests" except in terms of the overall peace. Poland should go through the motions of holding elections. But this was for U.S. domestic consumption: Stalin, Truman told Hopkins, should make some gesture "whether he means it or not to keep it before our public that he intends to keep his word."[60]

The immediate U.S. objective in summer 1945 was not rollback in Europe, but containment in east Asia. In late May, Grew told Harriman that once Russia was in the Pacific war, Mongolia, Manchuria, and Korea would slip into its orbit.[61] Earlier that month, the OSS gave Truman a report on the expected postwar situation. Eastern Europe was already lost. Things could be done in Asia, but the United States had to act quickly, since once Japan was defeated Russia's position in Asia would be greatly strengthened. If Washington failed to act, Russia might organize China as its ally.[62]

Until late July, however, Truman faced a problem: the atomic bomb might be a dud. Truman had been warned by the military in April that should the war stay conventional, Russia had to be brought in; otherwise, it would drag on to the Russians' benefit.[63] Meeting with Truman on 18 June, the Joint Chiefs confirmed that invading Japan would be costly. Russian entry, however, would likely lead to Japan's capitulation. Truman replied that, given this information, he would use the Potsdam conference to secure from Russia all possible assistance in the war.[64] Stalin's assurance that Russia would enter the war on 15 August was obtained on 17 July, the first day of the conference, much to Truman's satisfaction.[65]

What is interesting, however, is the change in U.S. policy after the bomb's true destructive power was revealed. When Truman obtained Russian agreement to enter the war, only a very initial report on the atomic test had been received. He therefore was focused primarily on the goal of ending the war quickly. Yet Truman's thinking shifted dramatically on 21 July, when General Leslie Groves's report on the test was formally presented. This report described in great detail how truly destructive the bomb was, and how its power had far exceeded even the most optimistic expectations of the scientists.[66]

When Stimson read the report to Truman, the president "was tremendously pepped up by it. . . . He said it gave him an entirely new feeling of confidence."[67] It showed. Churchill remarked the next day, after Stimson informed him of the report's contents, that he now understood why Truman the day before was a "changed man." He told the Russians "just where they got on and off and generally bossed the whole meeting."[68]

A critical change in the situation had occurred: the United States no longer needed Russia to bring about Japan's surrender. The bomb provided the magic formula both to end the war *and* to prevent any further consolidation of the Soviet sphere. Even when information on the atomic test was still fragmentary, Truman had told Pauley that the bomb "would keep the Russians straight."[69] On 20 July, with evidence arriving regarding the bomb's true power, Byrnes revealed to Walter Brown, his personal assistant, that he was now "determined to out-maneuver Stalin on China." Previously Byrnes had been pushing T. V. Soong, Chiang Kai-Shek's foreign minister, to negotiate a deal with Stalin over Manchuria to ensure Russia's early entry into the war. Now he sought to delay this agreement for as long as possible. From Brown's diary: Byrnes "hopes Soong will stand firm and then Russians will not go in [the] war. Then he feels Japan will surrender before Russia goes to war and this will save China."[70] Byrnes's faith in the bomb's coercive power seemed to know no bounds. On 28 July, he remarked that the success of the atomic test now gave him the confidence that the Soviets would agree to U.S. terms on the postwar peace. The next day, Byrnes argued that the bomb "had given us great power, and that in the last analysis, it would control."[71]

By late July, then, Washington was in a position to revise by force an agreement which had been in place for months, namely, that the Soviets would occupy Manchuria until Japan was defeated and its troops repatriated. At a 10 August cabinet meeting, Truman accepted a deal that would allow the Japanese to retain their emperor. Someone asked whether Washington should wait to hear back from the Soviets before implementing this compromise. Truman "interjected most fiercely" that the United States must proceed without Moscow. Stimson added that the Russians favored delay so they could grab as much of Manchuria as possible. Truman agreed. It "was to our interest," he argued, "that the Russians not push too far into Manchuria."[72]

The Beginning of Active Containment: China, August 1945

The bomb was not the only means to restrict Soviet consolidation in areas Washington had supposedly already conceded to the Soviet sphere. In August to September 1945, U.S. troops went into China to help Chiang Kai-Shek's Kuomingtang forces retake northern China and Manchuria.[73] The strategy was threefold. First, U.S. marines would help to patrol southern cities so that KMT troops could be redeployed north to fight Mao's Chinese Communist Party forces. Second, lend-lease would be secretly extended to help roll back the CCP, even as it was canceled for all other allies, including Russia. Finally, Washington would press Stalin to withdraw from Manchuria and hand over control only to the KMT.

On 10 August, the Joint Chiefs wrote to Commanding General of the China Forces Albert Wedemeyer that U.S. forces were preparing to secure key ports and communication points in China "for the purpose of assisting [the KMT]." Surrenders of Japanese forces would be to the KMT only, despite the CCP's equally important role in fighting Japan. Wedemeyer was also told to assist in the rapid transport of KMT forces to northern China where the CCP was strong.[74] There was no misunderstanding of Washington's intent. On 19 August, Wedemeyer replied that he would do everything in his power "to preclude [the] loss of advantages we now enjoy in Far East and to insure that favorable conditions are created for accomplishments of ultimate U.S. political and economic objectives." He warned, however, that the U.S. objective might be hard to hide: that while ostensibly he was facilitating Japanese surrender, "actually in effect . . . we are making an important contribution to preclude successful operations by Communist forces."[75]

Much more was to come. On 3 September, Byrnes informed Truman that Chiang wanted U.S. help in building a modern military force. Byrnes recommended this course, but noted that in peacetime such a Military Advisory Group was illegal. He thus suggested acting immediately, before the war was "legally terminated," to get around this restriction. The assistance sought was significant: Byrnes noted that about thirty KMT divisions had already been equipped by the United States, and that Chiang wanted sixty more. Truman was quick to respond. On 7 September, he told Soong, acting as Chiang's special envoy, that U.S. military advice would be provided.[76] Soon after, Washington was committed to building thirty additional KMT divisions.

The situation in China continued to deteriorate, however. By October, it was becoming apparent that Stalin was siding with the CCP in its effort to occupy Manchuria. U.S. troops were dispatched to northern China to receive surrender of Japanese troops, to help remove the "Communist menace which has been growing steadily since [the] war ended."[77] On 22 October, the State-War-Navy Coordinating Committee (SWNCC) submitted a report noting U.S. support through lend-lease would now include the equipping and training of a 39-division KMT army and support for its airforce. Quoting from a prior analysis, the SWNCC report was blunt:

"Continued support to China . . . should be carried on without hiatus in order best to preserve the present favorable position of the United States with respect to China." Our "present favorable position" in China, cannot . . . in the light of the present situation, be interpreted otherwise than as referring to our position as military collaborators with Chiang Kai-Shek.[78]

The report was approved and sent to the U.S. chargé in China on 7 November for implementation.

American aid to China was hardly insignificant: in the two months up to 15 October, it totaled more than 400 million dollars (approximately four billion in current dollars).[79] U.S. commitment to China was seen as critical to holding the line in all of Asia.[80] Truman understood the severity of the issue. In early December, he appointed General Marshall to find a solution on favorable terms. Marshall told Truman that should Chiang be unwilling to make concessions and America then failed to support him, "there would follow the tragic consequences of a divided China and of a probable Russian reassumption of power in Manchuria, the combined effect of this resulting in the defeat or loss of the major purpose of our war in the Pacific." Marshall then asked whether, in such circumstances, the United States should then just swallow its pride and support Chiang anyway, despite his antidemocratic ways. Truman and Byrnes agreed that it should.[81]

Thus U.S. containment in 1945 was not only active, but supported by a logic most scholars associate more with post-1947 policies. At the root was the premise that preserving America's "presently favorable" power position was essential to U.S. security.

Additional Measures in 1945

Efforts in 1945 to constrain the Soviet sphere were not confined to the Far East. By June, the Soviets were pressuring Turkey for better naval access to the Mediterranean Sea. A warm-water port on the Mediterranean had been a Russian geopolitical goal for centuries, and Stalin saw the end of war as the opportunity to realize it. In March, Moscow informed Ankara that the 1925 Turkish-Soviet treaty of nonaggression was no longer in force. In June, Molotov upped the ante, demanding in return for a new treaty joint control of the Dardanelles and the cessation of certain Turkish naval bases in the Mediterranean, at least in time of war. Ankara rejected these demands and sought U.S. help in countering Soviet pressure.[82]

For Washington, this pressure was part of a general Soviet effort to gain better access to the Atlantic Ocean, an effort that included Soviet demands in June for the internationalization of the Kiel canal. The canal had been built before 1914 to provide freer movement of German vessels between the North and Baltic Seas. Since the Soviets now controlled the ice-free port of Königsberg (renamed Kaliningrad), the canal's internationalization would give the Soviet navy year-round access to the Atlantic. On both issues, the canal and Turkey, Washington responded quickly.

On 6 July, the Strategy and Policy Group gave Assistant Secretary of Defense McCloy an analysis covering both the canal and the Dardanelles. Should Washington permit their internationalization, it might set a precedent undermining U.S. control over such waterways as the Panama canal. The report sympathized with Russia's problem, since it was "practically a land-locked nation." Given short-term weakness, however, Moscow would not take military action. Washington could thus take a strong stand, and "no concessions . . . need be made."[83]

A draft of Stimson's letter to Byrnes on the issue, dated 8 July, also acknowledged there was "considerable justification" for Soviet proposals, given Russian geography. Indeed, the argument that Washington must preserve control over Panama while denying Russian control of the Dardanelles might seem illogical. It was, however, "a logical illogicality." The Soviet Union was a "vigorous nation of unlimited potential." Should Washington concede on the Kiel-Dardanelles issue, this would give Russia greater power to realize possibly expansionist aspirations "without [us] knowing for certain that she is indeed free from them." Soviet control of these waterways must therefore be opposed.[84] As we will see, Truman and Byrnes held to a similar logic: although the jury might still be out on Soviet intentions, Russia's potential was already so huge that no further growth could be permitted.

Stalin introduced the waterways question at Potsdam on 22 July. Both Truman and Churchill were sympathetic to Russia's desire to revise the convention which had given Turkey control of traffic through the Dardanelles. Over the next few days, however, both leaders refused any substantive changes. Stalin eventually agreed to postpone the issue to a later conference.[85] The results on Kiel were similar. Truman and Churchill would grant the Soviets free access through the canal. Beyond that they would not go; Kiel would not be internationalized, but would remain under the Control Council for Germany's jurisdiction. This meant that the canal would remain firmly in the western Allied camp, as it was wholly within the British occupation zone.[86]

STAYING AHEAD REGARDLESS OF THE COSTS: U.S. POLICY AFTER NAGASAKI

After Nagasaki, Secretary of State Byrnes moved quickly to preserve the U.S. atomic monopoly. On 18 August, he told George Harrison, special assistant to Stimson, that since an atomic agreement was unlikely, "a continuation of all our efforts on all fronts to keep ahead of the race" was required. Scientists should therefore pursue their work full force, including work on the hydrogen bomb.[87] By this time, Stimson's attitude had moderated; he now favored some sharing of atomic secrets. When he sent McCloy in late August to discuss the issue, however, Byrnes remained "radically opposed" to sharing. The bomb for Byrnes was the perfect tool to shape the postwar peace on U.S. terms. As Stimson recorded, Byrnes was preparing for the foreign ministers' meeting "and wished to have the implied threat of the bomb in his pocket."[88]

On 12 September Stimson met with Truman to discuss a memorandum he had written on the issue. The atomic bomb was seen in many quarters, the report argued, "as a substantial offset to the growth of Russian [power]." Yet if the Soviets were not brought into an atomic partnership, the United States would be pursuing a policy of "maintain[ing] the Anglo-Saxon bloc over against the Soviet [bloc] in the possession of this weapon. Such a condition will almost certainly stimulate feverish activity on the part of the Soviet [bloc] toward the development of this bomb in what will in effect be a secret armament race of a rather desperate character." To negotiate with the bomb placed "rather ostentatiously on our hip" would only increase Soviet suspicions and distrust. Instead, an agreement had to be reached that could "sav[e] civilization not for five or for twenty years, but forever."[89]

Truman feigned sympathy, even agreeing that Washington should take Russia into its confidence.[90] His subsequent actions revealed something else. Truman supported Byrnes's strong stand at the foreign ministers' conference in September. He failed to support atomic sharing when Stimson and Under Secretary of State Dean Acheson argued their case in a 21 September cabinet meeting.[91] In a speech to Congress on 3 October, Truman deleted a section noting that atomic secrecy would not stop others from catching up in a comparatively short time, thus tacitly upholding the view that the secret could be preserved.[92] Then on 7 October, Truman made on-the-record remarks confirming he would not share the secrets. He sketched three levels of technical knowledge related to the bomb: basic scientific knowledge; engineering know-how; and the industrial capacity and resources needed to build the bomb. He used U.S. superiority on the second two levels to justify not sharing information on all three dimensions. If other nations such as Russia were to catch up to the United States, "they will have to do it on their own hook, just as we did." A few days later, an old friend asked Truman: "what it amounts to is this. That the armaments race is on, is that right?" The president replied in the affirmative but added that "we would stay ahead."[93]

By late October Byrnes's views were shifting somewhat. His failure to secure concessions in September apparently convinced him that Stimson was right—the Soviets would not cave in to atomic diplomacy. In a speech on 31 October, he argued that cooperation depended upon compromise, and expressed Washington's sympathy with Russia's special security interests in eastern Europe.[94] He departed for the Moscow conference of foreign ministers in December with a new plan for atomic cooperation. Still, the plan did not give away much: at most, he would offer information only at the first level of basic scientific knowledge.

Truman himself seemed to soften his stance in December. He let Byrnes take his new plan to Moscow, despite opposition from notable congressmen. Yet his harsh reaction to the deal Byrnes struck indicates that Truman still only sought cooperation that preserved America's overwhelming preponderance. On Byrnes's return, Truman took him aside to reiterate the need for a hard-line stance. The Russians understood force. Thus the United States had to rebuff any Soviet moves against Turkey and Iran, maintain control of Japan, and build a strong central government in China.[95]

Military planning during the fall continued to operate from the premise that Russia must be contained. On 29 August, at a meeting of the Joint Staff Planners, Vice Admiral Russell Willson read from his draft on the new military policy.

> When it becomes evident that forces of aggression are being arrayed against us by a potential enemy, we cannot afford, through any misguided and perilous idea of avoiding an aggressive attitude, to permit the first blow to be struck against us. Our government, under such conditions, should press the issue to a prompt political decision, while making all preparations to strike the first blow [if] necessary.[96]

This passage was incorporated in SWNCC 282, Basis for the Formulation of a U.S. Military Policy, approved by the Joint Chiefs on 19 September and forwarded to the SWNCC a week later. It specified as a key national policy the "maintenance of the United States in the best possible relative position with respect to potential enemy powers."[97]

Truman's hard-line views were no doubt reinforced in mid-October by a JCS report, forwarded to his chief of staff, Leahy, which emphasized the importance of maintaining a strict policy of atomic secrecy. America's "present advantageous position" must be preserved for as long as possible, and "most certainly during the present period of uncertainty" when Russian intentions were unclear.[98] A JCS report eleven days later, with Leahy again copied, gave the Americans at least a five-year head start on the bomb: "Security in peace and victory in any future major conflict requires, inter alia, that we make every possible effort to maintain this advantage and to advance more rapidly in scientific warfare than any other nation."[99]

Preserving conventional strength was also important, but Truman, like Roosevelt, was up against the public's desire for a return to peacetime normalcy, meaning a tiny standing army. Roosevelt and Forrestal had pushed for a new Service Bill before FDR's death. When a Senate vote on 3 April killed it, Forrestal got Stimson to agree to take up the campaign for universal military training. Stimson made the government's case to the House on 15 June.[100] Truman fully supported the idea.[101] So did the State, War, and Navy departments, which agreed on 16 October that it was highly inadvisable to continue rapid demobilization. Truman took the issue to the people on 23 October, arguing before a joint session of Congress that Americans had to face the fact "that peace must be built upon power, as well as upon good will and good deeds."[102] The UMT bill, however, never passed. Truman thus switched to strengthening the armed services through unifying the War and Navy departments. Speaking to the Senate on 20 December, he laid down another building block for his campaign to prepare public opinion for the coming struggle.[103]

> Now that our enemies have surrendered it has again become all too apparent that a portion of the American people are anxious to forget all about the war . . . [yet] the future peace of the world will depend in large part upon whether or not the United States . . . is willing to maintain the physical strength necessary to act as a safeguard against any future aggressor.

America, he added, also required industrial mobilization and greater scientific research for military purposes.[104]

In sum, the extent to which U.S. policy-makers sought to built a position of U.S. economic-military superiority in 1945 is clear. Domestic factors played a role, restricting the resources available for containment. Moreover, public expectations that American leaders should promote a moral liberal order limited Truman's ability to be forthright about U.S. actions, especially in China and Germany. To have acknowledged the full extent of the new containment policy in 1945 might have led the United States to be blamed for the subsequent cold war. Still, this does not give the domestic-level argument much explanatory power. It can only explain a constraint on U.S. leaders—why they sought to circumvent or subvert domestic obstacles to their strategy. It cannot explain what drove them to this strategy, namely, the same geopolitical fear compelling Germany earlier in the century: the fear of a rising Russian superpower.

THE TRAGEDY OF THE AMERICAN CONTAINMENT POLICY IN 1945

The evidence cited shows that U.S. leaders pursued active containment against Russia long before the "official" start of the cold war in 1946–47. This policy, as I discuss later, exacerbated Soviet suspicions and made a cold war essentially inevitable. The tragedy is that the policy sprang not from a conviction that the Soviets were unalterably hostile, but from fear of growing Soviet power should Washington not act. Moreover, Truman and Byrnes took a hard-line posture despite strong warnings that it would make cooperation with the Soviets almost impossible.

For theorists who emphasize the perceptions of hostile intentions, it is surprising that at the time Truman crystallized his containment strategy in mid-1945 he found Stalin not entirely disagreeable. On Potsdam's first day, he wrote in his diary: "I can deal with Stalin. He is honest—but smart as hell."[105] The next day he told his old friend Joseph Davies that Stalin was a "direct" man with whom he "got along fine."[106] Even though U.S. policy hardened after 21 July, Truman's view of the Soviet leader had not changed. On 28 July he told Forrestal that he "found Stalin not difficult to do business with." He wrote his wife the next day: "I like Stalin. He is straightforward. Knows what he wants and will compromise when he can't get it."[107] To another, Truman noted that Stalin was simply a good political boss, "as near like Tom Pendergast [Truman's mentor in Missouri] as any man I know."[108] Even twelve years later, in an unsent letter to Acheson, Truman acknowledged that during this period "I liked the little son of a bitch."[109]

Truman's main concern was not Stalin, but Stalin's successors. The Soviet system, he felt, had a fundamental flaw: without a clear means of succession, any militaristic oligarch could grab the reins of power. Truman told his cabinet in mid-May that his great fear was some Russian general would take over, acting like Napoleon.[110] Near the end of Potsdam, when Stalin canceled a meeting because he had a cold, Truman wondered what would happen if Stalin suddenly died. If some "demagogue on horseback" gained control of Russia's vast army "he could play havoc with European peace." Truman also wondered "if there is a man with the necessary strength and following to step into Stalin's place and maintain peace and solidarity at home." Dictators did not train successors, and he saw no one at the conference who could do the job.[111] Even in October, Truman noted that Stalin was "a moderating influence," and that it would be great catastrophe should he die.[112]

The other architect of containment, James Byrnes, felt the same way. He admitted to Davies in July that while Molotov was problematic, he had confidence in Stalin.[113] In September, Byrnes confided to his assistant that if Molotov was not ousted he would lead Russia to the same fate Hitler had led Germany. Stalin, on the other hand, "wants peace and [Byrnes] is fearful for the world if Stalin should die."[114] This explains his efforts in December to meet directly with Stalin to secure a modus vivendi over Molotov's head.[115]

In qualifying the postrevisionist view, it is also critical to note how keenly U.S. leaders saw that their actions would make cooperation more difficult.

As early as September 1944, advisers told Stimson it would be the "height of folly" to try to maintain the atomic monopoly, since it would only force Russia into a crash program.[116] Morgenthau warned the State Department in January 1945 that Moscow must be assured that America was not using Germany as a possible future ally against Russia.[117] Stimson also told the department that month that the trusteeship question for Pacific islands should not be broached with Moscow since it would "provoke a sense of distrust" and "call marked attention to our aims."[118] Nevertheless, U.S efforts to revive Germany and to control the islands were soon underway.

Truman understood the dangers. After berating Molotov on 23 April, he asked Davies whether he had gone too far. Davies spoke of the dangers of being too firm. Soviet foreign policy was driven by "fear of a hostile world," which, given recent history, was "abundantly justified." Truman sympathized, noting the many times Russia had been invaded. Davies argued that unless cooperation obtained, the United States would have to expect and prepare for a war in the near future. Truman "agreed entirely" that peace required a foundation of trust. Davies told him to keep fighting for peace. "Your conference with Molotov commanded their respect. You must now command their confidence in our good will and fairness."[119]

That Truman accepted this advice, and built it into his two-track strategy, is clear.[120] By mid-May he sent Hopkins to Moscow. He also sent Davies to explain his policy to Churchill, specifically why U.S. troops would be withdrawn from the Soviet occupation zones. The selection of Davies was deliberate. Since Davies was known to be sympathetic to the Soviets, sending him would end rumors that America and Britain were "ganging up" on Russia.[121]

Davies became one of Truman's most important confidants over the next few months. One of a select few invited by the president to Potsdam, he warned Byrnes just before the first meeting that to secure peace it was critical "to see the other fellow's point of view" specifically that "the first and dominant [Soviet] purpose . . . is their physical security."[122] By 29 July, as we have seen, Byrnes was convinced the bomb would control the peace. Davies warned him against this view. If the Russians felt excluded from atomic cooperation, "it would engender bad feeling—possible hostility, and ultimately a race in . . . armaments, which would culminate in the annihilation of one or the other [great powers], or perhaps both."[123]

The fact that Byrnes used Davies's idea on the Polish border question to end the conference on a cooperative note indicates that he did take some of Davies's concerns to heart.[124] This is also shown by a conversation on 1 August, when Byrnes told Davies of the impending atomic bombing of Japan. Davies asked whether this would not mean an atomic arms race. Byrnes agreed that it was "a serious danger." Given this, Davies argued, the president should secure an understanding with Stalin now, since the bomb was an "immediate . . . threat to [Soviet] security." Without an agreement, compromise on all other matters might be impossible. Byrnes agreed, but felt he needed more time to consider the issue.[125] Byrnes's dilemma was clear. Unless there was a partnership on the bomb, Moscow would feel betrayed. Yet Byrnes also believed that sharing the atomic secret would mean foregoing a critical tool needed to contain Soviet growth.

Given these warnings, Truman and Byrnes hardly moved to containment ignorant of its possible effects. Yet while Davies's language is the bluntest, the belief that hard-line policies might irretrievably damage cooperation was shared by many. For this reason, atomic sharing became one of the most debated issues of containment in the fall 1945.[126] On 22 September, the day after a cabinet meeting on the subject, Truman wrote to his wife that he faced conflicting advice—those on the right arguing for secrecy; those on the left arguing for sharing scientific knowledge. Truman knew he was at a crossroads, that his decision "is probably the most momentous one I'll make."[127] Within a week, however, his sense of prudence led him to choose a policy of complete secrecy.

Byrnes later regretted this strategy and sought to offer more carrots while upholding the two-track policy. By late 1945, however, Truman seemed to accept that a modus vivendi was now impossible; he thus emphasized the stick. For Truman, a cold war was unwanted, but it was better than allowing U.S. power to fall. In a meeting with Stettinius in October, he commented that the failure of the foreign ministers' conference did not upset him, since this was bound to occur at the end of the war, and that it was "perhaps better to [have it] happen out in the open at this stage."[128] By early 1946, Truman's attention was focused not on saving the peace, but on gaining the support of the American people for containment. This included not only recruiting Churchill to give his famous iron curtain speech in March, but the using of public forums to highlight Soviet violations of the spirit of Yalta. Within a year, world and U.S. public opinion would be primed for the Truman Doctrine and the official start of the cold war.[129]

STALIN'S REACTION TO U.S. POLICY AND THE SHIFT TO COLD WAR

Although relatively few Soviet documents on the 1945–49 period have been released,[130] the extant evidence shows that U.S. policies did indeed undermine postwar cooperation. Needless to say, Stalin was a brutal dictator. Moreover, he was highly suspicious of western countries, given Russia's historical experience. But out of simple geopolitical self-interest, he wanted good relations with the west: he needed breathing space to rebuild his war-ravaged country.[131] Thus in 1945 he offered little support for local Communists in western Europe and Greece and allowed Czechoslovakia and Hungary a moderate degree of freedom. Over Austria, Stalin had been pushing for joint control, not Soviet occupation, since 1944. He also quickly shifted to demobilization and industrial conversion. From 11.4 million men in May, the Red Army was reduced by 3 million by the end of 1945; by late 1947, the army was down to 2.9 million.[132] The U.S. military saw this trend. An October 1945 report noted that demobilization would cut the Soviet army to 4.4 million by spring 1946. Most of the divisions were needed to occupy eastern Europe; only 20 were capable of being used outside the Soviet sphere. Thus Russia would likely "avoid the risk of a major armed conflict for 5 to 10 years, except for purely defensive purposes."[133]

Note also that Stalin was at his most accommodating just as Truman was solidifying his containment strategy. In June, Stalin accepted the UN Security Council voting formula so important to the U.S. secretary of state.[134] As Truman's diary entries indicate, Stalin was a tough bargainer at Potsdam, but hardly uncooperative. Even hard-liners noticed Soviet efforts to accommodate. Forrestal noted in June that Grew had achieved significant progress in recent discussions with Moscow. McCloy indicated that Stalin had been compliant in a number of areas, including agreeing to make no territorial claims against China.[135] Reports from the military in Germany affirmed that Soviet commanders were cooperating; the problem, in fact, was not the Russians, but the French.[136]

Soviet policy began to harden only after August, as the U.S. strategy became increasingly obvious. Soviet fears were most manifest in their efforts to prevent Japan's remilitarization. As Stalin told his advisers at the time, Moscow had to "keep Japan vulnerable from all sides, north, west, south, east, then she will keep quiet."[137] At the foreign ministers' conference in September, Byrnes was taken aback by Molotov's strong concern for Japan. The Soviets were upset by the unilateral decision excluding them from an occupation role. At the first meeting, Molotov noted that the Japanese question was not on the agenda, even though Britain had promised it would be. He later requested an Allied Control Council for Japan, noting that the task of destroying Japanese militarism could not be left to the United States alone. Japan's highly militarized industrial structure, he argued, was "likely to lead to the renewal of Japanese aggression in the near future."[138] Byrnes dismissed these concerns despite Harriman's warnings that the Soviets were clearly fearful that America was preparing to use Japan against them.[139] Byrnes told Molotov that he refused to consider the issue at this conference. He later acknowledged that his tough stand had been a primary cause of the breakdown of the conference.[140]

By October, Soviet anxiety was tangible. When Harriman met with Stalin on 25 October, Stalin was angry that Truman was still ignoring the Japanese question.[141] The next day he was more blunt: if Washington continued to exclude the Soviets from the occupation, Moscow would pursue a "unilateral course" in Asia. In December, Byrnes offered a compromise. The Soviets were given a symbolic place on both the Far Eastern Commission in Washington (an advisory board to the U.S. occupation) and the smaller Allied Control Council in Japan (although MacArthur's decisions remained final).[142] Yet there is little doubt, as Harriman had warned, that U.S. resistance heightened Moscow's beliefs that Washington would use Japan as part of a broader policy to contain Russia.[143]

Although evidence on Stalin's response to other specific elements of containment is lacking, his negative reaction to Hiroshima is clear. Spies had revealed U.S. atomic research, but the demonstrated power of the bomb unnerved him. Just after Nagasaki, Stalin met with his top scientists and his commissar of munitions. He had one demand: with Hiroshima, the "equilibrium has been destroyed. Provide the bomb—it will remove a great danger from us."[144] As part of his overall policy of "catch up and overtake," Stalin proceeded to reorganize his country for this mission.[145]

As intended, the bomb gave the Russians new respect for American power. Two Russian scholars most familiar with the documents note that in August 1945 "the Americans vividly demonstrated to Stalin and many Russians that they could threaten the Soviet Union in the not-so-distant future." Thus, the "security belt of friendly regimes around the Soviet Union acquired a new urgency."[146] A scientist who helped develop the Soviet bomb recalled that "the Soviet government interpreted [Hiroshima] as atomic blackmail against the USSR, as a threat to unleash a new, even more terrible and devastating war."[147]

The American effort to shape the postwar peace through the implicit threat of atomic war had thus achieved more than mere containment. It had so frightened the Russians that all-out arms racing and cold war were now essentially inevitable. Truman of course had countenanced this eventuality. But as he noted in October, in the end the United States would stay ahead.

U.S. STRATEGIC PLANNING, 1945–1950

In the last part of this chapter, I focus on one question: Why did Washington not initiate a preventive war against Russia in the late 1940s, when American strategic superiority was apparently at its height? I show that U.S. leaders and officials, despite active consideration of preventive war,[148] rejected it for two reasons, both supportive of this book's theory. First, the United States had superiority in both potential and especially economic power.[149] Hence, compared to Germany before the two world wars, there was far less reason to believe that any U.S. military decline would be both deep and inevitable. Arms racing could "prevent" such a decline. Second, until the early 1950s, technical restrictions meant that the United States had too few atomic bombs to defeat Russia quickly and decisively in an all-out war. War plans consistently concluded that the west would have to sacrifice all of western Europe; a long, costly war would then follow in which Soviet surrender was far from assured. In short, containment was the better means to security: although it raised the likelihood of major war through inadvertence, it did not entail all the risks of actually choosing such a war. Security-maximizers are rational to choose major war only when no other feasible means of reversing decline exist.

American officials were well aware of Russia's ability to narrow the huge U.S. strategic advantage. A November 1945 military study predicted that as time went on, the Soviets would develop new weapons, including guided missiles, while improving their bomber force.[150] Another November analysis noted that, although the Soviet economy was weakened by the war, it possessed "tremendous war industrial potential." Since Moscow lacked an atomic bomb, however, it would not run the risk of a major war while rebuilding.[151]

Russia's potential for future military power was certainly unsettling. Yet all-out preventive war was not necessarily the best means to arrest its rise. That even the military saw arms racing from a position of U.S. economic superiority as a better first step is shown by a report on the atomic age written by the influential commanding general of the Manhattan project, General Groves. One version of the report was sent to the State Department in January 1946 to help shape civilian thinking. If the bomb could not be controlled by agreement, it argued, the world would enter into a vicious arms race. In such a race, the United States "must for all time maintain absolute supremacy in atomic weapons, including number, size and power, efficiency, means for immediate offense use and defense against atomic attack." Yet the report also seemed to temper the value of the arms-racing option.

> If we were truly realistic instead of idealistic, as we appear to be, we would not permit any foreign power with which we are not firmly allied, and in which we do not have absolute confidence to make or possess atomic weapons. If such a country started to make atomic weapons we would destroy its capacity to make them before it had progressed far enough to threaten us.

If Americans could be made aware of their true peril fifteen years later in a world of unrestricted atomic bombs, the report continued, they would demand one of two outcomes: either an agreement outlawing of atomic weapons forever or an exclusive U.S. monopoly. Since the latter, without the former, could only be achieved by war, the memorandum strongly implied that the Pentagon favored preventive war should diplomacy fail.[152]

Yet this was not the military's complete view. Groves's report to the civilians was taken word-for-word from an updated version of JCS 1477, a study of the impact of atomic weapons on national security.[153] Since JCS 1477 was for internal purposes, however, it contained the following passage excised from the civilian version. After noting that mutual trust was an essential requirement for an enforceable U.S.-Soviet agreement, JCS 1477 explained that "this will not be easy to obtain. Realistically, the second alternative [preventive war] will be equally difficult to achieve. Therefore, let us consider the probable effect on our armies of the future of an unrestricted atomic armaments race."[154] In short, the military did not tell the civilians that it had already concluded that decisive preventive war was simply too hard to achieve, and thus that arms racing was the most realistic means to security. The omission was no doubt deliberate. Pentagon officials likely worried that more dovish civilians might use any argument against preventive war to reject the course altogether, even if declining conditions later required this extreme step. Leaving preventive war in as a plausible alternative thus preserved U.S. options. Still, both the report to the State Department and JCS 1477 made clear that arms racing was the least of three evils considered. As the final sentences in both documents stated: "If there are to be atomic weapons in the world, we must have the best, the biggest, and the most."

January 1946 was thus a critical point in the decision against preventive war. Although calls for preventive war would continue for another fifteen years,[155] military planners realized that such a war, rather than being immoral, was simply infeasible. Every war plan created within the next five years showed that in the event of major war the Soviets would overrun Europe. This would force America to fight a long war from England, the Azores, and North Africa. Given these distances, and given the strong Soviet air-defense system, it would be very difficult to achieve a decisive victory.[156] Added to the problem was the small number of atomic bombs: until the successful "Sandstone" tests of the late 1940s, the United States had no way to mass-produce the weapon; in 1948, there were still only fifty bombs in the arsenal.[157] Set against an arms race founded on American economic preponderance, initiating major war was clearly not the rational means to security.

One might still wonder why, after the surprise Soviet atomic test in August 1949, Washington did not move immediately to preventive war. Preventive war was one of four alternatives considered as part of the NSC-68 process in early 1950. Yet once again, American leaders understood the rational choice: the U.S. economy was so preponderant that by simply spending more on the military, the United States could maintain military superiority.[158]

The shock of the Soviet test pushed the State Department's Policy Planning Staff into action in the fall of 1949. Its two key members were Kennan and Paul Nitze (until Kennan's departure in January 1950). At a PPS meeting in October, Kennan laid out the key question: "Are we holding our own?" Secretary of State Acheson stressed that the issue of future trends had to be studied carefully.[159] At a follow-up meeting in December, both Kennan and Nitze emphasized the importance of increasing conventional forces in Europe to prevent the Soviets from gaining the potential power of the area.[160]

One pillar of NSC-68's final recommendations grew out of this logic. The United States, to uphold preponderance, would need to deter Soviet territorial expansion and thus growth in Soviet potential power. For this, large-scale conventional military spending was required. The other pillar—massive increases in nuclear weaponry—was shaped by analyses from the Joint Chiefs and the CIA in early 1950. A 9 February JCS report argued that although the Soviets would gradually narrow the strategic gap, the overall power balance still favored the western camp—not only because of America's superior nuclear capability but also the superior Allied economic potential in support of a global major war.[161] The next day, the CIA issued a report that supported a nuclear buildup but also offered a warning. The Soviets were driven by fear. Overzealous steps to improve the U.S. position might cause them to believe the west was planning to attack Russia, which in turn might lead the Kremlin to launch a preemptive war.[162] Preventive war was thus quite unappealing versus the arms-racing option. Aside from the likelihood of an indecisive outcome, the very act of preparing for such a war could lead to a Soviet preemptive strike.

The arguments since autumn 1949 for a stronger containment posture culminated in NSC-68, presented to Truman in April 1950. The document was driven by the overarching belief that if America did not act soon to maintain its military preponderance, the Soviet Union might overtake it. Fortunately, the United States had four times the Soviet GNP. All Americans had to do, therefore, was to "summon up the potential within ourselves" and translate it into the military strength needed for a more vigorous containment policy.

The last part of the document considered four possible courses of action: continuation of current policies, isolation, preventive war, and an accelerated buildup of political, economic, and military strength. The fourth was chosen as the one best able to reverse the present trends and to maximize U.S. security. Continuing present policies or isolation would only allow Russia to dominate Eurasia, thus giving it "a potential far superior to our own."

The document recognized that in light of history the argument for preventive war made a powerful case. The argument fell apart on purely realist grounds, however: it was based on the faulty assumption that the United States could launch a decisive attack or win a long war. Atomic blows alone, however, would not cause the Kremlin to capitulate, and Russia would then go on to dominate most of Eurasia. Moral considerations are also noted, but even here the document's argument was purely expedient: the shock of U.S. responsibility for the war would make it difficult to establish a satisfactory international order after the war was over. Hence, even a military victory would not bring the United States closer to victory in the conflict with Communism.

In maximizing security, therefore, preventive war was inferior to the fourth option: using U.S. superiority in economic/potential power to maintain military dominance. The goal therefore was to construct "a successfully functioning political and economic system in the free world backed by adequate military strength." This would "postpone and avert the disastrous situation which, in light of the Soviet Union's probable fission bomb capability and possible thermonuclear bomb capability, might arise in 1954 on a continuation of our present programs."[163]

In sum, NSC-68 reflected two aspects of the theory's logic for bipolar systems. First, what drove the United States to accelerate the cold war rivalry after 1950 was the prospect of continued military decline in the absence of new, stronger action by Washington. Second, U.S. superiority in all three dimensions of power—military, economic, and potential—was critical to the sense of optimism regarding the future, notwithstanding current negative trends. In short, the United States possessed the strength to reverse the trends. In such circumstances, arms racing and economic revitalization are always more rational than preventive war.

As a postscript, it is worth noting that internal discussions of the merits of preventive war did not end in 1950. In 1953, President Eisenhower authorized a policy reappraisal, code-named Solarium, which had as one of its three alternatives preventive war.[164] In September, Eisenhower wrote a confidential letter to Secretary of State John Foster Dulles, observing that if America could not stay ahead of Russia, his duty to future generations might require initiating war "at the most propitious moment that we could designate."[165] Fortunately, by October, presentations to Eisenhower made clear that arms racing could indeed uphold U.S. nuclear superiority.[166] We can be thankful that Eisenhower, like Truman, did not opt for preventive nuclear war. But their reason for not doing so had little to do with democratic morality and almost everything to do with U.S. superiority in economic and potential power. So while German leaders earlier in the century had seen that decline would be deep and inevitable in the face of Russian industrialization, the United States had the luxury of being able to arms race its way to long-term security.

This chapter supports the book's contention that dynamic trends drive states to adopt policies that increase the chance of major war, all in order to reduce their prospects for long-term decline. American officials were more than aware of the Soviet system's capacity for evil, particularly against its own citizens. Yet significantly, Washington moved to containment even before it had determined the Kremlin's foreign policy intentions, and even though Truman and Byrnes saw Stalin as a businesslike geopolitician.

Contrary to traditionalists and classical realists, containment and the cold war were not results of a delayed American awakening to Soviet aggressive intentions. Nor were they, as revisionists and some liberal scholars argue, reflections of American greed or domestic economic structure. The U.S. policy-makers acted for national security, even as they saw the Soviets doing the same. Yet the postrevisionist view, which parallels aspects of neorealism, is also insufficient. This was not simply a spiral of misunderstanding fueled by the zero-sum nature of bipolarity. Bipolarity mattered, but because of dynamic trends. It was fear of decline in economic and potential power that compelled U.S. leaders to limit Moscow's consolidation of its realm and to prevent revolution in western Europe. Neorealism, which remains underspecified in its analysis of dynamic trends, cannot explain when bipolar systems will move from relative calm to intense rivalry and crisis. But the spiral-model aspect of postrevisionism is also incomplete in its understanding of the initial impulse to containment (even if it helps explain the subsequent action-reaction cycle). American policy-makers chose containment in mid-1945 not because they saw the Soviets as hostile in the near term—they knew the Kremlin wanted peace to rebuild after a devastating war. The fear was of the future: the authoritarian nature of the Soviet system meant that an expansionistic Napoleon-like character might wreak havoc down the road, if Russia was allowed to gain more power.[167] Restricting Soviet growth was thus a prudent step, even if it meant a heightened risk of inadvertent war.

A full explanation for the jump into cold war requires a different theoretical perspective. By separating power into three dimensions, dynamic differentials theory shows how fear of decline in economic and potential power led to such hard-line policies in the military realm. Containment served to protect the U.S. lead in economic/potential power, even at the cost of a hostile rivalry. Yet since the United States started the rivalry with superior economic/potential power, American leaders could hold off on preventive war until they saw whether arms racing and containment would indeed maintain U.S. military preponderance. The strategy helped "prevent" the kind of deep and inevitable decline that had, in the past, led other bipolar systems into total wars for survival. This suggests counterfactually that had the United States started in 1945 with the same military power but only the territorial mass of the original thirteen colonies, for example, American confidence in the future might have been closer to that of German leaders prior to the two world wars.

[7]

The Berlin and Cuban Missile Crises

What explains the shift within the early cold war from ongoing tension to periods of intense crisis? My focus here is on the three crises of greatest salience: the Berlin crises of 1948 and 1961 and the Cuban missile crisis of 1962 (with emphasis on the latter). These crises were, by almost all historical accounts, times when the risks of major war rose significantly. Such dramatic jumps in the probability of major war must be explained.[1] I show that perceptions of decline and fears for the future played a dominant role in all three crises.

There are three categories of explanation that have been applied, or could be applied, to the crises of the early cold war. The first focuses on personalities: variations across leaders in terms of beliefs, values, and character should lead to differences in the probability of their states initiating crises. Some actors, for example, are seen as inherently more risk-acceptant and therefore more likely to respond to a given domestic or external problem with dangerous policies.[2]

The second category examines domestic factors. In the bureaucratic politics model, policy results from the pulling and hauling of competing bureaucracies.[3] Each bureaucracy's position on an issue reflects its narrow organizational goals—protecting its mission, increasing its budget, and so forth—rather than the larger national interest. Variations in superpower behavior, such as shifts to crisis initiation, would thus follow from changes in the relative strengths of key bureaucracies over time. This logic is also found in theories of societal groups, whereby shifts to harder-line policies reflect changes in the relative power of various social groups. Soviet behavior, for example, might be explained according to battles between hardliners and moderates,[4] with American behavior explained according to White House–Congress and Democratic-Republican struggles for control.[5]

The third group captures systemic/realist explanations. For Waltzian neorealists, bipolarity explains the lack of major war during the cold war era.[6] Classical realism, assuming Soviet aggressiveness, would predict shifts in behavior following changes in the snapshot of power differentials.[7] Greater Soviet expansionism should therefore occur during periods of relative Soviet strength. Hegemonic stability theory would expect few crises during the period of U.S. hegemony, and instability only as Russia reaches a power-transition point in the early 1970s. Aggressive acts should be initiated by the rising power.[8]

Before turning to the evidence, I have a few comments on these positions to offer. One theory must be put aside because it lacks a variable: Waltz's argument for bipolar stability. Since bipolarity is a constant during the cold war, it alone cannot explain shifts in the likelihood of major war over time.[9] Dynamic changes in power differentials must be incorporated. Similarly, theories stressing psychological tendencies are limited. Because these tendencies are given by human nature, there is nothing to vary to explain shifts in behavior.[10]

I have had difficulty assessing the causal impact of bureaucratic and societal variables, for one reason: in thirty thousand pages of declassified documents and in work based on the recent documents, I found little evidence that these factors played a key role in U.S. and Soviet decisions.[11] This does not mean unit-level factors were unimportant. Yet given the abundant evidence showing the importance of declining power, bureaucratic and domestic forces appear to be less salient than systemic ones.

The other realist theories are inadequate as they stand. Hegemonic stability theory cannot explain why it was invariably the superpower fearing decline that initiated the crises. Classical realism and post-Waltzian neorealism are compatible with my argument to the extent that they incorporate the security dilemma and changing power differentials. Still, as we saw in chapter 2, these theories remain underspecified. Because they do not consider simultaneously the preventive and preemptive aspects of the security dilemma, they have no formal argument about how declining states grapple with the risks of inadvertent war when deciding whether to adopt harder-line policies.[12] Moreover, they tend to assume that if a great power seeks to maintain the power balance through measures internal to its sphere, such as arms racing and alliance building, it can. The evidence examined below shows that when actors view such measures as inadequate and therefore fear what would be otherwise exogenous decline, they initiate risky crises as the only means short of war to avert decline. Moreover, we see actors calibrating the severity (and thus the riskiness) of actions to the severity of decline and to the degree to which crisis initiation might coerce concessions mitigating that decline.

The crises of the early cold war reflected the third of three forms of decline discussed in the introductory chapter, namely, power oscillations. Unlike in the German cases, potential power was not the main problem; after U.S. actions in 1945–46, the two superpowers maintained a rough balance of population and basic resources.[13] Moreover, neither state feared entrenched stagnation, at least in the 1948–62 period.[14] Rather, the crises resulted from oscillations in the power balance caused by differential rates of success in the two sides' armament and alliance-building programs. Russia's power trends were generally upward after 1945 as it recovered from the war. But there were critical moments when the trend shifted downward because of the exogenous relative success of U.S. policies. At these moments, destabilizing crises broke out. In 1948, the anticipated impact of U.S. moves to incorporate western Germany into the western camp forced Stalin to act against Berlin. In 1961, the Soviets pressed on Berlin to stem the relative decline of eastern Europe. In October 1962, the United States was the one initiating the crisis, but for similar reasons. Khrushchev's deployment of missiles in Cuba could not be offset by internal U.S. measures in the short term. To avert a temporary but precipitous decline, Kennedy was compelled to bring on a crisis to compel Khrushchev to withdraw the missiles. In each case, the actors would not have taken such destabilizing actions had more moderate policies existed internally to avert decline.[15]

Note that in two of the crises—Berlin 1948 and Berlin 1961—the second-ranked great power brought on the crisis. Typically, it is the dominant military power in any system that initiates a major war or the crises that raise significant risks of such a war. As I argued in chapter 1, however, in bipolarity the second-ranked state can also do so when in decline, since there are no third parties to worry about. We would expect, however, that this actor would calibrate the severity of its actions to its power level, and this is borne out in the cases examined below. Khrushchev in mid-1961 was relatively bolder than Stalin in 1948, since he could rest on at least the perception of Soviet strategic strength. The Soviets' true inferiority in ICBMs was clear by early 1962, however. This gave Kennedy the confidence to move aggressively against the Cuban missiles later that year.

One other difference from the two world war cases should be noted. Washington and Moscow worried about expected decline in their larger geopolitical realms, not just shifts in U.S.-Soviet power per se. As I pointed out in chapter 1, when leaders calculate relative power, they analyze not only the resources they can mobilize within their borders, but also the power of small states within their spheres.[16] In 1914 and 1939, Germany's empire was so small that developments within it played little role in German decision-making. In the cold war, both superpowers' spheres were essential to overall security given their economic and potential power. Soviet decline in the critical European theater thus twice pushed Moscow to initiate crises over Berlin. Washington's concern in October 1962, in addition to the threat to the U.S. homeland, was that the western sphere's cohesion would deteriorate once the allies saw the shift in the power balance.

In sum, the evidence supports a dynamic systemic interpretation of the crises of the early cold war. Perceptions of declining power resulting from the anticipated success of the other's programs led to risky policies. Domestic factors cannot be completely dismissed. Yet given the lack of documentary evidence confirming their significance, their role appears to be relatively minor.

THE BERLIN CRISIS, 1948

The Berlin Crisis of 1948 and the Korean War shared a causal root. They reflected Moscow's reaction to U.S. policies that could not be countered by more intense arms racing and alliance tightening and that were thus leading to a relative deterioration of the Soviet sphere.[17] For Moscow in 1948, the trend in U.S.-to-Russian economic power was favorable as the Soviets rebuilt their devastated economy. Stalin's larger empire was in trouble, however, because of the anticipated impact of U.S. moves in Europe. Preventive motives were thus critical to Stalin's accepting the risks of escalation over Berlin. Most studies agree that Moscow was acting defensively, so I cover the crisis only briefly.[18]

Until even mid-1947, declassified documents show that Moscow still preferred détente to all-out cold war. This hope was undermined by Washington's announcement of the Marshall Plan to strengthen western Europe's economy.[19] The primary factor leading to the Berlin crisis was the London Conferences of January–March 1948, in which the United States, Britain, and France agreed to unite the German occupation zones and to hand political control over to an independent western German government.[20] This act left the Soviets facing a rising West Germany tied to the western bloc, a daunting prospect for a nation that had just lost so many lives fighting Germany. Berlin was both a means and an end for Moscow. As a means, the Soviets saw pressure on Berlin, particularly the blockade, as a way to convince the west to reverse the London agreements. As an end, the Soviets, by terminating the western presence in Berlin, hoped to stop the flow of refugees from the Soviet zone that was weakening the eastern German economy.

On 18 June, General Clay announced currency reform for the western zones, a first step in creating a unified West German state. The Soviets warned that they would act to protect their bloc's economy; on 24 June they blockaded all ground traffic to West Berlin. Washington realized the impact of currency reforms on the faltering eastern German economy. Political Adviser for Germany Robert Murphy wrote to the secretary of state on

19 June that Soviet measures to restrict traffic were "not unreasonable [given] the natural defensive action to protect [the] Soviet zone."[21] On 24 June, eastern bloc foreign ministers released a statement on the London Conferences revealing the larger Soviet fear: a resurgent West Germany. Among the problems to be settled, the statement noted, were Germany's demilitarization and control over heavy industry "with a view . . . to preventing the re-establishment of Germany's war potential."[22] In negotiations with Stalin and Molotov over the next two months, the concern for a rising Germany was a constant refrain.

On 3 July, Secretary of State George C. Marshall wrote to his ambassador in London that Moscow wanted to reopen the entire German question to reverse the recommendations of the London Conferences; he reiterated this opinion six days later.[23] U.S. leaders thus understood that Moscow's behavior reflected its concerns about the effect of western actions on the balance of power. American strategy was fixed, however: the London agreement would not be on the bargaining table.[24]

When negotiations began in early August, blocking the London agreements was still the primary Soviet goal. Only after Washington would not budge did Stalin shift to pushing the west out of Berlin. At the very least, he wanted to use Soviet currency reforms to absorb the city into the eastern economic sphere. This hierarchy of objectives was understood even before negotiations began. Ambassador Walter Bedell Smith in Moscow wrote on 24 July that Moscow might forgo a battle for Berlin, but only if the London agreements were canceled. The Soviets desired "a return to [the] *status quo ante.*" Since this was unlikely, they would fall back on their other aim, namely, liquidating Berlin as center of western reactionary influence.[25]

Talks began on 2–3 August, with Stalin pressing the question of a unified West Germany. Restrictions were placed on western access to Berlin, he said, because the London decisions and the currency reforms "had disrupted the economy of the [Soviet] zone." The London agreements should be suspended until after a four-power meeting. If they had already been put into effect, "there would be nothing left to discuss." Smith made it clear the London decisions would likely proceed. Stalin argued that he was still worried about the creation of the West German government, although he might allow some economic unification of the western zones.[26]

Smith reported on 3 August that the key Soviet concerns were the Berlin currency and the establishment of a West German government. The next day, Counselor to the State Department Charles Bohlen gave Marshall the consensus on Soviet actions: Stalin had retreated to some degree on the London agreements issue, but "he makes it entirely clear that [its] suspension is [his] objective . . . especially in respect of a Western zone government." If this could not be achieved, the Soviets would accept a divided

Germany, which would force the Russians to oust Allied troops from Berlin.[27]

In sum, the evidence shows that U.S. leaders knew that Moscow was defending against a declining situation resulting from the anticipated success of western policies, and was risking escalation as a means to reestablish the status quo ante. The struggle to reverse a negative power trend thus explains the Soviet risk-taking behavior. Domestic and personality approaches fall short. Not only was Stalin in complete control within the Russian hierarchy, but shifts in a given leader's behavior over time, barring physiological decay, are best explained by changes external to the actor.

THE BERLIN CRISIS, 1961

Next to Cuba 1962, the world probably never skated as close to the nuclear abyss as during the Berlin crisis of 1961. The June 1961 Kennedy-Khrushchev summit ended with a harsh exchange on the possibility of war over Berlin.[28] In July, Kennedy announced a conventional buildup in Europe and requested an additional $3.2 billion from Congress to signal U.S. resolve.[29] The construction of the Berlin Wall beginning on 13 August stemmed the refugee exodus, but the crisis was not over. Khrushchev's ultimatum that he would sign a treaty with East Germany, handing control over access to Berlin to the unstable East German regime, still stood.

On 31 August Khrushchev announced an end to Moscow's moratorium on nuclear testing, noting that any confrontation over Berlin would likely escalate to general war.[30] For Washington, the issue was U.S. access not only to West Berlin but also to East Berlin—whether the wall was designed to keep East Berliners in or Americans out.[31] As in 1948, Washington could not allow access rights to be trampled without a reputation loss. On 8 September, Kennedy asked his secretaries of defense and state to determine if NATO could mount a corps-sized probe to reopen access to Berlin. Over the next three days, war games were run indicating that NATO strategy required the "ability to manipulate the risks of undesirable consequences to both sides."[32] These risks were rising, as both sides committed arms and prestige. On 8–9 September, the Warsaw Pact announced measures to enhance its military strength, while Washington revealed that another 40,000 troops had been ordered to Europe.[33]

In mid-October, East German guards began denying access into East Berlin to U.S. nonuniformed personnel. Kennedy responded by authorizing commanders to use tanks to smash any barrier blocking access. On 23 October, he issued a memorandum which noted that if the crisis moved beyond a military buildup, conventional forces and then nuclear weapons would be used, with general war likely to follow.[34] On 25 October, East German guards again prevented a U.S. vehicle from crossing into East Berlin. U.S. tanks moved to the checkpoint. On 27 October, the Soviets moved twenty tanks to within 100 yards of the crossing; the Americans positioned their thirty tanks on the other side. This was the first and only direct confrontation of U.S and Soviet ground forces in the cold war. Fortunately, diplomacy pulled both sides back from the brink.

The preconditions for accidents and preemptive actions were clearly present. Moscow had information that American troops had been practicing using tanks to knock down a replica of the wall. A U.S. operational plan had indeed been designed to bring down parts of the wall.[35] Given committed reputations and the high tension, a misfired gun could easily have led to fighting. Such a clash, Khrushchev recalled, might have escalated to war.[36] Kennedy himself noted in early October, "The chances of settling this without war are not yet too good."[37] In sum, participant Paul Nitze's conclusion that "the risks were great and miscalculation on either side was our greatest potential enemy" seems justified.[38]

At issue is how the actors allowed themselves to get so far out on the slippery slope. The root of the crisis lies in Moscow's view of Berlin's role in the east-west power balance. Khrushchev's first move came in November 1958, when he announced that the wartime allies must turn Berlin into a "free city," meaning the allies must leave. Were this not done within six months, Moscow would sign a separate peace with the German Democratic Republic (GDR), making western access to Berlin contingent on East German kindness.[39] The threat was real: while Russia avoided responsibility, the East Germans could squeeze the United States, Britain, and France out of West Berlin though blockades and harassment. Khrushchev let his ultimatum slide in May 1959, but a struggle over Berlin's fate had begun.

Declassified documents reveal Moscow's motives.[40] The Soviets were acting defensively to protect their position in eastern Europe from the rise of West Germany and the steady decline of the GDR. In 1958, the main Russian concern was the growth of West Germany's army, particularly its nuclearization by the United States. By 1960–61, when the crisis reached its height, the key problem was the drain on East Germany's economy caused by the flight of refugees into West Berlin.[41] At stake was not just the European balance. Berlin and Germany were symbols of the whole cold war struggle, as Khrushchev noted. Moscow had to demonstrate the advantages of the socialist system of production. Should East Germany's economy collapse, it would have had repercussions for Russia's global position.[42] And that collapse, according to internal reports, seemed "inevitable" by mid-1961 unless something drastic was done.[43]

Soviet fears of decline had their origins in U.S. decisions in the early

1950s to make the Federal Republic of Germany (FRG) the key NATO conventional power and to nuclearize its army and NATO central-front forces in Germany. In 1957, Konrad Adenauer's government rejected all demands to suspend nuclearization. In October 1958, the Soviet ambassador in Bonn told East German leader Walter Ulbricht that Moscow's goal was at least to delay West German armament by two to three years.[44] The economic situation was also bad. West Germany's economic miracle was not only hurting GDR's relative power, but it was drawing away its most productive individuals. Reforms were having only a minimal effect. Ulbricht told Moscow in October 1958 that the 1957 passport law, while reducing the refugee total, had increased the number leaving through West Berlin from 60 percent in 1957 to over 90 percent by the end of 1958. Anticipated decline led to Khrushchev's first tentative probing through the ultimatum in November. Eisenhower stood firm, however. This led Khrushchev to retreat in March 1959 and call for a four-power conference to discuss the German question. But Khrushchev had not given up. As he told Ulbricht, "the conditions are not ripe as yet for a new scheme of things."[45]

The crisis was reignited by Khrushchev's announcement in June 1961 that a new six-month deadline existed to solve the Berlin question along the lines of the 1958 ultimatum. The Soviets were again responding to a deteriorating situation: the acceleration of East German economic decline. Moscow thus sought to halt the refugee exodus and in the process achieve de facto western recognition of both the GDR and the division of Europe.

The refugee situation and the GDR economy had been getting progressively worse through 1959–60. In November to December 1960, Khrushchev and Ulbricht met in Moscow to discuss the problem. Only a renewed threat of a peace treaty with East Germany, Khrushchev felt, would push the west to work out a stabilizing solution.[46] His position was straightforward: if there were no progress on Berlin, "the position of the West, particularly West Germany would be strengthened."[47] Ulbricht was so worried about his economy that he initially rejected an early treaty. Given East German dependence on the FRG, he explained, a treaty would lead to West German economic retaliation, which would only exacerbate East Germany's decline.[48]

Ulbricht wanted Soviet help. In late November, he had informed Khrushchev of measures needed to strengthen the GDR's economy. By the end of their meetings, Khrushchev agreed "to take over almost completely the East German economy . . . in order to save it."[49] Only then did Ulbricht accept the possibility of a peace treaty should other options fail. Khrushchev had his own price, however. Two years of economic reforms had not reduced the GDR's vulnerability to the West German economy; this dependence had to end, he argued.[50] Khrushchev's goals were thus twofold: to stem his satellite's economic decline—even at some short-term cost to Russia—and to ensure that if western powers would not leave Berlin, then at least a viable East German state would be secured. To achieve these goals without a major crisis was his preference.

Unfortunately, despite Khrushchev's renewed commitment the situation continued to deteriorate. From January to June 1961, 100,000 refugees left the GDR.[51] Three of every four were under the age of forty-five, and in addition to the flight of the intelligentsia, the GDR was losing its most skilled factory workers and engineers. These departures were having a devastating effect on the economy of East Germany.[52] For Khrushchev, this "unstable situation" was undermining the whole socialist movement.[53] Compounding this were the massive injections of economic aid: if the East German economy could not be stabilized soon, *Soviet* economic growth might be severely damaged.[54]

At the Warsaw Pact meeting in March, Ulbricht called for increased border controls, including a barbed-wire fence between the two Berlins. By mid-May, Moscow faced a new problem: the anxious East Germans might take independent action to close the border. This increased the risks of a military escalation that Khrushchev was hoping to minimize. On 19 May, Soviet ambassador Mikhail Pervukhin reported to Moscow that the East Germans wanted to reduce the exodus to prevent further economic decline. Yet in seeking an end to Berlin's occupation, "our German friends sometimes exercise impatience . . . not always studying the interests of the entire socialist camp."[55]

The June summit with Kennedy did not go well. Khrushchev's heavy-handed tactics failed to secure concessions. Afterward, the Soviet attaché in the GDR, Yuli Kvitsinsky, wrote that East German patience was growing thin. The East Germans believed it was now time to sign a peace treaty to resolve the West Berlin issue. They felt that this measure was "connected with a certain risk, but there is even more risk in further delay of the resolution of the issue, since any delay assists the growth of militarism in West Germany which increase the danger of a world war."[56] By early July, Ulbricht was talking as though the peace treaty would be soon signed, with East Germany then controlling all access routes to Berlin, *including* those in the air.[57] The threat to close air routes was especially worrisome to the Kremlin—in 1948 the Soviets had carefully avoided interfering with the western airlift to avoid a direct clash. The chance that East German impatience might cause an escalation to superpower war was rising.

The East Germans were in a good bargaining position, however, given the importance Moscow placed on the GDR's viability. In June, Anastas Mikoyan visited East Berlin for economic discussions, telling the East Germans that the GDR was critical to proving that Communism was the superior model. Hence, "We must do everything so that your development constantly and steadily goes forward. . . . We cannot and must not lose out to West Germany."[58] The primary means to stabilize East German decline was ending the refugee problem. Ambassador Pervukhin wrote to Foreign Minister Andrei Gromyko on 4 July that any peace treaty must establish a regime over movement between the two halves of Berlin. If necessary, the border should be closed, although Pervukhin thought this was both technically and politically a difficult step.[59]

Moscow, however, was becoming increasingly concerned with the growing time pressures caused by decline. In early July, Ulbricht informed Khrushchev that if the present situation continued, "collapse is inevitable" and he "could not guarantee that he could keep the situation under control this time." The East Germans themselves were beginning to worry about escalation. The problem, as the GDR secret police chief told officials on 7 July, was that western powers might overestimate their military power. Thus, "in spite of the [true] correlation of forces, the danger of open conflict exists."[60] Khrushchev needed a stop-gap measure to reduce the pressure. At the 3 August meeting of the Warsaw Pact, Ulbricht restated his demand to close the border between the two Berlins. Soon after, Khrushchev accepted the wall as the best way to avoid more extreme options, at least at this stage of the crisis.[61]

In acting, Khrushchev knew that he was taking risks. But the risks of doing nothing were even greater. In early August, Khrushchev told Warsaw Pact officials that without eastern bloc help, the GDR would not survive. Then "the [West German army] . . . would come closer to our Soviet border." Should this happened, "it would cost us . . . significantly more not only in the political, but also in the material [sense] than it [would cost] to help the GDR and strengthen it. By strengthening its position, we strengthen our position."[62] The Americans ultimately did not try to knock the wall down. Yet when Khrushchev decided to build it, a U.S. response was seen as likely. As Ulbricht told Khrushchev in mid-September, "the enemy took fewer countermeasures [over the wall] than expected."[63] The U.S. government was seen as potentially unstable since hawks were in a position to drive policy. "Hence everything is possible in the United States," Khrushchev told east European leaders in early August. "War is also possible. They can unleash it."[64]

In sum, the evidence upholds the hypothesis that leaders will accept significantly greater risks of major war when, because of the relative success of the other's policies, decline will continue unless stronger measures are taken. Other arguments find less support. To be sure, Khrushchev's personality affected his willingness to take risks. Yet information supporting the need for urgent action came from lower-level sources, and the rest of the Politburo apparently agreed with Khrushchev's actions. This consensus suggests that neither personality nor factional infighting was determinative.[65]

Classical realism and hegemonic stability theory can explain Soviet willingness to be more assertive: from Sputnik in 1957 to 1961, there was at least the perception of greater Soviet strategic power. Hegemonic stability theory, however, cannot explain why the Kremlin acted from the pessimism caused by anticipated decline. To the extent that classical realists and neorealists incorporate decline, they can explain the motives behind the Soviet moves. Yet, like Berlin 1948, the case illustrates how easily bipolar systems are upset by oscillations in the balance of power. It also reinforces the need for a more complete decision-making model, one that shows how declining states weigh the risks of continued decline against the risks of inadvertent escalation (factoring in the extent to which crisis initiation can help avert the decline).

KENNEDY, KHRUSHCHEV, AND THE CUBAN MISSILE CRISIS

The Cuban missile crisis is generally cited as the point in cold war history where the superpowers came the closest to all-out nuclear war. President Kennedy himself estimated the probability of nuclear war at the height of the crisis as between one-third and one-half, and two of his closest advisers agree.[66]

At issue is why, over missiles in Cuba, Kennedy would initiate a crisis that risked nuclear war, and why he would ratchet up the risk as the crisis progressed. Many might argue that Khrushchev initiated the crisis by placing missiles in Cuba, but this is incorrect. Khrushchev's move, while provocative, was technically a buildup of forces within the larger Soviet sphere. It was not only allowed by international law, but it was equivalent to the U.S. deployment of intermediate-range missiles in Turkey in 1961–62. We do not talk about the "Turkish missile crisis" of March 1962 because the Soviets, exposed in late 1961 as inferior in strategic nuclear power and lacking any viable means to prevent the U.S. deployment, chose to do nothing. Similarly, Kennedy could have done nothing in October 1962. Instead, he consciously raised the risk of an inadvertent escalation to nuclear war to compel Moscow to withdraw the missiles. U.S. nuclear predominance and naval superiority in the Caribbean gave him the confidence to think that Khrushchev would probably comply.

Washington brought on the crisis period for preventive reasons and with two main goals: (1) the protection of the U.S. homeland from a marked shift in the strategic balance, and (2) the maintenance of allied confidence in U.S. extended deterrence. The conventional view has been distorted by accounts from participants of Kennedy's ExComm, the select group established in the first week of the crisis to advise the president. These participants have overwhelmingly emphasized just the second objective. They likely did so to ensure alliance unity. To have revealed how much narrow security interests drove U.S. decision-making might have pushed allies toward neutralism, especially since NATO wishes were compromised by the secret trade of Turkish missiles. Nevertheless, participants have fostered the illusion that they believed Cuban missiles changed the balance of power only in perception, not in reality.[67]

The president himself was instrumental in propagating this account. In a nationally televised interview on 17 December 1962, he said: "The Soviets were not . . . intending to fire [the missiles], because if they were going to get into a nuclear struggle, they have their own missiles in the Soviet Union. But it would have politically changed the balance of power. It would have appeared to, and appearances contribute to reality." He then underscored Soviet unwillingness to accept a peaceful world of separate spheres.[68] The implication: the Cuban crisis was only about preventing Soviet gains on the periphery. America acted for the good of the alliance, not for itself.[69]

Preventing the disintegration of the alliance was indeed critical to U.S. actions. In the game of geopolitics, small states are essential, in their totality, to a great power's total resource base. Allowing Moscow to place missiles in the American backyard would have undermined allied confidence in U.S. power and resolve. Allies might have defected from the U.S. sphere, producing a dramatic shift in the balance of global economic and potential power.[70]

Yet U.S. policy-makers also worried about a significant and real shift in the nuclear balance. By the last week of the crisis, it was accepted that the missiles would mean at least a 50 percent increase in Soviet first-strike capability. Even more worrisome were future missile deliveries to Cuba. Without strong action, therefore, the United States faced a loss of superiority and even potential vulnerability to a first strike. Moreover, negating this vulnerability later might only make matters worse. An August report had warned that Soviet leaders might launch preventive nuclear war should they ever come to believe that they had temporary but waning superiority. Thus by late October, the ExComm was determined to prevent the missiles from becoming operational by any means, including an invasion of Cuba.

In what follows, I show that U.S. decision-making during the crisis was driven by the preventive logic of the model described in chapter 2.[71] Most critical was preventing a sharp negative oscillation resulting from the anticipated success of the Soviet deployment relative to any internal measures Washington could take to counter it. In acting, Kennedy and his advisers calibrated the risks of inadvertent nuclear war against the risks of decline and the anticipated likelihood that certain hard-line options would in fact avert decline. The severity of decline drove the severity of policy: the more U.S. officials believed that decline would be deep in the absence of stronger action, the more risks of nuclear war they were willing to accept.[72] Domestic-level factors had little influence on decision-making, except as occasional obstacles to the main goals. Kennedy and the ExComm weighed options according to what would further U.S. security, not what would serve the internal interests of any individual or group.

The Lead-up to the Crisis

To put U.S. behavior in October into context, one must understand the rising anxiety over the previous four months. On 9 July, Kennedy was given a new National Intelligence Estimate, which focused on strategic power trends. Its conclusions were not encouraging. The pace of the Soviet ICBM program had increased, and Soviet bombers were integrated into plans for a ballistic missile attack. These delivery vehicles were equipped with bombs hundreds of times more powerful than the Hiroshima weapon. The implications were stark: in a preemptive attack, Russia might soon be able to hit U.S. bases and still be able to respond to a U.S. retaliation.[73] Kennedy immediately asked that a special committee of key departments be formed to study the NIE's implications and report within a month.[74]

On 23 August, a detailed analysis signed by the secretaries of State and Defense, the CIA director, and the chairman of the Joint Chiefs was presented to Kennedy. Moscow was heightening efforts to achieve parity as soon as possible. Although U.S. superiority would likely continue as long as programs approved in 1961 were implemented, the biggest danger lay with Soviet perceptions. War might occur if Soviet leaders came to believe that they had achieved temporary military superiority that would then quickly erode. To avoid increased Soviet risk-taking driven by perceived decline, Washington had to act "to see to it that this military advantage does not occur."[75] The report thus underscored that should the Soviets ever see a marked shift in the strategic balance in their favor, subsequent U.S. efforts to catch up would increase the chance of war.[76]

Turning to pre-crisis preparations, we can trace American fears of Cuban missiles back to August 1962.[77] On 21 August, Kennedy's staff met to discuss accelerating Soviet aid to Cuba. From CIA director John McCone's minutes of the meeting:

> There was general agreement that the situation was critical. . . . There was discussion of various courses of action open to us in case the Soviets place MRBM [medium-range ballistic] missiles on Cuban territory. . . . It was felt that . . . drastic action on a missile site or other military installations of the Soviets in Cuba would bring about similar action by the Soviets with respect to our bases and numerous missile sites, particularly in Turkey and Southern Italy.[78]

On 23 August, the group met with the president, who asked about options against Soviet missiles in Cuba: whether "we [could] take them out by air or would a ground offensive be necessary."[79] A presidential National Security Action Memorandum was issued after this meeting. Reflecting the group's preventive thinking, it directed the Department of Defense to study "various military alternatives which might be adopted . . . to eliminate any installations in Cuba capable of launching nuclear attack on the US. What would be the pros and cons, for example, of pinpoint attack, general counter-force attack, and outright invasion?" With Cuba likely to grow stronger "with the passage of time," America had to be ready.[80]

A 19 September CIA estimate prepared for Kennedy noted that Soviet MRBMs and IRBMs (intermediate range—twice that of the MRBMs) in Cuba, acting as the equivalent of ICBMs, would represent "a significant strike capability" and "would increase the total weight of the attack which could be delivered against the U.S. in the event of general war."[81] The military would not be caught unprepared. Through September, the military developed two main contingency plans: OPLAN 312, or air strikes against Cuba; and OPLAN 316, a full-scale invasion seven days after air strikes began.[82] Secretary of Defense Robert McNamara and the Joint Chiefs met on 1 October to discuss the plans. They decided to prepare for a blockade of Cuba to support any required operation. The next day, McNamara told the Joint Chiefs, "The political objectives of the [plans] were defined as the removal of the threat of Soviet offensive weapon systems, and if, necessary, the removal of the Castro regime to assure the permanent removal of these weapons." On 6 October, OPLANs 316 and 312 were ordered to the highest state of readiness.[83]

In short, well over a week before the "surprise" discovery of the MRBMs and the official start of the Cuban missile crisis (Tuesday, 16 October), the United States was readying itself for preventive military action against missiles in Cuba. This was not due to inherent U.S. aggressiveness or a will to take risks; in September, Mongoose Plan B, calling for covert means to overthrow Castro, was still the main plan. The shift to emphasis on OPLANs 312 and 316 was simply the result of increasing evidence that Cuba was turning into a Soviet missile base.

The First Week of the Crisis

On Tuesday morning, 16 October, Kennedy was told that the existence of a MRBM base in Cuba had been confirmed. The first meeting of the Ex-Comm was held at 11:50 A.M. Significantly, given the common division of the ExComm into hawks and doves, every person held one and only one opinion—that immediate military action was necessary. Also significant is the tangible sense of time pressure, the feeling that action had to be taken before the missiles became operational. This feeling would grow until 28 October, the day Khrushchev agreed to remove the missiles. These two points support the argument that faced with an impending power shift, officials who see few options will support preventive measures that increase the risk of major war, regardless of their bureaucratic position.

In the first meeting, Kennedy's first major question was: "How long have we got . . . before it can be fired?"[84] McNamara noted that it was very critical in formulating plans to know "the time between today and the time when the readiness to fire capability develops." The best estimate was two weeks. This helps explain the relatively calm debate over the next two days and the shock felt on Friday when the CIA revealed not only that many more missiles existed, some of them ICBMs, but that some were already operational. Discussion for the rest of the meeting focused on which military option was most appropriate, not whether military action should be chosen. McNamara noted that any air strike must be "fairly extensive" and must happen before the missile sites became operational; "[this] is extremely important." Revealing prior planning, he said that the strike could be executed within days and that the military was prepared to follow it by "an invasion, both by air and by sea."

Halfway through the meeting, Kennedy switched to a discussion of Russian motives for deploying the missiles. His first remark, and the remarks that followed, are significant:

> JFK: What is the, uh, advant- . . . Must be some major reason for the Russians to, uh, set this up as a . . . Must be that they're not satisfied with their ICBMs. What'd be the reason that they would, uh . . .
>
> [Joints Chiefs of Staff Chairman] Taylor: . . . it'd make the launching base, uh, for short range missiles against the United States to supplement their rather defective ICBM system.

Secretary of State Dean Rusk added:

> Khrushchev . . . knows that we have a substantial nuclear superiority, but he also knows that we don't really live under fear of his nuclear weapons to the extent that . . . he has to live under fear of ours. Also we have nuclear weapons nearby, in Turkey and places like that.

This was the only discussion of Soviet motives in the first meeting.[85] It shows that ExComm members, including Kennedy, instantly grasped that the Soviets were using Cuban missiles as a quick means to strategic parity.[86]

In the last half of the meeting, the president summarized the policy options, all military ones: a surgical air strike, a general air strike, and an invasion. Reflecting the group's manifest sense of the declining trend, he told the ExComm: "I don't think we got much time on these missiles. . . . We can't wait two weeks while we're getting ready to roll. Maybe we just have to just take them out, and continue our other preparations [i.e., for invasion] if we decide to do that." He added: "We're certainly going to do [the surgical strike]; we're going to take out these missiles." The first meeting thus ended with Kennedy's tentative decision for immediate air strikes, possibly to be followed by a general air strike or invasion.

The blockade option that was eventually chosen was not introduced until the second meeting that day, beginning at 6:30 P.M. Significantly, when McNamara suggested it, no one took it up; discussion continued to focus on military options.[87] It was also in this meeting that McNamara, for the first time, broached the possibility that the Cuban missiles were not a real threat to the United States. National Security Advisor McGeorge Bundy, after observing that the group was now fixed on military action, had asked how gravely the Cuban missiles changed the strategic balance. McNamara's response: "not at all." In this opinion, McNamara stood alone. Only the next day would the idea gain even limited acceptance. In deflecting the common postcrisis argument that the missiles constituted not a real shift in the balance of power, only the perception of it, one should remember that when McNamara made his comment, and for the next two days, only 12 medium-range missile launchers had been spotted. Given the 75 ICBM launchers estimated for the Soviet arsenal, this was only a 16 percent increase in strategic missiles. By Saturday, however, 36 to 40 launchers, including IRBMs covering most of the United States, had been identified. This perceived increase of 50 percent was the figure accepted by Kennedy thereafter[88]—and this was only the first installment of Soviet missiles to Cuba.

Even in the Tuesday evening meeting, Joint Chiefs Chairman Maxwell Taylor instantly grasped the problem that the missile total could grow, telling McNamara:

> You're quite right in saying that these, these are just a few more missiles, uh, targeted on the United States. Uh, however, they *can* become a, a very, a rather important adjunct and reinforcement to the, to the strike capability of the Soviet Union. We have no idea how far they will go.

It was the president who then jumped in to agree:

> let's just say that, uh, they get, they get these in there and then you can't, uh, they get sufficient capacity so we can't, uh, with warheads. Then you don't want to knock 'em out [because], uh, there's too much of a gamble. Then they just begin to buildup those air bases there and then put [in] more and more.

Taylor continued that America would face "the same kind of, of pistol-pointed-at-the-head situation as we have [against] the Soviet Union at the present time." JFK replied that this "shows [why] the Bay of Pigs was really right," that is, why he had been right to try to eliminate Castro early on, before the situation got worse.[89] Kennedy later agreed that the missiles were also a challenge to U.S. resolve. The two U.S. objectives for opposing the missiles were now established: the protection of the U.S. homeland, and the maintenance of credible extended deterrence to ensure U.S. control over the periphery's potential power.

For the bureaucratic politics model, the behavior exhibited in this second meeting is puzzling. Attorney General Robert F. Kennedy, far from being a "dove from the start,"[90] was the most hawkish ExComm member; he tried to push the group toward the most extreme option—invasion. The secretary of defense and the chairman of the Joint Chiefs were more cautious. McNamara warned of the risks of military action. Although Taylor favored a general strike, he opposed invasion, and even stated that the Chiefs preferred no action to a limited strike, since the latter might invite Soviet retaliation. The president replied that he would not let the Chiefs' reluctance block the invasion option.[91]

The domestic-level argument also does poorly. Other than one comment by McNamara in the second meeting that the issue was a "domestic-political" one, there was no mention on 16 October that such considerations were important. McNamara's words are used by those arguing that domestic reasons, not national security, drove U.S. officials.[92] Yet the transcripts show that McNamara was just observing that Kennedy's public pronouncements, in which he had stated that he would "act" if offensive missiles were found in Cuba, did not mean only military options had to be considered. The blockade option was therefore still viable. In short, McNamara was not suggesting that the crisis be used to further the Democrats' chances for reelection, as the domestic argument contends. Rather, he was simply pondering the best means to national security and noting that domestic politics did not constrain U.S. choices.[93]

To summarize the first day, it is clear that, aside from McNamara in the second meeting, all participants maintained three core beliefs: first, the missiles constituted an unacceptable shift in the power balance, one that would directly threaten the U.S. homeland while undermining extended deterrence; second, the Soviets acted to shore up their weak strategic position; and third, preventive military action had to be taken quickly, since the missiles would soon be operational. Such thinking fits the predictions of dynamic differentials theory. Faced with impending decline, and with no internal or diplomatic options to reverse it, American officials readied themselves for a violent confrontation—despite the clear risks of escalation to major war.

For the next three days—from Wednesday until Friday—all but one of the ExComm meetings was held without JFK, who was away from Washington or busy with prearranged meetings. Debate revolved around two main options, the general air strike and the blockade. On Wednesday, a smaller ExComm met three times at the State Department. Here emerged a key point that would eventually shift the group toward the blockade—not the reaction of Moscow or the American people, but that of the allies. It became apparent that a surprise U.S. attack would damage one of the two objectives—the allies' allegiance. As RFK stated on Wednesday, the allies would see the United States as a "hysterical" great power if it attacked Cuba without trying some form of nonmilitary action first.[94]

The group adjourned Wednesday without a consensus on the best option.[95] Surprisingly (for the bureaucratic politics model), Secretary of State Dean Rusk was a strong hawk, arguing for immediate strikes against the missiles and then preparation for invasion. The president himself still leaned toward a quick military action.[96]

On Thursday morning, 18 October, an ExComm meeting was held with Kennedy.[97] Rusk began the discussion by arguing for military strikes. He reiterated the two key reasons: preventing a dangerous shift in the military balance, and avoiding losses on the periphery. Cuba would not be just "an incidental base for a few of these things," he stressed, but rather a "powerful military problem" both in any direct contest with Russia and in terms of the overall global struggle.

In recommending military action, Rusk acknowledged that it involved "very high risks indeed." Moscow might retaliate against Berlin or Korea, or even against the United States itself. A repetition of 1914 might occur, "where certain events brought about a general situation which at the time none of the governments involved could avoid." These comments show that even normally cautious individuals, faced with steep decline, are disposed to steps that knowingly risk inadvertent major war. Yet not all officials wanted to get this far out on the slippery slope, or at least not yet. A note from Charles Bohlen, former ambassador to Moscow, was read, stating that since action against Cuba "would greatly increase the probability of general war," he favored trying diplomacy first. Llewellyn Thompson, another former ambassador to Moscow, argued strongly for the blockade. Rusk found support from JCS Chairman Taylor, who stressed that Moscow were making Cuba into a "forward base of major proportions."

Kennedy wanted to know whether his option, a general air strike, might lead to nuclear weapons being used against the United States. McNamara felt that the Soviets would not authorize their use, but they might be unable to stop the Cubans from doing so. Escalation scenarios were discussed. Khrushchev would have to respond strongly to any attack on Cuba, McNamara argued. Kennedy said the United States might have to allow a Soviet occupation of Berlin, but others objected that Washington was required to defend the city. This might mean a clash of U.S. and Soviet troops, which, a number of ExComm members noted, would lead to "general war."

Kennedy summarized the dilemma: striking Cuba would hurt the alliance, since allies would feel that Washington was exposing them to the risks of general war. Yet if Washington failed to act, then the alliance would deteriorate. The latter problem was more dire, he concluded. Hence the real question was what action against the missiles would maintain alliance unity while "lessen[ing] the chances of a nuclear exchange which obviously is the final failure."[98]

The stark risks were evident. Yet through the meeting's last half, military action was simply assumed as the preferred option, with discussion focusing on how to implement it politically. The problem was again dynamic trends: the missile sites were under rapid construction, and, as RFK noted, the blockade was a slow means to the end. Assuming the general air strike as the course of action, the president said that he could announce on Friday that missiles were found, and call Congress back into session. Then, "we go ahead Saturday and take them out." After all, "The race is against those missiles."[99]

As the meeting ended, no formal decision was made. Two things were resolved, however: the limited strike and purely diplomatic options were out. Only two courses, the blockade and the general strike (with invasion likely to follow), were now up for consideration. It was agreed to have two groups investigate the options and report back to Kennedy after he returned from campaigning. Importantly, the blockade was seen at best only as a first step, since it was to be "followed by such further actions as appeared necessary as the situation evolved."[100]

Early on Friday morning, there was new information that additional sites existed, some with IRBMs. At 9:45 A.M., the Joint Chiefs briefed Kennedy on their views and recommended the general strike. Kennedy, wrestling with the tradeoffs, explained his dilemma: the strike would reduce the chance of missiles being used against the United States, while securing U.S. leadership in Latin America. Yet there was bound to be a reprisal from Moscow, which left him only the alternative of beginning a nuclear exchange. Yet Kennedy also noted a problem with the blockade. Its supposed advantage—that it reduced the risk of escalation to nuclear war—was false; Moscow would go after Berlin anyway, and the Cuban missiles would remain in place. Kennedy thus left the impression that he favored the military strike as the lesser of two horrific evils, even if he was now clearly concerned about the risks of escalation.[101]

By 11:00 A.M., when the ExComm met without Kennedy, Bundy undermined a consensus toward the blockade which had emerged the previous evening.[102] He related his meeting with the president that morning, observing that a blockade would only work over time while the military option was quick and effective.[103] Subsequent discussion showed a split between advocates of immediate military action (Bundy, Taylor, former Secretary of State Dean Acheson, Treasury Secretary Douglas Dillon) and those favoring the blockade (RFK and McNamara).

At the meeting the CIA unveiled the new evidence on the extent of the buildup. There were up to forty launchers in Cuba, not just twelve, and sixteen were IRBMs covering almost the whole of continental United States. Adding to the shock, at least two of the MRBM sites could now be considered "operational" (on Tuesday, the CIA had said it would take two weeks). After presenting this evidence, Arthur Lundahl, director of the National Photographic Interpretation Center, recalled that ExComm members became jittery and nervous.[104] Their anxiety was no doubt heightened by a CIA Special Estimate distributed that day. MRBMs and IRBMs in Cuba would increase limited Soviet ICBM capability, it indicated, since Cuban missiles could hit similar targets with equivalent warheads. Moreover, they were more accurate, while "for a preemptive or first strike, Cuban-based missiles would possess an advantage over Soviet-based ICBMs in that they would approach the U.S. with a shorter time-of-flight, and from a direction not now covered by U.S. BMEWS [Ballistic Missile Early Warning] capabilities." Then there was the problem of future installments. Should Washington accept the current missiles, Moscow would then simply add more MRBMs which it already had "in quantity." The report ended: "in the near future, therefore, Soviet gross capabilities for initial attack on U.S. military and civilian targets can be increased considerably by Cuban-based missiles."[105]

The impact of anticipated decline on the inner circle can be seen in a comment by Robert Kennedy that day. On Tuesday night, he had briefly mused about the possible advantages of fighting a nuclear war with Russia now rather than later.[106] In the Friday session, with the situation now more perilous, RFK expressed his opinion with more forcefulness. From the minutes:

> At different times the possibility of nuclear conflict breaking out was referred to. The point was made that once the Cuban missile installations were complete and operational, a new strategic situation would exist, with the United States more directly and immediately under the gun than ever before. . . . During this discussion, the Attorney General said that in looking forward into the future it would be better for our children and grandchildren if we decided to face the Soviet threat, stand up to it, and eliminate it, now. The circumstances for doing so at some future time were bound to be more unfavorable, the risks would be greater, the chances of success less good.[107]

The group's sense of a negative dynamic—of a terrible future situation that had to be prevented by present action—is tangible to say the least.

On Saturday 20 October, RFK and McNamara visited the National Photographic Interpretation Center to confirm the operational status of the IRBM sites. They were shown photos substantiating the rapid pace of site construction. Both men agreed, however, that the sites could still be eliminated if attacked soon.[108] At 2:30 P.M., a full National Security Council meeting began. The president had no doubts about the missiles' military significance: "In his view the existence of fifty [bombers] in Cuba did not affect the balance of power, but the missiles already in Cuba were an entirely different matter."[109] He still leaned toward the military option. A blockade, he argued, would allow more missiles to become operational, increasing the threat. RFK took a middle position: start with the blockade, but give Moscow only a short time to respond. If it did not immediately stop developing the bases, then the air strike should proceed. The president was convinced. He made the decision to initiate a blockade but still prepare for air strikes by Monday or Tuesday. He also authorized final preparations for a full-scale invasion of Cuba.[110]

The next morning Kennedy met Taylor, McNamara, RFK, and General Walter Sweeney (commander of Tactical Air Command) to discuss military details. McNamara confirmed the figure of forty launchers in Cuba, approximately a 50 percent increase in Soviet strategic missile power.[111] This figure, a product of CIA analysis,[112] became part of the discourse for the rest of the crisis. The missiles' significance was clear. The next day, Kennedy confided to the British prime minister that "the build-up in Cuba, if completed, would double the number of missiles the Soviets could bring to bear on the U.S. They would also overcome our warning system which does not face south. Furthermore, the short distance involving short times of flight would tempt them to make a first strike."[113] Policy-makers saw their dilemma. A military adviser briefed Vice-President Lyndon Johnson on Sunday that opinions varied as to whether Moscow would retaliate against U.S. bases in Turkey should America attack Cuba. "[The] risks involved in eliminating the situation are grave. Yet as time goes on, not only the risks but the magnitude and number of them are certain to increase. No amount of discussion . . . is going to moderate these unpleasant realities."[114]

On Monday, 22 October, Kennedy was not terribly optimistic. At 3:00 P.M., just hours before his national address, he told the National Security Council that despite the blockade, he might still end up having to invade Cuba. Even a blockade would force Khrushchev to respond, perhaps against Berlin or even against the United States.[115]

A meeting at 11:00 A.M. with core advisers revealed other concerns.[116] Discussion focused on reducing the risks of escalation to nuclear war if Cuba was hit. On Saturday, Kennedy had asked that U.S. personnel in Turkey manning the missiles be told not to fire back if fired upon. McNamara now explained that the Joint Chiefs assured him these instructions were already out. Kennedy replied that the message must be reinforced, "since as I say we may be attacking the Cubans, and the reprisal may come; and we don't want them firing on our nuclear weapons."[117]

Assistant Secretary of Defense Nitze then observed that "NATO's strategic concept requires the immediate execution of EDP in such an event [as an attack on Turkish missiles]." Kennedy asked, "What's EDP?" Nitze replied: "The European Defense Plan, which is nuclear war. So that means . . . " Kennedy, his voice rising in anger, cut Nitze off in mid-sentence: "Now that's why we ordered [them] to get on that," meaning why he wanted to ensure that any orders to respond were not carried out without his authorization. Kennedy could not have been pleased with what he was hearing. On the one hand, advisers were saying that standing instructions to U.S. personnel in Turkey were that they should not return fire. On the other hand, he was now told it was standard operating procedure to go to nuclear war should Turkish missiles be hit! The stark uncertainties associated with removing the Cuban missiles were now staring him in the face. Nonetheless, their continued construction would push Kennedy to assume such risks as the week wore on.

The Last Week of the Crisis

On Monday night, Kennedy announced to the world the existence of Soviet missiles and his planned steps to halt the buildup. He did not reveal that by Tuesday the Strategic Air Command would go to DEFCON 2, its highest level of alert in the cold war. He did warn, however, that he would regard any nuclear missiles launched from Cuba against any nation in the Western Hemisphere as an attack on the United States, requiring a "full retaliatory response upon the Soviet Union."[118]

The Soviets were not about to take this lying down. Back in September, Khrushchev had decided to support Russian troops in Cuba with tactical nuclear weapons and nuclear-tipped cruise missiles. The warheads for those weapons and for the MRBMs and IL-28 bombers had begun to arrive in Cuba on 4 October.[119] Now, on 22 October, Khrushchev faced a possible clash of U.S.-Soviet forces over Cuba. With word of Kennedy's impending speech, Khrushchev held a special Presidium meeting. Russia had to be ready for the worst, he said. "They can attack us, and we shall respond. . . . This may end in a big war."[120]

He outlined different scenarios, including a U.S. military attack or blockade on Cuba. With 41,000 Soviet troops on the island no match for the forces the Americans could throw at Cuba, the Presidium authorized the use of tactical nuclear weapons against any U.S. invasion. The Soviet commander in Cuba, General Issa Pliyev, could employ these weapons without first checking with Moscow. But he was not to fire MRBMs and IRBMs without a direct Kremlin order.[121] Since Kennedy had already decided to invade should diplomacy fail, the possibility of a nuclear exchange was very real.[122]

On Tuesday, the Kremlin received Ambassador Anatoly Dobrynin's analysis of U.S. motives. Confidential information indicated that Kennedy's advisers were worried about America's deteriorating position and were determined to stop any further decline. The U.S. military in particular feared that the American strategic advantage was being liquidated.[123] This report accurately captured the ExComm's preventive motivations. Yet by reinforcing 1960–62 reports that the U.S. military might want war,[124] it probably also strengthened Khrushchev's view that nuclear parity had to be reached—and soon. Yet as both sides made moves that further committed their reputations, the risks being taken to shape the strategic balance were now dangerously high.

On the Tuesday, Washington secured Organization of American States' approval of the blockade. The Russians confronted the U.S. Navy, but did not run the blockade. By Friday, site construction in Cuba was continuing at a feverish pace despite the quarantine, and Khrushchev showed every sign of trying to play for time. During the day Kennedy sent word to Khrushchev that he would soon take action to remove the missiles if Moscow did not. That night a private letter was received from Khrushchev indicating that he would withdraw the missiles if Washington pledged publicly not to invade Cuba. Optimism was dashed the next morning when a public announcement over Radio Moscow stated that, in addition to the pledge, Washington must also withdraw U.S. missiles from Turkey.

This upping of the ante, and the shooting down of a U2 over Cuba, created the profound pessimism of "Black Saturday," 27 October 1962. After much debate, the ExComm decided to respond formally only to the first letter, accepting Khrushchev's terms. Through RFK's backchannel with Dobrynin, however, a secret proposal was made Saturday night, offering Turkish missiles in exchange for the withdrawal of Cuban missiles. A select group had met at 8:00 P.M. to approve this plan, knowing many ExComm members opposed any trade. Should word leak that Washington had traded an ally's assets under pressure, the second U.S. objective—the credibility of extended deterrence—would be undermined.

Robert Kennedy relayed the offer to Dobrynin, and the group held their breath. Hopes were not high. Having made a public demand for the Turkish missiles, Khrushchev was unlikely to accept a private deal damaging the Soviet reputation. Moreover, many felt, particularly McNamara, that Moscow was simply buying time to make the missiles operational. McNamara's behavior that afternoon—his preoccupation with immediate military strikes, his lack of interest in further negotiations—suggests that he was now the ExComm's greatest pessimist.[125] Robert Kennedy later wrote that after he gave Dobrynin the 24-hour ultimatum and returned to the White House, "[the] President was not optimistic, nor was I. . . . He had not abandoned hope, but what hope there was now rested with Khrushchev's reversing his course within the next few hours. It was a hope, not an expectation. The expectation was a military confrontation by Tuesday and possibly tomorrow."[126] That U.S. policy-makers were in a position where military confrontation was now *expected* aligns with the theory: the need to remove the missiles was driving them to take extraordinary risks. If Khrushchev rejected the private offer, it would be hard for Kennedy to accept a public deal without destroying America's credibility and therefore its global position.[127]

Fortunately, Washington received word the next morning that Khrushchev would accept the private trade on Turkish missiles. The main part of the crisis was over. Dismantling of the missiles began soon after and, with the negative trend reversed, tension abated.

Much of this history of the last week of the crisis is well known. A few key details are not, mainly because ExComm members chose not to reveal them. The extent to which members were bombarded with information that the missiles were a significant and growing threat has been downplayed. Also minimized is the extent to which the State Department and White House collaborated, prior to Khrushchev's 27 October demand, to secure a secret deal on the Turkish missiles, knowing that NATO allies would not accept any such deal, public or private.

ExComm participants have argued that their focus was on maintaining the U.S. alliance system, while in fact they were equally concerned with the direct threat to the U.S. homeland. Yet here was the dilemma. It became clear through the last week that trading Turkish missiles was the key to getting rid of Cuban missiles and thus to achieving both U.S. ends. Yet this trade, should it have become known, would have undermined the extended-deterrence objective even as it maintained U.S. strategic preponderance. Hence the trade had to be denied for as long as possible. And when it was finally acknowledged,[128] participants had to make it appear that Kennedy had decided long before to remove the Turkish missiles, and that therefore there was no explicit "trade."

In what follows, I examine U.S. decision-making on a Turkish-Cuban missile deal as it occurred under the shadow of impending decline. The critical importance of the strategic balance was reinforced by two reports on Monday, 22 October. In the first, Bundy told Kennedy that in communicating with British Prime Minister Harold Macmillan, he should remember to include the point about future deployments, namely, that if the buildup in Cuba continued, "it would be a threat to the whole strategic balance of power, because really large numbers of missiles from this launch could create a first-strike temptation. . . . The missiles that are there now do not create this hazard, but a further build-up would."[129]

The second report was an analysis of Soviet motivations received by Walt Rostow, head of the ExComm Planning Subcommittee.[130] It concluded that the Soviets sought a military advantage to help them settle various regional problems, including Berlin, and to enable Moscow "to engage with maximum chance of success in a final military showdown with the U.S."[131]

At the 11:00 A.M. meeting on Monday, the group had discussed a Turkish-Cuban trade.[132] One hitch was noted in a report Bundy received that day: the United States retained only "custody" of the "warheads," meaning that the missiles themselves were the property of Turkey (the problem would be raised again on Saturday).[133] As for the attitudes of allies, including Turkey, reports were not favorable. On Tuesday, the U.S. ambassador to NATO, Thomas Finletter, sent word that the allies were upset over the lack of consultation. A delicate probing of Turkish feelings had begun after Monday night. On Wednesday, Rusk sent a telegram to both Finletter and Ambassador Raymond Hare in Ankara informing them that a negotiated solution might involve dismantling and removing the Jupiter missiles. Rusk noted that this would create serious politico-military problems for U.S.-Turkish relations within NATO. Hare was asked to assess the consequences of a removal, while Finletter was asked to comment on other allies' positions.[134]

In sending this telegram, Rusk knew that nothing was likely to occur quickly. On Tuesday he had received a report suggesting he press Turkey to announce a phase-out of the IRBMs as soon as a multilateral sea-based force (MLF) was in place.[135] Progress on MLF was a prerequisite to resolving the Turkish missile question, since Washington could not take any action which might make Ankara feel "pressed to give up the weapons against [its] will."[136]

Time, however, was of the essence. On Tuesday, the CIA reported that the three confirmed IRBM sites were under rapid construction.[137] On Wednesday, Rostow gave Bundy two analyses from his subcommittee, and Bundy no doubt forwarded their findings to Kennedy. The first argued that the issue of taking out the Cuban missiles was increasing in urgency, since Moscow was trying to settle for what was already on the island and what it could later smuggle in.[138]

The second report provided the subcommittee's view on Soviet motives and on U.S. policy. The recent American buildup had undermined Soviet calculations. Moscow "consequently needed quickly to redress the balance, and at the same time to convince the U.S. that it had been redressed, or more than redressed." Otherwise, it would face "a grave, and perhaps growing, disadvantage" in the cold war struggle. The Cuban missiles reversed this trend. Thus U.S. interests would be "seriously jeopardized" if Washington did "not follow up a refusal by the USSR to liquidate the bases by forcefully liquidating them ourselves." Three points supported the need for immediate action: the risk of escalation increased the longer the blockade continued; time worked in the Soviets' favor; and the Cuban missiles were a direct threat to U.S. strategic forces.[139] The sense of urgency was increasing. That night Kennedy told Macmillan that the Soviet buildup was continuing and he would have to decide soon whether to invade Cuba and take his chances, or wait until Khrushchev acted on Berlin and then go into Cuba. Waiting might reduce the risk of escalation, but if construction continued "the danger [of war] will be greater within 2 weeks."[140]

Behind the scenes, the State Department was probing a possible missile deal. A memo to Rusk from Rostow on Wednesday reiterated the need for Turkey and Italy to accept a phase-out of IRBMs once a multilateral force was in place.[141] There was a problem, however. The allies had never shown much enthusiasm for the MLF concept. Negotiating an agreement on it now, within the next few days, was infeasible—except through U.S. coercion, which would undermine alliance cohesion.

Hence, over the next three days, strenuous but subtle efforts were made to get the *allies* to propose an MLF, so that it would seem like a European initiative. The Europeans refused to take the bait. As for Turkey, equally subtle diplomacy was having equally unsuccessful results. On Thursday, Finletter reported that the Turks were wedded to the Jupiters as a symbol of NATO's resolve. He warned that a missile deal would undermine the alliance by showing that Washington would sell out European interests each time Moscow manufactured a crisis.[142]

The United States was on the horns of a dilemma. Khrushchev would not retreat unless shown the carrot of Turkish missiles as well as the stick of a possible invasion of Cuba. Yet trading away missiles that were unimportant to the Americans, but *were* important to the Europeans, would be seen as appeasement. The paradox was surreal: Kennedy needed missiles out of Cuba to maintain the material superiority for extended deterrence and U.S. security. The only way to do this without risking nuclear war was to trade away Turkish missiles. Yet the trade, if discovered, would destroy the ideational basis of the U.S. global position—America's reputation for resolve in the face of Soviet pressure.

By Friday, 26 October, a strategy to jump through the dilemma's horns was in place, but it was unlikely to succeed. Washington would deny rumors of a Turkish-Cuban trade. Simultaneously, it would offer Polaris submarines and MLF, explain the growing chance of escalation, and hope the Europeans got the message: that they had to propose a phasing out of Turkish and perhaps Italian missiles to avoid general war. This strategy was laid out in two memoranda, one from Rusk to the president and one from Rostow to Rusk.[143] The first told Kennedy he had to give Moscow a face-saving measure. Regarding European allies, Washington had to avoid any notion "that we are trading off pre-crisis allied or U.S. interests to secure removal of [Cuban missiles]." Failure on this point would undermine the alliance.[144]

Kennedy knew what face-saving measures were required. He and his brother, on their own, had made a critical decision earlier that week. On

Tuesday, journalist Frank Holeman relayed to Georgi Bolshakov, the Kennedy brothers' backchannel, that Robert Kennedy would consider trading Turkish for Cuban missiles.[145] This information was held up by Russian intelligence in Washington. Only on Thursday was it received in Moscow, and apparently it did not make it into Soviet leaders' hands until Friday.[146] These facts explain why Khrushchev rushed out a second letter on Saturday morning, demanding the Turkish missiles—he now had reason to believe Kennedy would throw them into the deal.

By Friday, the crisis was nearing its climax. At the NSC meeting that morning, Kennedy argued that time was running out. Work on the sites had to cease. Only two ways remained to remove the missiles: "to trade them out . . . [or] take them out."[147] He authorized that a subgroup of Operation Mongoose (the covert effort to overthrow Castro) be formed to discuss organizing a post-Castro government.[148] At 2:30 that afternoon, the Special Group (Augmented) on Operation Mongoose—augmented by the likes of McNamara, Taylor, and Bundy—met to coordinate the invasion.[149] The ExComm was readying for a major operation against Cuba, one that would involve 150–250,000 U.S. servicemen.

The next day was the most dangerous of the crisis. Three long meetings were held: at 10:00 A.M. to around noon, from 4:00 P.M. until almost 8:00, and then again from 9:00 P.M. until about 10:00.[150] In the morning, the group was discussing Khrushchev's first letter, offering removal of the missiles for a U.S. noninvasion pledge, when word was received of Khrushchev's public demand that the Turkish missiles be included in any deal. One of the stranger episodes of the crisis followed. The ExComm split into two. On one side were almost all key members, who ganged up on Kennedy to convince him not even to hint at a Turkish-Cuban trade. On the other side, arguing for the reasonableness of Khrushchev's new demand, were just two people—the Kennedy brothers. What at first is puzzling becomes understandable when one remembers that earlier that week the brothers had secretly broached a backchannel trade. The surprise demand by Khrushchev was thus no surprise to Kennedy—it was his earlier initiative that had apparently encouraged Khrushchev to up the ante.

Yet Kennedy was now in a corner. Khrushchev had turned what were supposed to have been secret discussions into a public demand. A deal now could destroy America's reputation. Kennedy asked the group about discussions with Turkey; he was told that the strategy was not to broach the question directly, but to feel out the Turkish response. After all, Under Secretary of State George Ball said, if Washington was the one bringing up the issue, "this would be an extremely unsettling business." Kennedy shot back: "Well *this* is unsettling *now* George." The United States might be taking military action against Cuba in the face of "reasonable" proposals. In discussions that followed, Bundy argued that even accepting the notion of a possible trade would undermine the alliance, and he was supported by Ball, Thompson, Rusk, and Dillon. Kennedy gave little ground.

The horns of the dilemma remained: go with Kennedy's wishes, and allies would sense a sell-out; refuse to discuss a trade and Khrushchev would stand firm, leading to a U.S. attack on Cuba and possible escalation to nuclear war—all for Turkish missiles only the Europeans thought had much value. And time, as RFK reiterated, was running out. The sense of impending doom was reinforced that day by a report on the missiles' military significance. Even the existing missiles represented "a serious dilution of U.S. strategic deterrent capability." Yet

> There is no reason why the Soviets could not, if unimpeded by an effective quarantine, literally multiply the number of launchers to a force large enough to threaten the entire strategic balance of power. The Soviets have deployed over 500 MRBMs and IRBMs on their own territory, and the lesser cost to ICBMs would make a major expansion in Cuba very attractive.[151]

As it turns out, this was not just a prudent warning. In May, Castro had privately informed the Russians that since the missiles strengthened the socialist camp, Cuba would accept as many missiles as necessary, "even 1,000, if you want to send so many."[152]

The Saturday report came on the heels of another CIA analysis emphasizing the rapid pace of site construction and Cuban mobilization.[153] In the morning meeting, the Kennedy brothers used the negative trends to argue that little time remained for hard-line negotiating—either the Turkish missiles were traded, or the invasion of Cuba would begin. The president conceded some ground, agreeing that publicly he would respond only to the first letter. Still, he wanted increased pressure on the Turks so Ankara would understand the impending danger, namely, that if the United States acted against Cuba, Khrushchev would act against Turkey. Rusk and Bundy now shifted somewhat to the president's side, probably because of the agreement to go with the first letter.

There was still a constraint, however: ownership of the missiles. Kennedy opined that Ankara would agree to relinquish the missiles, since they belonged to the Americans. The others corrected him: the missiles belonged to Turkey; just the warheads were in U.S. custody. So the United States could only withdraw the warheads? Kennedy inquired. McNamara responded that even this was not possible, since America was simply "custodians of the warheads [for the Turks]." In short, U.S. decision-makers had no legal right within the NATO IRBM agreement to withdraw the missiles unilaterally. Thus quite apart from the symbolic problem of "selling out" the allies, the goods they had to offer Moscow were not even theirs to sell!

Kennedy refused to be held back by such details: "we *cannot* permit ourselves to be impaled on a long negotiating hook while the work goes on at these bases," he argued.[154] He then prepared to leave the meeting to address the state governors on civil defense preparations.[155] Before leaving, he summarized his views:

> If the missiles in Cuba added 50% to Soviet nuclear capability, then to trade these missiles for those in Turkey would be of great military value. . . . From a political point of view . . . [w]e are in a bad position if we appear to be attacking Cuba for the purpose of keeping useless missiles in Turkey. We cannot propose to withdraw the missiles from Turkey, but the Turks could offer to do so. The Turks must be informed of the great danger in which they will live during the next week and we have to face up to the possibility of some kind of a trade over missiles.[156]

Given the risks of escalation, Kennedy was not going to let Turkish missiles preclude a negotiated settlement. Still, in accepting that the initiative had to come from the Turks, he was acknowledging that the United States could not be seen as selling out the allies under pressure.

Underlying discussions on Saturday afternoon was the recognition that, given the trends, the group would soon face a least-of-many-evils choice. At one point Kennedy was reiterating the need to move quickly given the pace of site construction. Either Moscow halted construction to allow time to bring the allies on board, or military strikes would begin. Bundy emphasized that it was the group's strong consensus that if Washington appeared to be trading away allied interests, "[we'd] just have to face a radical decline in the . . . " Kennedy cut him off by noting that

> as the situation is moving . . . this trade has appeal. Now if we reject it out of hand and then have to take military action against Cuba, then we also face a decline. . . . let's try to word [discussions with the allies] so that we *don't* harm NATO—but the thing that I think everybody would agree to [is that] . . . there should be a cessation of work. . . . If [the Soviets] don't agree to that . . . then we retain the initiative.[157]

As they grappled with the various options, three aspects of "decline" hovered over the discussion. Implicit for both Bundy and Kennedy was the significant increase in Soviet nuclear capability resulting from doing nothing. Bundy was also concerned about the decline the United States would face should the allies get wind of a trade (decline in the U.S. global position as the alliance crumbled). Kennedy accepted this, but emphasized the decline that would follow from military action against Cuba, namely, the risks of a superpower conflict which escalated to nuclear war—what he had called on 18 October the "final failure."

By Saturday evening, therefore, the goal was to minimize the total decline stemming from these three sources. On the negotiating spectrum, three positions remained to secure the withdrawal of Cuban missiles without war. From hard-line to soft-line, they were: (1) no deal on the Turkish missiles, and acceptance only of the "no-invasion" pledge; (2) a private deal to remove the Turkish missiles, plus the no-invasion pledge; and (3) agreement to Khrushchev's demand for a public deal on the Turkish missiles, plus the no-invasion pledge. From ExComm discussions and reports received that weekend on NATO/Turkish feelings, it is clear that Washington could go no further than the private deal without risking the alliance's disintegration. This, of course, was the deal offered that night through the backchannel.

Had Khrushchev turned down the deal and played for time—as he was expected to do—then military strikes against Cuba would have began early the next week. From there, Soviet retaliation against Europe was expected, compelling U.S. retaliation. Thus the world came frighteningly close to the escalation that could have led to nuclear war. No wonder McNamara wondered that night whether he would ever see another sunset.[158]

The documentary evidence provides solid support for the argument. The placement of missiles in Cuba—like U.S. deployments in Turkey—was a perfectly legal act within a superpower's sphere. Yet there was little internally the United States could do to match it in the short term. This meant, in the absence of a harder-line policy, a significant downward shift in the strategic balance, especially once Russia deployed additional missiles from its huge stock of MRBMs and IRBMs. Moscow would not only be better poised for a first strike, but subsequent U.S. efforts to reestablish America's nuclear position might push the Soviets into preventive war out of a belief that they possessed temporary but waning nuclear strength. Moreover, the loss of power would hurt extended deterrence, thus jeopardizing U.S. control over the vast economic and potential power of the periphery. To prevent this negative oscillation in the overall power balance, Kennedy and the ExComm embarked on a course that they knew entailed high risks of major war.

The evidence also upholds some of the nuances of the model outlined in chapter 2. Dominant states do not jump into preventive major war at the first sign of decline. Rather, they determine what measures short of war might be taken to alleviate the deteriorating situation. Rational actors, the model predicts, take more extreme steps only when they see no other options to prevent decline. On the first day of the crisis, when no other options seemed viable, immediate military action against Cuba was agreed to by all. Once the blockade option emerged as a useful first step, it was selected. Yet since it did not stop further construction on existing sites, by

26–27 October the ExComm readied itself for military strikes and invasion. Each step up the escalation ladder, each additional increase in the likelihood of inadvertent war, was weighed against the harm to U.S. security caused by accepting a permanent missile base in Cuba. As expected, greater and greater risks of an unwanted crash were assumed as the power situation continued to deteriorate.

The other theories find only minimal support. There is little declassified evidence indicating that domestic politics played an important role. In the main example—McNamara's remark on 16 October that the issue was a "domestic-political" one—McNamara was concerned about domestic obstacles to the achievement of security objectives, not about domestic goals per se.[159] The bureaucratic politics model also performs quite poorly. The documents show that ExComm members were obsessed with national security, not parochial needs; disagreements were almost exclusively over the best means to the agreed end.[160] Not only were actors' positions often opposite to those predicted by their bureaucratic standings—for example, the attorney general pressing for invasion on 16 October, while the secretary of defense warned of the risks of military action—but their positions shifted as new information on risks and benefits was received.

Personality had some bearing on individual behavior. Still, it was systemic pressures that pushed the ExComm to take such extraordinary risks. The personality approach works best at the margins—why, for example, Adlai Stevenson suggested diplomacy and Paul Nitze more hard-line action. But it cannot explain the broader consensus for strong action. Of existing realist theories, hegemonic stability theory does particularly poorly. It cannot explain why security fears drove American behavior or why expectations of decline led Kennedy to initiate the crisis period. Moreover, the United States took actions that increased the risk of major war despite having clear strategic superiority over Russia. Classical realism and neorealism, once preventive motivations are incorporated, can explain the U.S. desire to avert any anticipated decline in power. Still, these theories remain underspecified. To predict when states will shift to increasingly risky options, we need a model showing how leaders weigh the risks of allowing further decline against the risks of inadvertent major war associated with harder-line policies.

This chapter has tested one such model against three cold war crises. In each case, declining power stemming from the relative success of the adversary's arms and alliance policies led to the outbreak of a dangerous crisis. Trends and differentials of power were not the only factors shaping superpower behavior. Yet the strong salience of these factors relative to competing variables is confirmed.

It is appropriate to close this chapter by considering the thoughts of crisis participants on what was probably the single most dangerous 24-hour period in world history—Saturday evening and Sunday morning, 27–28 October 1962. All members of the ExComm were pessimistic, but McNamara—one of its more reasonable members—was perhaps the most so. Around 6:30 P.M., word of the U2 shot down over Cuba was received. McNamara reacted strongly. He agreed with Kennedy that this was a significant escalation. His suspicions were rising: even Khrushchev's first letter—which the ExComm had already accepted as a basis for negotiations—was merely "twelve pages of fluff," with "not a damned thing in it that's an offer." Khrushchev was stringing America along and nothing would be signed quickly; hence "[we] ought to be prepared for attack, all-out attack [on Cuba]."

He also outlined in stark detail the escalation scenario that would have brought the world to the brink of nuclear war. The United States had to be ready to attack quickly, with a general air strike against Cuba almost certain to lead to an invasion.[161] Then the Soviets "may, and I think probably will, attack the Turkish missiles." If they did that, "we *must* respond" with at least a NATO attack against Soviet warships and naval bases in the Black Sea. "Now that to me is the absolute minimum, and I would say that it is *damned dangerous*." In saying this, McNamara was not trying to dissuade the ExComm from attacking Cuba, only to warn them to be prepared for the consequences.[162] The fact that his efforts earlier had steered the group from an immediate military strike shows that McNamara was no warmonger. Systemic pressures had thus overridden his own propensity toward more moderate solutions.

By Saturday night the United States was ready to bear all the risks of escalation associated with an invasion of Cuba. And McNamara was not simply giving the worst-case scenario. In his memoirs, Khrushchev acknowledges that "if the Americans had started a war [over Cuba], we were not prepared to adequately attack the United States. In that case, we would have been forced to start a war in Europe. Then, of course, a world war would have begun."[163] President Kennedy that Saturday evening, piggybacking his brother's comments that Washington had to warn NATO that "on Tuesday we go in" should no agreement be reached, stated that NATO had to be prepared "for a disaster," since "the situation is deteriorating, and if we take *action*, we think there *will* be reprisals."[164]

In the end, the world avoided what JFK had called the final failure of nuclear destruction. Yet the ExComm was taking incredible chances as it made its moves, resting always on the hope that the Soviets would relent before things got out of hand. Behind such risk-taking was an overarching fact: the United States could not allow a fundamental shift in the balance of power. American policy-makers thus willingly accepted the short-term risk of an inadvertent nuclear holocaust in order to avert an oscillation that would have otherwise reduced long-term U.S. security.

[8]

Major War from Pericles to Napoleon

This chapter offers a brief survey of seven other important cases of major war. Given space constraints, the goal is not to engage established historical debates or to provide definitive evidence for or against particular arguments. Rather I seek, by what amount to plausibility probes, to test the salience of the theory's logic across time and space.

The cases represent the seven best-known examples of major war in Europe before the twentieth century.[1] Three are bipolar: the ancient Greek system; the Second Punic War between Carthage and Rome; and the French-Hapsburg conflict in the early sixteenth century. The other four are multipolar: the Thirty Years War; the wars of Louis XIV; the Seven Years War; and the Napoleonic Wars. Of these cases, the theory is well supported in all but one, the Seven Years War (for reasons to be explored). In each of the bipolar situations, war was initiated by the declining superpower even though it was only roughly equal in military power to the rising state. As with Germany in the twentieth century, decline was driven primarily by inferiority in potential power. Other realist theories find little support: classical realism cannot explain why two near-equal states fell into war; hegemonic stability theory, why the declining state attacked; and Waltzian neorealism, why major war broke out in bipolarity.

In each of the multipolar cases except the Seven Years War, the conflict was brought on by a state possessing significant military superiority but anticipating deep decline over the long term. This decline reflected entrenched stagnation relative to the rising state(s), as well as inferiority in certain dimensions of economic and potential power. Again, established realist arguments are not well supported. Classical realism accurately predicts the preponderant state as initiator, but it downplays the primary motive for war, namely, fear of decline rather than unit-level aggression.

Hegemonic stability theory cannot explain why a superior state attacked, or why it did so when declining rather than rising. Waltz's neorealism predicts war in multipolarity by miscalculation. Yet in each of the following cases, the initiator understood the risks and consciously unleashed war before its power fell any further.

Covering so many wars in so short a space leads to a focus on the wars themselves and therefore to some selecting on the dependent variable. To compensate, I try where possible to sketch the situations of the great powers in the periods prior to the wars. This allows us to see if incentives for war shifted as the causal variables did.[2]

THE PELOPONNESIAN WAR

The ancient Greek system up to the outbreak of the Peloponnesian War in 431 B.C. was dominated by two great powers, Sparta and Athens. Thucydides, our primary source, provides an argument that supports the theory. He contends that the real reason for the war lies not in complaints made by the Spartans and their allies about Athens before the war began. Rather, "what made war inevitable was the growth of Athenian power and the fear which this caused in Sparta."[3] In support of his thesis, Thucydides describes the growth of Athens through the gradual extension of imperial control over its former allies in the anti-Persian alliance, the Delian League.[4] He also argues that both sides were essentially equal in overall military power,[5] and this is supported by the fact that the war was a long, stalemated battle of the highest intensity.[6]

The Peloponnesian War is significant, since it is probably the singularly most "crucial case" against the argument that domestic-level forces push states into major wars.[7] It is clear, as I discuss, that Sparta initiated the war and that the Athenians sought to avoid it. This is directly contrary to what one would expect from knowledge of their internal dispositions. The Spartans needed their military at home to keep the helots, their slaves, from revolting; thus up until 432 B.C. they had been very reluctant to engage in major wars abroad.[8] Athens, on the other hand, was a vigorous power, as indicated by its massive empire-building efforts.[9] Hence a domestic-level approach should have predicted Athens as initiator, with Sparta the one seeking peace. Yet the result was the exact opposite.

Two points have been made to try to defeat Thucydides' argument, using his own evidence: first, that Athens, not Sparta, provoked the war;[10] second, that Athens had already peaked in relative power more than two decades before and therefore was not rising by 431.[11] Neither point is convincing. Sparta decided on major war a year before actual hostilities, just after the first public conference with its allies in summer 432 (it called a second conference soon afterward to secure allied ratification). Sparta spent the next year maximizing military preparedness.[12] Hence, the whole Greek world knew for almost a year that the Spartans were preparing to initiate a major war. Moreover, it was Sparta and its allies that launched an all-out attack on Athens in spring 431.

From the first conference until the end, Athens tried to dissuade Sparta from war. Athenian representatives at that conference, Thucydides relates, "hoped to divert their audience from the idea of war and make them incline towards letting matters rest."[13] Athens invoked the Thirty Years Peace of 445, which required that disputes be solved by arbitration, not force, and this was a constant Athenian refrain until war began.[14] The Spartans rejected all such nonviolent measures. Instead, they sent envoys to demand concessions under the threat of war. As Thucydides notes, this was done mainly to provide "a good pretext for making war" if Athens refused to capitulate.[15] It is clear therefore that Sparta must be held responsible for initiating the war.

The second critique argues that since the majority of the cities of what later became Athens's empire were under Athenian suzerainty by 460–457, Athens had peaked in power at this time.[16] This argument confuses a city's entry into the Athenian realm with the consolidation and growth of the realm itself.[17] It would be equivalent to saying that the United States peaked in power by 1867, simply because so few territories were added after that date. The treasury of the Delian League was not moved to Athens until 454 B.C., and it was not until peace with Persia in 448 that Athens shifted from simply leading an anti-Persian alliance to controlling, as hegemon, an imperial realm. Significantly, it was only around 447 that tribute payments by subject states began to be used to build the greatness of Athens (including the construction of the Parthenon). Moreover, trade within the Athenian empire, from all evidence, increased dramatically from 450 to 431 as the Persian threat declined. Athens grew significantly as a result.[18] Indeed, the period from 446 to 431 is now known as the acme of the Athenian state, the vaunted "Periclean Age."

Thus Thucydides' argument for the origins of the Peloponnesian War remains the most plausible, once Athens is eliminated as an aggressor, and given that Sparta had no unit-level reason for total war. This supports the theory's prediction that the declining great power in bipolarity will initiate war even when it is only equal to the rising state, out of fear for its long-term security.

THE SECOND PUNIC WAR

The major war between Carthage and Rome beginning in 218 B.C. closely follows the preventive logic of the Greek case.[19] Carthage had been the dominant western Mediterranean power for many centuries before the rise of Rome. Indeed, until 272 Rome was solely preoccupied with enemies on the Italian peninsula. That year Rome completed its domination of both central and lower Italy. In 264, a minor dispute over Messana in northern Sicily drew both Rome and Carthage into a struggle for control over this vital island lying directly between their homelands. This First Punic War, lasting from 264 to 241, reflected Carthage's first effort to prevent the expansion of the rising Roman power beyond its sphere.[20]

Carthage failed in its containment policy and in 241 was forced to sign a peace treaty relinquishing Sicily. Three years later, as the Carthaginian empire suffered a revolt of ethnic subjects, Rome forced its rival to surrender Sardinia. A glance at the map shows the significance of these losses: Carthage moved from domination of the western Mediterranean—indeed, Rome had no navy when conflict began in 264—to a situation where Rome ruled half the sea and was projecting power from islands dangerously close to Carthage itself. It did not take a genius to see that once Rome consolidated its new realm, it would easily overwhelm Carthage.[21]

With the loss of naval supremacy, only one way remained for Carthage to wage the preventive war necessary for its security: the land route over the Italian Alps. Already in 237, to compensate for the loss of Sardinia, Carthage had established a foothold in southern Spain. By 227, New Carthage was founded on the southern Spanish coast as a base for operations against the north. Rome, however, reacted to Carthage's northern expansion in order to protect Roman trading colonies along the French coast. With the 226 Ebro Treaty, Spain was divided into Roman and Carthaginian spheres of influence.

Carthage, however, could not remain satisfied with this status quo, so long as Rome continued to grow. This Roman rise began to appear inevitable by the end of the 220s. In 222, Rome scored a critical victory against Gaullic tribes occupying the one area of the Italian peninsula outside Roman control: northern Italy up to the Alps. If the Carthaginians had any illusions that Rome would not expand beyond Italy, these were dispelled by the Roman wars with the Illyrians (who occupied the coast of present day Croatia/Albania). In 228, Rome had achieved a partial victory against Illyrian cities. By 219 the Romans were intensifying their attacks on the Illyrian coast and showed every sign of overwhelming it.[22]

The writing was on the wall for the Carthaginians. Accordingly, like the Spartans, they proceeded to find a pretext for fighting all-out war before it was too late. This pretext was presented in the form of a valuable but vulnerable Spanish city under Roman protection: Saguntum. After 223, as the Carthaginians proceeded to conquer the countryside surrounding Saguntum, the city sought Roman aid. Initially reluctant, by 220 Rome decided to give Saguntum the assurance that it would act to uphold the city's security;

this was unequivocally communicated to the Carthaginians. Rome's reputation for defending small cities in its realm was now on the line. Carthage exploited this to its fullest advantage. By spring 219, with the full approval of the Carthaginian Senate, the young Carthaginian commander Hannibal began to besiege Saguntum, despite additional Roman warnings.

This was a full-scale assault on the credibility of Roman extended-deterrence commitments, and the Carthaginians no doubt expected, and desired, a vigorous Roman response. They got it in early 218, just after Saguntum fell to Hannibal. Roman envoys were sent to Carthage to demand the punishment of Hannibal, apparently assuming he had acted on his own and unaware of the Carthaginian Senate's support. Given the choice between peace and war, the Senate enthusiastically accepted war, and the Roman envoys departed. Soon after, Hannibal launched his famous attack across the Alps, plunging into the heart of Roman territory.

The ultimatum to Carthage in 218 seems to put some blame on Rome for the subsequent war, but two facts indicate that only Carthage was seeking all-out war using the pretext of Saguntum. First, the Romans clearly had no sense that Carthage would be foolish enough to besiege Saguntum after the unequivocal extension of Roman security commitments in 219. This is shown by the fact that Rome, before it received the news of Hannibal's attack on Saguntum in the summer of 219, elected to launch a large-scale offensive in the opposite direction, namely, against Illyria. Surely if the Romans had been seeking war with Carthage over Saguntum, they would not have diverted their forces from the western Mediterranean theater.[23] Second, Hannibal, in early 219—a year before major war began and around the same time he began his attack on Saguntum—secretly sent messengers to the Gauls in northern Italy to encourage revolt against Rome and to promise support. By spring 218 he received favorable replies.[24] This indicates that Hannibal was already planning a surprise attack against the Roman heartland before Rome was even aware that Saguntum had been besieged, that is, before Rome felt compelled to act to uphold its reputation. Given these facts, it is clear that Carthage used Saguntum as a means for bringing on preventive war against the rising Roman threat; the Romans, on the other hand, preferred to buy time to complete their expansion against the Balkan coast and to consolidate recent gains in northern Italy.[25]

In sum, the case supports the theory's predictions for bipolarity: war was initiated by the declining state despite its having only rough equality with the rising state.[26] This declining state, left inferior in potential power after the First Punic War and faced with an adversary still growing by internal consolidation and regional expansion, had to attack to avoid being overwhelmed in the long term. The fact that Carthage, despite early successes, ended up losing the war does not make its leaders any less rational; a risky preventive war was better than almost certain destruction later.

THE FRENCH-HAPSBURG WARS, 1521–1556

The third case of bipolarity is the European system from 1496 to 1556, dominated by France and the Hapsburg empire.[27] Major war between these two powers began in 1521, ended in 1556, and consisted of five separate wars. Three things are clear from the evidence: that France initiated all five wars; that France was the declining power; and that France and the Hapsburgs were essentially equal in relative military power, despite Hapsburg superiority in overall economic and particularly potential power.[28]

In the last half of the fifteenth century, the foundations for the modern unitary French state were laid. With the end of the Hundred Years War in 1453, France became the preeminent power of an essentially multipolar Europe. England, however, became seriously weakened by the devastating civil war, the War of the Roses (1455–85), to the point that by the early sixteenth century it was at best a middle power. The expansive Hapsburg realm of 1519 had not yet been formed; it emerged only gradually as a result of strategic marriages between the kings of Spain and Austria. It was the formation of this realm—indeed, the transformation of the system from multipolarity to bipolarity as Spain and Austria united—that undermined French security and led France to launch preventive war in 1521.

In 1469, Isabella of Castile and Ferdinand of Aragon had consolidated Spain to push back the Moors, a task accomplished by 1492. In 1496, their daughter married Philip, the son of Maximilian of Austria. For the French, this was a somber warning, for upon the death of Ferdinand and Maximilian, Philip would rule a united empire that would include not only Spain and Austria, but the Spanish Netherlands and Burgundy on France's eastern front. France would be effectively encircled. The date 1496 thus marks the shift from tripolarity (France, Spain, and Austria) to bipolarity (France and the Hapsburgs) in the European system, although the full realization of bipolarity would not come until 1519. In that year, Philip's nineteen-year-old son Charles became emperor of the united realm after Maximilian's death (Ferdinand having died three years before, and Philip in 1506). Significantly, in the same year, the twenty-five-year-old French king, Francis I, had lost out to Charles in his bid to become the Holy Roman Emperor. As a result, France faced a sprawling Hapsburg power whose possessions now included the German states on France's eastern border.

The French sun was clearly setting. Soon after the losses of 1519, Francis began planning for a surprise attack on three fronts against Charles.[29] All-out war began in the spring of 1521, when the French simultaneously invaded Navarre in northern Spain and Burgundy and the Netherlands; a French attack on Hapsburg possessions in Italy soon followed. It is important to realize how qualitatively different these actions were from previous wars in the 1453–1521 period. France had launched attacks on Italy before and indeed had been fighting for control of northern Italy since 1494. The war begun in 1521, however, was not a struggle over third parties, but an all-out assault on the core territory of the Hapsburgs. In fact, had the French succeeded in controlling Navarre, they would have been less than two hundred miles from the capital of Charles's empire, Madrid.

To understand the preventive motivations behind this assault, it is crucial to distinguish between short-term French military strength and the long-term economic and potential strength of the Hapsburgs. Charles had taken over an empire whose territory and population were about twice the size of France. Clearly, once this empire started to grow internally, it would overwhelm France. Moreover, with Cortés's defeat of Montezuma in 1520, the Spanish were poised to take over the riches of Latin America. As a military power, however, the Hapsburg empire was temporarily no stronger than the French. For one thing, the French state was unified, with an efficient centralized bureaucracy critical for sustained warfare. As with Germany in the twentieth century, France had all the advantages of strong internal lines of communication. The Hapsburg realm in 1521, on the other hand, was still a patchwork of different nationalities, with no strong overarching administration. Moreover, the Hapsburgs were temporarily weakened in the middle of 1520 by a major internal revolt in the core of the empire—Spain—led by nobles resentful of the new tax system.

The year 1521 was thus perfect timing for a French preventive war against an empire whose long-term growth seemed assured.[30] That the rest of Europe saw France as what F. C. Spooner calls the "first military power" is indicated by three facts.[31] First, when Francis and Charles attempted to bribe German electors in 1519 in their competition to become Holy Roman Emperor, Charles won even though his bribes were seen as less substantial; the German princes apparently selected Charles as the less threatening of the two candidates.[32] Second, Francis had won a significant battle in Italy in 1515—the battle of Marignano—thereby demonstrating not only French military prowess, but Francis's leadership skills. Third, Henry VIII of England signed a secret alliance treaty with Charles in 1520, renewed it in June 1522 when France was still doing well on the battlefield, but switched to an alliance with France after Francis's defeat at Pavia in 1525. This behavior—later known as England's traditional balance-of-power strategy— suggests that in 1521 European states feared a possible French victory against the temporarily disorganized Hapsburgs.

In addition, the war itself from 1521 to 1556 suggests that the French and the Hapsburgs were about equally matched. Francis's loss at Pavia in northern Italy—a defeat no one had expected, especially not Charles[33]— ended the first round of war, but France was far from finished. Over four subsequent wars, France fought the Hapsburgs to a stalemate. The French-

Hapsburg case thus nicely supports the theory: a declining France initiated major war once it realized that decline would be both deep and inevitable, and it did so even though it was only essentially equal to the rising state in military power.

THE THIRTY YEARS WAR

The Thirty Years War lasted from 1618 to the Peace of Westphalia in 1648. The puzzle addressed here is why a small revolt in Bohemia in 1618 against the Holy Roman Emperor led to a system-wide total war—the most destructive European war until the twentieth century. The Thirty Years War is often seen as the archetypical ideological conflict: the great powers, divided into Protestant and Catholic, fought to determine which religion would dominate in the German states. The war thus provides a "hard test" of any realist theory. If dynamic differentials theory works here, the salience of its logic is strongly supported.

The war was primarily driven by the fears of decline due to entrenched stagnation in the system's dominant military power: Spain.[34] It was Spanish intervention in the Bohemian crisis that caused the escalation to major war. No other great power wanted war; indeed, the rest sought to localize the conflict.[35] Spain alone exploited the crisis for a larger purpose, namely, to shore up its deteriorating position in Europe. Over the previous two decades, the Spanish elite had increasingly realized that economic and demographic power was shifting from Spain and its Italian possessions to northern Europe, specifically England, Holland, and France. Europe was going through a commercial revolution as Spanish bullion fueled a boom in interstate commerce. Yet the efficiency of the north was undermining Spain's historical economic dominance. Economic decline in turn was devastating its population. For Madrid, one country above all stood to gain from Spanish decay: Spain's traditional rival, France. Thus Spain intervened in Germany to bolster the overall position of the House of Hapsburg, despite awareness that this would likely lead to total war.

Religion played only a supporting role in the escalation to systemic war: it served to mobilize armies and for German princes provided the pretext for greater autonomy. Yet the critical divide in the system, a divide that determined the nature and scope of the war, was between France and Spain, two Catholic states. In the end, power politics trumped religious identification.

The war can be divided into two parts. From 1618 to 1627, the Spanish goal was to keep the Austrian cousins strong in eastern Germany while Spain, to maintain the encirclement of France, improved its position in the west and reduced Dutch strength. Spain had given Holland de facto independence in the truce of 1609. Yet the Dutch continued to hurt Spanish trade in the East and West Indies. With the truce set to expire in 1621, Spain used the 1618 crisis to increase its control in western Germany as it prepared to attack Holland.[36]

After 1627, Madrid shifted to a more direct strategy of reducing and then destroying the growing French threat. Planning for all-out war against France began after 1625, gaining steam as French and Spanish troops fought in northern Italy from 1628 to 1631 for control of Mantua. By 1634, Spain was readying forces for a three-pronged attack on France itself. In 1635, France preempted this preventive attack by a declaration of war. Spain plunged into France the next year and came within eighty miles of Paris before being stopped. A twenty-four-year war of attrition ensued, lasting until the 1659 Peace of Pyrennes.

The Thirty Years War was thus the second major war in a 250-year French-Hapsburg struggle for hegemony in Europe, the third being the wars of Louis XIV.[37] Spanish concerns about the rise of France increased after three decades of French internal religious strife ended in 1598. Mercantilist reforms under King Henry IV led to a marked French recovery by 1610.[38] In potential power, France's population of sixteen million was twice that of Spain's eight million, and France was more economically diverse and richer in natural resources (although Spain had a stronger colonial base).[39] Moreover, France's population grew rapidly after 1590, while Spain's was devastated by economic turmoil and plagues.[40]

With Henry's assassination in 1610, France entered a decade of uncertainty, as young King Louis XIII and his mother struggled for control and as internal clashes with Protestant Huguenots were renewed. Not until Cardinal Richelieu's ascendancy in 1624 did France reignite the consolidation process begun under Henry. In relative terms, however, while France's economy merely leveled off, Spain's continued to decline precipitously. Early seventeenth-century Europe experienced a period of general economic crisis. Yet it affected individual countries quite differently: depression began in Spain and the Mediterranean region in the late 1590s and Germany in the 1610s; after 1610, the French economy remained flat as northern states such as Holland and England grew. These differences reflected the relative cost-efficiency of French, Dutch, and English manufacturing.[41]

The Spanish elite were keenly aware of these trends. Beginning in 1600 and gaining force thereafter, economic writers, the *arbitristas*, began distributing analyses of Spanish *declinación*. They identified three key problems: a declining population, diminished national wealth, and falling levels of bullion from overseas colonies. The initial reaction was to hunker down and hope that peace with the Dutch would stem decline. By the late 1610s, however, as imports flooded Spain and bullion from the Americas fell by half, a pervasive sense of pessimism set in.[42] This mood, as John Elliott and Peter

Brightwell show, had much to do with Spain's increased willingness to accept the risks of major war.

The Thirty Years War traditionally begins with the revolt in May 1618 of Protestant Bohemian noblemen against the centralizing authority of Catholic Austria. Conflict between German Protestants and Vienna had been brewing for a decade, as the former sought greater autonomy. For Vienna, however, the challenge in May 1618, if allowed to stand, would have quickly undermined Austria's control over the Holy Roman Empire.[43] Any weakening of Austria was of great concern in Madrid. The two Hapsburg houses—Spain and Austria—had separated in the mid-sixteenth century, but familial bonds were strong and growing by the 1610s. Emperor Matthias was first cousin to Philip III of Spain. The ties were strengthened by the 1617 Oñate Treaty: Philip agreed to Ferdinand II's becoming Holy Roman Emperor upon Matthias's death, in exchange for territory in Italy and Alsace. Ferdinand was not only Philip's wife's brother, but was married to Philip's daughter.

The disintegration of the Austrian house would have jeopardized Hapsburg lands across Europe. In the early summer of 1618, however, the Spanish government was initially divided on the Bohemian crisis. One faction, led by the duke of Lerma, argued that Spain lacked financial resources and that intervention would spark a general war. This faction lost out to that led by Don Balthasar de Zúñiga, former ambassador at Vienna. Zúñiga was highly aware of the risks of escalation, but he argued that Spain could not let Austria fall. He also sought to position Spain for war against Holland as he protected the Spanish possessions on France's eastern border.[44]

As Brightwell shows, over the next year the Spanish made a series of reluctant lesser-of-two-evils decisions, knowing that they rendered general war almost certain. In July–August 1618, the first dispatches of money went out to Vienna. In April 1619, Matthias's death opened the succession question. In May Protestant forces marched on Vienna. Madrid responded by sending 7,000 troops from Flanders to fight on Austria's side, the first direct intervention by any great power. In the fall, the Spanish ambassador in Vienna, Iñigo Oñate, through promises of Spanish support, helped to reestablish the Catholic League, a band of German princes led by Maximilian of Bavaria. Another 7,000 Spanish troops were brought up from Italy in November. In August 1620, the crucial escalatory step was taken: Spain launched 20,000 troops against the Palatinate (in western Germany), partly to divert Protestant forces west, and partly to ensure Spain's control of the supply route from Italy.[45] This constituted a direct threat to France's position in the Rhineland.

By late 1620, Spanish troops represented half of the total Imperial army, and Madrid was paying half its expenses.[46] This support was critical to Imperial victories in November 1620 which dealt the rebels their first major defeat. Spain did not stop there. In 1621, it initiated war against Holland,

and spent the next eight years destroying Dutch trade with Germany when it could not defeat Holland outright.[47] From 1620 on, the rebels begged Paris to stop Spain, but the French were temporarily too weak. In late 1622, France finally aligned with Savoy to drive Spain out of Switzerland. In June 1624, France renewed its alliance with Holland and began subsidizing the Dutch war with Spain. In 1625, French, Dutch, and English subsidies allowed Denmark to intervene against the growing Hapsburg threat in eastern Germany.

The Spanish actions in 1618–22 which decisively escalated the war resulted from a pessimistic view that Spain had no choice. Zúñiga understood from July 1618 on that Spanish intervention would likely mean general war.[48] Yet without war, Holland would continue to undermine Spanish commerce. In spring 1619, he noted that while conquering Holland outright would be difficult, Spain had to act: "Affairs can get to a certain stage where every decision taken is for the worse, not through lack of good advice, but because the situation is so desperate that no remedy can conceivably be found."[49] Against arguments that Spain could not afford to aid Austria, Zúñiga countered that "the occasion demands that we should make all those supreme efforts that are normally made when one is confronted by total disaster." His plea to do everything possible despite the obstacles prevailed after careful consideration by Philip's council.[50]

From 1624 to 1627, Hapsburg forces scored important victories. Yet Spain's decline continued. Yearly receipts of New World bullion after 1610 were one-third to one-half of the peak of the late sixteenth century; after 1625 receipts dropped even further, and in 1628 they fell to zero when the entire silver fleet was captured by the Dutch.[51] Pessimism intensified. A minister in 1629 went so far as to say that the crown's finances had been in "continuous *declinación*" for his thirty-nine years of service. The same year, Count-Duke Gaspar de Guzmán Olivares, who ran the Spanish state after 1622, wrote that Spain's problems in its Italian war with France were just another setback to a nation "which still continues on its decline."[52]

Aware that Spanish industry could not compete, Olivares sought to reform the economy along northern mercantilist lines. Yet here was the dilemma: he needed peace to give reforms a chance, but Spain could not allow France and others to grow as Spain put its economic house in order.[53] Olivares faced increasing internal pressure after 1625 to launch a preventive war against France.[54] He initially balked, knowing that all-out war would kill his reform program. The conflict in Italy from 1628 to 1631, however, exacerbated the downward spiral while increasing mistrust of French intentions. Sweden's intervention in 1630 further drained Hapsburg resources.[55] By 1631–32, Olivares resigned himself to the need for total war against France, using the next three years to prepare for it.[56]

Richelieu meanwhile moved to protect the invasion "gates" from Germany into France.[57] After 1632, the frontier became an armed camp. In 1634, Olivares readied Spanish forces for a three-pronged attack on France: from Germany, the Spanish Netherlands, and northern Spain. This was Olivares's "master plan," a plan involving the coordinated operations of two fleets, four armies, and upwards of 100,000 men—what R. A. Stradling calls "the most ambitious military conception of early-modern Europe."[58] Time was of the essence. As a Spanish envoy told the king of Hungary in October 1634, "any more delay [in attacking France] would cause great damage" to the Hapsburg cause.[59]

Logistical problems forced the invasion's postponement. Olivares was anxious; he knew Richelieu would try to buy time to further French growth. In January 1635, he told colleagues that given the size of Spain's forces, the attack should succeed. Yet "everything must begin at once, for unless they are attacked vigorously, nothing can prevent the French from becoming masters of the world, and without any risk to themselves."[60] Paris was indeed reluctant to fight, but decided that the Spanish attack had to be preempted.[61] In February, France renewed its alliance with Holland and in April secured Swedish support; in May it declared war and crossed into the Spanish Netherlands. The next month, Olivares gave King Philip details on his master plan. Spain had reached a crossroads. The plan would either "lose everything irretrievably or enable us to save the ship." If Spain did not have the strength to finish France off, "let us die in summoning it, for it is better to die than to fall under the sway of [the French heretics]. . . . Thus everything will come to an end, or Castile will be the leader of the world."[62]

Preventive thinking was at the heart of Olivares's calculations. As Elliott summarizes, he "knew as well as anyone that he was engaged in a desperate race against time. If France could be beaten quickly, the future would still be his." Only then could he implement the reforms needed to revitalize Spain's economy.[63] The Spanish plunge into war in 1618 and the subsequent escalation to an all-out war of elimination again illustrates the tragic dimension of international politics. Neither Zúñiga nor Olivares, the two individuals most responsible for Spain's hard-line policy, were inherently aggressive individuals. Yet they felt compelled by geopolitical circumstances to take actions that they knew might lead to Spain's destruction as a great power.

THE WARS OF LOUIS XIV

For France and Spain, the Thirty Years War continued until the peace of 1659. The French-Hapsburg rivalry was still not over, however. From 1660 to 1685, France under Louis XIV rose to a level of marked preponderance, but the French felt anything but secure. Eastern borders were open to attack from the system's new rising power: Austria. This Hapsburg monarchy had been quietly consolidating its strength in the latter half of the century. After 1683, it became a significant future threat. In September 1683, Austria halted a Turkish assault on Vienna, and then over the next five years drove the Turks out of Hungary, Serbia, and northern Romania. This not only doubled Austria's size, but it meant that Vienna might turn its battle-hardened forces westward once Turkey sued for peace.

Two other factors were critical in leading France to launch its preventive war in the fall of 1688, a war that but for a temporary pause (1697–1700) would last a quarter century. First was the Spanish succession question, which since the birth of the sickly Carlos II in 1661 had hung over almost every dimension of Austro-French relations. Both France and Austria had claims on Spanish possessions upon Carlos's death. After 1685, however, Paris saw increasing signs that Vienna would make a grab for the crown. Should it succeed, France would face a united Hapsburg realm, the very thing that had driven Francis into war in 1521. Second, after 1680 the French economy suffered from entrenched relative stagnation, due in part to the success of English and Dutch mercantilism. France's own mercantile policy, begun under Colbert in the 1660s, had failed by the 1680s.

Louis and his advisers thus saw preventive war against the Austrian sphere and the Spanish Netherlands as a way not only to protect France's vulnerable eastern border, but to position France for a later fight for the vast Spanish possessions. Absorbing at least some of these possessions would help France compete against English and Dutch commerce, especially in the lucrative Levant-Mediterranean trade. Even more important, it would prevent these territories from falling into the hands of the rising Austrian state.[64]

The Spanish succession issue was Louis's constant obsession after he assumed power in 1661. His marriage to Maria Teresa, the eldest daughter of Philip IV of Spain, connected France to the Spanish throne, but Maria had renounced her direct claim as part of the marriage agreement. This meant that upon the deaths of Philip and his son Carlos, the crown might go to Philip's second daughter Margaret Teresa, who was married to Leopold I, ruler of Austria. From his birth Carlos was expected to die at any moment. By hanging on until 1700, he provided a focal point for four decades of Franco-Austrian conflict. The French could not permit the reunification of the House of Hapsburg. In 1663, after Louis's reevaluation of French policy, Colbert privately wrote:

As for foreign affairs, since it is only the [House of Hapsburg] that must always be considered, either to draw the advantages resulting from its weakness, or because of fear of its elevation, he [Louis] decided to do everything possible to hold it always in check, both at the center and at the two extremities of its states.[65]

Louis was particularly worried about the Hapsburg presence in western Germany and the Spanish Netherlands, at some points less than two hundred miles from Paris. In 1664, he decided to "apply myself more than ever ... to prevent the Emperor [Leopold] from maintaining considerable forces on foot [in Germany]."[66] In 1667, his forces invaded the Spanish Netherlands, with Louis claiming that since Spain had never paid Maria's dowry, he deserved compensation. When this provoked an alliance of England, Holland, and Sweden, Louis retreated. His conciliatoriness partly reflected a secret deal with Leopold in January 1668 to divide Spain's territories upon Carlos's death. The agreement shows Louis's concern for France's border and its Mediterranean trade: France would receive the Spanish Netherlands and Franche-Comté (on the eastern border), Naples, and Sicily, as well as African and Asian colonies; Austria would receive Spain and the American colonies.

In the 1660s, under Colbert, Paris sought to reduce English and Dutch trade dominance though mercantilism. This policy included large tariff jumps in 1664 and 1667 and government support for global trading companies. In 1672, France attacked Holland after isolating it diplomatically. The goal was to use the attack to facilitate the occupation of the Spanish Netherlands, a point of vulnerability. Louis also hoped to reduce Dutch commercial strength.[67] The war did not go as planned: the Dutch opened their dikes to stop the French onslaught, and within a year Spain and Austria were pulled into a war lasting until 1679.[68] The war's costs contributed to the decline of France's economy in the 1680s.

After the Dutch War, Louis sought to absorb a number of fortresses and cities on the border with Germany (his policy of *Réunion*). Like Richelieu, Louis saw these points as "gates" facilitating a Hapsburg invasion of France. By incorporating them into the French sphere, he could achieve the long-standing French dream: a defensible frontier.[69] By 1684, many important positions, including Strasbourg and Luxembourg, had been captured. In August, with the treaty of Ratisbon, Austria recognized the possessions France had acquired since 1681, including Strasbourg. Two problems remained, however: the parties to the treaty agreed only to a twenty-year truce, not to a permanent transfer of territory; and the critical "gate" of Philipsburg still remained in Hapsburg hands.

Louis also had to worry about economic and demographic trends. Until the late 1670s, France's economy had been expanding. By the mid-1680s, however, it had stagnated while the rest of Europe continued to grow.[70] Part of the problem was the relative success of English and Dutch mercantile policies.[71] France was also suffering a population crisis: by the early 1680s, deaths began to outnumber births.[72] French leaders were aware of the problems. After 1683, there was increasing criticism of the economic system at the highest levels. In 1687, as the agrarian crisis intensified, the government began investigating the causes of rural poverty.[73]

Geopolitical trends were also negative. France was clearly the preeminent military power in Europe in the 1680s.[74] Yet as Geoffrey Symcox notes, during the decade "the balance of power began to tip in favor of Louis' enemies."[75] As it fought Turkey, Austria's army grew in size and experience. Vienna also launched reforms improving the empire's cohesiveness. Moreover, military inventions that had given France a qualitative edge in the 1670s had diffused to adversaries. These facts so unnerved War Minister Louvois that in 1687 that he interrogated officers who had served in Austria's eastern army and sought new ways to increase his army's firepower.[76]

Of primary concern were Austria's consistent victories against Turkey. Aside from the huge increases in Austrian territory, Paris feared that once Turkey sought peace, Austria would turn west to reclaim its lost border areas. Louis sought to turn the twenty-year truce into a permanent agreement; Vienna refused. As Austrian victories continued, Louis hastily erected further frontier fortifications.[77]

Louis feared invasion above all, but he also worried that Leopold would use his new-found strength to enforce his claim to the Spanish throne. A 1685 memorandum for an envoy to Madrid noted that should Leopold hear that Carlos's health was failing, he would "make peace with the Turk . . . to be able to have all his troops march toward the Rhine." This was a recurring concern over the next few years.[78] From 1685 until the start of war in 1688, Louis worked diligently to shape Carlos's choice of successor. Expecting Carlos's death, he drew up a manifesto claiming the whole Spanish inheritance for his family. Despite the influence of Louis's sister, the Spanish queen, French efforts came to naught. Louis's concerns were not helped by rumors in late 1687 that Vienna might have Joseph, heir to the Austrian throne, raised in Madrid as successor to Carlos.[79]

After 1686, the French position unraveled faster than Louis could have anticipated. In August 1687 came word of the Turkish defeat at Mohács. Louvois wrote Vauban, the man in charge of French military installations, that the news had made Louis "judge it necessary to bring his frontier towards Germany to the last stage of perfection."[80] Through the first eight months of 1688, Louis sought the pope's approval for his candidate for the ecclesiastical principality of Cologne, a strategic point on the Rhine. Paris received reports in June that Holland and Brandenburg-Prussia were mobilizing to block this move. In July, to increase pressure, Louis's envoy told the pope that France was reluctant to take advantage of "favorable circumstances" if war broke out as a result of the pope's decisions.[81] Nevertheless, in August the pope decided in favor of Austria's candidate.

The key report came on 15 August from Louis's ambassador in Istanbul. The Turks, driven back to Belgrade, were ready to make peace. On 20 August, Louis met with his advisers. The decision was made: France would attack Austrian positions in Philipsburg and the Palatinate.[82] French forces struck in late September; by that fall the Spanish Netherlands would be added to the list. Within a year, France would be battling a coalition of all the key great powers.

Louis made his goals public in a declaration to Vienna in September 1688. He had acted to prevent the emperor's "long-established plans to attack France as soon as he could have peace with the Turks." France had to attack the forts "which would give the Emperor easy possibility to . . . sustain war against France."[83] This was propaganda, but it also reflected Louis's true logic. Marshal Villars wrote that the court in August was forced to decide between halting the effort of Holland's William of Orange to capture the English throne and preventing Turkey from making peace with Austria, "which the next moment would bring down on us all the forces of the Emperor."[84] Detailed work by John Wolf, Symcox, and others shows that Louis was acting defensively to protect France from an impending shift in the balance of power.[85]

Louis hoped for a short war that would force Austria to make territorial concessions securing France's frontier. But he recognized the high risk of all-out systemic war. In a letter to his ambassador in Istanbul in late August, Louis noted that his move would mean a "general war in all Europe" from which Turkey could draw advantages.[86] The risks had been clear for some time. In October 1686, Spain, Austria, Sweden, Bavaria, and Saxony had formed the League of Augsburg to protect Germany against further French incursions. By attacking this area, France was invoking alliance commitments from all members.

By the third year, the war fell into a stalemate. In 1697, a peace treaty was signed, but the issues had not been solved. France was still vulnerable on its eastern border, and Louis still worried that the Spanish inheritance would fall into Austria's hands. In October 1698, France signed an agreement with England and Holland that on Carlos's death, Prince Joseph Ferdinand of Bavaria would receive the inheritance. While this deal did not benefit France, it averted a marked increase in Austrian power. Unfortunately, Joseph Ferdinand died in February 1699. In March, a new deal was negotiated with England and Holland. To avoid another coalition, Louis was more than reasonable: Spain, its colonies, and the Spanish Netherlands would go to Archduke Charles of Austria, while France received Naples, Sicily, and Lorraine. Leopold refused this generous settlement. With confidence bolstered by fresh victories over Turkey, he now worked to uphold his claim to the whole inheritance.[87]

In November 1700, Carlos finally died. To everyone's surprise, his will designated that the entire inheritance would go to Louis's grandson Philip. If France turned down this offer, it would go to Austria. In late November, Louis and his advisers debated two unpleasant options: accept, and face war with Austria and probably another Grand Alliance; reject, and allow

Austria to recreate the realm of Charles V. After much discussion, Louis decided to accept the offer. War was inevitable in either case, since France could not permit Austria to gain so much territory. And France's acceptance would at least provide the legal basis for absorbing Spain and its colonies, a move that among other things would improve France's ability to compete in foreign trade.[88]

Thus Louis's logic for initiating the second half of the twenty-five-year major war (the War of Spanish Succession) parallels his reasoning in the first. Austria's 1698–1700 victories over Turkey not only reestablished the Austrian threat, but Vienna's insistence on the entire Spanish inheritance meant that if France did *not* act, it would soon be surrounded by a state of overwhelming power. Louis was not motivated by a lust for *gloire* as much as by a drive for security. As Wolf notes, no one reading Louis's letters can fail to notice his life-long fear of invasion.[89]

THE SEVEN YEARS WAR

The Seven Years War from 1756 to 1763 is the one case of major war studied in this book that does not work well for dynamic differentials theory. Although declining trends were critical to its origins, the war broke out even though the key players were relatively equal in military power. The case thus contradicts my assertion that general war in multipolarity requires a significantly superior military state. Moreover, the war shows that occasionally declining and near-equal great powers can overcome the collective-action problem to organize coalitional preventive war against a rising state. The reasons for these deviations from the typical pattern are thus of interest: they help us understand the conditions under which the theory might be wrong.

The origins of the Seven Years War are straightforward. Historians agree that the primary provocateur was Austria, assisted by Russia. Both states feared the rise of Frederick the Great's Prussia, an upstart state led by a man who had clearly demonstrated a penchant for territorial expansion. Their plan, germinating in 1748–49 but gaining steam in 1755–56, was to eliminate this rising threat before it did any more damage; the spoils would then be divided between themselves and other disaffected states. In the summer of 1756, as Frederick saw Austria and Russia preparing for offensive war, he reluctantly decided to launch a preemptive strike. In late August, he plunged his army into Saxony, leading to a seven-year stalemate in which tiny Prussia, assisted by Britain, hung on against the poorly coordinated efforts of Austria, Russia, and their recent ally France.

Austrian-Russian fears of Prussia were sparked by Frederick's surprise victories over Austria in 1740–44 during the War of Austrian Succession, which led to Prussia's annexation of Silesia.[90] Prussia was a young power: it arose out of the wars of Louis XIV and up until 1740 was not even considered a true great power by most capitals. It had a very small territory, and its population of four million was less than one-third of Austria's and one-fifth of France's.[91] Prussia offset these disadvantages by having the most efficient and well-trained army in Europe.[92] These qualitative strengths could be shown only on the battlefield; thus only after its military successes in 1740–44 was Prussia seen as a growing menace.

As the War of Austrian Succession wound down, "the perception of relative decline . . . infused the Habsburg decision-making system," writes the historian Dennis Showalter.[93] In 1746, Austria and Russia formed a defensive alliance against Prussia which provided the basis for later negotiations. In March 1749, a secret conference of Austria's high council was held to discuss foreign policy. The future chancellor Count von Kaunitz offered a position that would guide his policies during the critical years 1755–56. Austria must never resign itself to the loss of Silesia, "and [must] regard the King of Prussia as the greatest, most dangerous . . . enemy of the dynasty." Accordingly, Austria's constant concern must be to defend itself against Frederick's aggressions and to "limit his power" while retrieving lost lands.[94]

Kaunitz's strategy over the next seven years, both as ambassador to France and as chancellor, was to resolve the centuries-old French-Hapsburg conflict and then to draw France and Russia into a coalition to eliminate Prussia.[95] France's assistance was necessary for two reasons: Austria could not attack Prussia if it had to worry about a French response (especially since France and Prussia had been allies since the 1730s); and France could supply the subsidies needed to ensure that the cash-poor Russian army attacked Prussia's eastern flank. Until May 1756, however, Paris was reluctant to further the designs of its historical adversary. What changed its mind was British-Prussian diplomacy over the winter of 1755–56. Britain and France had already begun a long war over control of North America and India. London worried that Prussia might use the British-French conflict to grab Hanover, the homeland of the British king.

To deter Frederick, London and Petersburg agreed in September 1755 to cooperate against Prussia, with Britain providing 100,000 pounds a year to support the Russian army. When Frederick found out, he decided to mend relations with London to reduce the chance of Russian attack. In January 1756, Prussia and Britain signed the Treaty of Westminster, in which both parties agreed to defend Germany territory against any aggressors. The treaty upset both Paris and Petersburg. The French saw it as a stab in the back: they were relying on attacks on Hanover to divert British forces from the colonial arena. In February, the French decided against renewal of the Franco-Prussian alliance. In March–April, the Russian council agreed to mobilize for war against Prussia and to promise Austria an offensive alliance that would include Sweden and Saxony.

Things were falling into place for Kaunitz, but he had to be careful. To guarantee subsidies for Russia, he wanted France as an active and not just neutral player. In May 1756, the first step in the "diplomatic revolution" was achieved: France agreed to a defensive alliance. If Austria were attacked by Prussia, France would provide 24,000 troops. Vienna still had two problems, however. First, to ensure France acted, it had to get Prussia to appear the aggressor.[96] Second, Kaunitz did not feel the Austrian army was quite ready for war. Thus he sought to postpone the Austro-Russian attack until spring 1757.

Russia was itching for war in 1756, and had 80–120,000 troops mobilized for the job. Austria had only 65–80,000 battle-ready troops, but by the next spring Kaunitz expected another 40–50,000 would be available. Since Prussia had upwards of 150,000 men, a short delay in the invasion made sense.[97] In June 1756, Kaunitz convinced Petersburg to hold off its attack until early 1757. Nevertheless, to ensure that Prussia would be seen as the aggressor, Vienna used diplomacy to provoke Frederick into a preemptive strike. In June–July, Frederick's spies informed him of Russia's mobilization and the coming Austro-Russian attack, but also told him that it would be delayed until the spring.[98] Frederick had no desire for war; he was still consolidating gains from the previous conflict.[99] Yet he also knew that with Vienna and Petersburg determined to eliminate his state, he could not afford to wait until their mobilizations were complete.

In July, Frederick mobilized the Prussian army even as he sought a diplomatic solution. Four times between July and late August, he instructed envoys in Vienna to ask Austrian leaders to declare that they had no current or future intention, alone or with Russia, of attacking Prussia. In his later entreaties, he presented evidence of the Austro-Russian plans and promised to recall his army if only Vienna would declare its peaceful intentions. Each time, the Austrians either denied the allegations or gave "vague and haughty" replies that only affirmed Frederick's suspicions.[100] On 25 August, his patience running out, Frederick wrote to his sister that he had not received a response to his fourth demarche, but that with Austria mobilizing he was "more certain of war than ever." Since he was "expecting a response that was either defiant or ambiguous," the latter on which he "could not rely," he had arranged to leave with his troops on Saturday.[101] On 29 August, Prussian forces invaded Saxony. By this act, Austria achieved its goal of appearing the victim of Prussian aggression. France would enter the war on Austria's side and would provide millions of livres in subsidies to aid the Russian army.[102]

The Seven Years War supports this book's theory insofar as it was fear of decline rather than unit-level factors that drove Austria to organize a preventive war against Prussia. Yet neither Austria nor its partner Russia was militarily superior to Prussia, contrary to the prediction that only markedly superior military powers will initiate major wars of elimination. Unique geopolitical circumstances in the mid-eighteenth century explain how Vienna and Petersburg could overcome the collective-action problem to aggregate their strength against the common threat. First, Prussia was viewed by all as a new power that had upset the established structure. Dividing it up between Austria, Russia, Sweden, and Saxony (with France receiving compensations in the west) could thus be seen simply as a return to the old status quo, rather than as a challenge to the system.[103]

Second, history and Prussia's small territory reduced the universal problem of relative gains in dividing up spoils. Austria, Sweden, and Saxony would be receiving territory taken from them by past Prussian aggression. Moreover, with Russia receiving parts of East Prussia/Poland, no state in 1756 could envision a dramatic shift in the balance of power caused by any subsequent boundary disputes. This is dramatically different from the other multipolar cases, where the rising state was territorially large enough that its elimination would have created significant fears of relative loss.

Third, one must take into account the other powers' extreme suspicion of Frederick as leader of Prussia. He had betrayed his own ally France twice in the War of Austrian Succession, even as he sliced off pieces of Austria. His militarism, arrogance, and love of war for the sake of glory were legendary. As early as 1743, he had declared as a basic rule of geopolitics that all states, no matter how small, must continuously expand to avoid falling behind. His political testament of 1752 outlined specific territories in Germany that should be eventually annexed.[104] In the face of such an extreme character, the deep Austrian-Russian interest in eliminating the menace helped overcome the problems of coordinated offensive war.[105]

In sum, the Seven Years War suggests that coalitional preventive major war by near-equals in multipolarity can be achieved, but only under a narrow set of conditions. The rising state must be seen as highly expansionistic, and it must be a territorially small upstart, such that its elimination would be viewed not as undermining the system, but as stabilizing it. It is hard to think of many periods besides the mid-eighteenth century where these conditions were met.[106]

THE NAPOLEONIC WARS

The period from 1792 to 1815 witnessed two distinct wars: the wars of the French Revolution (1792–1801) and the Napoleonic Wars (1803–15). The former period was not a major war by my definition: while involving many great powers, it was not a conflict that threatened the existence of those powers, but instead a war to reestablish the system's ideological homogeneity. France sought to maintain the new revolutionary government; the other states sought to replace it with a traditional royalist one.[107] The period after 1802, however, was clearly one where the survival of great powers was at stake. France was seeking hegemony, specifically the destruction of Britain and the reduction of others to the status of vassal states.

Yet the roots of the Napoleonic Wars lay not in ideology or in Napoleon's personality, but in the eighteenth-century British-French struggle for global dominance. For a century, France and Britain had fought over trade, industry, and colonies. By 1800, the British had won. They had a far larger colonial realm, one that included India, the jewel of any imperial crown. Moreover, Britain was decades ahead in the industrial revolution. For the French, these developments were alarming. Britain's larger resource base and massive industrial growth, tied to its trade supremacy, meant the long-term devastation of the French economy. This would leave France vulnerable to attack either from giant land powers such as Russia, or from Britain itself. Throughout his career, destroying Britain before it was too late was Napoleon's primary focus. Napoleon's obsession with Britain was hardly new. He simply carried on the tradition of French leaders for the previous half-century—of viewing French survival as a function of the British question.

Since 1700, Britain and France engaged in an unremitting struggle for colonies and trade. The turning point was the Seven Years War. Britain emerged as the war's only victor. It now controlled most of North America and India and had made important gains in western Africa and the West Indies. British trade took off. Even the loss of the American colonies (facilitated by France) did not slow this growth; Britain simply turned America into a supplier of raw materials and a market for its industrial goods. Britain was significantly superior in the technology of the first industrial revolution, and it used this superiority to undersell competitors and to build its dominance in shipping. British trade from 1780 to 1800 tripled, while from 1773–74 to 1800 the size of the merchant marine doubled.[108]

The French economy did not fair so well. French officials, even as they tried to copy British innovations, were constrained by the entrenched practices of the *ancien régime* economy. The revolution did not help: the celebration of economic individualism reinforced a preference for small-scale farming and manufacturing. In fact, despite Napoleon's reform efforts, France would not experience a true industrial takeoff until 1850.[109] The resulting trends were ominous. France's share of total European manufacturing from 1750 to 1800 fell from 17.2 to 14.9 percent, while Britain's rose from 8.2 to 15.3 percent. By 1800, Britain's industrialization per capita was twice that of France.[110] To make matters worse, the demographic trends were against France. France's population in 1800 of 28 million was almost twice Britain's 16 million (not counting colonies). By the 1780s, however, France had entered a period of slower absolute growth as birth rates fell; the British population meanwhile was growing at 10 percent a decade, a trend that would continue for 130 years.[111]

Napoleon's concern for the rising British threat was not unique. After the Seven Years War, senior French officials flirted with a plan to invade Britain, but realized they lacked the power.[112] In early 1798, the Directory running France actively considered such an invasion but was convinced by Napoleon of its current infeasibility; to hurt Britain in another way, Napoleon was sent to conquer Egypt, in preparation for a possible attack on British India.[113]

Napoleon's desire to eliminate Britain remained a constant. In 1788, at age nineteen, he observed that land powers like Sparta and Rome usually destroyed wealthy sea powers, as long as they fought on the latter's territory.[114] In October 1797, having defeated Austria in Italy, Napoleon wrote to the minister of foreign affairs that while the Austrians were a dull lot, the English were a productive people. It was therefore critical to eliminate England, "or France must expect itself to be destroyed by the corruption and intrigues of those active islanders." Once England was defeated, "Europe will be at our feet."[115] In March 1800, now ruler of France, Napoleon issued a proclamation that London desired to reduce France to a second-rate power and to divide Europe in order to seize its commerce.[116] Three months later, he told the British king that it was England, not France, which threatened the balance of power, because of its monopoly on global trade.[117] In these views, Napoleon was not alone: as Arnold Harvey shows, it was widely felt throughout Europe after 1800 that British power had grown too strong.[118]

Napoleon offered the most revealing insights into his thinking in 1803, as war with Britain was reignited after the short-lived Peace of Amiens (March 1802 to May 1803). On 23 August, Napoleon used a letter to Foreign Minister Talleyrand on Russian mediation to detail his geopolitical views. France and England both had interests in the East Indies and in the Americas. But to reright the balance in these areas, England would have to "limit its power." England's unwillingness to evacuate even tiny Malta—one of the sticking points that had led to renewed war—"made clear its intention to add the Mediterranean to its almost exclusive commercial sphere of the Indies, America, and the Baltic." Of all the calamities that could arise, "there is none comparable to this." War, therefore, "however unfortunate it may be," was necessary, and would "never reduce the French people to bowing before this arrogant nation, who make a game of all that is sacred on the earth, and who have, especially in the last twenty years, assumed an ascendancy and temerity which threatens the existence of all nations in their industry and commerce, the lifeblood of states."[119] England's destruction would satisfy more than just the French. That fall, he wrote that "all the evils, all the plagues that afflict mankind come from London."[120] To General Augereau he would state: "I have reason to hope that, within a reasonable time, I will achieve the objective that all of Europe desires. We have six centuries to avenge."[121]

Napoleon's strategy for major war after 1800 was flexible, evolving as circumstances changed, but destroying England remained its objective. By the Treaty of Lunéville in February 1801, Austria recognized French control of the western bank of the Rhine and Belgium and the independence of the Helvetian Republic (Switzerland). Only Britain remained in the war, and Napoleon wanted breathing space to prepare for major war. In October 1801, with his position in Egypt deteriorating, he pressured London into an initial peace, a peace that was finalized in March at Amiens. War-weary Britain gave up most of the colonial conquests made over the previous decade, except Trinidad and Ceylon, and agreed to evacuate Egypt and Malta.

Napoleon's initial strategy was to use the peace to revitalize France's economy, to achieve military superiority, and to hurt British commerce as he rebuilt French colonial trade. Historians agree that after 1804 Napoleon's army was significantly superior to any other state's, primarily owing to mass conscription, better mobility, and Napoleon's leadership skills.[122] Eliminating England, however, required a navy plus the craft for transporting troops, and here he knew that he needed more time to prepare.[123] In late 1801, Napoleon moved to retake Haiti from the rebel leader Touissant Louverture. Haiti had been France's most important colony before the slave revolt in 1791. Napoleon planned to use it and Louisiana (recently reacquired from Spain) as the basis for a reinvigorated West Indies trade policy.[124] A letter to Navy and Colonial Minister Decrès in April 1802 showed he had other goals as well: he instructed Decrès to prepare to reestablish a French position in India. Having failed to get at British India via Egypt in 1798–99, Napoleon would now do so the long way—around the Cape of Good Hope.[125]

By early 1803, relations with Britain were again rocky, and for one main reason. Napoleon, like Hitler in the late 1930s, was positioning his country for major war by occupying the small states on his border. Britain, also as in the 1930s, could not tolerate this expansion if it hoped to stop its rival from achieving continental hegemony. Napoleon had annexed Piedmont and occupied Switzerland in the fall of 1802. Most worrisome, however, was France's continued occupation of Holland. By the treaty of Lunéville, France promised to evacuate Holland after a general peace. The treaty of

Amiens created this general peace, but Napoleon refused to leave, knowing that the Dutch fleet was critical to any invasion of Britain.[126] London was also upset by Napoleon's exclusion of British goods from France. In late January 1803, Napoleon allowed an internal French report to be made public, indicating that France could retake Egypt with a few thousand troops. His goal of hurting British economic power as he prepared for major war was clear. London thus refused to evacuate Malta to restrict France's ability to do harm in the Mediterranean.

Napoleon knew he could not meet London's core demand—a withdrawal from Holland—without sacrificing his ability to wage major war. He thus sought to isolate Britain as he prepared to invade it. In March 1803, he lambasted the British ambassador in front of the entire diplomatic corps, blaming Britain for seeking war.[127] Reports from his ambassador in London showed that the British did not want war.[128] Nevertheless, in late March he ordered his soldiers north and in April gave orders to ready French forces, including those on the French coast.[129] With his troops failing to retake Haiti, he sold Louisiana to the United States to raise money for his military buildup and to position America as a "maritime rival" that could divert British forces.[130]

In May 1803, Paris and London declared war. For the remainder of the year, Napoleon poured money into the navy and began to develop invasion plans. By December 1804, he had 2,000 craft and 177,000 men in northern France, ready for invasion.[131] The plan that evolved by 1805 was risky but ingenious. France was far superior on land, but even with Dutch ships it could only barely match the English navy. Napoleon therefore would have his Mediterranean fleet, led by Admiral de Villeneuve, move across the Atlantic to draw Lord Nelson's southern fleet to the Americas. Villeneuve would then race back to France and join up with the northern fleet at Brest. This temporary naval strength would allow French troops to jump the Channel and quickly defeat the weak English army.

The plan's execution began in May 1805 and was going well until late July, when Villeneuve, instead of turning north after recrossing the Atlantic, turned south and stationed his fleet at Cadiz in southern Spain. Napoleon spent an anxious August awaiting word that Villeneuve had met up with the northern fleet, aware that Austria and Russia were moving westward in support of Britain. The moment of destiny had arrived. On 13 August, he wrote Villeneuve: "Never had a fleet faced such risks for a more important object. . . . For the sake of aiding the invasion of a power which for six centuries has oppressed France, we might all die without regret."[132] As late as 20–23 August, Napoleon still thought he could destroy England once and for all if Villeneuve were to arrive.[133] Yet to Napoleon's chagrin, he never did. On 23 August, Napoleon broke his camp on the north coast and quickly moved his 200,000 man army into Germany to meet the Austrians.

His new strategy was to defeat the continental states first, in order to use Europe as a base for undermining British commerce while he prepared for another invasion of the island.[134] By December France had decisively defeated Austria at Austerlitz. In October 1806, Prussia was beaten. The next month, Napoleon announced the Berlin Decree—a blockade on all British goods. This formed the basis for the Continental System, Napoleon's attempt to destroy Britain's economy by creating an exclusive French economic sphere in Europe.[135] In June 1806, having defeated Russia's forces, he compelled Czar Alexander to agree to close all Russian ports to British goods and to help France force smaller states like Sweden and Denmark to observe the Continental System.

Eliminating England remained Napoleon's main objective up until he attacked Russia in 1812. In September 1807, he outlined plans for another invasion of England, and in early 1808, he reinforced his camp in northern France for that purpose.[136] Britain was still hanging on by 1810, but its economy was faltering. French relations with Russia, however, had turned sour. The Continental System had devastated Russia's economy.[137] Moreover, Petersburg was worried by Napoleon's supply of arms to his recent creation, the Duchy of Warsaw. Napoleon knew of Britain's efforts to save its economy by smuggling goods through Russia. He thus pressured Petersburg to tighten its trade restrictions. In December 1810, the czar not only refused, but he issued a decree imposing tariffs on French goods while opening ports to neutral shipping—which in practice meant British goods would flood into Europe, ending any hope of forcing England to its knees.[138] In July, Napoleon had stated that he would go to war with Russia the moment it made peace with Britain.[139] In June 1812, he invaded Russia to bring a reduced Russia back into the Continental System. Conquering Russia could also provide a direct route to attacking British India.[140]

This analysis shows that fear of a rising Britain was Napoleon's main reason for initiating all-out major war. If England was not eliminated, it would gradually strangle France's economic growth, leaving it vulnerable to invasion by England or by huge land powers such as Russia. Other more personal factors—Napoleon's lust for glory and power, his confidence in his own abilities—cannot be ignored. Yet once we put Napoleon's calculations within the context of a century of French-British rivalry, we see that his concern with Britain's rise was neither new nor irrational. Britain was decades ahead in the industrial revolution, and its long-term global dominance in manufacturing and trade seemed assured—unless war was waged.

This chapter has shown the remarkable continuity in the causes of major war over the millennia. Notwithstanding wide variations in regime-type and leaders' personalities, we saw that fear of deep decline drove each of the seven key major wars of the ancient, early modern, and modern west-

[233]

ern world prior to 1900. The first three cases demonstrate how fragile bipolar systems can be: in each case, war broke out even though the declining state was only roughly equal to the rising state in military power. In three of the four multipolar cases, it was a declining state with significant military superiority that brought on systemic war. Even in the one anomalous case, the Seven Years War, fears of decline were instrumental in pushing Austria to organize a war of elimination against Prussia. The case does suggest that under a narrow set of conditions—the rising state is an aggressive upstart with little territory—major war might break out in multipolarity among states with roughly equal military power. Overall, however, the weight of history strongly upholds the logic of dynamic differentials theory.

[9]

The Implications of the Argument

This book has sought to provide a dynamic realist theory of major war that represents a Lakatosian progressive problem shift within the realist paradigm. The evidence of the empirical chapters suggests that the theory has moved toward this goal: it explains the empirical facts covered by existing theories, while also accounting for evidence left unexplained by these theories.[1] The theory reaches this goal by synthesizing the systemic strengths of current realist arguments, while avoiding the tendency to dip down to the unit level to explain individual cases. This approach helps us to reexamine Kenneth Waltz's popular distinction between theories of international political outcomes and theories of foreign policy. For Waltz, systemic theories explain continuities in outcomes within bipolar or multipolar systems; to understand differences in behavior across states and over time, he argues, one must go down to the unit level.[2] This view has encouraged most scholars to assume that systemic theory can only establish the broad constraints on state behavior, and that for greater explanatory power one must automatically incorporate domestic- and individual-level variables.

The book shows the limitations of this perspective. At any point in time, states face specific systemic constraints reflecting their unique trends and differentials of power. This fact allows us to make predictions about how individual states will act without necessary consideration of their unit-level characteristics.[3] Indeed, strong predictions on outcomes like major war can be made only with a theory that predicts when and why particular states will initiate actions making such outcomes likely. A good systemic theory of foreign policy, therefore, is a prerequisite for a good theory of international political outcomes. Thus while Waltz's neorealism does not seek to explain when major wars will break out, but only why they might recur, this book offers falsifiable predictions about when states will either initiate major wars or take the hostile steps that greatly increase the risks of such a war. Moreover, as the evidence shows, the key major wars, as well as "near-misses" such as the Berlin and Cuban missile crises, were indeed driven by the dynamics of relative power. Unit-level forces can be significant, as I discuss below. But a crucial first step in theory building is establishing a deductively consistent systemic argument—the goal being to determine to what extent behavior and international outcomes can be explained solely with reference to systemic constraints. Such a theory will then set the context and boundaries for the causal role of unit-level variables.

This chapter first considers some of the implications of the argument for both realist and liberal international relations theory. I then examine the book's practical implications for the great power dynamic that will likely dominate the next three decades or more—the relationship between the United States and China.

REALISM AND MAJOR WAR

By fusing the strengths of current realist theories, this book makes three main contributions to realist theory. First, it examines the importance of power shifts across bipolar and multipolar systems. Classical realism and neorealism emphasize polarity; hegemonic stability theory and preventive war arguments stress the importance of dynamic power trends. Yet polarity and the problems of decline have not been brought together in one theory. Dynamic differentials theory shows that polarity affects whether declining states will take actions that could lead to major war. In multipolarity, the declining state must have a significant level of military superiority to consider risking major war. In bipolarity, it may launch major war or crises threatening such a war whether superior or merely equal to the rising state—indeed, it may do so even if somewhat inferior, as we saw with the two Berlin crises.

Considering polarity and power trends simultaneously helps to eliminate anomalies in the existing theories. Classical realism has trouble explaining why war would break out in bipolar systems like Sparta-Athens, Carthage-Rome, and France-Hapsburgs, when both states were essentially equal (that is, when there was a "balance of power"). For neorealism, the very fact that war occurred in bipolarity is surprising. Hegemonic stability theory, with its view that superiority makes for peace, cannot explain why in each of the major wars from 1600 to 1945—with the exception of the Seven Years War—war would be initiated by a state with marked military superiority.[4] The fact that decline occurred in a multipolar context provides the answer.

The second contribution is the building of an argument which can explain when and why a state might take hard-line measures that increase the probability of war through inadvertent means. Many realists emphasize the problem of declining power. Crisis and security-dilemma theorists, including defensive neorealists, underscore the risk that hard-line policies can provoke inadvertent spiraling. No established theory, however, combines these two dimensions into a comprehensive decision-making model.

By developing such a model, this book can make predictions of why, even in the nuclear age, states would ever get themselves into cold wars or crises that risk all-out destruction. States will accept such risks only when continuing with established policies will not stem decline but stronger actions hold out the promise of stabilizing their power position. Yet in moving to harder-line policies, they will weigh the risks of further decline against the risks of provoking an inadvertent spiral to major war. This argument helps us to explain not only why great power crises with a high risk of major war are so rare, but also why they occasionally occur. The two Berlin crises and the Cuban missile crisis only broke out when one of the two superpowers believed that internal measures alone would not reverse decline, but that crisis initiation might achieve this objective.

The book's third contribution is its analysis of three different forms of decline and their varying effects on declining states. Entrenched relative stagnation has been studied by countless scholars. Less well studied are the problems of power oscillations and of disjunctures in economic/potential power and military power. Negative power oscillations occur when the other state's policies are relatively more successful over at least the short term. The declining state will not only worry about the loss of power, but will anticipate that its subsequent effort to catch up may push the *other* state into preventive policies, perhaps even war. Depending on the size of the oscillation, strong action now to ameliorate decline can be rational. This dynamic was at work, as we saw, in the three cold war crises. Most realists ignore power oscillations or do not integrate them with the risks of inadvertent spiraling. Consequently, they do not offer complete explanations for the occasional but dangerous risk-taking witnessed in the cold war.

The separation of economic/potential power from military power is particularly valuable in explaining cases where states embark on the most extreme measures to uphold their security. Probably the most destabilizing situation in world politics is one where a state is militarily superior, but inferior in economic and especially potential power. This was Germany's problem prior to both world wars: it possessed marked military superiority, yet it faced a Russia with three times its population and forty times its land mass. Without war, the German civilian and military leaders believed that Russia would eventually overwhelm Europe; *with* war, Germany might not only eliminate the threat, but it could grab the territory needed for long-term security. Inferiority in potential power was also at the heart of the problem in a number of other important cases, particularly Carthage-Rome and France-Hapsburgs and to a lesser degree in the ancient Greek case and the Napoleonic Wars.

Current realist theories, by overlooking the importance of disjunctures in economic/potential power and military power, provide less comprehensive systemic explanations across the various cases. Classical realists and neorealists recognize Germany's insecure geographic position in the center of Europe, but they tend to fall back on Hitler's personality and Nazi hypernationalism to explain the specific motives for the Second World War. Classical realists have trouble explaining the First World War, given the balance of power between the two alliance blocs. Neorealists invoke miscalculation in multipolarity to account for war in 1914. Yet multipolarity is a constant that cannot explain the changing incentive for major war over time. More to the point, World War I was *not* a war of miscalculation; Berlin wanted war for preventive reasons and did everything necessary to bring it on under the best possible conditions.

In sum, realist theories as they stand remain disconnected and incomplete. Classical realism rightly emphasizes power differentials; neorealism, polarity and the security dilemma; hegemonic stability theory and preventive war theories, the problem of dynamic trends. By synthesizing and reformulating these elements, dynamic differentials theory provides an argument with greater explanatory power across the full range of cases.

Regime-Type, Liberal Theory, and Major War

The book's argument also has implications for liberal arguments, particularly those that stress the role of domestic-level causes of major war. The theoretical chapters held such unit-level factors constant to isolate the role of shifts in the differentials of power. By relaxing that assumption, we can examine how certain domestic forces might operate under properly specified systemic conditions. Overall, the empirical chapters showed that unit-level factors were less important in causing major wars and crises than is commonly supposed. Yet this book does not deny the importance of such factors in history. They can be expected to have two separate effects independent of relative power changes.

First, even though the theory's power conditions are almost always necessary conditions for major war, they may not be sufficient: chapter 2 noted that declining states will sometimes initiate major conflict for aggressive nonsecurity motives. One cannot ignore the Genghis Khans of history who seem to be propelled more by glory and greed than by concerns about rising neighbors. It is worth reiterating, however, that such examples do not falsify the theory, only qualify its salience.[5] Moreover, the fact that so many of the key cases of the twentieth century and of previous centuries were driven primarily or exclusively by fears of decline shows the strong salience of the dynamic differentials argument.

Second, domestic forces may affect the probability of major war through variations on the regime-type of the *rising* state. In the theoretical chapters, I assumed that the declining state was fundamentally uncertain of the future intentions of the rising state. That is, the declining state assumed either that the other was just as likely as not to attack later at its peak (a 50–50 chance), or that the other's propensity to attack was a function of how far it rose. This assumption allowed us to isolate the interactive effects of other more systemic causal factors, while showing how conflict might arise even when all states sought only their own security. A declining state's analysis of the other's regime-type, however, should have some influence on its estimate of the other's likelihood of attacking later (the third parameter from chapter 2). A declining authoritarian state will probably be just as suspicious of a rising democracy as of a rising nondemocracy. Declining democracies, however, are likely to place some importance on the domestic characteristics of the rising state—but not always in ways consistent with the hypotheses of the liberal "democratic peace" literature.

By the logic of the democratic peace, a declining democracy should be less likely to attack a rising democracy at time t_0 if it has strong reason to believe that the rising state will remain democratic after it peaks at time t_1. At t_1, the (formerly) rising state should be disinclined to attack because of its respect for the other's democratic ways and because of legislative constraints on its ability to make war.[6] Anticipating this fact, the declining state at t_0 will lower its estimate of the rising state's likelihood of attacking later and thus be less inclined to preventive war.

Note, however, that there is a key condition underpinning the logic here: the relative stability of the rising state's regime-type. What really matters is not whether the rising state is currently democratic, but whether it will *still be* democratic years down the road, after it peaks. If Russia were rising today, for example, the fact that it is democratic would be of little comfort; given Russia's fragile democratic structure, it seems hard to predict its regime-type in ten or fifteen years. This suggests an important implication of this book's argument for liberal democratic peace theory, at least as this theory relates to great powers and major war: in dynamic power environments, peace will be robust primarily between established, stable democracies.

This discussion suggests that to strengthen liberal theory, we need to combine the dynamics of domestic politics with the dynamics of systemic power changes. Since what matters to a declining state is its estimate of the *future* "democratic-ness" of the rising state, the former will base this estimate primarily on the internal trends within the latter. If the rising state is a democracy showing increasing signs of instability, there will be less confidence about its future type. If, however, the rising state is currently authoritarian but undergoing democratization, this should give the declining state greater confidence that by the time the other peaks, it will have become democratic enough to be relatively peaceful.[7] This leads to a second and surprising implication of dynamic differentials theory: declining and democratic states may be *more* likely to initiate preventive moves against unstable democracies than against authoritarian states that show a strong trend toward democracy.[8]

In sum, systemic realist arguments do not need to reject the insights of liberal theory. Regime-type can matter. Yet if declining power is as critical a causal force as the empirical chapters suggest, liberal theories need to address the twin problems of domestic instability and future intentions. Declining states know that the rising state, regardless of its regime-type, has little reason to attack while still rising. But they worry about the other's intentions years into the future once it is more powerful. In the context of relative decline, therefore, the stability of the rising state's current regime-type should provide one important means for estimating these future intentions.[9]

PRACTICAL IMPLICATIONS

What are the argument's implications for the prospects for peace in the post–cold war world? Neorealists who predict instability in Europe and Asia due to the emergence of global and regional multipolarity are unnecessarily pessimistic.[10] Multipolar systems are less likely to fall into major war than bipolar ones, since the conditions for war are less permissive.[11] As we have seen, major wars can occur in bipolarity when states are either equal or unequal in military power, but in multipolarity the initiator requires marked superiority to consider attacking the system. Hence, the presence of many regional powers in Europe and Asia will help moderate the behavior of any particular state. Even a resurgently nationalistic Germany would be deterred from taking on the European system again, since costly bilateral wars would harm its relative power position versus third parties. The same holds for China or Japan in the Far East.

Multipolarity in the twenty-first century will not be the problem. The problem is the risk of significant shifts in the power balance. Major wars and destabilizing crises occur when dominant states anticipate deep decline. Dynamic differentials theory thus focuses our attention on powers that are most likely to rise against the established states. Concerns about the relative rise of China are particularly evident, and for good reason. Since the early 1980s, China's economy has been growing consistently at an annual rate of two to three times that of any other great power. Simple extrapolation suggests that China could catch up to America in total GNP within a couple of decades. The worry, of course, is that China's rising economic strength will eventually be translated into the kind of military power that could threaten U.S. security. To the extent that China emerges as the only challenger in what would become a strongly bipolar world, this worry will be intensified.[12]

Will China's relative growth undermine the stability the global system now enjoys? Behind this issue lurk the questions of why exactly the system has been essentially stable since the early 1990s (with stability defined as a low probability of major war) and which state is most likely to initiate a new round of cold wars and crises.

For liberals, the stability since 1991 has a number of roots: the end of an ideological battle between capitalism and socialism;[13] the spread of democracy;[14] increasing economic interdependence;[15] and a growing web of economic and political institutions.[16] This book does not dismiss the potential effects of such unit-level and nonpower systemic variables. Yet just as liberal theories miss one of the core causes of conflict over the millennia—the fear of long-term decline—they also overlook what may be both the necessary and sufficient conditions for the recent peace: that unlike in previous eras, there is no reason to believe that the dominant great power, the United States, is declining deeply and inevitably. Should such a belief arise and gain widespread acceptance, history indicates that all of the liberal causes of peace combined would have little restraining value.

The United States, compared to potential rivals, currently occupies a unique historical position. Unlike Britain in the nineteenth century, which was superior in at most industrial production, the United States is supremely dominant in all three dimensions of power: military, economic, and potential.[17] With the once-vaunted Red Army now in tatters, the United States is clearly the world's only remaining conventional global superpower. Although Russia still retains a large strategic-missile force, its economy is so weak that the main fear is not Russian attack, but the government's inability to maintain control of its nuclear weapons. China's nuclear arsenal is still a small fraction of America's, as are the British and French stockpiles.

Economically, China's historically strong growth rate is a concern. But to explain the stability from 1991 to 2000 and the stability that will likely continue for at least the next decade, we should note the crucial differences between recent Chinese growth and the rise of Russia after 1945. After World War II, U.S. leaders had good reason to fear Soviet economic growth. Russia, owing to reforms starting in the nineteenth century, was by 1945 poised to become an industrial superpower. Moreover, the years after 1945 were a period when total industrial output, particularly in "heavy" goods like steel and machinery, was still a critical basis for economic and military power. Thus the fear that the Soviets might become the Americans' economic equal (or better) was a reasonable one.

Behind Russian economic strides lay the state's potential power: a huge reserve of raw materials and a population equal to that of the United States. Most important, however, were Russian technological strengths. The Russians not only matched the Manhattan Project within four years, but were the first to launch an ICBM and a satellite. Moreover, from 1945 to 1962 U.S. second-strike capability was not necessarily assured. Potential Soviet technological achievements, backed by massive spending in basic research, thus represented a real threat to long-term U.S. security.[18]

The potential rising Chinese threat has a number of important differences from the situation in the early postwar years. First, China, despite recent gains, is still in many ways a developing nation. Eighty percent of its population still works in agriculture, using highly labor-intensive technology. China must now move beyond an expertise in light manufacturing into the second stage of development: advanced industrial production. Yet with the United States immersed in the third stage of high-tech production, China will have to scramble to compete in the information age.[19]

It is in the dimension of potential power that China's real strength remains the most ambiguous. With a territory equal to the United States, China has an adequate resource base. Moreover, such a large area permits the dispersion of nuclear missiles. Such a dispersion is a critical condition for becoming a nuclear superpower, since it allows the nation to absorb a counterforce first-strike without necessarily destroying itself in the process.[20]

In other aspects of potential power, however, China faces important obstacles. Although historically a large population brings increased economic strength, in China's case it is clearly too big for its own good. Superpowerdom requires a per capita surplus over basic consumption that can be devoted to ongoing research and investment, global power projection capability, and high-tech weaponry. China's economic growth may give it a total GNP equal to or greater than that of the United States within a decade or so. But with four times the population, per capita income will remain a fraction of America's for some time to come. This places clear restrictions on China's ability to shift greater funds to the military prerequisites of superpowerdom.

China also remains inferior in probably the most important element of potential power in the modern world: technology. The United States (and Japan) lead the world in almost all technological areas. China is far from narrowing the current gap, including that in military technology. So while in the 1950s U.S. leaders could rightly worry that Russia might overtake

America in technological know-how—a superiority that might be translated into military superiority—there seems little reason at present to think China could achieve this goal. Moreover, the United States now possesses a large and secure second strike. Given the diversity of the U.S. bomber, submarine, and missile forces, only a breakthrough on an anti-missile defense system could undermine the U.S. nuclear deterrent. Yet the Americans remain second to none in such technology.

This analysis helps explain the global stability of the 1990s and why the subsequent few years should also be relatively peaceful.[21] Note that liberal arguments have difficulty accounting for this stability, at least in terms of the key great power relationship: the United States and China. China remains authoritarian, so democratic peace arguments do not apply. By the turn of the new century, China was still outside the institutional framework that supposedly fosters peace (Organization for Security and Cooperation in Europe, NATO, Partnership for Peace, WTO).[22]

The issue at hand, therefore, is under what conditions we would expect a deterioration in U.S.-Chinese relations over the next two decades.[23] Since rising states wish to avoid conflict, the theory would expect China to continue to be relatively peaceful (especially since economic engagement is helping to fuel its growth). If destabilizing policies are to be initiated, the perpetrator will likely be a declining United States.[24] Chapter 2 outlined three variables and three parameters that help predict when a declining state will shift from peaceful engagement to hard-line strategies. Two of the variables focus on the depth and inevitability of decline in the absence of strong action. We have seen that Washington over the last few years has had little reason to believe that decline would be either deep or inevitable. Given this, and given the real risks involved in reigniting a new cold war through containment, engagement has made sense.

Over the next two decades, however, intense debates between hawks and doves over the depth and inevitability of decline—and what the United States can do about it—will likely increase, especially if China can sustain high growth rates.[25] As I argued in chapter 2, however, both groups will likely agree on the basic causal logic, disagreeing only over estimates of variable/parameter values. Hawks will tend to reject engagement because they are more pessimistic about the depth of the U.S. fall. Downplaying arguments as to why Chinese economic growth should peter out, such individuals will focus on China's potential to become the world's largest economy and to translate this economic power into military strength. While acknowledging that hard-line strategies will likely produce a new cold war, hawks will probably have lower estimates than doves of the likely spiraling effects (parameter two). The risks of letting China rise would therefore be greater than the risks of inadvertent war.

Two other parameters from chapter 2 will also animate the hawks-doves debate. The first is the likelihood of China attacking the United States later at its peak, if permitted to grow. Hawks undoubtedly will perceive China, given its Communist leadership, as a future threat (and democratic-peace theorists should agree). Moderates and doves will point to the existence of nuclear weapons and America's secure second strike as a powerful deterrent even if China becomes preponderant.[26] The other parameter is the extent to which a hard-line strategy short of war can actually overcome U.S. decline. Agreement is likely here that through U.S. adoption of containment, Chinese economic growth can be moderated: given China's need for trade and investment, CoCom-like restrictions would clearly hurt. But the value of such restrictions must be balanced against the real risk of unleashing a new cold war that would increase the chance of inadvertent war.

How does a president, in the midst of such tradeoffs, choose a policy to maximize the nation's long-run security? The president's task is to establish the best estimates for the variables and parameters described above, and then to balance off the benefits, costs, and risks for each option along the soft-line/hard-line spectrum. Over time, as more information is received, a rational president will update his or her estimates and adjust policy accordingly. Currently, China's long-term rise to superpower status may not seem inevitable if engagement continues. Within the next decade, however, if China's relative growth continues, estimates will have to be revised and policy can be predicted to gravitate toward the hard-line end of the spectrum.

In short, a wait-and-see policy is rational now given the risks of a new cold war, but in another decade U.S. leaders may find themselves back in Truman's dilemma of 1945. Truman, despite warnings that a hard-line strategy would spark a destabilizing rivalry, moved to restrict Soviet growth. In ten years' time, U.S. policy-makers will likely face a similarly profound choice. Whether they move to containment will depend less on China's friendliness, and more on the updated estimates of the depth and inevitability of decline, the degree to which decline can be averted by strong action, and the likelihood of war as a result of such action.

This book's theory is a theory on the effects of decline, not on its causes per se.[27] It thus offers predictions on state behavior for different future scenarios, but it cannot predict which scenario will transpire. China might have an internal revolution tomorrow that halts its growth, whereas Russia might get its economic act together to become the new rising state. By establishing the variables and parameters affecting a state's expected probability of survival, however, the theory shows the interaction between the key causal factors that determine a state's rational policy. Moreover, by isolating the effects of differentials and trends in relative power, the theory helps leaders understand the systemic framework for their policies before they plunge into all the complications of the unit level.

Existing realist theories remain at odds because of limitations in their deductive structures. They thus offer policy-makers few predictions that are not challenged by opposing views within the realist camp.[28] Dynamic differentials theory, by synthesizing their strengths into one causal logic, helps to resolve this intrarealist conflict. No systemic argument will explain and predict everything; rational leaders will still want to consider domestic and personality factors in their decision-making process. Yet given the evidence demonstrating how strongly and how often systemic variables override such factors, leaders can ignore systemic constraints only at their own peril.

This book has shown the explanatory and predictive value of taking a dynamic realist approach to the analysis of great power behavior and major war. Unit-level factors no doubt still play important causal roles. Yet by emphasizing dynamic trends in the power balance, this study reinforces the tragic dimension of world politics. Even good security-seeking states will be inclined to hostile acts in the face of deep and inevitable decline. Moreover, the problem for declining states is less the other's present characteristics than its future characteristics once it grows to preponderance. And since rising states have an incentive to project peaceful intentions, declining states have difficulty estimating future intentions based on the other's current behavior.

The intractable problems of decline suggests new research agendas for both realist and liberal scholars. Realists have to abandon the sterile debate over whether equality or inequality between great powers is destabilizing. As we have seen, both may be problematic, depending on polarity and on the depth and inevitability of the dominant state's projected decline. The real question is therefore under what conditions does equality or inequality lead to war. This book helps to answer this question.

Realists must also go beyond their primary focus on relative power as an exogenous force that actors simply accept, and act upon. Dynamic differentials theory provides a framework allowing actors to adopt hard-line policies short of war that stand a chance of reversing decline. This framework offers important theoretical advantages. By facilitating predictions on when cold war rivalries and great power crises will occur, it permits predictions on the probability of major war as a continuous variable. Valid arguments on the risks of spiraling to inadvertent war within rivalries and crises can thus be integrated with a broader realist theory of major war.

The dilemma of decline also requires a shift in focus for liberal scholars and those employing modern game theory. Too much emphasis has been placed upon comparative statics—on examining snapshots of actor characteristics and of the information each side possesses regarding those characteristics. This book indicates that the problem is less one of determining the other's present type than of estimating its future type in environments of shifting power. Large-N quantitative studies of the behavior of democratic versus authoritarian states have not captured this. Moreover, to the extent that games of incomplete information focus on how costly signals reveal the other's current type, they miss the core problem: the declining state's anxiety regarding the other's type many years down the road. This future type is something about which the rising state's signaling practices, even before one considers its incentive to misrepresent, can reveal little.

I end with a call for theoretical cooperation between realist and liberal paradigms. For too long these paradigms have been unnecessarily at odds with each other, with realists stressing the primacy of power while liberals counter with domestic factors, international norms, and psychological pathologies. Yet as I suggested in chapter 2, there exists an underlying causal logic on which both camps can agree. Since both groups want to help security-seeking states (in particular, the United States) make rational decisions, both can recognize the problem that decline poses but also the problem of the rising state's future type and of the risk that hostile policies can bring on an inadvertent war. Dynamic differentials theory, in order to build a strong systemic realist theory, has isolated the role of changing power on a rational state's decision-making process. Relaxing the theory's parameters and assumptions, however, illuminates how shifts in non-power variables should affect state behavior within any particular dynamic power environment. Realists and liberals can then dispense with debates over whether power or nonpower variables "matter." They can move to the more fruitful question of the conditions under which they matter, and to what extent. They can also examine when and to what extent power variables will work with nonpower variables to create their effects, and when in fact power might override other factors (or vice versa).

Beginning with this common framework, empirical analyses would then not seek to score definitive coups against the other paradigm. Rather, since empirical counterexamples can always be identified for every argument, the task would be to show how often power factors trumped nonpower variables (or the converse), and how often only a mixture of variables explains the events in question. This book has demonstrated the significant influence of declining power on state behavior across time. Yet to provide guidance on issues such as the rise of China, scholars must offer leaders coherent arguments for how power differentials and trends interact with other parameters to shape a state's rational policy. Dynamic differentials theory offers one such argument.

Appendix

Table A.1 reproduces the figures on national strength during the first years of war from Jacek Kugler and William Domke's article "Comparing the Strength of Nations," *Comparative Political Studies* 19 (April 1986): 39–70. The authors construct an overall index of actualized power that takes into account not only a nation's economic resource base (as measured by GNP) but also its political capacity to mobilize this resource base.

Kugler and Domke's figures of "national strength" are a function of a nation's "internal capabilities" plus its "external capabilities." Internal capabilities in turn equal the "societal resource base" (GNP) multiplied by the "relative political capacity" of a state (a separate index measured as a ratio of the state's actual extraction of resources versus its expected extraction). External capabilities equal the foreign aid the state receives to fight a war multiplied by its relative political capacity.

Kugler and Domke do not provide separate figures for the Soviet Union 1939–41 and Britain 1941–42. Neither do they provide separately Germany's total national strength for 1941 and 1942. I have calculated those German figures by taking the authors' total for the Axis alliance in 1941 and 1942 and subtracting from it the power figures for Italy and Japan. On the eastern front in particular, Germany's index of strength was 153.2 in 1941 and 165.5 in 1942.

Tables A.2–A.4 provide each state's percentage share of resources over five different indices of power in the Correlates of War data set (University of Michigan). While the data to calculate these relative balances were not necessarily available to the leaders of any of these states at the time and are often distorted by questionable national-accounting practices and fluctuating exchange rates, the figures do provide a rough check on the accuracy of leader perceptions of the distribution of power across time. The population column captures one aspect of a state's potential power; the figures for iron and steel production and energy consumption capture two dimensions of a state's economic power; and the defense expenditures and defense personnel statistics are one part of the military power balance (although they measure neither the qualitative aspects of military power nor relative strategic acumen).

The COW data set, before calculation of the percentages, is provided in the following units: population—thousands of individuals; iron-steel production—thousands of tons; energy consumption—thousands of coal-ton equivalents; defense expenditures—thousands of current-year British pounds (table A.2) or U.S. dollars (tables A.3 and A.4); and defense personnel—thousands of men.

Figures do not capture the resources of the smaller states within each great power's empire or sphere of influence. Columns may not add to 100 percent owing to rounding.

Table A.1. Kugler/Domke's statistics on actualized power, 1914–1915 and 1939–1941

World War I

	Britain	France	Russia	Total Allies	Germany
1914	30.6	33.2	48.9	112.7	107.0
1915	78.3	47.0	100.1	225.4	268.0

World War II

	Britain	France	Total	Soviet Union	Germany
1939	10.5	42.0	52.5	—	121.5
1940	27.4	79.6	107.0	—	162.1
1941	—	—	—	176.4	209.7
1942	—	—	—	148.5	234.1

Table A.2. Statistics on relative power balance, 1820–1914

	Population	Iron-Steel Production	Energy Consumption	Defense Expenditures	Defense Personnel
1820					
Britain	14.2	48.1	n/a	29.0	9.5
France	20.8	18.2	n/a	23.3	13.8
Russia	36.3	18.2	n/a	23.1	51.0
Prussia	7.7	6.4	n/a	9.2	8.6
Austria	21.1	9.1	n/a	15.4	17.1
1830					
Britain	14.8	53.0	n/a	23.3	8.6
France	20.1	20.8	n/a	34.5	15.9
Russia	35.9	14.6	n/a	21.4	50.7
Prussia	8.0	4.6	n/a	8.5	8.0
Austria	21.0	6.9	n/a	12.3	16.8
1840					
Britain	15.3	64.0	n/a	19.8	10.3
France	19.7	15.9	n/a	36.4	27.2
Russia	35.9	8.6	n/a	25.9	38.0
Prussia	8.4	5.0	n/a	6.7	8.2
Austria	20.6	6.4	n/a	11.0	16.2
1850					
Britain	15.0	69.7	n/a	18.8	9.7
France	19.5	12.2	n/a	27.2	21.1
Russia	36.6	7.3	n/a	30.1	42.0
Prussia	8.9	4.0	n/a	5.6	6.3
Austria	20.0	6.7	n/a	18.2	20.9
1860					
Britain	15.0	66.4	69.2	29.6	14.9
France	19.4	15.4	12.4	30.3	26.2
Russia	39.5	6.0	0.9	22.1	37.1
Prussia	9.3	6.8	14.0	5.4	8.6
Austria	16.8	5.3	3.5	12.5	13.2
1870					
Britain	13.9	65.8	61.7	13.2	12.7
France	17.1	12.8	12.7	39.2	22.4
Russia	37.6	3.9	0.9	13.2	36.6
Germany	15.4	13.0	18.5	28.5	15.8
Austria	15.9	4.3	6.2	5.9	12.5
1880					
Britain	13.5	60.6	57.4	18.7	10.3
France	14.6	13.3	13.3	28.7	22.6
Russia	39.0	3.4	2.5	26.6	37.8
Germany ·	17.6	19.0	21.6	16.9	17.9
Austria	15.1	3.5	5.2	9.0	11.4
1890					
Britain	13.2	50.2	51.2	20.2	10.9
France	13.5	12.3	12.9	25.1	23.3
Russia	41.1	5.8	3.8	20.6	33.0
Germany	17.3	25.6	25.1	25.5	19.8
Austria	15.0	6.1	6.9	8.7	13.0

	Population	Iron-Steel Production	Energy Consumption	Defense Expenditures	Defense Personnel
1895					
Britain	13.1	45.6	48.5	23.5	11.3
France	12.8	11.6	12.4	23.6	21.4
Russia	41.9	8.4	5.6	23.7	33.9
Germany	17.3	27.8	26.0	20.3	22.0
Austria	14.8	6.6	7.5	9.0	11.4
1900					
Britain	12.9	30.4	43.7	46.1	15.3
France	12.2	9.6	12.2	15.7	19.5
Russia	42.6	13.4	7.8	16.6	35.9
Germany	17.6	39.5	28.8	15.3	19.6
Austria	14.7	7.1	7.4	6.2	9.7
1905					
Britain	12.7	27.4	41.2	16.6	9.1
France	11.6	10.4	12.2	12.5	14.4
Russia	43.5	10.5	8.8	50.9	54.4
Germany	17.8	44.9	30.1	13.8	14.9
Austria	14.5	6.8	7.6	6.2	7.2
1910					
Britain	12.4	22.7	38.5	23.9	11.0
France	10.9	12.0	11.4	19.3	19.2
Russia	44.9	11.6	8.6	24.2	40.7
Germany	17.8	46.0	33.0	23.5	19.8
Austria	14.0	7.6	8.5	9.0	9.3
1914					
Britain	12.2	25.5	38.2	25.4	12.2
France	10.6	9.0	11.8	18.7	18.2
Russia	45.4	14.3	9.5	13.0	30.4
Germany	17.7	44.2	36.5	27.1	19.8
Austria	14.1	6.9	3.9	15.8	19.3

Note: Defense personnel measures the standing army and does not include trained reserves that can be put into action upon mobilization (thus Germany's relative number of military men in 1914 is understated).

Defense expenditures in certain years prior to 1914 reflect the costs of specific conflicts, in particular 1870 (Franco-Prussian war), 1900 (Boer war), and 1905 (Russo-Japanese war).

I have not included either the United States or Italy, given their low military significance for the interactions of the main European great powers.

Table A.3. Statistics on relative power balance, 1920–1941

	Population	Iron-Steel Production	Energy Consumption	Defense Expenditures	Defense Personnel
1920					
Britain	16.0	41.6	45.6	43.3	9.8
France	13.3	12.2	14.0	10.6	24.1
Soviet Union	43.2	0.9	3.1	34.7	50.4
Germany	14.6	41.9	34.2	2.3	1.9
Italy	12.9	3.5	3.2	9.0	13.9
1925					
Britain	14.3	24.4	38.8	21.8	19.1
France	12.8	24.2	16.9	12.2	26.5
Soviet Union	44.6	6.1	5.3	54.4	31.4
Germany	15.9	39.5	35.0	5.6	6.4
Italy	12.4	5.8	4.1	6.0	16.7
1930					
Britain	13.3	20.2	33.6	10.3	18.3
France	12.1	25.6	17.8	10.1	23.6
Soviet Union	45.5	15.6	11.9	70.9	32.3
Germany	17.2	33.9	32.4	3.4	6.6
Italy	11.9	4.7	4.4	5.4	19.2
1933					
Britain	12.9	23.8	32.5	8.3	14.8
France	11.6	21.9	16.2	13.0	21.1
Soviet Union	45.8	23.0	19.3	58.7	41.5
Germany	18.0	25.4	27.8	11.2	5.5
Italy	11.6	5.9	4.2	8.7	17.0
1934					
Britain	12.8	23.3	31.7	9.2	13.2
France	11.4	15.9	14.5	12.0	19.1
Soviet Union	46.1	25.1	21.4	59.0	39.3
Germany	18.0	30.9	28.0	12.0	13.2
Italy	11.6	4.8	4.4	7.7	15.1
1935					
Britain	12.7	21.0	30.6	7.1	8.0
France	11.3	13.2	13.3	9.5	13.7
Soviet Union	46.4	26.5	23.1	60.2	32.4
Germany	18.0	34.6	28.3	17.6	11.5
Italy	11.6	4.7	4.7	5.6	34.4
1936					
Britain	12.6	21.3	30.1	10.7	10.6
France	11.2	11.9	12.6	12.0	18.6
Soviet Union	46.7	29.1	24.7	35.3	41.1
Germany	18.0	34.1	29.0	28.1	18.8
Italy	11.5	3.6	3.5	13.8	10.8
1937					
Britain	12.5	21.7	29.0	12.3	10.1
France	11.0	13.0	12.8	8.8	17.7
Soviet Union	47.0	29.2	23.9	34.1	41.4
Germany	17.9	32.7	30.2	32.6	17.4
Italy	11.5	3.4	4.1	12.2	13.4

Table A.3. (*continued*)

	Population	Iron-Steel Production	Energy Consumption	Defense Expenditures	Defense Personnel
1938					
Britain	12.4	17.7	27.5	11.4	9.9
France	11.0	10.3	11.8	5.6	15.3
Soviet Union	47.2	30.2	24.8	33.2	41.3
Germany	17.9	37.9	31.9	45.3	20.6
Italy	11.5	3.9	3.9	4.6	12.8
1939					
Britain	12.5	20.4	26.9	28.6	6.5
France	10.9	12.1	10.3	3.7	9.5
Soviet Union	44.5	26.7	24.5	21.7	29.4
Germany	20.7	37.3	34.8	43.5	45.1
Italy	11.5	3.5	3.6	2.4	9.5
1940					
Britain	12.3	21.8	27.0	22.8	6.7
France	10.7	7.3	9.7	13.1	33.0
Soviet Union	43.8	30.3	24.8	14.1	27.7
Germany	21.8	36.9	35.0	48.6	21.8
Italy	11.3	3.7	3.5	1.4	10.8
1941					
Britain	13.8	22.3	29.2	23.7	16.9
Soviet Union	48.8	27.8	28.4	14.5	30.9
Germany	24.7	46.3	38.7	60.7	52.2
Italy	12.7	3.7	3.7	1.1	n/a

Note: I have not included the United States, given its low military relevance to the inter-actions of the main European great powers (even in 1939, it was still spending only 1.6 per-cent of its GNP on defense). The United States does of course matter to the outcome of the war given its huge economic and potential power. For the Correlates of War relative per-centages from 1930 to 1940 when America and Japan are included, see Randall Schweller, *Deadly Imbalances* (New York: Columbia University Press, 1998), table 1.1.

Table A.4. Statistics on relative power balance, 1945–1962

	Population	Iron-Steel Production	Energy Consumption	Defense Expenditures	Defense Personnel
1945					
United States	45.4	85.5	84.3	91.3	49.2
Soviet Union	54.6	14.5	15.7	8.7	50.8
1946					
United States	45.6	81.8	83.6	83.7	53.5
Soviet Union	54.4	18.2	16.4	16.3	46.5
1947					
United States	45.3	84.1	83.1	55.3	35.7
Soviet Union	54.7	15.9	16.9	44.7	64.4

	Population	Iron-Steel Production	Energy Consumption	Defense Expenditures	Defense Personnel
1948					
United States	45.3	81.2	82.0	45.4	31.9
Soviet Union	54.7	18.8	18.0	54.6	68.1
1949					
United States	45.4	75.2	79.3	49.2	30.4
Soviet Union	54.6	24.8	20.7	50.8	69.6
1950					
United States	45.5	76.2	80.1	48.4	24.4
Soviet Union	54.5	23.7	19.9	51.2	75.6
1951					
United States	45.5	75.2	79.9	62.4	38.0
Soviet Union	54.5	24.8	20.1	37.6	62.0
1952					
United States	45.5	71.0	78.7	68.6	40.0
Soviet Union	54.5	29.0	21.3	31.4	60.0
1953					
United States	45.5	72.7	78.0	66.0	36.3
Soviet Union	54.5	27.3	22.0	34.0	63.7
1954					
United States	45.6	65.9	75.7	60.4	34.7
Soviet Union	54.4	34.1	24.3	39.6	65.3
1955					
United States	45.6	70.1	75.1	57.8	32.0
Soviet Union	54.4	29.9	24.9	42.2	68.0
1956					
United States	45.6	68.2	75.0	61.0	33.8
Soviet Union	54.4	31.8	25.0	39.0	66.2
1957					
United States	45.7	66.6	73.1	61.7	36.6
Soviet Union	54.3	33.4	26.9	38.3	63.4
1958					
United States	45.7	58.5	71.2	60.1	38.2
Soviet Union	54.3	41.5	28.8	39.9	61.8
1959					
United States	45.7	58.6	71.3	57.3	39.3
Soviet Union	54.3	41.4	28.7	42.5	60.7
1960					
United States	45.6	58.0	70.9	55.1	39.1
Soviet Union	54.4	42.0	29.1	44.9	60.9
1961					
United States	45.6	55.7	70.4	52.3	43.5
Soviet Union	54.4	44.3	29.6	47.7	56.5
1962					
United States	45.9	53.3	70.0	51.2	46.4
Soviet Union	54.3	46.7	30.0	48.8	53.6

Notes

1. This position tends to be most associated with liberal and constructivist scholars.

2. Extending my argument in this direction is beyond the scope of this book, but for an initial discussion, see Dale C. Copeland, "From Structural Realism to Dynamic Realism," paper delivered at the International Studies Association annual meeting, Toronto, March 1997.

3. In this vast literature, see esp. Robert Gilpin, *War and Change in World Politics* (Cambridge: Cambridge University Press, 1981); Paul Kennedy, *The Rise and Fall of the Great Powers* (New York: Random House, 1987); Geir Lundestad, ed., *The Fall of Great Powers* (Oxford: Oxford University Press, 1994); Joseph S. Nye, *Bound to Lead* (New York: Basic Books, 1991); and Michael Mann, ed., *The Rise and Decline of the Nation State* (Oxford: Basil Blackwell, 1990).

4. The declining state will also anticipate that its very ability to later reverse the power trends after suffering this short-term loss can drive the other to preventive war. Note that power oscillations are deeper than the small "blips" in power referred to earlier.

5. This long-standing division has been recently manifested, with caveats, in the debate between offensive realists and defensive realists. For references, see Eric J. Labs, "Beyond Victory: Offensive Realism and the Expansion of War Aims," *Security Studies* 6 (summer 1997): 1–47, and Benjamin Frankel, "Restating the Realist Case," *Security Studies* 5 (spring 1996): xiv–xviii.

6. For summaries of nonrealist theories, see Jack S. Levy, "The Causes of War: A Review of Theories," in Philip E. Tetlock et al., eds., *Behavior, Society, and Nuclear War*, vol. 1 (New York: Oxford University Press, 1989); Stephen Van Evera, "Causes of War" (Ph.D. diss., University of California, Berkeley, 1984), pt. 2, chaps. 7–10, and his forthcoming *Causes of War*, vol. 2 (manuscript, Massachusetts Institute of Technology).

7. Following Kenneth Waltz, this book employs the term "unit level" to refer to causal factors that are internal to the state: regime-type, the struggles of social groups and bureaucracies, domestic upheaval, psychological dimensions of individuals, and the like (*Theory of International Politics* [New York: Random House, 1979], chaps. 2–4).

8. In particular, I examine the significance of declining power for the theory of the democratic peace and for the emergence of China as the century's new superpower.

1. Rethinking Realist Theories of Major War

1. Because of space constraints, this book does not provide complete references on the vast literature on major wars and crises. For more detailed chapter-by-chapter references for both the theoretical and empirical materials, see my web site at the University of Virginia Department of Government and Foreign Affairs, <www.people. virginia.edu/~dcc3a>.

2. Hans J. Morgenthau, *Politics among Nations*, 5th rev. ed. (New York: Alfred A. Knopf, 1978); Edward V. Gulick, *Europe's Classical Balance of Power* (New York: W. W. Norton, 1962); Raymond Aron, *Peace and War* (New York: Praeger, 1966); Martin Wight, "The Balance of Power," in Herbert Butterfield and Martin Wight, eds., *Diplomatic Investigations* (Cambridge: Harvard University Press, 1966); Michael Sheehan, *The Balance of Power* (London: Routledge, 1996).

3. See esp. Morgenthau, *Politics among Nations*, chaps. 3–5, 16, and Morgenthau, *Scientific Man versus Power Politics* (Chicago: University of Chicago Press, 1946). This pessimistic view of human nature is followed by Arnold Wolfers, who repeats Lord Acton's dictum that "power corrupts, and absolute power corrupts absolutely" (*Discord and Collaboration* [Baltimore: Johns Hopkins University Press, 1962], 121). For recent "neoclassical" realist arguments on these lines, see Randall L. Schweller, *Deadly Imbalances* (New York: Columbia University Press, 1998), and Fareed Zakaria, *From Wealth to Power* (Princeton: Princeton University Press, 1998).

4. Morgenthau, *Politics among Nations*, chaps. 11–14; Gulick, *Europe's Classical Balance of Power*, chap. 1; Aron, *Peace and War*, chap. 5; Karl W. Deutsch and J. David Singer, "Multipolar Power Systems and International Stability," *World Politics* 16 (April 1964): 390–406.

5. For a recent use of differentials, see Emerson M. S. Niou, Peter C. Ordeshook, and Gregory Rose, *The Balance of Power* (New York: Cambridge University Press, 1989).

6. For confirmation of their thesis, classical realists tend to rely on examples such as the 1930s, where alliances against the potential hegemon were less than complete; see Michael Joseph Smith, *Realist Thought from Weber to Kissinger* (Baton Rouge: Louisiana State University Press, 1986).

7. See Morgenthau's drawings in chaps. 11–14 in *Politics among Nations*.

8. See ibid., 216–17. Morgenthau does seem aware, however, that dynamic trends might call into question the whole notion of the balance of power as a stabilizing force.

9. Kenneth N. Waltz, *Theory of International Politics* (New York: Random House, 1979), 65–69, 117–28; Waltz, "The Origins of War in Neorealist Theory," in Robert I. Rotberg and Theodore K. Rabb, eds., *The Origins and Prevention of Major Wars* (Cambridge: Cambridge University Press, 1989); Barry Buzan, Charles Jones, and Richard Little, *The Logic of Anarchy* (New York: Columbia University Press, 1993).

10. See Waltz, *Theory of International Politics*, chap. 8; Waltz, "The Stability of a Bipolar World," *Daedelus* 93 (summer 1964): 881–909; John J. Mearsheimer, "Back to the Future: Instability in Europe after the Cold War," *International Security* 15 (summer 1990): 5–56; Thomas J. Christensen and Jack Snyder, "Chain Gangs and Passed Bucks: Predicting Alliance Patterns in Multipolarity," *International Organization* 44 (spring 1990): 137–68; Barry R. Posen, *The Sources of Military Doctrine* (Ithaca: Cornell University Press, 1984); Stephen Van Evera, "Primed for Peace: Europe after the Cold War," *International Security* 15 (winter 1990/91): 7–57; and Benjamin Miller, *When Opponents Cooperate* (Ann Arbor: University of Michigan Press, 1995). For additional references and a

critique, see Dale Copeland, "Neorealism and the Myth of Bipolar Stability: Toward a New Dynamic Realist Theory of Major War," *Security Studies* 5 (spring 1996): 29–89.

11. On tragedy in international relations, see Robert Jervis, *Perception and Misperception in International Politics* (Princeton: Princeton University Press, 1976), chap. 3, and Michael Spirtas, "A House Divided: Tragedy and Evil in Realist Theory," *Security Studies* 5 (spring 1996): 385–423.

12. In his core work, Waltz does not consider differentials of power within a system as a structural cause, but instead assumes states to be "near equals" (*Theory*, chaps. 5 and 8, esp. 167–68). This assumption is used to avoid the complications of shifting structure that arise when differentials are introduced, as Posen points out (*Sources of Military Doctrine*, 64; see also Van Evera, "Primed for Peace," 36). In later work, Waltz does consider differentials of power in terms of their implications for the future peace. See Waltz, "The Emerging Structure of International Politics," *International Security* 18 (fall 1993): 44–79.

13. Waltz, *Theory*, 69, 71. Thus his theory "does not explain why particular wars are fought," but only "war's dismal recurrence through the millennia" (Waltz, "Origins of War," 44).

14. See esp. Mearsheimer, "Back to the Future."

15. See Barry R. Posen, "The Security Dilemma and Ethnic Conflict," in Michael E. Brown, ed., *Ethnic Conflict and International Security* (Princeton: Princeton University Press, 1993); James D. Morrow, "A Twist of Truth: A Reexamination of the Effects of Arms Races on the Occurrence of War," *Journal of Conflict Resolution* 33 (September 1989): 500–529; and Robert Jervis, "Arms Control, Stability, and Causes of War," in Emanuel Adler, ed., *The International Practice of Arms Control* (Baltimore: Johns Hopkins University Press, 1992), 187. On preventive war, see esp. Jack Levy, "Declining Power and the Preventive Motivation for War," *World Politics* 40 (October 1987): 82–107; Emerson M. S. Niou and Peter C. Ordeshook, "Preventive War and the Balance of Power," *Journal of Conflict Resolution* 31 (September 1987): 387–419; Alfred Vagts, *Defense and Diplomacy* (New York: King's Crown, 1956), chap. 8; Stephen Van Evera, "Causes of War" (Ph.D. diss., University of California, Berkeley, 1984), chap. 2; Randall L. Schweller, "Domestic Politics and Preventive War: Are Democracies More Pacific?" *World Politics* 44 (January 1992): 235–69; Woosang Kim and James D. Morrow, "When Do Power Shifts Lead to Wars?" *American Journal of Political Science* 36 (November 1992): 896–922; and Richard Ned Lebow, "Windows of Vulnerability: Do States Jump through Them?" *International Security* 9 (summer 1984). For a recent review of preventive war theory, which also goes under the name "window theory," see Stephen Van Evera, *Causes of War: Power and the Roots of Conflict* (Ithaca: Cornell University Press, 1999), chap. 5.

16. Other names for the argument include power preponderance theory and power transition theory. For hegemonic stability theory as a theory of international political economy, see David Lake, "Leadership, Hegemony, and the International Economy: Naked Emperor or Tattered Monarch with Potential?" *International Studies Quarterly* 37 (December 1993): 459–89.

17. Organski is quite clear that the rising state brings on the war. See *World Politics*, 2d ed. (New York: Knopf, 1968), 367–71; Organski and Jacek Kugler, *The War Ledger* (Chicago: University of Chicago Press, 1980), 27–28; and Kugler and Organski, "The Power Transition," in Manus I. Midlarsky, ed., *Handbook of War Studies* (Boston: Unwin Hyman, 1989), 171–94. Gilpin certainly puts most of the blame on the rising state (*War and Change in World Politics* [Cambridge: Cambridge University Press, 1981], chaps. 1–2, especially 33, 94–95, and 186–87), but he also believes declining states occasionally begin major wars for preventive reasons (ibid., 191). He later suggests that who is responsible for war is not really of concern ("The Theory of Hegemonic War," in Rotberg and Rabb, eds., *Origins and Prevention of Major War*, 26). This ambiguity reduces the the-

ory's deductive rigor while making it less falsifiable. Hence, I focus on Gilpin's core discussion in *War and Change* which emphasizes the rising state's desire to change the system through war. For a formal analysis drawing from Organski's argument, see Robert Powell, *In the Shadow of Power* (Princeton: Princeton University Press, 1999), chaps. 4–5. For further references and for discussion of other dynamic approaches, including George Modelski and William Thompson's long cycle theory and Charles Doran's power cycle theory, see Copeland, "Neorealism and the Myth of Bipolar Stability," 36; Copeland, "Realism and the Origins of Major War" (Ph.D. diss., University of Chicago, 1993), chaps. 1–2. For analysis of recent extensions of hegemonic stability theory, see Jonathan M. DiCicco and Jack S. Levy, "Power Shifts and Program Shifts: The Evolution of the Power Transition Research Program," *Journal of Conflict Resolution* 43 (December 1999): 675–704.

18. On this, see Levy, "Declining Power and the Preventive Motivation for War," 84.

19. One might contend that rising states become impatient, discounting the value of future payoffs versus present ones. Incorporating such a psychological variable, however, is inconsistent with hegemonic stability logic, which assumes that the rising state is a patient, rational actor as it rises, since it realizes more power is needed to achieve its ends. There is no reason a priori to expect it suddenly to become impatient just because it reaches near equality with the declining state. If it has been patient that long, it should continue to wait until after the transition point (and Organski and Kugler's own evidence indicates that that is exactly what rising states do: *War Ledger*, 58–61).

20. Gilpin, for example, when he argues that Thucydides' insights can be applied to any system, does not distinguish between bipolar and multipolar ones ("Theory of Hegemonic War," 19–28).

21. The initiator's military preponderance is also clear in three of the four major wars between 1600 and 1900 (chapter 8).

22. Organski and Kugler, *War Ledger*, 58–59.

23. Jacek Kugler and William Domke, "Comparing the Strength of Nations," *Comparative Political Studies* 19 (April 1986): tables 5–6, and discussion 60–65. I reproduce their results in table A.1 of the appendix (see also tables A.2 and A.3). Randall Schweller's calculations of the military balance in 1938–39 indicate that Germany was stronger than Britain and France combined, and 40 percent stronger than the Soviet Union (*Deadly Imbalances*, table A-8). The Correlates of War data set shows Germany in 1941 having larger defense expenditures and higher defense personnel levels than Britain and Russia combined (table A.3 of this book's appendix).

24. Organski and Kugler, *War Ledger*, 60. Note that they explicitly reject alliances as integral to their power transition logic (25–26).

25. Woosang Kim, "Power Transitions and Great Power War," *World Politics* 45 (October 1992): 153–73, and Kim and Morrow, "Do Power Shifts Lead to Wars?" See Kugler and Organski, "Power Transition," 184, for their reworking of the theory to accommodate this fact.

26. Another associated myth—that British "hegemony" in the mid-nineteenth century explains the relative peace of that period—has been exploded by the statistics of Joseph S. Nye and Paul Kennedy. Britain at most had a lead in naval and industrial economic power only; it was never the largest European state in total GNP and was inferior to others in total military capability. See the statistics in Nye, *Bound to Lead* (New York: Basic Books, 1991), chaps. 1–2; Kennedy, *The Rise and Fall of the Great Powers* (New York: Random House, 1987), chaps. 4–5; and table A.2 of this book's appendix.

27. Although this variable has two aspects—the size of the differential and the trend—powerful predictions about state behavior can be made only by considering size and trend simultaneously. That is, the gap between states in relative power means

little unless one knows whether the gap is growing, narrowing, or stable, while trends are meaningless without knowledge of relative power positions.

28. The role of these and other core assumptions, which act as ceteris paribus boundary conditions for the causal logic, is explained in the methodology section.

29. I focus on preventive wars driven solely by security fears, but states with unit-level aggressive motives are also rational to wait until their power is declining before attacking.

30. For a full discussion of the instability of bipolarity, see Copeland, "Neorealism and the Myth of Bipolar Stability."

31. This loss of relative power to sideline-sitters is known as the "dilemma of the victor's inheritance": Richard Rosecrance, *Rise of the Trading State* (New York: Basic Books, 1986), 34, and Geoffrey Blainey, *The Causes of War*, 3d ed. (New York: Free Press, 1988), chap. 4. Neither author considers the implication of such a relative loss for the stability of bipolar versus multipolar systems.

32. Cf. Van Evera, "Primed for Peace," 36–37.

33. The small states in bipolarity do matter in the aggregate; thus each great power will be unwilling to permit the other from grabbing the small states one by one. But it is very difficult to get small states *voluntarily* to switch sides en masse, since their current great power patron is strong enough to enforce loyalty (consider the Soviet Union and eastern Europe in the cold war). Thus, in bipolarity, both rising and declining great powers have a hard time drawing enough new powers to their side via diplomacy to change their blocs' relative power levels in a big way. Yet since they can enforce loyalty within their sphere, they are likely to include small states presently in their sphere as part of their overall power when determining whether to launch preventive war.

34. This reinforces the inherent instability of bipolarity compared to multipolarity. See Copeland, "Neorealism and the Myth of Bipolar Stability."

35. The dependent variable—the probability of major war—reflects the viewpoint of the analyst making predictions; at this point, states are assumed to have only a dichotomous choice between war and not-war. Chapter 2 goes further by allowing states to choose hard-line policies that knowingly increase the probability of an inadvertent slide into major war.

36. The more detailed logic behind this conclusion proceeds as follows. In the absence of any dynamic trends, a state will expect that its relative power and therefore its probability of winning any war that does occur will remain the same into the future. If the state initiates the war now, its expected probability of survival (EPS) is simply this probability of winning. If it holds off from war, however, it knows that the others might not attack later. For even the smallest likelihood that the others will not choose war later, the EPS for holding off is always greater that the EPS of initiating war now (assuming no offensive advantage).

37. In a situation where the second-ranked state in bipolarity is in decline (such as t_3), we can predict that the probability of major war will be moderate to high, depending on this state's relative military power and the severity of its decline.

38. Note that this is essentially a mixed system-type, half-way between bipolarity and multipolarity. It is the "bipolar" element, however, that makes it less stable than at time t_2: the lower-ranked great powers are simply not as able to deter the declining state's attack on the system as compared to the more purely multipolar situation. This point highlights the value of using a continuous independent variable like differentials of power to explain a continuous dependent variable like the probability of major war. If one keeps in mind that it is the degree of power inferiority or superiority that matters, there is no need to establish arbitrary criteria for cut-offs between unipolar, bipolar, and multipolar systems; mixed types are allowed. These power differentials can

then be used to make finer-grained predictions about the stability of any particular real-world system than are possible in more narrowly structural theories focusing on ideal-type polarity alone.

39. To reiterate, potential power embodies all the capital and resources that could be eventually translated into economic output, but have not yet been so translated (including such things as population size, raw materials reserves, technological levels, and unused fertile territory). For other authors' considerations of the concept of potential power, see Copeland, "Neorealism and the Myth of Bipolar Stability," 54, n. 76.

40. It is worth remembering that in calculating relative power, leaders will not simply compare the resources that their great powers can mobilize within their borders. The military, economic, and potential power of small states within a great power's sphere must also be considered. This is particularly important with regard to economic/potential power, since the small states often supply critical resources and territory needed for the great power's military security. Thus, when we consider the empirical cases, we will see that the differentials and trends across the larger spheres had much to do with the changing likelihood of major war over time. Germany in 1913 and 1938–39 remained significantly inferior to Russia and Britain in overall potential power because of the latter states' past imperial policies. In mid-1945, fear of decline in America's Eurasian position led Truman to initiate policies that led to the cold war. Decline in the Soviet position in eastern Europe twice led Moscow to provoke severe crises over Berlin.

41. Empirical studies often use the Correlates of War (COW) data set, which provides data for military, economic, and demographic power: see J. David Singer, Stuart Bremer, and John Stuckey, "Capability Distribution, Uncertainty, and Major Power War, 1820–1965," in Singer et al., eds., *Explaining War* (Beverly Hills: Sage, 1979). Almost invariably when the data set is used, these three categories are collapsed into one index of overall power: see William B. Moul, "Measuring the 'Balances of Power,' " *Review of International Studies* 15 (April 1989): 101–21. I avoid this tendency when I reproduce the COW data in tables A.2–4 of the appendix.

42. There is a plethora of quantitative studies on this first question, but since these studies look at all types of war, not just major wars, they have little relevance here. It is worth noting, however, that the results of these large-N analyses are decidedly mixed: see James Fearon, "War, Relative Power, and Private Information," Typescript, University of Chicago, 1992.

43. These cases, each of which is covered below, are: the French-Hapsburg bipolar conflict (1521–56); the Thirty Years War (1618–48); the wars of Louis XIV against the European "Grand Alliances" (consisting of the War of the League of Augsburg, 1688–97 and the War of the Spanish Succession, 1701–13); the Seven Years War (1756–63); the Napoleonic Wars (1799–1815); the First World War, and the Second World War.

44. See the statistics in Kennedy, *Rise and Fall*, chaps. 4–5.

45. In chapters 2 and 9, I express this possibility through a parameter that takes into account the expected future unit-level characteristics of the rising state.

46. See chapter 8 and Thucydides, *The Peloponnesian War*, trans. Rex Warner (Harmondsworth: Penguin, 1954), 1.101–2, 1.118, 4.41.

47. This point follows directly from the tragedy of the security dilemma. See, in particular, Robert Jervis, "Cooperation under the Security Dilemma," *World Politics* 30 (January 1978): 167–214, and Charles L. Glaser, "The Security Dilemma Revisited," *World Politics* 50 (October 1997): 171–201.

48. Moreover, as Fearon notes, owing to anarchy the rising state has a hard time committing itself to being peaceful later: "Rationalist Explanations for War," *International Organization* 49 (summer 1995): 401–9.

49. On the problem of changing future intentions, see Jervis, "Cooperation under the Security Dilemma," 168; Robert J. Art and Robert Jervis, "The Meaning of Anarchy," in Art and Jervis, eds., *International Politics* (Boston: Little, Brown, 1985), 3; and Mearsheimer, "Back to the Future."

50. In chapter 9, I discuss the implications of this logic for the new world order, including the conditions for conflict when the rising and declining states of interest are democratic.

51. For arguments that multipolar systems will be stable unless one state (or an offensive coalition) possesses over 50 percent of the system's resources, see Niou, Ordeshook, and Rose, *Balance of Power*, chap. 3.

52. The following is only a sketch of the collective action problem in alliances, not an in-depth analysis of alliance politics. For the latter (and for the alliance literature), see Stephen M. Walt, *The Origins of Alliances* (Ithaca: Cornell University Press, 1987), and Glenn H. Snyder, *Alliance Politics* (Ithaca: Cornell University Press, 1997). For further discussion of buckpassing and chainganging in multipolarity, see Copeland, "Neorealism and the Myth of Bipolar Stability," 38–47.

53. On the fear of "abandonment," see Glenn H. Snyder, "The Security Dilemma in Alliance Politics," *World Politics* 36 (July 1984): 461–95.

54. Cf. Mearsheimer, "Back to the Future," 16. My argument draws on, but differs from, standard neorealist buckpassing arguments (Waltz, *Theory*, 164–65; Posen, *Sources of Military Doctrine*, 63–64; Snyder, *Alliance Politics*; Snyder, "Security Dilemma") based on Mancur Olson's seminal work on the collective action problem (*The Logic of Collective Action* [Cambridge: Harvard University Press, 1965], and Olson and Richard Zechhauser, "An Economic Theory of Alliances," *Review of Economics and Statistics* 68 [August 1966]: 266–79). Olson assumes actors seeking to maximize absolute gains. When the group is large, they free ride since the marginal costs of contributing exceed the marginal benefits. Most buckpassing arguments in neorealism likewise assume that states focus on absolute costs. The states therefore may not only fail to ally, but may also neglect internal military spending (Posen, *Sources*, 64). As I have noted elsewhere, self-help in an anarchic world means that states are unlikely to neglect their military spending (Copeland, "Neorealism and the Myth of Bipolar Stability," 44–47). But concern about relative loss through war can reduce the willingness to commit fully to a coalition.

55. This argument provides a first-cut explanation for the fluctuations in coalitional unity during the wars of Louis XIV and Napoleon. See Paul W. Schroeder, *The Transformation of European Politics, 1763–1848* (Oxford: Oxford University Press, 1994), and Schroeder, "History Reality vs. Neorealist Theory," *International Security* 19 (summer 1994): 108–48.

56. This argument builds on Glenn Snyder's point that allies in multipolarity fear "entrapment" in committing to others, although he focuses solely on defensive alliances ("Security Dilemma"). The only counterexample to the above rule I have found is Austria's efforts to form an offensive alliance with Russia in 1755–56 to eliminate a rising Prussia. As chapter 8 discusses, this led to Prussia's preemptive attack in August 1756. Because Prussia attacked before Austria and Russia could consolidate the offensive alliance, we shall never know if indeed they would have been able to launch their offensive preventive war.

57. The situation is somewhat different in bipolarity. The declining superpower may launch coalitional preventive war against the rising state by bringing together as many of the small states in its sphere as possible. The intense collective action problem does not manifest itself here, given the declining superpower's ability to coerce its small clients to join the coalition. Hence, a coalitional preventive war in bipolarity, led by the declining superpower, is quite likely since defection from the coalition is greatly

minimized. Thus Sparta and Carthage could start their respective major wars with their allies firmly behind them. During the cold war, it was clear that any major conventional war between the United States and Russia would have almost certainly involved all the NATO and Warsaw Pact countries.

58. What follows draws inspiration from, but goes a few steps further than, Jervis's discussion in "Cooperation under the Security Dilemma."

59. In Rousseau's famous staghunt analogy, each hunter prefers to work together to capture the stag (CC), but fears others will defect to catch a rabbit, leaving him with nothing (CD). As mistrust grows, more actors will defect if only to preempt, and cooperation becomes difficult.

60. A similar logic prevails in multipolarity.

61. On the problem of oscillations, see Van Evera, "Causes of War," chap. 2, and Morrow, "Twist of Truth," 506–7. In chapter 2, I elaborate on this problem.

62. On this, see Manus I. Midlarsky, "Systemic Wars and Dyadic Wars: No Single Theory," *International Interactions* 16 (December 1990): 171–81. For a critique, see Bruce Bueno de Mesquita, "Big Wars, Little Wars; Avoiding Selection Bias," *International Interactions* 16 (December 1990): 159–69.

63. This is usually an element of other scholars' definitions, even if only implicitly; see Jack S. Levy, "Theories of General Wars," *World Politics* 37 (April 1985): 344–74.

64. See esp. Martin van Creveld, *Fighting Power* (Westport, Conn.: Greenwood, 1982); Trevor N. Dupey, *Numbers, Predictions, and War*, rev. ed. (Fairfax, Va.: Hero, 1985); Allan R. Millett and Williamson Murray, eds., *Military Effectiveness*, 3 vols. (Boston: Allen and Unwin, 1988); and Charles A. Kupchan, "Setting Conventional Force Requirements," *World Politics* 41 (July 1989): 536–78.

65. See inter alia Gary Becker, *The Economic Approach to Human Behavior* (Chicago: University of Chicago Press, 1976), chap. 1, and Mark Blaug, *The Methodology of Economics* (Cambridge: Cambridge University Press, 1980), chap. 6.

66. This is the equivalent in physics to assuming a perfect vacuum to predict the behavior of falling objects, or in economics to assuming fixed prices of other goods to predict how changes in a product's price will affect demand. See Blaug, *Methodology of Economics*, chap. 3, and John Neville Keynes, "The Scope and Method of Political Economy," in Daniel M. Hausman, ed., *The Philosophy of Economics* (Cambridge: Cambridge University Press, 1984), 85–93. I specify some additional parameters in chapter 2.

67. In game-theoretical terms, they have fundamentally incomplete information about the other's future type: see James Morrow, *Game Theory for Political Scientists* (Princeton: Princeton University Press, 1994).

68. Note that it does not mean that declining state automatically assumes "worse case" (i.e., that the other *will* attack). Rather, it means that, all things being equal, the other is as likely to attack as not (a 50–50 chance), or that the other's likelihood will be a function of how far it rises, rather than a function of internal qualities of the state.

69. On disturbing causes, see J. S. Mill, "On the Definition and Method of Political Economy," in Hausman, *Philosophy of Economics*, and Blaug, *Methodology of Economics*, chap. 3.

70. See Blaug, *Methodology of Economics*, 79–80.

71. In social sciences, of course, no single disconfirming example would truly falsify a theory; all theories are probabilistic. This book holds itself to a higher standard than microeconomics, however. The latter tests hypotheses in the aggregate; we do not ex-

pect all individuals to buy less when the price rises, only that most will (see Fritz Machlup, "On Indirect Verification," in Hausman, *Philosophy of Economics*, 204). My cases, on the other hand, consider the behavior of specific actors.

72. See Jeffrey C. Alexander, ed., *The Micro-Macro Link* (Berkeley: University of California Press, 1987).

73. For similar reasoning, see William Curti Wohlforth, *The Elusive Balance* (Ithaca: Cornell University Press, 1993).

74. Objective evidence can also be valuable as a fallback in measuring variables when there is little (or unreliable) internal documentation on actor beliefs and perceptions. The assumption would then be made that since we do not know how the actors really thought, we can presume that they saw this objective evidence clearly. I do this, for example, when looking at the pre-modern cases in chapter 8. It must be reiterated, however, that this is only a second-best method.

75. See Waltz, *Theory*, 99–101.

76. Peter J. Katzenstein, ed., *The Culture of National Security* (New York: Columbia University Press, 1996), chaps. 1–2.

77. To the extent that constructivism tries to subsume all beliefs as part of its canon, it becomes tautological. Since all human action is a function of beliefs, after the fact such a constructivism could describe and explain all behavior; nothing could falsify the argument.

78. See, for example, Organski and Kugler, *War Ledger*, and most of the theorists who build on their argument (references in DiCicco and Levy, "Power Shifts").

79. See Gary King, Robert O. Keohane, and Sidney Verba, *Designing Social Inquiry* (Princeton: Princeton University Press, 1994), 217–23 (cited herein as KKV).

80. The war in the Far East starting in 1941 is not considered, since it was a large-scale war in a subsystem, rather than a major war as defined. Moreover, its outbreak was shaped by war in the core system: documents show that Japan would not have attacked had France, Britain, and Russia—three important Asian powers—not been drawn away or defeated by Hitler. Japanese actions, however, do provide powerful support for my causal logic. Japan was declining precipitously in 1940–41 as a result of U.S. economic sanctions. As the subsystem became more bipolar owing to the European war, Japan's slight military edge over the United States gave it the possibility of a successful war; deep decline made it a necessity. See my U.S.-Japan case study in Copeland, "Modeling Economic Interdependence and War," paper delivered at the American Political Science Association annual meeting, Chicago, 1995, and the documents in Nobutake Ike, ed., *Japan's Decision for War* (Stanford: Stanford University Press, 1967).

81. After 1965, as Mutually Assured Destruction became more entrenched, both sides were increasingly cautious about risking major war. Still, dynamic trends were important. The end of détente and the coming of a "second cold war" in the early 1980s reflected the belief that Russia might overtake the United States in first-strike capability unless Washington acted quickly. The fact that the "Reagan buildup" actually began under Carter, a man predisposed toward peace, shows the overriding power of systemic pressures. For a brief discussion of the end of the cold war, see chapter 2 and Copeland, "Neorealism," 71–72, n. 125. On the post–cold war era, see chapter 9.

82. See KKV, 129–37.

83. Given space constraints, however, a full empirical analysis of the behavior of each of the great powers across time cannot be undertaken here.

84. The book seeks to survey close to the "universe" of major wars, at least in western history. Footnotes in chapter 8 briefly discuss why some well-known wars should

not be considered major wars, and also note the significance of some non-western major wars not examined in the main text.

85. On hard tests, see Harry Eckstein, "Case Study and Theory in Political Science," in Fred I. Greenstein and Nelson W. Polsby, eds., *Handbook of Political Science* (Reading, Mass.: Addison-Wesley, 1975); KKV, 209–12; Waltz, *Theory of International Politics*, chap. 1 and pp. 124–25.

86. Indeed, for theories like the bureaucratic politics model, the cold war constitutes their best case. Showing that such theories have little explanatory power even under such "most likely" circumstances constitutes a crucial test of their value. See Eckstein, "Case Study," and KKV, 209–12.

87. KKV, 168–82.

88. A final potential problem is that of endogeneity, whereby changes in state behavior affect the levels of power, rather than vice versa (KKV, 185–96). Chapter 2 shows how one can turn this problem into an opportunity for stronger systemic theories of major war.

2. FOREIGN POLICY CHOICES AND MAJOR WAR

1. See esp. Glenn H. Snyder and Paul Diesing, *Conflict among Nations* (Princeton: Princeton University Press, 1977), 11–12, 342–47, 363–68; Richard Ned Lebow, *Between Peace and War* (Baltimore: Johns Hopkins University Press, 1981), 61–62; and Zeev Maoz, *Paths to Conflict* (Boulder, Colo.: Westview, 1982), 2–3, 89–90. See also Stephen Van Evera, *Causes of War* (Ithaca: Cornell University Press, 1999), 79–80.

2. See Robert Jervis, "Cooperation under the Security Dilemma," *World Politics* 30 (January 1978): 167–214, and references in Charles L. Glaser, "The Security Dilemma Revisited," *World Politics* 50 (October 1997): 171–201.

3. See esp. Jervis, "Cooperation under the Security Dilemma"; Glaser, "Security Dilemma Revisited"; Glaser, "Realists as Optimists," *International Security* 19 (winter 1994–95): 50–90; Barry R. Posen, "The Security Dilemma and Ethnic Conflict," in Michael E. Brown, ed., *Ethnic Conflict and International Security* (Princeton: Princeton University Press, 1993); and Van Evera, *Causes of War*, chaps. 3–4.

4. Thus for Waltz and Mearsheimer, there is no real downside to adopting a hardline policy; system stability is undermined only when states fail to balance *enough* (because of collective-action problems in multipolarity, for example). Waltz argues for miscalculation in multipolarity, but this reflects the number of powers, not spiraling within a security dilemma: Waltz, *Theory of International Politics* (New York: Random House, 1979), chap. 8; Mearsheimer, "Back to the Future," *International Security* 15 (summer 1990): 15–19.

5. Of course, this does not mean that rising states, like all states, will not sometimes seize an opportunity to expand when the risks are low. But as soon as the risks of major war rise, they should be far more cautious than declining powers.

6. In chapter 9, I consider how different types of rising states might influence the state's calculus. The key security problem, however, is the ascending state's future intentions if permitted to grow, not its present intentions. Thus the declining state's knowledge of the other's present regime-type will matter less than the estimated long-term stability of this regime-type (an estimate largely independent of diplomatic interaction).

7. Since chapter 1 covers the implications of dynamic change for bipolar versus multipolar systems, the model here focuses for simplicity on just two actors, the declining state and the rising state that constitutes its main threat.

8. The discussion sets up these options as discrete choices, but one should remember that there are *degrees* of severity attached to each one. A state choosing containment, for example, must decide exactly how strong to make such a policy.

9. Cf. Alexander L. George's definition in George, ed., *Avoiding War: Problems of Crisis Management* (Boulder, Colo.: Westview, 1991), xi, 545.

10. Fully specified, this probability must be compared to the likelihood of the other attacking later if its growth is hindered by hard-line policies, allowing for the effect of these policies on the other's level of mistrust.

11. A rising state that grows to a relative power differential of 70–30, for example, might be expected to attack with a 70 percent likelihood.

12. The analogue in economics is firms selecting the option that, all things considered, provides the highest level of expected net profit.

13. Expressed formally: assuming that victory means survival (1.0), and defeat means elimination as a state (0), the EPS for any option will equal $1 - p_w + p_w p_v$, where p_w is the probability of war, and p_v is the probability of victory. (An outright victory or a stalemated war preserving the state's existence both constitute "victory" here.) This formalization follows from two logical steps: first, whether war occurs or not; and second, how likely the state is to win *if* war occurs. The costs of war are not included, since I assume states are willing to accept such costs in order to survive. War costs can still play two roles, however: in a world of conventional weapons, they shape the p_v vis-à-vis third parties; in a nuclear world, they greatly reduce the probability of meaningful victory (that is, war where the society survives). For pushing me to think along these lines, I thank Andrew Kydd (see his "Sheep in Sheep's Clothing: Why Security Seekers Do Not Fight Each Other," *Security Studies* 7 [autumn 1997]: 121–22 for a slightly different formulation).

14. See Dale C. Copeland, "A Formal Model of Preventive War," typescript, University of Virginia, May 1999.

15. In the above formula, if $p_w = 1.0$, then the EPS is reduced to simply the p_v.

16. Thus the conclusion from chapter 1 that major wars are more likely to be initiated by dominant military powers in either bipolarity or multipolarity. In a nuclear world, relative power per se is less important than the probability, given the strategic balance, of a splendid first strike.

17. To work, crisis initiation must be expected to address the *specific source* of decline. Thus while Khrushchev in 1961 could reasonably think that a crisis over Berlin might avert eastern Europe's economic deterioration, the Soviets in the mid-1980s could not expect crisis initiation to solve the main problem—the widening technological gap vis-à-vis the west (more about this later).

18. My analysis does not adopt the position of "prospect theory" that actors facing potential loss tend psychologically to be more risk-acceptant (see Barbara Farnham, ed., *Avoiding Losses/Taking Risks* [Ann Arbor: University of Michigan Press, 1994]). The actors are still assumed to be risk-neutral; they are simply rationally comparing the risks of not acting versus the risks of hard-line policies.

19. On justification crises, see Lebow, *Between Peace and War*, chap. 2.

20. Formally, deadlock preferences are DC > DD > CC > CD, where DC represents a state's attack which goes unreciprocated (or simply where the state gets in the first blow); DD is all-out war where both parties begin fighting at essentially the same time; CC is the current peace; and CD is allowing the other to make the first move, either by a direct attack or war against a third party. In figure 6, the fact that crises have no independent causal force is indicated by the direct line from "preventive motives" to major war.

21. Chapter 8 shows that the first pathway was also dominant in the Second Punic

War of Carthage-Rome, the French-Hapsburgs war of 1521, the Thirty Years War, the wars of Louis XIV, and the Napoleonic Wars.

22. As with the first pathway, the fact that the crisis has no independent effect is shown by the line directly from aggressive motives to war.

23. On inadvertent war, see esp. George, *Avoiding War*; Richard Ned Lebow, *Nuclear Crisis Management* (Ithaca: Cornell University Press, 1987), chaps. 2–4; Daniel Frei, *Risks of Unintentional Nuclear War* (New York: UN Institute for Disarmament Research, 1983); Robert Powell, *Nuclear Deterrence Theory* (Cambridge: Cambridge University Press, 1990), chaps. 5–6; Barry R. Posen, *Inadvertent Escalation* (Ithaca: Cornell University Press, 1991); and Robert Jervis, *Meaning of the Nuclear Revolution* (Ithaca: Cornell University Press, 1989), 144–47.

24. Geoffrey Blainey, *The Causes of War*, 3d ed. (New York: Free Press, 1988), chap. 9; Scott D. Sagan, *The Limits of Safety* (Princeton: Princeton University Press, 1993); Bruce G. Blair, *The Logic of Accidental Nuclear War* (Washington, D.C.: Brookings, 1993); Paul Bracken, "Accidental Nuclear War," in Graham T. Allison, Albert Carnesale, and Joseph S. Nye, eds., *Hawks, Doves, and Owls* (New York: W. W. Norton, 1985); Bracken, *The Command and Control of Nuclear Forces* (New Haven: Yale University Press, 1983).

25. Formally, staghunt preferences are CC > DC > DD > CD (compare to deadlock preference rankings in n. 20).

26. See Van Evera, *Causes of War*, chap. 3; Powell, *Nuclear Deterrence Theory*, 111–12; Thomas Schelling, *The Strategy of Conflict* (Cambridge: Harvard University Press, 1960), 209–29; Richard Betts, "Surprise Attack and Preemption," in Allison, Carnesale, and Nye, *Hawks, Doves, and Owls*, 57–58; Lebow, *Nuclear Crisis Management*, chap. 2; and Steven J. Brams and D. Marc Kilgour, "Threat Escalation and Crisis Stability," *American Political Science Review* 81 (September 1987): 833–50.

27. Preemptive war therefore depends on technology and geography; the system must be offense-dominant. Preventive war is a function of a different independent variable, namely, shifting power differentials.

28. See Sagan, *Limits of Safety*, chaps. 2–3.

29. See Dan Reiter, "Exploding the Powder Keg Myth: Preemptive Wars Almost Never Happen," *International Security* 20 (fall 1995): 5–34.

30. Snyder and Diesing, *Conflict among Nations*, 242–43.

31. Reiter, "Exploding the Powder Keg Myth," 16–25; Allen S. Whiting, "The U.S.-China War in Korea," in George, ed., *Avoiding War*; Janice Gross Stein, "The Arab-Israeli War of 1967: Inadvertent War through Miscalculated Escalation," in ibid.

32. Analysts almost universally agree that preemption is the most likely means to nuclear war; see Jervis, *Meaning of the Nuclear Revolution*.

33. See Lebow, *Nuclear Crisis Management*, chap. 4; Thomas Schelling, *Arms and Influence* (New Haven: Yale University Press, 1966), 44, 93; Richard Smoke, *War: Controlling Escalation* (Cambridge: Harvard University Press, 1977), chaps. 9–10; Patrick M. Morgan, "Saving Face for the Sake of Deterrence," in Robert Jervis, Richard Ned Lebow, and Janice Gross Stein, *Psychology and Deterrence* (Baltimore: Johns Hopkins University Press, 1985); and references in Dale C. Copeland, "Do Reputations Matter?" *Security Studies* 7 (fall 1997): 33–71.

34. See James D. Fearon, "Threats to Use Force" (Ph.D. diss., University of California Berkeley, 1992), chaps. 2–4; Fearon, "Rationalist Explanations for War," *International Organization* 49 (summer 1995): 379–414; Powell, *Nuclear Deterrence Theory*; and D. Marc Kilgour and Frank C. Zagare, "Credibility, Uncertainty, and Deterrence," *American Journal of Political Science* 35 (May 1991): 305–34.

35. Chicken preferences are DC > CC > CD > DD (compare to staghunt and dead-lock preferences, nns. 20 and 25).

36. Cf. Schelling, *Arms and Influence*, chaps. 2–3.

37. Snyder and Diesing, *Conflict among Nations*, 242–43.

38. For most analysts, crises by definition involved a higher probability of war be-tween the actors. See James L. Richardson, *Crisis Diplomacy* (Cambridge: Cambridge University Press, 1994), 10–12; Michael Brecher and Jonathan Wilkenfeld, *A Study of Crisis* (Ann Arbor: University of Michigan Press, 1997), 3–4; and Brecher and Wilken-feld, "Crises in World Politics," *World Politics* 34 (April 1982): 382–83.

39. Schelling, *Arms and Influence*, chap. 3.

40. Cf. Stephen Van Evera, "Causes of War" (Ph.D. diss., University of California, Berkeley, 1984), chap. 2, and James D. Morrow, "A Twist of Truth: A Reexamination of the Effects of Arms Races on the Occurrence of War," *Journal of Conflict Resolution* 33 (September 1989): 500–529.

41. It should be remembered that conciliation is a highly rational strategy for rising states, regardless of their motives. Note also that when the power trends are essentially flat (no state rising or falling), then reassurance policies are wise, since they avoid pro-voking an escalatory spiral.

42. The fact that United States was a democracy may have made the alignment that much easier, but it is worth recalling that U.S.-British relations in the nineteenth cen-tury were anything but amicable. Not only did the two countries compete for territory in North America, but in 1896 they almost came to blows over Venezuela. That Eng-land after 1900 also put aside outstanding problems with an authoritarian Japan (not to mention Russia) indicates that geostrategic factors more than regime-type were driving the process. Cf. Randall L. Schweller, "Domestic Politics and Preventive War," *World Politics* 44 (January 1992): 235–69.

43. For an analysis of accommodation which assumes the power transition hypoth-esis that the rising state is the one most likely to attack, see Robert Powell, "Uncer-tainty, Shifting Power, and Appeasement," *American Political Science Review* 90 (De-cember 1996): 749–64.

44. Fearon, "Rationalist Explanations for War." See also Jervis, "Cooperation under the Security Dilemma"; and Robert J. Art and Robert Jervis, "The Meaning of Anar-chy," in Art and Jervis, eds., *International Politics* (Boston: Little, Brown, 1985) on the problem of future intentions.

45. I summarize the evidence in Copeland, "Trade Expectations and the Outbreak of Peace: Détente 1970–74 and the End of the Cold War 1985–91," *Security Studies* 9 (au-tumn 1999/winter 2000): 15–58.

46. For references on enduring rivalries, see Paul F. Diehl, ed., *The Dynamics of En-during Rivalries* (Urbana: University of Illinois Press, 1998).

47. Gary Goertz and Paul Diehl's statistical analysis indicates that states are far more likely to fall into war if part of an enduring rivalry than if not: "Empirical Impor-tance of Enduring Rivalries," *International Interactions* 18 (1992): 158–59.

48. On the spiral and deterrence models, see esp. Robert Jervis, *Perception and Mis-perception in International Politics* (Princeton: Princeton University Press, 1976), chap. 3; Charles Glaser, "Political Consequences of Military Strategy: Expanding and Refin-ing the Spiral and Deterrence Models," *World Politics* 44 (July 1992): 497–538; and An-drew Kydd, "Game Theory and the Spiral Model," *World Politics* 49 (April 1997): 371–400.

49. Thus since 1990, China has maintained a relatively moderate policy, so as to re-duce any American incentive for trade sanctions and preventive actions. A rising state,

of course, can be expected to respond to hostile actions by the other, if only avoid power losses and to ensure deterrence against attack.

50. This is true even when, as I assume, the system is neither offense or defense dominant. Of course, the more offense dominates, the more a given deterrence action will undermine the other's security; see Jervis, "Cooperation under the Security Dilemma."

51. See Jervis, *Perception and Misperception*, chap. 3; Jervis, "Cooperation under the Security Dilemma"; Glaser, "Political Consequences"; Russell J. Leng, "Reciprocating Influence Strategies in Interstate Crisis Bargaining," *Journal of Conflict Resolution* 37 (March 1993): 3–41; and Jonathan Bendor, "In Good Times and Bad: Reciprocity in an Uncertain World," *American Journal of Political Science* 31 (August 1987): 531–58.

52. See esp. Glaser, "Political Consequences"; Glaser, "Security Dilemma Revisited"; Jervis, *Perception and Misperception*, chap. 3; Lebow, *Beyond Peace and War*; Richard Ned Lebow and Janice Gross Stein, *We All Lost the Cold War* (Princeton: Princeton University Press, 1994); and Posen, "Security Dilemma and Ethnic Conflict."

53. This argument builds on Jervis's point that the two models are not necessarily incompatible, since they work from differing assumptions about the adversary's intentions. When the adversary is aggressive, the deterrence model applies; when the adversary is a status-quo security seeker, the spiral model applies (Jervis, *Perception and Misperception*, chap. 3). My argument links the two models with variables and parameters other than the adversary's intentions. Moreover, in the third parameter I focus more on the rising state's future intentions than its current intentions.

54. Cf. Jervis, "Hypotheses on Misperception," in G. John Ikenberry, ed., *American Foreign Policy*, 2d ed. (New York: HarperCollins, 1996), 516.

55. On the difference between falsification and salience, see the methodology section of chapter 1. The term "falsification" should be used advisedly here; it simply means that the evidence contradicts the causal logic of the theory in a particular case (a "disconfirmation"). Since we are dealing with probabilistic theories, no single empirical disconfirmation should lead to a theory being discarded. Theories, as per Lakatos, should be evaluated against one another for their relative explanatory power—the amount of evidence supporting a theory's logic versus the amount of evidence disconfirming it.

56. For a more extensive test of this proposition, see Dale Copeland, "Neorealism and the Myth of Bipolar Stability," *Security Studies* 5 (spring 1996): 29–89. To the extent that neorealists implicitly capture the point that states take increased risks of inadvertent war to avoid decline, they would agree with hypothesis 1 of dynamic differentials theory.

57. This is based on the original arguments of Organski/Gilpin, before later adjustments for alliance blocs (see chapter 1).

3. German Security and the Preparation for World War I

1. For ease of exposition, henceforth I will refer to the Austro-Hungarian state simply as "Austria."

2. See esp. Fritz Fischer, *The War of Illusions* (New York: Norton, 1975); Fischer, *Germany's Aims in the First World War* (New York: Norton, 1967); Fischer, *From Kaiserreich to Third Reich* (London: Unwin Hyman, 1986); Luigi Albertini, *The Origins of the War of 1914*, 3 vols. (Oxford: Oxford University Press, 1952); John C. G. Röhl, *The Kaiser and His Court* (Cambridge: Cambridge University Press, 1994); V. R. Berghahn, *Germany and the Approach of War in 1914* (London: St. Martin's, 1973); and Imanuel Geiss, *German Foreign Policy, 1871–1914* (London: Routledge, 1976).

3. Scholars closest to this position are Fritz Stern, "Bethmann Hollweg and the War," in Stern, *The Failure of Illiberalism* (New York: Columbia University Press, 1992), and David E. Kaiser, "Germany and the Origins of the First World War," *Journal of Modern History* 55 (September 1983): 442–76. Neither, however, would see security as the sole driving force behind German policy.

4. Karl Dietrich Erdmann, "War Guilt 1914 Reconsidered," in H. W. Koch, ed., *The Origins of the First World War*, 2d ed. (London: Macmillan, 1984); Egmont Zechlin, "Cabinet versus Economic War in Germany," and "July 1914: A Reply to a Polemic," both in ibid.; Andreas Hillgruber, *Germany and the Two World Wars* (Cambridge: Harvard University Press, 1981); John W. Langdon, *July 1914* (New York: Berg, 1991), 109–29.

5. See esp. Robert Jervis, *Perception and Misperception in International Relations* (Princeton: Princeton University Press, 1976), chap. 3. This perspective was shaped by revisionist historians of the late 1920s (see Langdon, *July 1914*, chap. 2).

6. Richard Ned Lebow, *Between Peace and War* (Baltimore: Johns Hopkins University Press, 1981), chap. 5.

7. Stephen Van Evera, "The Cult of the Offensive and the Origins of the First World War," *International Security* 9 (summer 1984): 64, 71–78; Jack Snyder, "Civil-Military Relations and the Cult of the Offensive, 1914 and 1984," *International Security* 9 (summer 1984); Snyder, *The Ideology of the Offensive* (Ithaca: Cornell University Press, 1984). Van Evera also argues that faith in the offensive made expansion more tempting, increasing the risk of preventive war.

8. See esp. Albertini, *Origins*, vol. 2; Van Evera, "Cult of the Offensive"; Snyder, "Civil-Military Relations"; and Joachim Remak, "1914—The Third Balkan War," in Koch, ed., *Origins*, 93–95. For a critique, see Marc Trachtenberg, "The Meaning of Mobilization in 1914," *International Security* 15 (winter 1990–91): 120–50.

9. Paul Kennedy, *The Rise of Anglo-German Antagonism, 1860–1914* (London: George Allen and Unwin, 1980), chap. 14.

10. See esp. Woodruff D. Smith, *The Ideological Origins of Nazi Imperialism* (Oxford: Oxford University Press, 1986), chaps. 4 and 8, and Otto Hammann, *The World Policy of Germany, 1890–1912* (London: Allen and Unwin, 1927).

11. Snyder, *Myths of Empire* (Ithaca: Cornell University Press, 1991), 31–49, chap. 3; Eckart Kehr, *Economic Interest, Militarism, and Foreign Policy* (Berkeley: University of California Press, 1970). See also Charles A. Kupchan, *The Vulnerability of Empire* (Ithaca: Cornell University Press, 1994), chap. 6.

12. Fischer, *War of Illusions*, viii. On the primacy of domestic politics, see esp. Wolfgang J. Mommsen, "Domestic Factors in German Foreign Policy before 1914," in Mommsen, *Imperial Germany, 1867–1918* (London: Arnold, 1995), chap. 9; Hartmut Pogge von Strandmann, "Germany and the Coming of War," in R. J. W. Evans and Strandmann, *The Coming of the First World War* (Oxford: Clarendon, 1988); Michael Gordon, "Domestic Conflict and the Origins of the First World War," *Journal of Modern History* 46 (June 1974): 191–226; and Arno J. Mayer, "Internal Causes and Purposes of War in Europe, 1870–1956," *Journal of Modern History* 41 (September 1969): 291–303.

13. Fischer, *War of Illusions*, 470. For arguments that Austria's aggressiveness and fear of decline drew others into war, see Samuel R. Williamson, *Austria-Hungary and the Origins of the First World War* (New York: St. Martin's, 1991), and Paul W. Schroeder, "World War I as Galloping Gertie," *Journal of Modern History* 44 (1972): 319–45.

14. Kenneth Waltz, *Theory of International Politics* (New York: Random House, 1979), 167; Thomas J. Christensen and Jack Snyder, "Chain Gangs and Passed Bucks: Predicting Alliance Patterns in Multipolarity," *International Organization* 44 (spring 1990): 137–68. Like the first category, this explanation sees war as inadvertent. Yet states are drawn into war less as a function of irrational beliefs, and more as a rational response

to systemic imperatives. See Scott D. Sagan, "1914 Revisited: Allies, Offense, and Instability," *International Security* 11 (fall 1986): 151–75.

15. See chapter 2. Both Gilpin and Organski also believe Germany initiated war to gain the prestige and benefits that it had been denied.

16. Recall that a war of preemption results from the belief that the other seeks to attack now, while a war of prevention is a function of decline and the belief that the other might attack later after it has accumulated greater power.

17. *DD*, doc. 629. Except for corrections, my translations from *DD* follow those in Max Montegalas and Walther Schücking, eds., *The Outbreak of the World War: German Documents*, collected by Karl Kautsky (New York: Oxford University Press, 1924).

18. See especially Lebow, *Between War and Peace*; Fischer, *War of Illusions*; and Fischer, *Germany's Aims*. Those showing that German leaders, including Bethmann, did *not* count on British neutrality include Erdmann, "War Guilt," 363–64; Mommsen, "Domestic Factors"; and Hillgruber, *Germany*, 26.

19. See inter alia Kennedy, *Rise of British-German Antagonism*, and Smith, *Ideological Origins*.

20. See William L. Langer, *European Alliances and Alignments, 1871–1890*, 2d ed. (New York: Knopf, 1962), 38–48, 109.

21. Paul Kennedy, *The Rise and Fall of the Great Powers* (New York: Random House, 1987), chap. 4.

22. Langer, *European Alliances*, 38–39, 48–49.

23. The fact that no other great power tried to take on the system after 1815 is easily explained. As noted in chapter 1, no state ever achieved the level of marked military superiority needed for a bid for hegemony; only Russia came close in terms of troop numbers, but the quality of its army always remained inferior (see the statistics in table A.2 of the appendix and in Joseph S. Nye, *Bound to Lead* [New York: Basic Books, 1991], chaps. 1–2, and Kennedy, *Rise and Fall*, chaps. 4–5). Thus, despite many domestic changes, including the rise of many questionable leaders, the nineteenth century avoided major war. Relative equality served as a powerful constraint. Leaders thus sublimated their desires into imperialism in the south and localized battles for position in Europe, such as the Crimean War.

24. Quoted in Fischer, *War of Illusions*, 45. Bülow continues that Russia would be truly weakened only when it had lost the areas to "the west of the line Onega Bay—Valdayskaya heights—Dnieper" (ibid.). This territory, constituting most of eastern Russia, is essentially what Germany received in 1918 by the Treaty of Brest-Litovsk.

25. Quoted in ibid., 38.

26. Gerhard A. Ritter, *The Schlieffen Plan* (New York, 1958); Fischer, *War of Illusions*, 54.

27. Quoted in Fischer, *War of Illusions*, 55.

28. See L. C. F. Turner, "The Significance of the Schlieffen Plan," in Paul Kennedy, ed., *The War Plans of the Great Powers, 1880–1914* (Boston: Allen and Unwin, 1979), 207–10; Fischer, *War of Illusions*, 55–60; and Holger Herwig, "Imperial Germany," in Ernest R. May, ed., *Knowing One's Enemies* (Princeton: Princeton University Press, 1986), 77.

29. Graydon A. Tunstall, *Planning for War against Russia and Serbia* (Boulder, Colo.: Social Science Monographs, 1993), chap. 4; Albertini, *Origins*, 1:436–37.

30. Quoted in Fischer, *War of Illusions*, 61.

31. David G. Hermann, *The Arming of Europe and the Making of the First World War* (Princeton: Princeton University Press, 1996); Tunstall, *Planning for War*.

32. Quoted in Fischer, *War of Illusions*, 62.

33. Hermann, *Arming of Europe*, 135.

34. Quoted in ibid., 135–36.
35. Quotations in Fischer, *War of Illusions*, 84–86.
36. Quoted in ibid., 86.
37. Quoted in ibid., 139.
38. Quoted in Berghahn, *Germany*, 186.
39. Hermann, *Arming of Europe*, 161, 165.
40. Quoted in ibid., 166; David Stevenson, *Armaments and the Coming of War: Europe, 1904–1914* (Oxford: Clarendon, 1996), 201–2.
41. Quoted in Hermann, *Arming of Europe*, 166–67.
42. Quoted in ibid., 169. See also Stevenson, *Armaments*, 202–3.
43. Fischer, *War of Illusions*, 124–25. See also Geiss, *German Foreign Policy*, 137–38, and documents in B. De Siebert, ed., *Entente Diplomacy and the World* (New York: Knickerbocker, 1921), chap. 7.
44. *GP*, vol. 39: doc. 15612.
45. See Fischer, *War of Illusions*, chap. 9; John C. G. Röhl, "V. Admiral Von Müller and the Approach of War, 1911–1914," *Historical Journal* 12 (1969): 651–73; Röhl, *Kaiser*, chap. 7; and Geiss, *German Foreign Policy*, 142–45.
46. From Admiral Müller's diaries, quoted in Röhl, *Kaiser*, 162.
47. Quoted in ibid., 162–63, 177. Müller's notes are corroborated by reports by the Saxon and Bavarian military attachés and the notes of a confidant of Tirpitz. See ibid, 165; Fischer, *War of Illusions*, 161–63; and Röhl, "Admiral Müller," 663.
48. Quoted in Röhl, "Admiral Müller," 663.
49. Quoted in Röhl, *Kaiser*, 175–76.
50. Fischer is the strongest supporter of this view, although his own evidence shows that Bethmann saw the likelihood of British neutrality as very slim (*War of Illusions*, chap. 9).
51. Ibid., 166 (see also 69).
52. Quoted in Röhl, *Kaiser*, 162–63.
53. Quoted in Fischer, *War of Illusions*, 164; Röhl, "Admiral Müller," 664.
54. Fischer's summary, *War of Illusions*, 164.
55. On Italy, see ibid., 170.
56. Ibid., 169.
57. Ibid., 173.
58. Hermann, *Arming of Europe*, 221–25.
59. For some quantitative data, see tables A.1 and A.2 of the appendix.
60. General Friedrich von Bernhardi, *Germany and the Next War* (London: Edward Arnold, 1914), 20, 53, and chaps. 5 and 9.
61. Quoted in Hermann, *Arming of Europe*, 181–85. These arguments were passed on to Bethmann (ibid., 182).
62. Ibid., 183.
63. Norman Stone, *The Eastern Front, 1914–1917* (New York: Scribner's, 1975), 37.
64. Quoted in Fischer, *Kaiserreich*, 47.
65. William C. Fuller, "The Russian Empire," in May, ed., *Knowing One's Enemies*, 113.
66. Quoted in Hermann, *Arming of Europe*, 191–92.
67. *DD*, Appendix IV: doc. 27.
68. The accuracy of German perceptions is upheld by Jacek Kugler and William Domke's evidence, which shows Germany in 1914 to be almost equal in actualized military power to Britain, France, and Russia combined (see table A.1 of this book's appendix). The Correlates of War data set (table A.2) indicates that while Germany was not quantitatively superior in troop numbers, it was very dominant, especially

versus France and Russia, in the iron and steel production so necessary to Germany's war machine.

69. Contrary to the social-imperialist argument, social cohesion was seen as the *means* to a successful war for security, not as the end of a victorious war. Thus it was critical to achieve this cohesion *before* the war broke out.

70. Quoted in Fischer, *War of Illusions,* 192–93.

71. See Fischer's extensive evidence, ibid., 190–99.

72. Although estimates generally assumed a short war, a longer war was also considered, and financial preparations for it were actively discussed (ibid., 200).

73. Ibid., 203.

74. See esp. L. L. Farrar, *The Short War Illusion* (Santa Barbara, Calif.: ABC-Clio, 1973).

75. Quoted in Fischer, *War of Illusions,* 203.

76. See Turner, "Significance of the Schlieffen Plan," 211–12; Otto Friedrich, *Blood and Iron* (New York: Harper Collins, 1995), 235; and Snyder, *Ideology of the Offensive,* 111, 153–54. Bernhardi, recognizing that Germany would be opposed by Britain, France, and Russia, had advised in 1912: "We must therefore prepare not only for a short war, but for a protracted campaign" (*Germany and the Next War,* 154).

77. Quoted in Friedrich, *Blood and Iron,* 229. See also Snyder, *Ideology of the Offensive,* 153–55. It is important to note that the German military was aware that tactically (on the battlefield) defense held the advantage. It was for this reason that the strategic concentration of forces in the north was emphasized, to overcome France's defense through sheer numbers. See ibid., chap. 5, esp. 138–39. So while Snyder and others see German adherence to Schlieffen's plan in the face of acknowledged defense dominance as a product of irrational motivated bias, there is a simpler and more plausible explanation: political motives—the need to destroy a rising Russia—required an offensive plan to take territory from Russia. Since France was allied with Russia, the Schlieffen Plan was the *only* plan that held any possibility of achieving the political goals in the face of defense dominance.

78. Quoted in Fischer, *War of Illusions,* 262; see also 371 on fears of Russian financial reforms.

79. William C. Fuller, *Strategy and Power in Russia, 1600–1914* (New York: Free Press, 1992), 437. On Russia's massive industrial and military growth before the war, see Peter Gatrell, *Government, Industry, and Rearmament in Russia, 1900–1914* (Cambridge: Cambridge University Press, 1994), chaps. 3–7.

80. Fischer, *War of Illusions,* 371.

81. Quoted in ibid., 372–73. For other newspaper articles on the rising Russian threat, see ibid., 374–77.

82. Quoted in ibid., 381. See also Berghahn, *Germany,* 180.

83. Fischer, *War of Illusions,* 388.

84. Quoted in ibid., 397.

85. Quoted in ibid., 402. See also William C. Wohlforth, "The Perception of Power: Russia in the Pre-1914 Balance," *World Politics* 39 (April 1987): 362.

86. Quoted in Albertini, *Origins,* 1:437. Jagow was sympathetic to Moltke's views. The main problem, he felt, was the kaiser, who would oppose such a war and therefore had to be manipulated into it (Fischer, *War of Illusions,* 402).

87. Albertini, *Origins,* 1:375.

88. Quoted in ibid., 381.

89. Williamson, *Austria-Hungary,* 128.

90. Ibid., 130.

91. It cannot be argued that Russian mobilization in 1912–13 was only partial and

therefore was not seen as a threat in Berlin. As we will see, in 1914 Germany threatened Russia with general mobilization in response to only partial Russian mobilization, invoking alliance commitments to Austria as the pretext.

92. Williamson, *Austria-Hungary*, 133.

93. Quoted in Albertini, *Origins*, 1:436.

94. Quoted in ibid., 437.

95. Ibid., 440–47.

96. Ibid., 454.

97. The first quotation is Albertini's paraphrase; the second is from the documents; ibid., 455.

98. Quoted in ibid., 456. On 7 July and then on the 8th, Jagow reinforced the theme of nonintervention to the Austrians.

99. In addition to citations in n. 12, see Hans-Ulrich Wehler, *The German Empire, 1871–1918* (Leamington Spa, U.K.: Berg, 1985); Hans Mommsen, "The Topos of Inevitable War in Germany in the Decade before 1914," in Volker R. Berghahn and Martin Kitchen, eds., *Germany in the Age of Total War* (London: Croom Helm, 1981); Willibald Gutsche, "The Foreign Policy of Imperial Germany and the Outbreak of the War, in the Historiography of the GDR," in Gregor Schöllgen, ed., *Escape into War?* (Oxford: Berg, 1990); and Schöllgen, "Introduction," in ibid., 5–12.

100. See esp. Wehler, *German Empire*, and Schöllgen, "Introduction," 6–8.

101. Smith, *Ideological Origins*, chap. 4.

102. See esp. Wehler, *German Empire*, and Fischer, *War of Illusions*.

103. Quoted in Berghahn, *Germany*, 56.

104. Quoted in ibid., 82.

105. Quoted in Kaiser, "Germany," 456.

106. Quoted in Berghahn, *Germany*, 97–98.

107. Ibid., 65.

108. Quoted in Arno J. Mayer, *The Persistence of the Old Regime* (New York: Pantheon, 1981), 319.

109. Ibid., passim.

110. David Blackbourn and Geoff Eley, *The Peculiarities of German History* (Oxford: Oxford University Press, 1984); Eley, *Reshaping the German Right* (Ann Arbor: University of Michigan Press, 1991), xiii–xxvi, 1–16.

111. See chapter 4.

112. Berghahn, *Germany*, 152–53, chap. 8. See also Wehler, *German Empire*, 97–99, who agrees that the *Sammlung* between the elites essentially fell apart after 1910.

113. Konrad H. Jarausch, *The Enigmatic Chancellor* (New Haven: Yale University Press, 1973), chap. 4; Berghahn, *Germany*, chaps. 7–8; James Retallack, "The Road to Philippi: The Conservative Party and Bethmann Hollweg's 'Politics of the Diagonal,' 1909–14," in Larry Eugene Jones and Retallack, eds., *Between Reform and Resistance* (Oxford: Berg, 1993).

114. Snyder's argument that a cartelized German elite began to internalize earlier strategic myths and thus initiated war out of fear of encirclement (*Myths of Empire*, chap. 3) can help deal with the dearth of evidence showing that German leaders chose war to solve a domestic crisis. Note, however, that this argument affirms that security, rather than domestic cohesion, was the primary motive for the war. The remaining debate thus simply concerns the issue of whether German leadership had any rational reason to worry about its neighbors. Given that Germany faced a Russia of three times its population and forty times its land mass, one whose industrialization program would have continued regardless of Germany's policies, it is hard to argue that Berlin's fear of the rise of Russia was divorced from reality.

4. The July Crisis and the Outbreak of World War I

1. See Wolfgang J. Mommsen, "The Debate on German War Aims," *Journal of Contemporary History* 1 (July 1966): 47–74; John Moses, *The Politics of Illusion* (London: Harper and Row, 1975); John Langdon, *July 1914* (New York: Berg, 1991), chaps. 4–5; Dwight Lee, ed., *The Outbreak of the First World War*, 4th ed. (Lexington, Mass: Heath, 1975); and H. W. Koch, ed., *The Origins of the First World War*, 2d ed. (London: Macmillan, 1984).

2. See Jack S. Levy, "Preferences, Constraints, and Choices in July 1914," *International Security* 15 (winter 1990–91): 151–86.

3. Austria thus did not get the outcome it most preferred, namely localized war against Serbia with Russian implicit acquiescence, but rather an outcome it preferred only to war with Russia without German support, namely world war with German support.

4. Levy, "Preferences," 153–63.

5. In actual fact, of course, German leaders thought in terms of *degrees* of support for both possibilities, from low to high, but for simplicity we can think in terms of a dichotomy.

6. Most of the options revolved around variations of the "Halt in Belgrade" proposal suggested by the kaiser on 28 July. The core debate between Austria and Russia was over the degree to which Serbia, Russia's ally, would be destroyed by a negotiated settlement: Austria wanted a higher degree, and Russia a lesser degree. Also of significance was how the settlement would appear to other states, especially Russia's Balkan and French allies. Russia could not be seen to be giving away the farm, even if, as its proposals in the final days indicate, it was willing to do so. Finally, the means to a settlement was important. Russia preferred a European-wide conference, since this would bring to bear the weight of other powers. Austria wanted at most German mediation. Both, however, were somewhat amenable to direct Austro-Russian talks, perhaps mediated by Germany.

All of this led to eight possible outcomes that were heatedly discussed in the final days. From Austria's to Russia's most preferred, they were: (1) Austro-Serbian localized war; (2) temporary occupation of Serbia to force compliance to Austrian demands (*DD*: docs. 380, 433; 29 and 30 July); (3) a Halt in Belgrade and "other places" to force Serbian compliance to Austrian demands (*DD*: doc. 323; 28 July); (4) a Halt in Belgrade and "other places" plus German mediation (*DD*: docs. 395, 396; 30 July); (5) a Halt in Belgrade and "other places," overseen by all the great powers (*DD*: doc. 460; 30 July); (6) Austrian military operations, but Austrian willingness to accept some modifications on its demands and to state that it is a European affair (Sazonov's "formula," *DD*: doc. 421; 30 July); (7) a negotiated peace through a four-power conference ("*à quatre*") (*DD*: docs. 236, 248; 26 and 27 July); (8) an Austrian capitulation and return to status quo. I shall show how Berlin used these proposals so that it appeared to want peace, while ensuring that Austria and Russia would never reach a peaceful solution.

7. The purely-localized-war outcome was slightly higher in ranking to this negotiated peace. But since German leaders knew that it was unlikely from the beginning of July and next to impossible by its end, it cannot count as a serious possibility. Even so, statements by Bethmann discussed below indicate that general war with domestic and Austrian support was preferred to localized war. While the debate between Fischer and his critics now seems to revolve around whether Germany preferred localized war to continental war (with Fischer now arguing that continental war was preferred; Langdon, *July 1914*, chaps. 4–5), the real debate between the camps concerns whether Germany preferred negotiated peace to continental war. The calculated risk notion of

the critics makes little sense unless one assumes that Berlin preferred a negotiated peace to continental war but risked the possibility of things getting out of hand (continental war or worse) to achieve the best option of a localized war.

8. Imanuel Geiss, ed., *July 1914* (New York: Scribner's, 1967), 70.

9. Quoted in Hartmut Pogge von Strandmann, "Germany," in R. J. W. Evans and Strandmann, eds., *The Coming of the First World War* (Oxford: Clarendon, 1988), 115. Bethmann also told Hoyos that "if [general] war was to become inevitable, the present moment would be more favorable than a later one." Quoted in Fritz Fellner, "Die 'Mission Hoyos,'" in Wilhelm Alff, ed., *Deutschlands Sonderung von Europa, 1862–1945* (Frankfurt: Lang, 1984), 295; see also *ÖA*, vol. 8, doc. 10076.

10. Geiss, *July 1914*, doc. 4.

11. Ibid., doc. 5. The military's pessimism was reinforced by two reports received on 5 July from the general staff, titled "The Completion of the Russian Railway Network" and "The Growing Power of Russia" (Konrad H. Jarausch, *The Enigmatic Chancellor* [New Haven: Yale University Press, 1973], 468, n. 9).

12. Kurt Riezler, *Tagebücher, Aufsätze, Dokumente*, ed. Karl D. Erdmann (Göttingen: Vandenhoeck und Ruprecht, 1972), 182–83 (except for minor changes, my translation here follows Wayne C. Thompson, *In the Eye of the Storm* [Iowa City: University of Iowa Press, 1980], 74–75).

13. Quoted in Norman Stone, *The Eastern Front, 1914–1917* (New York: Scribner's, 1975), 42.

14. Riezler, *Tagebücher*, 187.

15. Theodor Wolff, *Tagebücher 1914–1919*, ed. Bernd Sösemann (Boppard: Harald Boldt, 1984), 64. On 17 February 1915, Stumm told Wolff that in July 1914 "we were not bluffing"; "We were reconciled to the fact that we would have war with Russia" and if it had not come, "we would have had it in two years' time under worse conditions" (ibid., 166–67).

16. Wolff, *Tagebücher*, 19 July 1917, 521–22. This was no post-hoc reconstruction of events. Just after Bethmann's statement that he feared war was inevitable, Wolff replied: "I know, I spoke to you then; you told me of your fear."

17. Quoted in Fritz Fischer, *Germany's Aims in the First World War* (New York: Norton, 1967), 51.

18. Quoted in Wolfgang J. Mommsen, *Imperial Germany, 1867–1918* (London: Arnold, 1995), 281, n. 67.

19. Quoted in ibid.

20. Riezler, *Tagebücher*, 184.

21. Geiss, *July 1914*, p. 89.

22. Geiss, *July 1914*, docs. 7 and 15.

23. Ibid., doc. 33.

24. The Austrian prime minister, Karl von Stürgkh, had remarked a day before that Vienna ran "the risk that by a policy of hesitation and weakness it could later on no longer be so certain of Germany's unqualified support." And Emperor Franz Joseph, as Berchtold records, on 9 July approved of a strong policy against Serbia, noting that he was "anxious that weak behavior would discredit our position vis-à-vis Germany." All quotations from Fritz Fischer, *War of Illusions* (New York: Norton, 1975), 480–81.

25. *DD*: doc. 19.

26. *DD*: doc. 49, 14 July.

27. *DD*: doc. 106; Fischer, *Germany's Aims*, 58.

28. Riezler, *Tagebücher*, 185. The word "liberation" likely refers to Riezler's prewar writings, where he argued that Germany had to "liberate itself from the nightmare of coalitions" against it (see Moses, *Politics of Illusions*, 33).

29. Riezler, *Tagebücher*, 186.

30. See John C. R. Röhl, "V. Admiral Von Müller and the Approach of War, 1911–1914," *Historical Journal* 12 (1969): 673, n. 105.

31. Fischer, *War of Illusions*, 483.

32. *DD*: doc. 74.

33. Quoted in Fischer, *War of Illusions*, 483.

34. Riezler, *Tagebücher*, 189–90.

35. Ibid., 189–91. On other secret preparations, see Wolff, *Tagebücher*, 153.

36. See D. C. B. Lieven, *Russia and the Origins of the First World War* (New York: St. Martin's, 1983), 140–45, and Luigi Albertini, *The Origins of the War of 1914*, 3 vols. (Oxford: Oxford University Press, 1952), 2:290–94.

37. Geiss, *July 1914*, doc. 71; *DD*: doc. 138.

38. *DD*: Appendix 4, doc. 2.

39. *DD*: doc. 257; Albertini, *Origins*, 2:455.

40. Quoted in Albertini, *Origins*, 2:460.

41. Inadvertent war theories require this notion in order to show that German leaders did not want war but could not prevent events from getting out of hand. Fischer requires it because he believes that Bethmann, counting on British neutrality, panicked when he saw that Britain would indeed oppose Germany.

42. They are thus often referred to as the "world-on-fire" telegrams. See Marc Trachtenberg, "The Meaning of Mobilization in 1914," *International Security* 15 (winter 1990/91): 120–51. Trachtenberg's position is similar to mine, in that he argues that the military did not usurp control, nor were preemptive motivations important (147–50). But Trachtenberg sees the telegrams as a genuine attempt by Bethmann to pull back from war, taken in response to Russian mobilization, not British warnings. When Bethmann failed, he did not lose control; rather, he "abdicated" it, allowing the military take over (142–43). Yet this leaves unexplained why Bethmann would simply give up when he still had time to negotiate. Trachtenberg's argument thus seems to rely ultimately on Bethmann's weak personality.

43. *DD*: doc. 3.

44. *DD*: doc. 72.

45. 25 July 1914, Wolff, *Tagebücher*, 64.

46. *DD*: doc. 456 (second part is drawn from Fischer's translation, *War of Illusions*, 492). See also *DD*: docs. 242, 291, 445.

47. *DD*: doc. 160.

48. *DD*: doc. 194.

49. See Riezler's entry on 23 July, recording Bethmann's view that the war will come through Russian mobilization. Once this occurred, "the whole nation will feel the danger and rise up": *Tagebücher*, 190.

50. *DD*: doc. 219.

51. See Albertini, *Origins*, 2:481–82. When the French ambassador, Jules Cambon, reminded him of his pledge later that week, Jagow admitted that he had made it, but stated that "the words . . . did not constitute a firm commitment on his part." *DDF*, vol. 11: doc. 380.

52. *DD*: doc. 236.

53. *DD*: doc. 238.

54. *DD*: doc. 237.

55. *DD*: docs. 258, 266, and 265.

56. See esp. Richard Ned Lebow, *Between Peace and War* (Baltimore: Johns Hopkins University Press, 1981), chap. 5.

57. Riezler, *Tagebücher*, 192.

58. *DD*: doc. 277.

59. Recall that Riezler had recorded that day Bethmann's belief that if Russia mobilized, "the whole nation will feel the danger and rise up" (n. 49).

60. *DD*: doc. 293 (kaiser's emphasis removed).

61. The proposal, in essentially the same form, was also put forward by England on 28 July.

62. *DD*: doc. 323.

63. *DD*: doc. 335. Wilhelm communicated with Vienna only through the chancellor, which allowed Bethmann to monitor and revise his messages.

64. *DD*: doc. 229.

65. *DD*: doc. 338.

66. It had been decided upon in secret by the czar and his advisers only at around 6:00 the night before, and Pourtalès had not yet been informed, nor had it been implemented.

67. *DD*: docs. 341 and 342.

68. Lieven, *Russia and the Origins*, 145–46; Albertini, *Origins*, 2:552–61.

69. *DD*: doc. 343.

70. See Geiss, ed., *Julikrise und Kreigsausbruch 1914*, vol. 2 (Hannover: Verlag für Literatur und Zeitgeschenen, 1964), doc. 676. See also Fischer, *War of Illusions*, 494; Albertini, *Origins*, 2: chap. 11.

71. *DD*: doc. 357. See *DD*: doc. 355 for a similar telegram received at 4:34 P.M.

72. *DD*: doc. 365.

73. See *DD*: doc. 377 and its n. 3.

74. *DD*: docs. 365A, 369, 370, and 376A.

75. *DD*: doc. 380.

76. From *DD*: doc. 359, sent to the czar at approximately 6:30 P.M. on 29 July; and doc. 335.

77. *DD*: doc. 332.

78. *DD*: doc. 387. There is also no question that the chancellor was responsible for these two telegrams: the original documents were in his own handwriting (see *DD*: doc. 383, n. 1; *DD*: doc. 387, n. 1).

79. *DD*: doc. 384.

80. See *DD*: doc. 357.

81. *DD*: doc. 384.

82. *DD*: doc. 385.

83. *DD*: doc. 342. Note that the passage reinforces the point that Bethmann knew that Russian mobilization was different, that it did not force Germany to preempt. See also Geiss, *Julikrise*, doc. 676, on Bethmann's 29 July conference with the generals, when he told them that he was "of the opinion that . . . the mobilization of Russia did not mean war."

84. *DD*: doc. 385.

85. *DD*: doc. 323.

86. At 10:15 P.M., 10:30 P.M., and 12:30 A.M.

87. *DD*: doc. 388.

88. *DD*: doc. 365 from Pourtalès, arriving at Berlin at 8:29 P.M., 29 July.

89. From *DD*: doc. 368. The missing fifth paragraph indicates that Grey believed that he could "secure for Austria every possible satisfaction." Because Bethmann did not send this to Austria, Vienna would not be encouraged to consult further with the English; all mediation would go through Berlin.

90. *DD*: doc. 395.

91. This interpretation may seem less plausible than the simpler explanation: that Bethmann truly wanted Austria to back down and agree to a deal with Russia. Yet while both interpretations are possible, the latter remains inconsistent with all of Bethmann's actions surrounding this telegram.

92. *DD*: doc. 365.

93. *DD*: doc. 396.

94. From his diary, quoted in Röhl, "Admiral Müller," 669. The Austrian naval attaché in Berlin wrote to Vienna the same day that "people here await all possible complications with the utmost calm and regard the moment as very favorable for a big settlement" (quoted in Fischer, *War of Illusions*, 487).

95. Jarausch, *Enigmatic Chancellor*, 169.

96. *DD*: doc. 456.

97. Riezler, *Tagebücher*, 193.

98. *DD*: doc. 407.

99. *DD*: doc. 408.

100. Geiss, *Julikrise*, doc. 1089.

101. *DD*: doc. 420; German White Book in *CDD*: exhibit 23.

102. This is not the only instance of tampering with times in the White Book to show Russia's responsibility. Compare Exhibits 20 and 21 of *CDD* to *DD*: docs. 335 and 332 respectively.

103. *DD*: doc. 422 in particular indicated that Russia was preparing along both the Austrian and German borders.

104. See Lieven, *Russia and the Origins*, chap. 5; Albertini, *Origins*, 3: chap. 1.

105. Why Berlin needed to provoke Petersburg first, and Paris second, is clear. Russia had the slowest mobilization schedule by far; hence, Germany, as the fastest mobilizer, could allow it to go first. France's mobilization, although not as quick as Germany's, was relatively efficient, so it had to be delayed until the last minute. This would allow Germany to claim that it was only responding to French mobilization, while still leaving the French army relatively unprepared for war. Berlin was playing a finely tuned game here: while trying to maximize the blame falling on Russia and France, which required others to mobilize first (or at least appear to have done so), Berlin had to ensure that their actual preparedness was low in order to increase the chance of victory. What is remarkable is how effectively the German leaders played this game, considering that the two objectives—blame and adversary preparedness—were pulling in different directions.

106. *DD*: docs. 433 and 465; see also 441.

107. *DD*: doc. 441.

108. Albertini, *Origins*, 2:673.

109. Ibid., 3:23–27.

110. *DD*: docs. 451 and 464.

111. *DD*: doc. 473.

112. From "Neue Dokumente zu Kriegsausbruch und Kriegsverlauf," documents collected by B. Schulte, *Militärgeschichtliche Mitteilungen* 25 (1979): 140. Wenninger continues: "From Vienna, still no answer to yesterday's telegram [presumably Moltke's to Conrad]. Again uncertainty, until we finally put this to bed."

113. Albertini (*Origins*, 3:39–45) is the sole exception I could find, although he draws different conclusions.

114. Bethmann's alterations are shown in the footnotes of Kautsky's original publication of the documents (*DD*).

115. *DD*: doc. 490.

116. *DD*: doc. 491 (emphasis added).

117. *DD*: doc. 491, n. 4.

118. What if the French actually agreed to remain neutral? This would have destroyed the plan to attack France as an act of self-defense, while forcing Germany to turn against just Russia. Its western front would then be exposed to French attack. To avert this possibility, Bethmann attached to the telegram instructions that if France did

declare its neutrality, the ambassador was to "demand the turning over of the fortresses of Toul and Verdun as a pledge of neutrality," which Germany would occupy until the war with Russia was over (*DD*: doc. 491). This condition was so manifestly outrageous as to guarantee that Paris would reject neutrality and mobilize.

119. *DD*: doc. 492.

120. *DD*: doc. 492, n. 9.

121. *DD*: doc. 488 and its n. 6.

122. *DD*: doc. 479.

123. Albertini, *Origins*, 2:671–74 and 3:45–46.

124. *DD*: docs. 396 and 465.

125. Buchanan's paraphrase, in *My Mission to Russia*, vol. 1 (Boston: Little, Brown, 1923), 209.

126. Geiss, *Julikrise*, doc. 1000(d).

127. *DD*: doc. 542, n. 3.

128. *DD*: doc. 542. The ultimatum's demands were also clearly designed to be unacceptable to Russia (*DD*: doc. 490). Germany asked Russia to cancel not just general or partial mobilization, but all "measures." This was contrary to the 29 July promise that Germany would allow Russia to mobilize against Austria as long as it refrained from hostilities (*DD*: docs. 380 and 392). Moreover, given Russia's size, the demand was technically impossible to implement in twelve hours. Finally, the ultimatum offers no concessions despite Sazonov's previously conciliatory measures (*DD*: docs. 421 and 460; *BD*: vol. 11, doc. 340).

129. *DD*: doc. 542.

130. *DD*: doc. 542, n. 5.

131. *DD*: doc. 562.

132. Albertini, *Origins*, 3:171.

133. One might think Jagow had read only the initial section of a partially decoded telegram which indicated the telegram's importance, but not its contents. Yet not only was the telegram short, but the key information about possible English and French neutrality appears in the first two sentences (*DD*: doc. 562).

134. *DD*: doc. 612.

135. Quoted in Albertini, *Origins*, 3:177.

136. Ibid., 191–92.

137. Quoted in ibid., 195–96.

138. Quoted in ibid., 47.

139. Quoted in ibid., 47–48.

140. Quoted in ibid., 48.

141. Ibid., 48. Austrian civilian leaders were not so informed, for obvious reasons.

142. Quoted in ibid., 48.

143. Quoted in Röhl, "Germany," 27.

144. *DD*: doc. 629.

145. *DD*: doc. 662.

146. *DD*: docs. 667, 693, and 703.

147. *DD*: doc. 734.

148. Indeed, the British forces barely made it in time to help turn back the German tide.

149. Quoted in Fischer, *War of Illusions*, 505.

150. Elsewhere, I discuss a factor that intensified German perceptions of long-term decline, namely, their negative expectations regarding the global trading environment: Copeland, "Economic Interdependence and War: A Theory of Trade Expectations," *International Security* 20 (spring 1996): 5–41.

5. The Rise of Russia and the Outbreak of World War II

1. Works exposing the military's prewar cooperation with Hitler include Wilhelm Deist, *The Wehrmacht and German Rearmament* (Toronto: University of Toronto Press, 1981); Klaus-Jürgen Müller, *The Army, Politics, and Society in Germany, 1933–45* (Manchester: Manchester University Press, 1987); and Michael Geyer, "The Dynamics of Military Revisionism in the Interwar Years," in Wilhelm Deist, ed., *The German Military in the Age of Total War* (Leamington Spa, U.K.: Berg, 1985). Even these works, however, end up accepting that by 1938–39 the military was unable to alter Hitler's extreme plans. For the generals' cooperation in Nazi genocide on the eastern front, see Omer Bartov, *The Eastern Front, 1941–45* (London: Macmillan, 1985).

2. The "continuity" of German policies across the wars has been noted by some scholars, although almost exclusively with a focus on domestic politics: see Konrad H. Jarausch, "From Second to Third Reich: The Problem of Continuity in German Foreign Policy," *Contemporary European History* 12 (March 1979): 68–82. Realists have identified Germany's central position in Europe as a common cause of both wars, but have not stressed the rising Russian threat (an exception is Stephen Van Evera, *Causes of War* [Ithaca: Cornell University Press, 1999], 97–98).

3. On the roots of Hitler's genocidal obsession, see Ian Kershaw, *The Nazi Dictatorship*, 3d ed. (London: Arnold, 1993), chap. 5.

4. See Geoffrey Stoakes, *Hitler and the Quest for World Dominion* (Leamington Spa, U.K.: Berg, 1986), chap. 5.

5. This is a relaxation of the third parameter from chapter 2, whereby rising states that are seen as inherently hostile are more likely to provoke preventive war by the declining state.

6. Considering German war-weariness, one might argue that Nazi ideology was essential to mobilizing the people for one final shot at hegemony. Although plausible, this argument suggests only that some form of hypernationalism—perhaps one similar to that employed in Japan—was needed as a means to the geopolitical end.

7. For references on the social history of Nazism, see Kershaw, *Nazi Dictatorship*, chaps. 2–4 and 7.

8. Cf. John J. Mearsheimer, "Back to the Future," *International Security* 15 (summer 1990): 25–26.

9. See references in Kershaw, *Nazi Dictatorship*, chap. 6, and John Hiden and John Farquharson, *Explaining Hitler's Germany* (London: Batsford, 1983), chap. 5; particularly Klaus Hildebrand, *The Foreign Policy of the Third Reich* (Berkeley: University of California Press, 1973); Eberhard Jäckel, *Hitler's World View* (Cambridge: Harvard University Press, 1981); Andreas Hillgruber, *Hitlers Strategie* (Frankfurt: Berhard, 1965); and Hillgruber, *Germany and the Two World Wars* (Cambridge: Harvard University Press, 1981).

10. See references in Kershaw, *Nazi Dictatorship*, chap. 6; Hans Mommsen, "National Socialism: Continuity and Change," in Walter Laqueur, ed., *Fascism* (Harmondsworth: Penguin, 1979), 151–92; Martin Broszat, *The Hitler State* (London: Longman, 1981); and Tim Mason, *Nazism, Fascism, and the Working Class* (Cambridge: Cambridge University Press, 1995).

11. This parallels A. J. P. Taylor's argument that Hitler had no set plan for total war, but Taylor sees Hitler more as an opportunistic geopolitician (*The Origins of the Second World War* [Harmondsworth: Penguin, 1963]); for powerful critiques, see Esmonde M. Robertson, ed., *The Origins of the Second World War* (London: Macmillan, 1971).

12. See Kershaw, *Nazi Dictatorship*, chap. 4.

13. Ibid., chaps. 2–4; Hiden and Farquharson, *Explaining Hitler's Germany*, chap. 3.

14. See Kershaw, *Nazi Dictatorship*, chap. 6.

15. Moreover, Hitler did not perceive Germany's economic difficulties as constituting a threat to the party's hold on power. As he told his military in the fall of 1939, "revolution from within" was essentially "impossible" (quoted in R. J. Overy, " 'Domestic Crisis' and War in 1939," *Past and Present* 116 [August 1987]: 159).

16. Alan Bullock, *Hitler*, rev. ed. (New York: Harper and Row, 1964), 806–7.

17. Kenneth N. Waltz, *Theory of International Politics* (New York: Random House, 1979), chap. 8; Mearsheimer, "Back to the Future."

18. See Mearsheimer, "Back to the Future," 24–25 and 29, and Barry R. Posen, *The Sources of Military Doctrine* (Ithaca: Cornell University Press, 1984), 193 and chap. 6.

19. See references in chapter 1, especially Hans Morgenthau's *Scientific Man versus Power Politics* and *Politics among Nations*.

20. Morgenthau, *Politics among Nations*. This argument for Germany's aggressive "revisionism" is upheld by Randall L. Schweller, *Deadly Imbalances* (New York: Columbia University Press, 1998).

21. See references in chapter 1.

22. Quoted in Walter Laqueur, *Russia and Germany* (New Brunswick, N.J.: Transaction, 1990), 25.

23. See Michael E. Brown, Sean M. Lynn-Jones, and Steven E. Miller, eds., *Debating the Democratic Peace* (Cambridge: MIT Press, 1996).

24. Quoted in Fritz Fischer, *Germany's Aims in the First World War* (New York: Norton, 1967), 174–75, 634.

25. Hans W. Gatzke, *Stresemann and the Rearmament of Germany* (Baltimore: Johns Hopkins University Press, 1954), 18.

26. Quoted in Elmer Bendiner, *A Time for Angels* (New York: Knopf, 1975), 215–16. See Stresemann diary, 7 September 1925, in Eric Sutton, ed., *Gustav Stresemann: His Diaries, Letters and Papers*, vol. 2 (New York: Macmillan, 1937), 503–5.

27. Quoted in Gatzke, *Stresemann*, 35.

28. Stresemann diary, Sutton, *Stresemann*, 2:504–5.

29. On German war preparations in the 1920s and 1930s prior to Hitler's assumption of power, and the expansionist goals of Stresemann's successors, see esp. Gaines Post, *The Civil-Military Fabric of Weimar Foreign Policy* (Princeton: Princeton University Press, 1973), and Edward M. Bennett, *German Rearmament and the West, 1932–1933* (Princeton: Princeton University Press, 1979).

30. See Stoakes, *Hitler*, chap. 5, and Woodruff D. Smith, *The Ideological Origins of Nazi Imperialism* (New York: Oxford University Press, 1986).

31. Hitler, *Mein Kampf*, trans. Ralph Manheim (Boston: Houghton Mifflin, 1925), 641–67 (in the block quotation, Hitler italicizes the whole text). See also *Hitler's Secret Book* (New York: Grove, 1961), 145 (written in 1928).

32. In the late 1920s, Hitler briefly saw America as an even bigger long-term threat, because of its huge population and land mass (*Secret Book*, 103–4). The American Depression significantly lowered his estimate of U.S. future growth, however, causing him to switch his focus back to Russia. See Gerhard Weinberg, "Hitler's Image of the United States," in his *World in the Balance* (Hanover, N.H.: University Press of New England, 1981), 53–74.

33. Henry Ashby Turner, ed., *Hitler: Memoirs of a Confidant* (New Haven: Yale University Press, 1985), 173; see also 91, 162, 53. This aligns with recollections of Hermann Rauschning, another associate of the time: Rauschning, *The Voice of Destruction* (New York: Putnam's, 1940), 130, 133.

34. NDR: doc. 472. See Gerhard Weinberg, *The Foreign Policy of Hitler's Germany: Diplomatic Revolution in Europe, 1933–36* (Chicago: University of Chicago Press, 1970), 27, and Deist, *Wehrmacht*, 26.

35. Weinberg, *Foreign Policy*, 27.

36. Quoted in Deist, *Wehrmacht*, 26.

37. General Eugen Ott later acknowledged that Hitler's February 3 speech on securing *Lebensraum* in the east "seemed to me at the time a crucial declaration." Other generals were alarmed, he claims, but discounted the speech as a "boundless scheme" that would soon be seen as unrealistic (quoted in Weinberg, *Foreign Policy*, 27, n. 8). There is no contemporary evidence that they discounted Hitler's plan. Indeed, it seems difficult to believe that the military could think that Hitler's declaration was crucial and alarming, and yet go on to dismiss it.

38. Deist, *Wehrmacht*, 28; Müller, *Army, Politics*, 54–59.

39. Wilhelm Deist, "The Rearmament of the Wehrmacht," in Deist et al., *Germany and the Second World War* (Oxford: Clarendon, 1990), 1:414.

40. Deist, *Wehrmacht*, 33.

41. Hitler also wanted SA leader Ernst Röhm eliminated for internal reasons. Still, had he thought the SA was the best tool for war, he could have built up the organization, instead of turning to the traditional military.

42. Quoted in Robert J. O'Neill, *The German Army and the Nazi Party, 1933–39* (London: Cassell, 1966), 40–41. After the war, Weichs acknowledged that "Hitler had set forth his complete foreign policy programme and already intimated the probability of aggressive war." Moreover, "the only detail which did not correspond to later developments was the actual timing" of the war, which came earlier than the generals expected (ibid., 41).

43. *NCA*, 7:443–49.

44. Klaus-Jürgen Müller, "Military and Diplomacy in France and Germany in the Inter-war Period," in Müller, ed., *The Military in Politics and Society in France and Germany in the Twentieth Century* (Oxford: Berg, 1995), 116–18.

45. In the meeting, an assistant argued that the link between industry and the military should not be put in writing so that "the military purpose may not be traceable." Beck immediately promised a decision. *NCA*, 7:448–49. Word filtered down to regional command. Future Army Commander-in-Chief Walther von Brauchitsch, then posted in East Prussia, wrote Berlin in September to reiterate that a military buildup in East Prussia was not possible without economic recovery; "both of these together form the basis for a *policy directed toward the East*": *NCA*, 6:280.

46. Deist, "Rearmament," 423.

47. Ibid., 421–22; see also Geyer, "Dynamics of Military Revisionism," 132.

48. Deist, "Rearmament," 422–23.

49. See notes of meeting on 3 February 1933, *NDR*, doc. 472.

50. On the buying of time as a conscious policy, see *NDR*, doc. 494.

51. *NCA*, 7:450–52. This is indicated by the group's consensus that a law providing for "total mobilization" was necessary for "the conduct of the war and the achievement of victory." Fighting war, rather than deterring it, was the objective.

52. Deist, *Wehrmacht*, 40–41.

53. See Klaus-Jürgen Müller, *General Ludwig Beck: Studien und Dokumente* (Boppard: Harald Boldt, 1980), doc. 34, and Geyer, "Dynamics of Military Revisionism," 136.

54. Geyer, "Dynamics of Military Revisionism," 137.

55. See Deist, "Rearmament," 433–35.

56. Quoted in Geyer, "Dynamics of Military Revisionism," 137.

57. Quoted in ibid., 138; Deist, *Wehrmacht*, 42.

58. Ibid., 42–43.

59. The corresponding period before World War I, 1905–13, was somewhat longer since Germany's economic position versus Russia was less precarious. Hitler and the military were more aware that Germany's economic gains from 1935 to 1939 could not be sustained given Stalin's massive industrialization program; thus the rush to maximize military superiority.

60. See Dale C. Copeland, "Economic Interdependence and War: A Theory of Trade Expectations," *International Security* 20 (spring 1996): 5–41.

61. *NDR*: doc. 185. See also Hermann Göring's briefing of the Cabinet on the "showdown with Russia," *NCA*, 7:471–73.

62. Quoted in Hans-Erich Volkmann, "The National Socialist Economy in Preparation for War," in Deist et al., *Germany*, 280. In the fall of 1936, Hitler began building the populace's support for preventive war against Russia. See Norman H. Baynes, ed., *The Speeches of Adolf Hitler*, vol. 1 (London: Oxford University Press, 1942), 673.

63. Goebbels's diaries, quoted in Kershaw, *Nazi Dictatorship*, 124–25.

64. All quotations are from Colonel Friedrich Hossbach's minutes, *DGFP*, series D, vol. 1: doc. 19.

65. Quoted in Deist, "Rearmament," 442–44.

66. Deist, *Wehrmacht*.

67. Deist, "Rearmament," 452–53.

68. America was expected to support Britain, but given its weak military, Hitler saw it mainly as a long-term threat to be dealt with after Germany conquered the continent. See Weinberg, *World in the Balance*, 53–74.

69. *NDR*: doc. 508.

70. *DGFP*, series D, vol. 2: doc. 221; see also doc. 235.

71. *NDR*: doc. 521.

72. *DGFP*, series D, vol. 2: doc. 235.

73. Quoted in O'Neill, *German Army*, 153–57; Williamson Murray, "Net Assessment in Nazi Germany," in Murray and Allan R. Millett, eds., *Calculations: Net Assessment and the Coming of World War II* (New York: Free Press, 1992), 76.

74. Murray, "Net Assessment," 78.

75. Ibid., 78–79; Major-General Alfred Jodl's diary, 10 August 1938, in *NCA*, 4:364; Deist, *Wehrmacht*, 98–99; Telford Taylor, *Munich* (Garden City, N.Y.: Doubleday, 1979), 698.

76. Beck himself told Brauchitsch on 30 May that Czechoslovakia's existence was "intolerable" and that it must be eliminated by war if necessary. Manfred Messerschmidt, "Foreign Policy and Preparation for War," in Diest et al., *Germany*, 658.

77. See esp. Harold C. Deutsch, *Conspiracy against Hitler in the Twilight War* (Minneapolis: University of Minnesota Press, 1968); Deutsch, *Hitler and His Generals* (Minneapolis: University of Minnesota Press, 1974); and Correlli Barnett, ed., *Hitler's Generals* (New York: Quill, 1989).

78. *DGFP*, series D, vol. 1: doc. 19.

79. *NDR*, 690–91; Taylor, *Munich*, 306–7. In summer 1937 he had issued a directive for "the concerted preparation of the armed forces for war" that noted "an unprovoked offensive deployment . . . was not excluded, where the risks remained calculable." Quoted in Müller, *Army, Politics*, 26.

80. Taylor, *Munich*, 316–21; Walter Görlitz, "Blomberg," in Correlli, ed., *Hitler's Generals*, 135–37. Even Deutsch affirms that the generally accepted view—that Hitler was surprised and disappointed by the revelations—is probably the correct one (*Hitler and His Generals*, 106–7).

81. See Taylor, *Munich*, 301–4, 313–30, and Matthew Cooper, *The German Army, 1933–1945* (New York: Stein and Day, 1978), 59–63.

82. Quoted in Cooper, *German Army*, 38.

83. I cover it in more detail in Copeland, "Deterrence, Reassurance, and Machiavellian Appeasement," paper presented to conference on Deterrence in Enduring Rivalries, Naval Postgraduate School, Monterrey, Calif., September 1995.

84. John Charmley, *Chamberlain and the Lost Peace* (Chicago: Ivan Dee, 1989), chaps. 11–13; Keith Middlemas, *Diplomacy of Illusion* (London: Weidenfeld and Nicolson,

1972), chaps. 11–13; R. A. C. Parker, *Chamberlain and Appeasement* (New York: St. Martin's, 1993), chaps. 7–8.

85. See Williamson Murray, *The Change in the European Balance of Power, 1938–1939* (Princeton: Princeton University Press, 1984), 204–5.

86. *NCA*, 4:365. Hitler was also intensely angry over Munich, believing that Chamberlain had cheated him out of his invasion. Invasion was preferred since it would give the military a chance to hone its efficiency, while stirring up the population for future tasks. See Taylor, *Munich*, 934–36.

87. See Taylor, *Munich*, 876–97. Moreover, there were signs that Washington might not stay neutral if Hitler did not accept the deal (*DGFP*, series D, vol. 2: docs. 453, 632, and 651; and Taylor, *Munich*, 890).

88. *NCA*, 7:476–78.

89. *DGFP*, series D, vol. 6: doc. 149.

90. *DGFP*, series D, vol. 6: doc. 52, and also doc. 205. In January 1939 Hitler began to shift more resources toward the navy. See *NDR*, 728–29 on the "Z-Plan."

91. *DGFP*, series D, vol. 6: doc. 211.

92. See Charmley, *Chamberlain and the Lost Peace*, chaps. 16–17, and Middlemas, *Diplomacy of Illusion*, chap. 14.

93. *DGFP*, series D, vol. 6: doc. 188.

94. Quoted in Anthony Read and David Fischer, *The Deadly Embrace* (London: Michael Joseph, 1988), 77. On the military's concurrent recognition of the Soviet buildup and Hitler's resolve to destroy it, see *NCA*, vol. 6: pp. 887–91.

95. On the German-Russian discussions, see *DGFP*, series D, vol. 6: docs. 215, 325, 351, 406, 414, and 424.

96. *DGFP*, series D, vol. 6: doc. 185.

97. *DGFP*, series D, vol. 6: doc. 433.

98. *NDR*: doc. 540.

99. *DGFP*, series D, vol. 7: docs. 192 and 193. See also 13 June memorandum on the belief that British-French intervention was very likely; *DGFP*, series D, vol. 6: appendix I, doc. 11.

100. Quoted in Alan Clark, *Barbarossa* (New York: Quill, 1985), 25. On the widespread perception in August that Germany's position was one of marked but waning military superiority, see Albert Speer, *Inside the Third Reich* (New York: Macmillan, 1970), 163. See also General Georg Thomas's view that the economy, owing to supply problems, had peaked and could only decline: Volkmann, "Nationalist Socialist Economy," 369.

101. *DGFP*, series D, vol. 7: doc. 200.

102. See Donald Cameron Watt, *How War Came* (New York: Pantheon, 1989), chap. 26, esp. 489–90.

103. *DGFP*, series D, vol. 7: doc. 271. See also Watt, *How War Came*, 491–92.

104. Tokyo also told Berlin in late August that it would not enter the war.

105. The OKW (*Oberkommando der Wehrmacht* or High Command of the Armed Forces) replaced the War Ministry in early 1938 and served as Hitler's coordinating agency.

106. Watt, *How War Came*, chaps. 26–27. Watt shows that Ribbentrop and Hitler did not want another Munich and therefore prevented Polish diplomats from gaining access to German leaders. In Hitler's words: "I only fear that at the last moment some swine will lay a plan of negotiations before me" (quoted in Murray, *Change in European Balance*, 205).

107. In multipolarity, the initiator always prefers to pick his adversaries off one by one.

108. Indeed, through the fall he overestimated their likelihood of attacking Germany.

109. See Copeland, "Deterrence, Reassurance, and Machiavellian Appeasement."

110. See John J. Mearsheimer, *Conventional Deterrence* (Ithaca: Cornell University Press, 1983), chap. 4.

111. General Franz Halder diary, *KTB*, vol. 1, 27 September 1940. Apart from corrections, my translations follow Charles Burdick and Hans-Adolf Jacobsen, eds., *The Halder War Diary, 1939–1942* (Novato, Calif.: Presidio, 1988).

112. *NCA*, 7:800–814.

113. Mearsheimer, *Conventional Deterrence*, chap. 4.

114. *NCA*, 3:572–77.

115. B. H. Hart, *The German Generals Talk* (New York: Morrow, 1948), 33–34.

116. *NCA*, 7:250–54. Thomas worried that Germany was prepared for a war in breadth, not depth. Its superiority was in fighting quick, decisive wars; if war dragged out, the superiority of the others' resources would prove decisive. Thomas's concerns were valid, but they were beside the point. Given Germany's inferior potential-power base, fighting a war in breadth was the only chance Germany had to grab the territory needed to overcome this inferiority.

117. Mearsheimer, *Conventional Deterrence*, 99–100; Martin van Creveld, *Fighting Power* (Westport, Conn.: Greenwood, 1982). This conclusion is supported by the Correlates of War data set (table A.3, appendix), which shows Germany in 1939–40 having defense expenditures and personnel greater than Britain's and France's combined. Jacek Kugler and William Domke's calculation of Germany's actualized military power finds a similar result (table A.1 of the appendix); see also Schweller, *Deadly Imbalances*, table A-8.

118. Mearsheimer, *Conventional Deterrence*, 100. Mearsheimer downplays Germany's marked qualitative superiority in the forces that mattered: tanks and airplanes. The Luftwaffe's performance in the west shows its overwhelmingly dominance in tactical air warfare compared to the outmoded French air force. Since in blitzkrieg warfare air superiority is key, once Germany secured it in the initial days the battle was essentially over (as the British immediately recognized). Moreover, strategic acumen must be factored into the military balance, and as Mearsheimer shows, German leadership skills were far superior: ibid., chap. 4.

119. Cooper, *German Army*, 117, 131–32, 154.

120. Remember that in multipolarity, the preponderant state is working against the combined rearmaments of the others. See Speer, *Inside the Third Reich*, 163, for the German understanding of this equation.

121. Halder diary, *KTB*, 27 September 1939.

122. See Clark, *Barbarossa*, 34, on the incredible devastation Stalin wrought.

123. Read and Fischer, *Deadly Embrace*, 417. Cooper agrees that the German army had "superior quality" to the Soviet army; it lost only because Russia's winter stopped the German advance (Cooper, *German Army*, 214–15, 117, 283–84).

124. Quoted in Robert Cecil, *Hitler's Decision to Invade Russia, 1941* (London: Davis-Poynter, 1975), 143.

125. Helmuth Groscurth, *Tagebücher Eines Abwehroffiziers, 1938–1940*, ed. Helmut Krausnick and Harold C. Deutsch (Stuttgart: Deutsche Verlags-Anstalt, 1970), docs. 64 and 66.

126. Ibid., doc. 68.

127. Ibid., doc. 70, pt. A.

128. Deutsch, *Conspiracy*, 205–7.

129. As Cooper summarizes: "The generals were keen to end the traditional Slavonic rivalry for the domination of Eastern Europe," and "constantly expressed their fears" regarding future Soviet intentions (*German Army*, 252).

130. See Mearsheimer, *Conventional Deterrence*, 118–26. Confidence was high. As Hitler informed Mussolini in March, "The sense of superiority over our Western opponents animating both officers and troops is absolute and unqualified"; yet given British rearmament, Germany had to act now. *DGFP*, series D, vol. 8: doc. 663.

131. Quoted in Barry A. Leach, *The German Strategy against Russia, 1939–1941* (Oxford: Clarendon, 1973), 48; Clark, *Barbarossa*, 24.

132. In mid-July, Halder noted that Hitler was puzzled by Britain's unwillingness to make peace. Using force against Britain was "against his grain," since Britain's defeat would only allow Japan and America to grab its empire. Halder diary, *KTB*, 13 July 1940.

133. Halder's hostility toward Russia mirrored that of his predecessor, Beck. See Leach, *German Strategy*, 53.

134. Halder diaries, *KTB*, 3 July 1940, translation by Leach, *German Strategy*, 56.

135. Leach, *German Strategy*, 50, 56.

136. Halder diaries, *KTB*, 22 July 1940; Leach, *German Strategy*, 58–60.

137. Walter Warlimont, *Inside Hitler's Headquarters, 1939–45* (Novato, Calif.: Presidio, 1962), 112; Leach, *German Strategy*, 64.

138. Quoted in Warlimont, *Inside Hitler's Headquarters*, 111–12 (Warlimont was one of the four subordinates). The navy was also in agreement: Leach, *German Strategy*, 151.

139. Halder diary, *KTB*, 31 July 1940.

140. Quoted in Leach, *German Strategy*, 250–52. This was not blind optimism: the plan assumed that the Russians, if rational, would fall back to defensive positions behind Russia's great rivers; Moscow had no such plans. See Cecil, *Hitler's Decision*, 116–17.

141. Halder diary, *KTB*, 5 December 1940. War-game exercises in late 1940 had affirmed Russian inferiority in armored warfare, artillery, and air power. Yet the difficulties were not ignored; the exercises also recognized the danger of overextension due to geographic distance and the problem of flank attacks: Leach, *German Strategy*, 105.

142. Halder diary, *KTB*, 4 November and 5 December 1940; *OKW KTB*, 5 December 1940.

143. *DGFP*, series D, vol. 11: doc. 532.

144. See Cecil, *Hitler's Decision*, chap. 11.

145. Read and Fischer, *Deadly Embrace*, 498–99.

146. *DGFP*, series D, vol. 11: doc. 630; *OKW KTB*, 253–58; Halder diary, *KTB*, 16 January 1941.

147. Quoted in Leach, *German Strategy*, 132.

148. *NCA*, 3:627 (quotation underlined in original).

149. *IMT*, 20:577–78.

150. *OKW KTB*, 3 February 1941.

151. *IMT*, 20:577–78.

152. Halder diary, *KTB*, 5 May 1941.

153. Halder diary, *KTB*, 7 April 1941; Leach, *German Strategy*, 174.

154. Quotations from Alexander Werth's account, *Russia at War, 1941–1945* (New York: Carroll and Graf, 1964), 122–23. Werth was a journalist in Moscow during this time and was given classified details on the speech after the German invasion (122). Since Werth's book is fairly sympathetic to the Soviets, this revelation of Stalin's future intentions we can take as genuine.

155. *NCA*, 6:1000. See also Halder diary, *KTB*, 14 June 1941, and Read and Fischer, *Deadly Embrace*, 611.

156. Warlimont, *Inside Hitler's Headquarters*, 147. For additional references to Hitler's desire to destroy Russia before it could grow further, see *NCA*, 1:795, 819–20; H. R. Trevor-Roper, ed., *Hitler's Secret Conversations, 1941–1944* (New York: Octagon, 1976), 150, 537–38; and Trevor-Roper, *The Testament of Adolf Hitler* (London: Cassell, 1961), 33–34, 59, 107.

157. See Leach, *German Strategy*, appendix IV.

158. Halder diary, *KTB*, 17 February 1941.

159. Quoted in Leach, *German Strategy*, 173–74, 156. Hitler later admitted to his

aides, "On 22 June a door opened before us, and we didn't know what was behind it . . . the heavy uncertainty took me by the throat" (ibid.).

160. This information is from the Soviet 1960 study *History of the War*, in Werth, *Russia at War*, 133–40.

161. Some estimation mistakes were made. In particular, the military should have taken rumors of new Soviet heavy tanks more seriously (see Leach, *German Strategy*, 172–73). Still, even here the analysis was fairly rational: the generals were indeed worried by these rumors (Clark, *Barbarossa*, 26), and as Hitler later noted, the reports of massive Russian tank production helped push him even more quickly into war (Trevor-Roper, *Hitler's Secret Conversations*, 150).

162. In mid-June 1941, Washington and London expected Russia to last only six to seven weeks against a German onslaught; this remained the assumption through the early weeks of the conflict: Cecil, *Hitler's Decision*, 121.

163. On German fears of U.S. growth, see Weinberg, *World in the Balance*, 53–74.

164. See Copeland, "Deterrence, Reassurance, and Machiavellian Appeasement."

6. Bipolarity, Shifting Power, and the Cold War

1. Traditionalists include Arthur Schlesinger, Herbert Feis, Adam Ulam, Philip Mosely, George Kennan, and Henry Kissinger. For references, see Howard Jones and Randall B. Woods, "Origins of the Cold War in Europe and the Near East," *Diplomatic History* 17 (spring 1993): 251–310, and Melvyn P. Leffler, "Interpretative Wars over the Cold War, 1945–60," in Gordon Martel, ed., *American Foreign Relations Reconsidered, 1890–1993* (London: Routledge, 1994). John Lewis Gaddis has recently moved to the traditionalist camp: *We Now Know: Rethinking Cold War History* (Oxford: Oxford University Press, 1997). Traditionalists emphasizing Stalin's pursuit of power and security over ideological ends are Woods and Jones, *The Dawning of the Cold War* (Athens: University of Georgia Press, 1991), and Vojtech Mastny, *The Cold War and Soviet Insecurity* (New York: Oxford University Press, 1996).

2. Revisionists include Gabriel Kolko, William Appleman Williams, Thomas McCormick, and David Horowitz. For references, see Jones and Woods, "Origins of the Cold War," and Leffler, "Interpretive Wars."

3. Postrevisionists include John Lewis Gaddis (until recently), Geir Lundestad, Daniel Yergin, and Robert Pollard. For references see Gaddis, "The Emerging Post-Revisionist Synthesis on the Origins of the Cold War," *Diplomatic History* 7 (Summer 1983): 171–90; Jones and Woods, "Origins of Cold War"; and Leffler, "Interpretive Wars."

4. See Robert Jervis, *Perception and Misperception in International Politics* (Princeton: Princeton University Press, 1976), chap. 3, and references in chapter 2 of this book.

5. This position draws upon another aspect of the security dilemma: the fear that the other's intentions may change (Robert J. Art and Robert Jervis, "The Meaning of Anarchy," in Art and Jervis, eds., *International Politics* [Boston: Little, Brown, 1985], 3; Jervis, *Perception and Misperception*, 62).

6. This is more true of spiral models based on psychological variables; a purely rationalist spiral model is closer to my argument. See Jervis, *Perception and Misperception*, chap. 3, and Charles L. Glaser, "The Security Dilemma Revisited," *World Politics* 50 (October 1997): 171–201.

7. Melvin P. Leffler, *A Preponderance of Power: National Security, the Truman Administration and the Cold War* (Stanford: Stanford University Press, 1992); Leffler, "The American Conception of National Security and the Beginnings of the Cold War," *American Historical Review* 89 (April 1984): 346–81; Leffler, *The Specter of Communism* (New York: Hill

and Wang, 1994); Leffler, *The Struggle for Germany and the Origins of the Cold War*, Occasional Paper no. 16 (Washington, D.C.: German Historical Institute, 1996); Leffler, "Inside Enemy Archives: The Cold War Reopened," *Foreign Affairs* 75 (July–August 1996): 120–35.

8. See Dale C. Copeland, "Neorealism and the Myth of Bipolar Stability: Towards a New Dynamic Realist Theory of Major War," *Security Studies* 5 (spring 1996): 29–89.

9. Cf. Leffler, *Preponderance of Power*.

10. *FRUS, 1945, Malta and Yalta*: 107–8. The letter was made part of the State Department briefing book for the Potsdam conference. See *FRUS, 1945, Potsdam* I:265.

11. See George F. Kennan, *Memoirs, 1925–1950* (Boston: Little, Brown, 1967), 225–30 and appendix A.

12. Ibid., 506.

13. On Kennan's influence on Harriman, see Harriman and Elie Abel, *Special Envoy to Churchill and Stalin, 1941–1946* (New York: Random House, 1975), ix–x.

14. Quoted in David McCullough, *Truman* (New York: Touchstone, 1992), 372.

15. NA, JCS 1313/1, 16 April 1945, RG 218, CCS 092 USSR (3–27–45), Sec. 1.

16. Leffler, *Preponderance*, 60–61.

17. Quoted in Lynn Etheridge Davis, *The Cold War Begins* (Princeton: Princeton University Press, 1974), 221.

18. See Grew's 19 May report, in Joseph C. Grew, *Turbulent Era*, 2 vols. (Boston: Houghton Mifflin, 1952), 2:1446; Stimson and Marshall's discussion, appendix V, Martin J. Sherwin, *A World Destroyed* (New York: Vintage, 1987), 350–53; and Byrnes's comments to assistant Walter Brown, Brown diary, 24 July, Clemson University.

19. Wallace diary, 4 May 1945, in John Morton Blum, ed., *The Price of Vision: The Diary of Henry A. Wallace, 1942–1946* (Boston: Houghton Mifflin, 1973), 441–42.

20. Quoted in Woods and Jones, *Dawning*, 42. See also Michael S. Sherry, *Preparing for the Next War* (New Haven: Yale University Press, 1977), 181.

21. Most historians now agree that Roosevelt was as much a realist as an idealist by his last year in office. See inter alia Warren F. Kimball, *The Juggler: Franklin Roosevelt as Wartime Statesman* (Princeton: Princeton University Press, 1991); Sherry, *Preparing for the Next War*; Sherwin, *World Destroyed*; Daniel Yergin, *Shattered Peace*, rev. ed. (Harmondsworth: Penguin, 1990); and John Lewis Gaddis, *United States and the Origins of the Cold War, 1941–1947* (New York: Columbia University Press, 1972).

22. Appendix L, "Notes of the Interim Committee Meeting, 31 May 1945," in Sherwin, *World Destroyed*, 300–301.

23. Sherry, *Preparing for the Next War*, 42.

24. NA, JSSC 9/1, "Post-War Military Problems—with Particular Relations to Air Bases," RG 218, CCS 360 (12–9–42), Sec. 1, Box 269, p. 10.

25. NA, RG 218, CCS 092 USSR.

26. Sherry, *Preparing for the Next War*, 44–47.

27. JCS 570/4 and "Supplemental Instructions to the State Department Concerning Post-War Military Bases." NA, JCS 570/4, RG 218, CCS 360 (12–9–42), Sec. 2.

28. Stimson Diary, LC, 18 March 1945, p. 2.

29. See for example, JCS 570/17, 14 May 1945, "Overall Examination of U.S. Requirements for Post-War Military Bases," NA, RG 218, CCs 360 (12–9–42) Sec. 5; and JPS 684/4, 4 June 1945, of same title, NA, RG 218, CCS 360 (12–9–42), Sec. 6, Box 271.

30. JWPC 361/4, 25 August 1945, "Overall Examination of U.S. Requirements for Military Bases," NA, RG 218, CCS 360 (12–9–42), Sec. 7, Box 271.

31. *FRUS, 1945, Malta and Yalta*: 153.

32. Gaddis, *United States*, 123–31. On JCS 1067's development, see also Bruce K. Kuklick, *American Policy and the Division of Germany* (Ithaca: Cornell University Press,

1972), chaps. 2–5, and John H. Backer, *Winds of History* (New York: Van Nostrand Reinhold, 1983), chaps. 1–3.

33. Leffler, *Struggle*, 16.

34. Stimson Diary, LC, 17 and 29 March 1945.

35. Quoted in Leffler, *Struggle*, 16–17. See also Stimson Diary, LC, 19 April 1945.

36. Stimson Diary, LC, 16 May 1945. See also Gaddis, *United States*, 236–37.

37. Leffler, *Struggle*, 17.

38. *FRUS*, 1945, Potsdam I:628, n. 3.

39. Ibid., 612; see also 613, 623.

40. See Clay's letters to Washington on 29 June and 5 July, in Jean Edward Smith, ed., *The Papers of General Lucius D. Clay*, 2 vols. (Bloomington: Indiana University Press, 1974), 1:41 and 48. On Clay's ignoring of the directive, see John Gimbel, *The American Occupation of Germany* (Stanford: Stanford University Press, 1968), 5–9, and Carolyn Woods Eisenberg, *Drawing the Line* (Cambridge: Cambridge University Press, 1996), chaps. 4 and 6.

41. See Leffler, *Struggle*, 21; *FRUS*, 1945, Potsdam I:585–97.

42. Stimson Diary, LC, 3 July 1945, p. 2.

43. On the largely reactive way the Soviets dealt with their occupation of eastern Germany, see Norman M. Naimark, *The Russians in Germany* (Cambridge: Harvard University Press, 1995).

44. See Leahy diary, LC, 20 April 1945.

45. Stimson Diary, LC, 11 May 1945.

46. *FRUS*, 1945, vol. 5:999–1000.

47. See ibid., 1000–1011, and Yergin, *Shattered Peace*, 94.

48. See *FRUS*, 1945, vol. 5:1018–21.

49. Ibid., 1031–33.

50. See *FRUS*, 1945, Potsdam I:491–571, esp. 523, 537, 545–47.

51. See Charles L. Mee, *Meeting at Potsdam* (New York: Evans, 1975), 188–89, 191, and 266–67, and Eisenberg, *Drawing the Line*, 100–120.

52. Eisenberg, *Drawing the Line*, 100.

53. See especially Gar Alperovitz, *Atomic Diplomacy*, rev. ed. (London: Pluto, 1994), and Alperovitz, *The Decision to Use the Atomic Bomb* (New York: Vintage, 1995).

54. For the literature, see J. Samuel Walker, *Prompt and Utter Destruction* (Chapel Hill: University of North Carolina Press, 1997).

55. Stimson Diary, LC, 10 May 1945.

56. Ibid., 14 May 1945.

57. Ibid., 15 May 1945.

58. Publicly Truman explained the delay as due to domestic budgetary issues. But as he confided to Joseph Davies, a former ambassador to Moscow and a close friend, on 21 May, "I have another reason which I have not told anybody," namely, "the atomic bomb." Davies Diary and Journal entries, Davies Diaries, LC, 21 May 1945, box 17; see also Stimson Diary, LC, 6 June 1945.

59. Quoted in Len Giovannitti and Fred Freed, *The Decision to Drop the Bomb* (New York: Coward-McCann, 1965), 65–66. See Ronald Takaki, *Hiroshima* (Boston: Little, Brown, 1995), 7, and Sherwin, *World Destroyed*, 202.

60. Quoted in Robert James Maddox, *From War to Cold War* (Boulder, Colo.: Westview, 1988), 65. This aligned with Leahy's advice to Truman that Washington should focus on giving Poland the "external appearance" of independence (Leahy Diary, LC, 23 April 1945). The agreement reached with Stalin in June reveals U.S. acquiescence. Stalin agreed to include London Poles in the interim Polish government until elections were held, but only as a minority part of the government. Truman then immediately recognized the

new Polish government even before any guarantee that elections would be held (they never were). Finally, Truman made no objections in July when Stalin proceeded to try sixteen leaders of the Polish opposition. See Davis, *The Cold War Begins*, 237–48; George McJimsey, *Harry Hopkins* (Cambridge: Harvard University Press, 1987), 386; and Marc Trachtenberg, *A Constructed Peace* (Princeton: Princeton University Press, 1999), 12–14.

61. Memorandum, 19 May 1945, in Grew, *Turbulent Era*, 2:1446.

62. Leffler, *Preponderance*, 60–61.

63. *FRUS*, 1945, vol. 5:254–56.

64. Barton J. Bernstein and Allen J. Matusow, eds., *The Truman Administration: A Documentary History* (New York: Harper and Row, 1966), 7–8.

65. Truman diary, 17 July 1945, in Robert H. Ferrell, ed., *Off the Record: The Private Papers of Harry S. Truman* (Harmondsworth: Penguin, 1980).

66. *FRUS*, 1945, Potsdam II:1362–65.

67. Stimson Diary, LC, 21 July 1945.

68. Ibid., 22 July 1945.

69. Quoted in Alperovitz, *Decision*, 252.

70. Brown Diary, Clemson University Library, 20 July 1945.

71. Davies journal and diary, Davies Diaries, LC, 28 July 1945, Box 19; 29 July 1945.

72. Wallace diary, 10 August 1945, in Blum, *Price of Vision*, 474. See Michael Schaller, *The American Occupation of Japan* (New York: Oxford University Press, 1985), 17–18.

73. Until recently, this campaign was largely unknown, mainly because it was kept out of public view or painted as part of normal postwar occupational duties. See Odd Arne Westad, *Cold War and Revolution* (New York: Columbia University Press, 1993); Marc S. Gallicchio, *The Cold War Begins in Asia* (New York: Columbia University Press, 1988); Kenneth S. Chern, *Dilemma in China* (Hamden, Conn.: Archon, 1980); and Michael Schaller, *The U.S. Crusade in China, 1938–1945* (New York: Columbia University Press, 1979). The memoirs of Truman and Byrnes (respectively, *Year of Decisions* [Garden City, N.Y.: Doubleday, 1955], and *Speaking Frankly* [New York: Harper, 1947]) make almost no mention of the campaign, despite the 800 million dollars in military and economic aid given to the KMT between August 1945 and December 1946 (see Schaller, *Crusade*, 271–72).

74. *FRUS*, 1945, vol. 7:527–28.

75. Ibid., 532–33.

76. Ibid., 547–48, 551.

77. From chargé in China Robertson's reports to Byrnes, 9 and 14 October, ibid., 578–80.

78. Ibid., 585–88.

79. Schaller, *Crusade*, 272.

80. See note by secretaries of War and Navy to Byrnes, *FRUS*, 1945, vol. 7:670–78; and meeting of departments of State, War, and Navy in early November, ibid., 606–7.

81. *FRUS*, 1945, vol. 7:768.

82. Harry N. Howard, *Turkey, the Straits, and U.S. Policy* (Baltimore: Johns Hopkins University Press, 1974), 216–25.

83. NA, 6 July 1945, "Internationalization of the Kiel Canal and Russian Interest in the Dardenelles," RG 165, ABC 093 Kiel, Sec. 1–A (6 July 45), Box 102.

84. NA, "U.S. Position re Soviet Proposal on Kiel Canal and Dardanelles," RG 165, ABC 093 Kiel, Sec. 1–A (6 July 45), Box 102.

85. See *FRUS*, 1945, Potsdam II:256–67, 301–5, 365–67, 372–73.

86. See ibid., 313–14, 453, 649–56, 1423–24.

87. From Harrison's record of the meeting, appendix Q, Sherwin, *World Destroyed*, 315. See also David Holloway, *Stalin and the Bomb* (New Haven: Yale University Press, 1994), 121.

88. Stimson Diary, LC, 12 August to 3 September 1945, p. 3; and 4 September 1945.
89. Ibid., letter and memorandum, 11 September 1945; diary, 12 September 1945.
90. Ibid., 12 September 1945.
91. Wallace diary, 21 September 1945, in Blum, *Price of Victory*.
92. Gregg Herken, *The Winning Weapon* (New York: Vintage, 1982), 35.
93. Quoted in Herken, *Winning Weapon*, 35–39. See also Alperovitz, *Decision*, 434–35.
94. *Documents on American Foreign Relations*, vol. 8, 1945–1946 (Princeton: Princeton University Press, 1948), 8; see also Forrestal diary, 6 November 1945, quoted in Herken, *Winning Weapon*, 59.
95. Truman letter, 5 January 1946, in Ferrell, *Off the Record*, 79–80; Herken, *Winning Weapon*, 88–89.
96. JPS 216th meeting, 29 August, NA, RG 218, CCS 334 (8–2–545), Box 217. See also JPS 219th meeting, 12 September 1945, NA, RS 218, CCS 334 (8–2–45), Box 217.
97. SWNCC 282, in *DAPS*, pp. 39–44.
98. JCS 1471/2, 19 October 1945, NA, RG 165, ABC 471.6 ATOM (17 August 45), Sec. 1.
99. JCS 1477/1, 30 October 1945, "Overall Effect of Atomic Bomb on Warfare and Military Organization," NA, RG 165, ABC 471.6 ATOM (17 August 45), Sec. 2.
100. Stimson Diary, LC, 4 April 1945; 15 June 1945.
101. See his private letter, 23 October 1945, in Ferrell, *Off the Record*, 71–72. See also Stimson Diary, LC, 7 September 1945, and Forrestal diary, 7 September 1945, in Walter Millis, ed., *The Forrestal Diaries* (New York: Viking, 1951) for intracabinet discussions.
102. Forrestal diary, 16 October 1945, in Millis, *Forrestal Diaries*, 102; Robert J. Donovan, *Conflict and Crisis* (New York: Norton, 1977), 136–37; Michael J. Hogan, *The Cross of Iron* (Cambridge: Cambridge University Press, 1998), chap. 4.
103. On Truman's conscious efforts to mold public opinion in support of containment, see Jones and Woods, "Origins of the Cold War," 268; Gaddis, *United States*, 350–52; Thomas G. Paterson, *Meeting the Communist Threat* (New York: Oxford University Press, 1988), chap. 3; Richard M. Freeland, *The Truman Doctrine and the Origins of McCarthyism* (New York: New York University Press, 1985); and Sherwin, *World Destroyed*.
104. Quoted in Millis, *Forrestal Diaries*, 120.
105. Truman diary, 17 July 1945, in Ferrell, *Off the Record*.
106. Davies diary, Davies Diaries, LC, 18 July 1945.
107. Forrestal diary, 28 July 1945, in Millis, *Forrestal Diaries*; Truman letter to wife, 29 July 1945, in Robert Ferrell, ed., *Dear Bess* (New York: Norton, 1983), 522.
108. Quoted in Alonzo L. Hamby, *Beyond the New Deal* (New York: Columbia University Press, 1973), 115.
109. Truman letter to Acheson, 15 March 1957, in Ferrell, *Off the Record*, 349.
110. Wallace diary, 18 May 1945, in Blum, *Price of Victory*, 451.
111. Truman diary, 30 July 1945, in Ferrell, *Off the Record*.
112. Gaddis, *United States*, 274–75.
113. Davies diary, Davies Diaries, LC, 22 July 1945.
114. Brown diary, Clemson University Library, 21 September 1945.
115. See Robert L. Messer, *The End of Alliance* (Chapel Hill: University of North Carolina Press, 1982); Patricia Dawson Ward, *The Threat of Peace* (Kent, Ohio: Kent State University Press, 1979); and Maddox, *From War to Cold War*.
116. Takaki, *Hiroshima*, 58.
117. *FRUS*, 1945, vol. 3:391.
118. Stimson diary, LC, 23 January 1945.
119. Davies diary, Davies Diaries, LC, 30 April 1945.
120. His genuine concerns for peace at this time are shown by his diary entries. In late May, he wrote that "to have a reasonably lasting peace the three great powers must

be able to trust each other and they must themselves honestly want it" (Truman diary, 22 May 1945, in Ferrell, *Off the Record*). In a 7 June entry he lashed out against those who endangered the peace by adopting a knee-jerk anti-Russian stance (ibid.).

121. Davies diary, Davies Diaries, LC, 30 April 1945.

122. Davies diary-journal, ibid., 16 July 1945.

123. Davies diary, ibid., 29 July 1945.

124. See Davies diary, ibid., 28 and 29 July 1945.

125. Quoted from two versions of Davies's diary written for 1 August, ibid.

126. For warnings from the scientists, see the Jeffries report of November 1944 and the Franck report of June 1945. Appendix R in Sherwin, *World Destroyed*, 316, and doc. 4 in Barton J. Bernstein, ed., *The Atomic Bomb* (Boston: Little, Brown, 1976), 12, respectively.

127. Truman letter to wife, 22 September 1945, in Ferrell, *Dear Bess*, 523.

128. Quoted in Herken, *Winning Weapon*, 53–54.

129. Freeland, *Truman Doctrine*; Woods and Jones, "Origins of the Cold War," 268.

130. By comparison, there has been a flood of documents on the 1950–80 period; see *CWIHPB*, Issues 1–11.

131. That the released documents indicate initial Soviet desires for a postwar modus vivendi is discussed in William C. Wohlforth, "New Evidence on Moscow's Cold War," *Diplomatic History* 21 (spring 1997): 229–42; Vladislav Zubok and Constantine Pleshakov, *Inside the Kremlin's Cold War* (Cambridge: Harvard University Press, 1996), 275–77; Scott Parrish, "The USSR and the Security Dilemma" (Ph.D. diss., Columbia University, 1993); and Parrish, "Marshall Plan, Soviet-American Relations, and the Division of Europe," in Norman Naimark and Leonid Gibianskii, eds., *The Establishment of Communist Regimes in Eastern Europe, 1944–1949* (Boulder, Colo.: Westview, 1997). It is worth noting that recent analyses that argue that evil Soviet intentions caused the cold war rely almost exclusively on evidence of hard-line Soviet behavior *after* 1945, that is, after Washington had moved to a provocative containment policy (see, for example, Gaddis, *We Now Know*, and Douglas J. MacDonald, "Communist Bloc Expansion in the Early Cold War: Challenging Realism, Refuting Revisionism," *International Security* 20 [winter 1995–96]: 152–88). Whether Moscow would have become more hard-line in the absence of a strong U.S. policy is very much an open question.

132. See Vojtech Mastny, *Russia's Road to the Cold War* (New York: Columbia University Press, 1979), 281–82; Michael M. Boll, *Cold War in the Balkans* (Lexington: University Press of Kentucky, 1984), 118–25; Caroline Kennedy-Pipe, *Stalin's Cold War* (Manchester: Manchester University Press, 1995), 56, 87–88; and Holloway, *Stalin*, 151–52.

133. NA, JIS 80/10, 25 October 1945, RG 218, CCS 092 USSR (3–27–45) Sec. 2, Box 208. See Matthew Evangelista, "Stalin's Postwar Army Reappraised," *International Security* 7 (winter 1982–83): 110–38.

134. See Townsend Hoopes and Douglas Brinkley, *FDR and the Creation of the U.N.* (New Haven: Yale University Press, 1997).

135. See Millis, *Forrestal Diaries*, 67–68.

136. See Eisenberg, *Drawing the Line*, 169; Clay to McCloy, 3 September 1945, in Smith, *Papers of Lucius Clay*, 1:62–68.

137. Quoted in Holloway, *Stalin*, 124. For Soviet concerns in August, as expressed to Harriman, see his *Special Envoy*, 499–505.

138. *FRUS*, 1945, vol. 2:118, 357, 367.

139. Ward, *Threat of Peace*, 39–40.

140. Byrnes, *Speaking Frankly*, 108; see also 102. On Stalin's angry reaction to U.S. behavior at the conference and his growing suspicions, see Vladimir O. Pechatnov, " 'The

Allies Are Pressing on You to Break Your Will . . . ': Foreign Policy Correspondence between Stalin and Molotov and Other Politburo Members, September 1945–December 1946," CWIHP, Working Paper no. 26, September 1999, pp. 5–8.

141. During October, Harriman told Washington that Soviet security concerns in the Far East were legitimate, and had recommended giving the Soviets at least a role on the pattern of the Balkan commissions (Schaller, *American Occupation*, 59).

142. Schaller, *American Occupation*, 60–61; Chern, *Dilemma in China*, 121.

143. On the Russian reaction, see Khrushchev, *KR: GT*, 81–83, and Pechatnov, "Allies Are Pressing," 6–10.

144. Quoted in Richard Rhodes, *Dark Sun: The Making of the Hydrogen Bomb* (New York: Touchstone, 1995), 179. See also Holloway, *Stalin*, 132–33.

145. Holloway, *Stalin*, 132–33 and chaps. 6–8.

146. Zubok and Pleshakov, *Inside the Kremlin's Cold War*, 42–43.

147. Quoted in ibid., 42. These accounts align with evidence collected by a western journalist in Moscow during the war. His sources indicated that it "was clearly realized that this was a New Fact in the world's power politics, that the bomb constituted a threat to Russia." After a brief spell of bewilderment, "all the bombs did, in effect, was to create on the Russian side a feeling of anger and acute distrust vis-à-vis the West. Far from becoming more amenable, the Soviet Government became more stubborn": Alexander Werth, *Russia at War, 1941–1945* (New York: Carroll and Graf, 1964), 1037–44. On Stalin's fears in the early postwar period, see Jeffrey Robinson, *The End of the American Century* (London: Simon and Schuster, 1997), 61–63.

148. For a pathbreaking study on this, see Marc Trachtenberg, "A 'Wasting Asset': American Strategy and the Shifting Nuclear Balance, 1949–54," in *ISR*. See also Russell D. Buhite and Christopher Hamel, "War for Peace: The Question of an American Preventive War against the Soviet Union, 1945–55," *Diplomatic History* 14 (summer 1990): 367–84.

149. The Correlates of War data set (table A.4, appendix) shows that American perceptions of marked economic superiority were accurate.

150. JIC 329, *APWASU*.

151. JIC 250/6, *APWASU*.

152. *FRUS*, 1946, vol. 1:1197–1203; Trachtenberg, "Wasting Asset."

153. This document was issued to all the top military leaders, including Nimitz and Eisenhower. Eisenhower, while he considered Groves's views "perhaps extreme in some respects," had a favorable overall impression of the paper (Trachtenberg, "Wasting Asset," 69).

154. JCS 1477/6, 21 January 1946, "Effect of Atomic Weapons on National Security and Military Organizations," NA, CCS 471.6 (8–15–45), Sec. 2, RG 218.

155. Trachtenberg, "Wasting Asset."

156. See *APWASU*, and Steven T. Ross, *American War Plans, 1945–1950* (New York: Garland, 1988).

157. David Alan Rosenberg, "Toward Armageddon: The Foundations of United States Nuclear Strategy, 1945–1961" (Ph.D. diss., University of Chicago, 1983), 89–90, 119–22.

158. On the development of NSC 68, see esp. John Lewis Gaddis, *Strategies of Containment* (Oxford: Oxford University Press, 1982), chap. 4, and Samuel F. Wells, "Sounding the Tocsin: NSC 68 and the Soviet Threat," *International Security* 4 (fall 1979): 116–58.

159. *FRUS*, 1949, vol. 1:399–402.

160. Ibid., 413–14.

161. JIC 502/1, 9 February 1950, "Implications of Soviet Possession of Atomic Weapons," NA, CCS 471.6, USSR (11–8–49), Sec. 1, RG 218.

162. CIA, ORE 91–49, 10 February 1950, NA, CD 11–1–2, RG 330 (1947–50 series).

163. All NSC-68 quotations are from *DAPS*, pp. 385–442.

164. See Trachtenberg, "Wasting Asset," for a thorough analysis.

165. *FRUS*, 1952–54, vol. 2:461.

166. Trachtenberg, "Wasting Asset." For more on U.S. decision-making during the 1950–53 period, see Copeland, "Realism and the Origins of Major War" (Ph.D. diss., University of Chicago, 1993), chap. 5.

167. Unit-level factors mattered, therefore, but in terms of the *rising* state's characteristics, not the declining state's. (This is a relaxation of the third parameter in chapter 2.)

7. THE BERLIN AND CUBAN MISSILE CRISES

1. Given space constraints, I focus on the immediate run-ups to the crises. Although this leads to some selecting on the dependent variable, the broader patterns of behavior and shifts in stability during the 1945–62 period are analyzed elsewhere: Dale C. Copeland, "Realism and the Origins of Major War" (Ph.D. diss., University of Chicago, 1993), chaps. 5–7, and Copeland, "The Security Dilemma and the Missile Gap Controversy, 1955–61" (typescript, University of Virginia, August 1998).

2. This approach is most evident in the standard cold war textbooks, where chapters are organized around the leaders in question: for example, Seyom Brown, *The Faces of Power* (New York: Columbia University Press, 1994), and John Lewis Gaddis, *Strategies of Containment* (Oxford: Oxford University Press, 1982).

3. For analysis and references see Graham T. Allison and Philip Zelikow, *Essence of Decision*, 2d ed. (New York: Longman, 1999), and David A. Welch, "The Organizational Process and Bureaucratic Politics Paradigm," *International Security* 17 (fall 1992): 112–46.

4. See esp. Matthew Evangelista, "Internal and External Constraints on Grand Strategy: The Soviet Case," in Richard Rosecrance and Arthur A. Stein, ed., *The Domestic Bases of Grand Strategy* (Ithaca: Cornell University Press, 1993); Jack Snyder, "International Leverage on Soviet Domestic Change," *World Politics* 42 (October 1989): 1–30; James G. Richter, *Khrushchev's Double Bind* (Baltimore: Johns Hopkins University Press, 1994); Carl Linden, *Khrushchev and the Soviet Leadership* (Baltimore: Johns Hopkins University Press, 1990); and Robert M. Slusser, *The Berlin Crisis of 1961* (Baltimore: Johns Hopkins University Press, 1973).

5. See Brown, *Faces of Power*; Thomas E. Mann, ed., *A Question of Balance: The President, the Congress, and Foreign Policy* (Washington, D.C.: Brookings, 1990). Perhaps the most developed argument here is Snyder's coalitional politics model, which sees shifting degrees of social cartelization as critical to U.S. and Soviet behavior (*Myths of Empire* [Ithaca: Cornell University Press, 1991], chap. 7).

6. Kenneth N. Waltz, *Theory of International Politics* (New York: Random House, 1979), chap. 8. See also John Lewis Gaddis, *The Long Peace* (New York: Oxford University Press, 1987), and John J. Mearsheimer, "Back to the Future," *International Security* 15 (summer 1990): 5–56. All three note that nuclear weapons also played an important deterrent role.

7. The most notable example is Louis J. Halle's *The Cold War as History* (New York: Harper and Row, 1967).

8. See Jacek Kugler and A. F. K. Organski, "The Power Transition," in Manus I. Midlarsky, ed., *Handbook of War Studies* (London: Unwin Hyman, 1989), 185–90, for a brief look at the cold war. I have found no sustained cold war analyses by hegemonic stability theorists.

9. For a critique of neorealism's general claim that bipolarity is more stable than multipolarity, see Dale C. Copeland, "Neorealism and the Myth of Bipolar Stability," *Security Studies* 5 (spring 1996): 29–89.

10. Deborah Welch Larson, for example, argues that U.S. leaders were slow to move

to containment because of predispositions to hold onto past beliefs: *Origins of Containment* (Princeton: Princeton University Press, 1985). Such an argument can explain only continuity, not change; the source of altered beliefs is external to the actor.

11. More evidence of domestic pulling and hauling exists for noncrisis issues, such as internal debates over arms buildups. See esp. Michael H. Armacost, *The Politics of Weapon Innovation* (New York: Columbia University Press, 1969), and Desmond Ball, *Politics and Force Levels* (Berkeley: University of California Press, 1980). One explanation for this difference is that crisis-initiation decisions, given the risks, force participants to focus on national security over parochial interests, while pushing leaders to resist bureaucratic arguments.

12. Thus while classical and neorealists may find chapter two's model plausible, there are few realists who provides case studies of the cold war crises from this perspective.

13. See appendix, table A.4, for the relative population balance. Washington did worry about Soviet technological growth and therefore took active steps to uphold its superiority (see Copeland, "Security Dilemma and Missile Gap").

14. This would change for the Soviets by the 1980s; see chapter 2.

15. In other perceived negative oscillations for the United States over the period, such as 1957–60 fears of a future missile gap, more moderate policies such as increased arms spending did exist; crisis initiation was therefore not necessary. See Copeland, "Realism and the Origins of Major War," chap. 5–6, and Copeland, "Security Dilemma and the Missile Gap."

16. Chapter 1, n. 40.

17. Given space constraints, I cover the Korean War crisis elsewhere: Copeland, "When Containment Backfires: The Dynamic Origins of the Korean War" (typescript, University of Virginia, July 1998). Contrary to the traditional view that Washington's lack of interest gave Stalin a green light in early 1950, I argue that Stalin approved the North Korean attack because of growing evidence that America was becoming *more* involved in Asia. By January–March 1950, the U.S. strategy was to remilitarize Japan while building up South Korea and Southeast Asia as part of a growing east Asian sphere. Newly declassified documents show that Stalin was reluctant to sanction North Korea's invasion, and did so only once U.S. policies implied a deep decline in his Asian position.

18. See Michail M. Narinskii, "The Soviet Union and the Berlin Crisis," in Francesca Gori and Silvio Pons, eds., *The Soviet Union and Europe in the Cold War, 1943–53* (London: St. Martin's, 1996); Marc Trachtenberg, *A Constructed Peace* (Princeton: Princeton University Press, 1999), 78–91; Avi Shlaim, *The United States and the Berlin Blockade, 1948–1949* (Berkeley: University of California Press, 1983); James L. Richardson, *Crisis Diplomacy* (Cambridge: Cambridge University Press, 1994), 192–203; Thomas Parrish, *Berlin in the Balance, 1945–1949* (Reading, Mass.: Addison-Wesley, 1998), chap. 12; and Ann Tusa and John Tusa, *The Berlin Airlift* (New York: Atheneum, 1988), chaps. 5–7.

19. See Scott Parrish, "The Turn to Confrontation: The Soviet Reaction to the Marshall Plan, 1947," CWIHP, Working Paper no. 9, March 1994; Parrish, "The USSR and the Security Dilemma" (Ph.D. diss., Columbia University Press, 1993), chap. 4; and William C. Wohlforth, "New Evidence on Moscow's Cold War," *Diplomatic History* 21 (spring 1997): 229–42.

20. On the London Conferences, see *FRUS*, 1948, vol. 2.

21. Ibid., 910.

22. U.S. Department of State, *Documents on Germany* (Washington, 1985), p. 150.

23. *FRUS*, 1948, vol. 2:947, 955.

24. See ibid., 949, 950, 954, 961.

25. Ibid., 984–85.

26. Ibid., 999–1003; Narinskii, "Soviet Union," 68–69.

27. *FRUS*, 1948, vol. 2:1007–13.

28. Parish, "USSR," 382.

29. NSA (*BC*), Chronology, p. 119.

30. NSA (*BC*), Chronology, p. 128.

31. Paul H. Nitze, *From Hiroshima to Glasnost* (New York: Grove Weidenfeld, 1989), 199.

32. Quoted in NSA (*BC*), Chronology, pp. 129–30.

33. See NSA (*BC*), Chronology, p. 135.

34. NSA (*BC*), Chronology, pp. 135–36. See Nitze, *From Hiroshima*, 202–4 on the development of this directive.

35. William Burr, "New Sources on the Berlin Crisis, 1958–1962," *CWIHPB*, Issue 2:23; Richter, *Khrushchev's Double Bind*, 142; *KR*, 506–9; *KR: LT*, 506–7; Michael R. Beschloss, *The Crisis Years* (New York: Harper Collins, 1992), 334–35.

36. *KR: GT*, 169–70. This pessimism at the highest levels is confirmed by a senior Soviet official (see Beschloss, *Crisis Years*, 334–35).

37. Quoted in Beschloss, *Crisis Years*, 320.

38. Nitze, *From Hiroshima*, 204–5.

39. See Department of State, *Documents on Germany*, pp. 542–46 and 552–59.

40. Hope Harrison's documentary work on the Soviet view during the crisis is the most complete, and it strongly shapes my analysis: Harrison, "The Bargaining Power of Weaker Allies in Bipolarity and Crisis: The Dynamics of Soviet-East German Relations, 1953–1961" (Ph.D. diss., Columbia University, 1993); Harrison, "The Exercise of Power in Soviet-East German Relations, 1953–1961" (typescript, Russian Research Center, Harvard University, February 1994); and Harrison, "Ulbricht and the Concrete 'Rose': New Archival Evidence on the Dynamics of Soviet-East German Relations and the Berlin Crisis, 1958–1961," CWIHP, Working Paper no. 5, May 1993.

41. Soviet fears of West German nuclearization were also important in 1961–62, as Trachtenberg shows: *History and Strategy* (Princeton: Princeton University Press, 1991), chap. 5, and *Constructed Peace*, 252–55; see also David Murphy, Sergei Kondrashev, and George Bailey, *Battle Ground Berlin* (New Haven: Yale University Press, 1997), 359–61. But the bulk of the evidence (particularly Harrison's) shows that East German economic decline was Moscow's more dominant concern in the 1961 crisis.

42. *KR: GT*, 164–65.

43. See Vladislav Zubok and Constantine Pleshakov, *Inside the Kremlin's Cold War* (Cambridge: Harvard University Press, 1996), 251.

44. Harrison, "Ulbricht," 12; see also Vladislav Zubov, "Khrushchev and the Berlin Crisis (1958–1962)," CWIHP, Working Papter no. 6, May 1993: 5.

45. Quoted in Harrison, "Ulbricht," 16–21.

46. Harrison, "Bargaining Power," 182–85.

47. Quoted in Richter, *Khrushchev's Double Bind*, 140.

48. Harrison, "Ulbricht," 28–29.

49. Harrison's words, "Ulbricht," 28; Harrison, "Bargaining Power," 185–86.

50. Harrison, "Ulbricht," 27–29.

51. Honoré Catudal, *Kennedy and the Berlin Wall Crisis* (Berlin: Berlin Verlag, 1980), 164, 184.

52. Norman Gelb, *The Berlin Wall* (London: Joseph, 1986), 62–71.

53. *KR: GT*, 168.

54. See Zubok and Pleshakov, *Inside the Kremlin's Cold War*, 248–49.

55. Quoted in Harrison, "Ulbricht," 36.

56. Quoted in ibid., 38.

57. Ibid., 38, 42.

58. Quoted in Harrison, "Bargaining Power," 207–8.

59. Harrison, "Ulbricht," 43; Murphy, Kondrashev, and Bailey, *Battle Ground*, 367.

60. Quoted in Harrison, "Ulbricht," 47; Harrison, "Bargaining Power," 219–24.

61. See Harrison, "Ulbricht," 50; Murphy, Kondrashev, and Bailey, *Battle Ground*, 374–75.

62. Quoted in Harrison, "Bargaining Power," 233–34. Khrushchev's concern regarding West Germany was genuine. Bonn had long talked about absorbing East Germany. A December 1956 Soviet report stated that a stronger West Germany might convince Poland to eject Russian troops. In 1957, Mikoyan noted that Khrushchev correctly saw that if East Germany was not strengthened, "then our army will be surrounded by fire." Moscow had no choice: either prop up the East German economy, or "lose the GDR altogether": Zubok and Pleshakov, *Inside the Kremlin's Cold War*, 195–98.

63. Quoted in Harrison, "Exercise of Power," 42.

64. Quoted in Richter, *Khrushchev's Double Bind*, 141.

65. An up-to-date analysis of domestic infighting is Richter, *Khrushchev's Double Bind*, but it offers little evidence that such struggles were at work over Berlin in 1958–61.

66. Theodore C. Sorensen, *Kennedy* (New York: Harper, 1965), 705; Arthur M. Schlesinger, *Robert Kennedy and His Times* (New York: Ballantine, 1978), 570. On Mc-George Bundy and Robert McNamara's agreement, see Richard Ned Lebow, *Nuclear Crisis Management* (Ithaca: Cornell University Press, 1987), 15.

67. For representative quotations, see Robert F. Kennedy, *Thirteen Days* (New York: Norton, 1968), 36; Schlesinger, *Thousand Days* (Boston: Houghton Mifflin, 1965), 796–97; and Secretary of Defense McNamara's interview with Richard Neustadt, NSA (CC): doc. 3307, p. 342, where he argues that "we didn't believe that it had [changed the military balance], but rather that if we failed to react, [everyone] would believe the political balance had changed." National Security Advisor Bundy's and Secretary of State Rusk's memoirs came after the declassified documents, so they were more willing to give equal weighting to both objectives (respectively, *Danger and Survival* [New York: Random House, 1988], 415–17, and *As I Saw It* [Harmondsworth: Penguin, 1990], 230). But in the same Neustadt interview from the early 1980s, Bundy supported McNamara's emphasis on the political balance.

68. Robert A. Divine, ed., *The Cuban Missile Crisis*, 2d ed. (New York: Marcus Wiener, 1988), 109.

69. This emphasis on alliance credibility over immediate security is still embedded in most of the recent analyses. See Robert Smith Thompson, *The Missiles of October* (New York: Simon and Schuster, 1992); Aleksandr Fursenko and Timothy Naftali, *"One Hell of a Gamble": Khrushchev, Castro, and Kennedy, 1958–1964* (New York: W. W. Norton, 1997); Richard Ned Lebow and Janice Gross Stein, *We All Lost the Cold War* (Princeton: Princeton University Press, 1994); Beschloss, *Crisis Years;* and Dino A. Brugioni, *Eyeball to Eyeball: The Inside Story of the Cuban Missile Crisis* (New York: Random House, 1991). A recent series of oral histories involving Soviet and U.S. participants have generally reinforced the myth: James G. Blight and David A. Welch, eds., *On the Brink*, 2d ed. (New York: Noonday, 1990); Bruce Allyn, Blight, and Welch, eds., *Back to the Brink* (Lanham, Md.: University Press of America, 1992); and Blight, Allyn, and Welch, eds., *Cuba on the Brink* (New York: Pantheon, 1993). A more balanced view is Mark J. White, *The Cuban Missile Crisis* (London: Macmillan, 1996).

70. Moreover, as Allison and Zelikow have argued, Khrushchev would have been poised to press his demands on Berlin. This would have increased the probability of major war down the road. It was thus rational to confront Khrushchev at that point, while the United States possessed superior strategic power: Allison and Zelikow, *Essence of Decision*, 99–107.

71. I cover Soviet reasons for putting missiles in Cuba elsewhere ("Neorealism and the

Myth of Bipolar Stability," 73–76). Consistent with most accounts, I argue that the goal was primarily to close a perceived widening in the strategic gap, and only secondarily to defend Cuba. Washington had released evidence in late 1961 dispelling Khrushchev's boast that Russia was equal in nuclear missiles. Khrushchev needed a stop-gap measure to secure deterrence until second-generation ICBMs were deployed en masse. Copying U.S. actions in Turkey, he saw medium- and intermediate-range missiles in Cuba as the solution. The Presidium unanimously agreed to the plan in May 1962. A recent book on Russian decision-making (Fursenko and Naftali, *Hell of a Gamble*) supports this account, but sees defending Cuba as equally critical. The book, however, shows that in April 1962 when Khrushchev conceived his plan, KGB reports indicated that the United States was unlikely to invade Cuba and would rely on subversion (159–60). Achieving parity on the cheap was thus the more powerful motivating force behind the missile deployment.

72. Scott Sagan's detailed work on complex organizations and the Cuban crisis, *The Limits of Safety* (Princeton: Princeton University Press, 1993), indicates that the objective risks of inadvertent war through an accident were even greater than ExComm members believed.

73. National Intelligence Estimate (NIE) 11-8-62, 6 July 1962, NSA (*SE*): doc. 372.

74. *FRUS*, 1961–63, vol. 8:342–43.

75. Ibid., 355–78, esp. 358, 366.

76. Washington's fear of oscillations and Soviet preventive motivations was also prevalent during the 1950s (see Copeland, "Security Dilemma").

77. The possibility that Moscow might put nuclear missiles in Cuba had been noted as early as February 1962, in a working draft on the forces needed to overthrow Castro, written under the names of McNamara and Rusk (26 February 1962, "Project Cuba," in NSA [CMCR, 1992], no file number). For authors propagating the myth that ExComm members were completely surprised in October by the existence of Cuban missiles, see Sorensen, *Kennedy*, chap. 24; Bundy, *Danger*, chap. 9; and Schlesinger, *Thousand Days*, chap. 30.

78. CIA (CC): doc. 6.

79. McCone's minutes, *CIA (CC)*: doc. 8.

80. NSA (CC): doc. 295; CIA (CC): doc. 9.

81. NSA (CC): doc. 425.

82. NSA (CC): doc. 3087, pp. 17–23.

83. NSA (CC): doc. 2925, pp. 1, 7–9; doc. 3087, p. 40.

84. Kennedy secretly taped many ExComm meetings. Quotations from these tapes for 16 and 27 October are taken largely from Bundy's transcriptions (NSA [CC]: docs. 622, 623, and 1544), supplemented where necessary by transcriptions released recently by Ernest May and Philip Zelikow (*KT*). The former better preserves the stops and starts of the actual discussions. For the other taped meetings, I rely on *KT* except where my own transcriptions capture words missing from *KT*.

85. There was a brief discussion of the Kremlin's motives in the second meeting, which paralleled this discussion.

86. See n. 71 on Soviet motives. Also understood was the Turkish-Cuban parallel. As Bundy observed, "as [Rusk] says, [this] has many comparisons between Cuba and [U.S. missiles in] Italy, Turkey and Japan."

87. McNamara reintroduced the idea near the meeting's end, but even then no one jumped in to support it.

88. As only Khrushchev and a few others knew, the real Soviet ICBM launcher total was only 20. Accordingly, the 40 launchers in Cuba, covering the same targets in less time and without warning, constituted a tripling of Soviet strategic missiles almost overnight: Allen, Blight, and Welch, *Back to the Brink*, 53.

89. As we will see, JFK's concern that the missile total would grow substantially was well founded. Castro told the Russians in May that he would accept as many as 1,000 missiles if necessary: Carlos Lechuga, *In the Eye of the Storm* (Melbourne: Ocean, 1995), 35.

90. Schlesinger, *Robert Kennedy*, 546.

91. *KT*, 97–98.

92. See Lebow, "Domestic Politics and the Cuban Missile Crisis," *Diplomatic History* 14 (fall 1990): 471–92, and Thompson, *Missiles*, 353.

93. See *KT*, 112–16.

94. *CIA (CC)*: doc. 57. Discussion that day on Soviet motives reinforced the view that Moscow sought to improve its strike capability against North America and to undermine the U.S. position in Europe and Latin America: *CIA (CC)*: docs. 52, 53, and 57.

95. Memoranda on the pros and cons of various alternatives offered no recommendations. See "Possible Courses of Action," NSA (CMCR, 1992–93), CMC I, no file number, and "Some Possible Subsequent Courses of Action and Counter-Action," NSA (DOS CMCR, 1992), CMC-8702125.

96. McCone's notes, *CIA (CC)*: doc. 55.

97. Quotations are from JFKL Presidential Recordings, 18 October 1962, Tapes 30.2 and 30A.1 (my transcription), and *KT*. See also McCone's record, *CIA (CC)*: doc. 60.

98. This follows my transcription (*KT* has Kennedy stating that a nuclear exchange would be a "prime failure").

99. Interestingly, even at this early stage, the idea of trading off Turkish missiles to achieve a peaceful resolution was discussed.

100. McCone's meeting notes, *CIA (CC)*: doc. 60.

101. See *KT*, 173–88. There was an interesting exchange on the missiles' significance. Army Chief of Staff Earle Wheeler stressed that the missiles greatly increased the Soviet ability to attack the United States. Marine Corps Commandant David Shoup replied that the global public might not understand this fear, since it would expect Moscow to have the equivalent number of ICBMs in a few years. Kennedy agreed that Russia would later have many ICBMs. Still, he argued, while Cuban missiles might not increase Russia's total future power, they do " create a danger right there now" (ibid.). Kennedy thus understood that the Soviets would eventually move toward parity. Yet by increasing their power so significantly and so quickly, they would hurt the U.S. ability to stay ahead according to the 1961 buildup plan. This would not only hurt extended deterrence; it might create a Soviet perception of temporary but declining superiority that could push Moscow into preventive war.

102. For the Thursday night discussion, see *KT*, 171–72.

103. Meeting minutes, NSA (*DR*): doc. 21. By the way he spoke, he implied that the president shared his opinion. That JFK still leaned to military action is shown by his behavior the next day and by his asking his close aide Theodore Sorensen on Thursday to draw up ultimata to Khrushchev and Castro to justify a military strike. See NSA (*CC*): doc. 676 and "To: F.C. [Fidel Castro]," JFKL, Sorensen Papers, Box 49, "Cuba-Subjects Standing Committee, 9/62–10/62 and undated." There were no equivalent letters for the blockade option; Sorensen would not begin to work on the blockade speech until Saturday (see Sorensen, *Kennedy*, 686–93).

104. Brugioni, *Eyeball to Eyeball*, 303; NSA (*CC*): doc. 3302.

105. NSA (*CC*): doc. 696.

106. See NSA (*CC*): doc. 623.

107. NSA (*DR*): doc. 21.

108. Brugioni, *Eyeball to Eyeball*, 311–13.

109. Minutes of NSC meeting, 20 October, RFK Papers, quoted in Schlesinger, *Robert Kennedy*, 550. The CIA Special Estimate that day affirmed that the missiles would make "an important contribution to [Soviet] total strategic capability": NSA *(DR)*: doc. 24.

110. *FRUS*, 1961–63, vol. 11:126–36. That night Kennedy assured McCone that Moscow would have only seventy-two hours to dismantle the missiles or military action would begin (ibid., 137–38 and 132).

111. NSA *(DR)*, doc. 25.

112. NSA *(CC)*: doc. 736.

113. *FRUS*, 1961–63, vol. 11:164.

114. "Cuba," 21 October 1962, NSA (CMCR, 1992), CMC I, no file number.

115. JFKL Presidential Recordings, 22 October 1962, 3:00 P.M. NSC meeting.

116. All quotations are from JFKL Presidential Recordings, 22 October 1962, 11:00 A.M., Tapes 32.1 and 32.2 (my transcriptions) (*KT* puts this meeting at 11:30).

117. Kennedy's words are somewhat blurred at the end, so he might be saying "we don't want them firing on us with nuclear weapons."

118. Theodore C. Sorensen, ed., *"Let the Word Go Forth"* (New York: Bantam Doubleday, 1988), 272–75.

119. Fursenko and Naftali, *Hell of a Gamble*, 206–17.

120. Quoted in ibid., 240–41.

121. Ibid., 241–42.

122. The risk that this would lead to all-out nuclear war was understood. The next day, the Soviet Defense Ministry, fulfilling an order from the Council of Ministers, took "supplementary measures to support the Armed Forces at the highest state of military readiness," including the troops of the strategic rocket forces. See Defense Minister Rodion Malinovski's report to Central Committee, 24 October 1962, in *CWIHPB*, Issue 5:73.

123. Telegram from Dobrynin to Moscow, 23 October 1962, *CWIHPB*, Issue 5:70–71.

124. See Fursenko and Naftali, *Hell of a Gamble*, 51–52, 155, 185.

125. On Thursday, showing skepticism for negotiated solutions, he told the group: "I never have thought we'd get them out of Cuba without the application of substantial force": *KT*, 417.

126. Kennedy, *Thirteen Days*, 109; see also *KT*, 609. The day before, the president noted that of the two options left—a negotiated solution and military action—"I doubt [the former] is going to be successful" (*KT*, 476).

127. Rusk recently "revealed" that on Saturday night Kennedy agreed to consider a plan created by Rusk (and known to no one else), now dubbed the "Cordier ploy." Andrew Cordier, president of Columbia, was to have asked U Thant, secretary-general of the UN, to make a public proposal for the removal of both Turkish and Cuban missiles. This would have provided another option should Moscow reject the private deal (*As I Saw It*, 240–42). This revelation implies that Kennedy would have backed away from invading Cuba in the crunch. More recent evidence, however, shows that Rusk's recollections were incorrect. Rusk did contact Cordier, but on *24–25 October*, and only about UN monitoring *after* any Turkish-Cuban missile deal, not about a pre-deal offer (see *KT*, 606, n. 3, and White, *Cuban Missile Crisis*, 202–3).

128. Robert Kennedy, *Thirteen Days*.

129. NSA *(CC)*: doc. 842.

130. This group of experts from various departments was established to study the future and advise the ExComm. Its crucial role after 21 October has been little discussed by ExComm members.

131. NSA *(CC)*: doc. 819. See also Harriman's report to Under Secretary of State

George Ball (NSA ([CC]: doc. 816), and a report by Raymond Garthoff, the State Department's Special Assistant for Soviet Bloc Political/Military Affairs to Rostow (NSA [CC]: doc. 940). On the Berlin connection, see *KT*, 678–80, and Allison and Zelikow, *Essence of Decision*, 99–107.

132. *KT*, 216–17.

133. "Memorandum for Mr. McGeorge Bundy," 22 October 1962, JFKL NSF, Box 226, Folder "Nato Weapons, Cables—Turkey."

134. NSA (CC): docs. 953 and 1080; Telegram to Hare and Finletter, 24 October 1962, JFKL NSF, Box 226, Folder "Nato Weapons, Cables—Turkey."

135. The MLF idea involved mostly submarine-based divisions made up of three or more nationalities, and was designed to reinforce extended deterrence by giving Europeans some sense of controlling the nuclear decision.

136. "SUBJECT: Cuba," 23 October 1962, NSA (CMCR, 1992–93), CMC I, no file number.

137. "Current Intelligence Memorandum," NSA (CC): doc. 905; see also *KT*, 348.

138. NSA (CC): doc. 1192.

139. NSA (CC): doc. 1164.

140. *KT*, 385–88.

141. "SUBJECT: Cuba," 25 October 1962, JFKL NSF, Box 226, Folder "NATO Weapons Cables—Turkey."

142. *FRUS, 1961–63*, vol. 11:213–15; NSA (CC): doc. 1328.

143. NSA (CC): docs. 1446 and 1448.

144. NSA (CC): doc. 1446.

145. Fursenko and Naftali, *Hell of a Gamble*, 249–50. Cf. Dobrynin's telegram to Moscow, 24 October 1962, *CWIHPB*, Issue 5:71–73.

146. Fursenko and Naftali, *Hell of a Gamble*, 250, 273–75.

147. *KT*, 461–64. See also *FRUS, 1961–63*, vol. 11:225. A Department of Defense report that day noted that the missiles' "military significance is that, in a Soviet no-warning attack on U.S. strategic forces, the Cuban missiles already there could reduce by about 30 per cent the number of our surviving vehicles, and by about 40 per cent the number of weapons that we could deliver on Soviet targets" (NSA [CC]: doc. 1398).

148. Meeting minutes, in *FRUS, 1961–63*, vol. 11:221 and 229–31. See also *KT*, 443–44, and CIA Deputy Director Marshall Carter's memorandum to McCone, 25 October 1962, *CIA (CC)*: doc. 93.

149. *FRUS, 1961–63*, vol. 11:229–31.

150. Quotations for these meetings, unless otherwise noted, are from Bundy's transcripts (NSA [CC]: doc. 1544), supplemented where necessary with *KT*, 492–628.

151. Raymond L. Garthoff, *Reflections On the Cuban Missile Crisis*, rev. ed. (Washington, D.C.: Brookings, 1989), 202–3.

152. Quoted in Lechuga, *In the Eye*, 35. Since IRBMs could reach all of the U.S. ICBM sites, even half this total could have quickly undermined U.S. deterrence. Moreover, as the August report had emphasized, the greatest hazard facing the United States was the possibility that Soviet leaders might *think* they had achieved a temporary but waning period of nuclear superiority.

153. NSA (CC): doc. 1492.

154. Kennedy's emphasis.

155. The fact that civil defense preparations had been actively pursued that week, and that Kennedy would leave such a critical meeting to inform the governors, shows the extent to which he believed that nuclear war might be unavoidable in the end.

156. Since the tape recording ended at this point, the passage is taken from the minutes, *ISR*, 318.

157. Kennedy's emphasis.

158. Interview with Neustadt, NSA (*CC*): doc. 3307.

159. In the few other examples where domestic public opinion was mentioned, barring one exception, the comments again revolved around public opinion as a potential constraint on what had to be done (*KT*, 127, 133, 200, 557). The exception is Kennedy's agreement with his brother's comment on 23 October that he would have been impeached if he had not acted (*KT*, 342–43). For two reasons, this exchange should not be overemphasized. First, in the prior discussion, JFK is focused on the global repercussions of allowing Khrushchev to deploy the missiles. Hence his agreement to RFK's comment is a side point to the main discussion. Moreover, since this exchange comes late in the crisis, after the key steps had already been taken, Kennedy's agreement seems more to reflect an attempt to bolster previous decisions, rather than indicating that he was driven by domestic motives. So even if staying in power was one of the president's goals (as it surely was), the vast bulk of the evidence shows that security concerns were his primary obsession.

160. Bureaucratic and organizational factors were important more in information-gathering and in the implementation of ExComm directives than in the actual decision-making. See Allison and Zelikow, *Essence of Decision*, chaps. 4 and 6.

161. Dillon: "Unless you get a cease-fire"; Bundy: "Or a general war."

162. Indeed, he immediately argued that Washington might minimize the escalation risk by "defus[ing] the Turkish missiles *before* we attack Cuba." Quotations from Bundy's transcripts, *NSA* (*CC*): doc. 1544 (McNamara's emphasis).

163. *KR: GT*, 182. On Khrushchev's growing fears on 27–28 October, see Fursenko and Naftali, *Hell of a Gamble*, 271–87. See also the alarming letters from Castro on Saturday, calling for a nuclear first strike against the United States, in Blight, Allyn, and Welch, *Cuba on the Brink*, appendix.

164. Bundy's transcripts, NSA (*CC*): doc. 1544 (Kennedy's emphasis).

8. Major War from Pericles to Napoleon

1. Inevitable limits on time prevent me from covering instances of major war in the historical Chinese and Indian systems. Initial impressions suggest that the theory does not work terribly well for the most infamous of these cases: the hegemonic triumphs of Genghis Khan and his successors in the multipolar thirteenth century. The Mongols certainly possessed military superiority, but greed and glory rather than security seem to have been their dominant motives. The theory does better in the multipolar Warring States period in China (403–221 B.C.). Jockeying for position went on for a century and a half until the Qin empire, exploiting its superior cavalry forces and internal organization, achieved the military preponderance needed for an all-out war for hegemony. The Mongol and Qin victories show that bids for hegemony in multipolarity can succeed, although they apparently require the relative disunity of opponents.

2. I have not come across periods where states met my conditions and yet did *not* initiate major wars. Still, such periods may exist, and more research is needed.

3. Thucydides, *The Peloponnesian War*, trans. Rex Warner (Harmondsworth: Penguin, 1954), 1.23; see also 1.88 and 1.118.

4. Ibid., 1.89–117.

5. Ibid., 1.1; 2.8–11. The Spartans understood that war would be long and costly (1.80–88; 2.11).

6. See Peter J. Fliess, *Thucydides and the Politics of Bipolarity* (Baton Rouge: Louisiana University Press, 1966).

7. See Harry Eckstein, "Case Study and Theory in Political Science," in Fred I.

Greenstein and Nelson W. Polsby, eds., *Handbook of Political Science* (Reading, Mass.: Addison-Wesley, 1975).

8. Thucydides, *Peloponnesian War*, 1.101–2; 1.118; 4.41.

9. Differences in the two sides' characters are amply shown in book 1 of Thucydides. Corinth, a Spartan ally, for example, chides the Spartans that while Athenians take risks to build their empire, Spartans stay at home and avoid conflict (1.69–70). On these differences, see Peter R. Pouncey, *The Necessities of War: A Study of Thucydides' Pessimism* (New York: Columbia University Press, 1980), 57–68.

10. On the history of this debate and a decisive riposte in Thucydides' favor, see G. E. M. de Ste. Croix's carefully argued and detailed analysis, *The Origins of the Peloponnesian War* (Worcester, U.K.: Duckworth, 1972).

11. On this, see Donald Kagan, *The Outbreak of the Peloponnesian War* (Ithaca: Cornell University Press, 1969), and Richard Ned Lebow, "Thucydides, Power Transition Theory, and the Causes of War," in Lebow and Barry S. Strauss, eds., *Hegemonic Rivalry: From Thucydides to the Nuclear Age* (Boulder, Colo.: Westview, 1991), 125–68.

12. See Thucydides, *Peloponnesian War*, 1.83–88; 1.118–25.

13. Ibid., 1.72.

14. One should not conflate Athens's clear imperial ambitions (ibid., book 1, passim) with a desire for major war. The Athenians certainly sought to absorb as many small states as possible into their tribute-paying empire. But Athens had no reason for wanting all-out war with Sparta if it could expand on the periphery without such a war. That Athens, as the rising power, did not desire major war in 431 is reinforced by Pericles' strategy of keeping Athens on the defensive and not adding to the empire during the war (2.65).

15. Ibid., 1.126.

16. See Lebow, "Thucydides, Power Transition Theory," 128.

17. See Jacqueline de Romilly, *Thucydides and Athenian Imperialism* (Oxford: Basil Blackwell, 1963), 19–20.

18. Russell Meiggs, *The Athenian Empire* (Oxford: Oxford University Press, 1972), chaps. 6–14; John V. A. Fine, *The Ancient Greeks* (Cambridge: Harvard University Press, 1983), chaps. 9–11.

19. The following synopsis is based on Polybius, *The Rise of the Roman Empire* (Harmondsworth: Penguin, 1979); R. M. Errington, *The Dawn of Empire* (Ithaca: Cornell University Press, 1972); Donald Kagan, *On the Origins of War* (New York: Doubleday, 1995); Tenny Frank, *Roman Imperialism* (New York: Cooper Square, 1972); Cyril E. Robinson, *History of the Roman Republic* (New York: Crowell, 1965); and T. A. Dorey and D. R. Dudley, *Rome against Carthage* (Garden City, N.Y.: Doubleday, 1972).

20. The war began solely as a struggle for control over a third party; only much later did it evolve into a war threatening either power's homeland. The First Punic War thus provides a powerful example of how the overcommitment of reputations and emotions in peripheral conflicts can lead to major war. Since neither side entered the conflict expecting an escalation to total war, however, all theories of major war remain incomplete in this case.

21. On Rome's increased potential power, see Dorey and Dudley, *Rome*, 26–28.

22. Scholars agree that Rome was acting defensively at this time, seeking to eliminate threats to its client states (Kagan, *Origins*, 262–74).

23. Moreover, Rome was woefully unprepared for war with Carthage in this period, to the point of neglecting to organize a third army for use in the west (ibid., 267). One might argue that the Romans were building up for war with Carthage by first eliminating threats at their rear, but this only reinforces the point: Carthage needed to act

before Rome got any stronger; and the Romans' move against Illyria indicates that they did not want war with Carthage for some time. Carthage's hostility was not a preemptive move in the face of imminent Roman attack, but a preventive move against long-term Roman growth.

24. Errington, *Dawn of Empire*, 62.

25. Laying responsibility at Carthage's door is consistent with our most objective source, Polybius, *Rise of the Roman Empire*, 3.30. Although Polybius refers to personal revenge as one of Hannibal's motives, the "pressure of circumstances," including the losses of Sardinia and Sicily, is also crucial (3.28; 2.30; 9.22–25). Modern historians also blame Carthage, but many too easily accept the revenge motive, forgetting that Hannibal acted on the Senate's instructions (Frank, *Roman Imperialism*, 122–25; Robinson, *History*, 105–10).

26. Near equality is again shown by the length and ferocity of the war, and how close Carthage came to winning. It is also the conclusion of Livy, *The War with Hannibal*, trans. Aubrey de Selincourt (Harmondsworth: Penguin, 1965), 21.1.

27. This characterization aligns with traditional diplomatic history (see n. 28). The Ottoman empire occupied a role similar to Persia's in the Greek case and Macedon's in the Rome-Carthage case: it was an extrasystemic actor which, because of geography, had a difficult time projecting power into the core system, but which occasionally affected events in the core. For an argument that the system was bipolar between the Hapsburgs and the Ottomans, see Ted Hopf, "Polarity, the Offense-Defense Balance, and War," *American Political Science Review* 85 (June 1991): 475–93. For a critique showing that Hopf's figures support the traditional position, see Dale Copeland, "Neorealism and the Myth of Bipolar Stability," *Security Studies* 5 (spring 1996): 67, n. 117.

28. These conclusions and the historical account are drawn from: R. J. Knecht, *Renaissance Warrior and Patron: The Reign of Francis I* (Cambridge: Cambridge University Press, 1994); Knecht, *Francis I* (Cambridge: Cambridge University Press, 1982); David Jayne Hill, *A History of Diplomacy in the International Development of Europe*, vol. 2 (New York: Howard Fertig, 1967); Manuel Fernández Alvarez, *Charles V* (London: Thames and Hudson, 1975); D. B. Wyndham Lewis, *Charles of Europe* (New York: Coward-McCann, 1931); H. Koenigsberger, "The Empire of Charles V in Europe," in G. R. Elton, ed., *The New Cambridge Modern History*, vol. 2 (Cambridge: Cambridge University Press, 1958), 310–33; F. C. Spooner, "The Hapsburg-Valois Struggle," in ibid., 334–58; and Francis Hackett, *Francis the First* (London: William Heinemann, 1934).

29. See Hackett, *Francis*, 222–54.

30. This argument dovetails with what Knecht calls the standard textbook explanation for the beginning of thirty-five years of warfare, namely, the French need to break out of an ever-tightening Hapsburg encirclement (*Renaissance Warrior*, 176).

31. Spooner, "The Hapsburg-Valois Struggle," 343.

32. See Hill, *History*, 323–49.

33. Alvarez, *Charles V*, 60.

34. That Spain was the preponderant military power of the time, and was seen as such, is discussed in M. S. Anderson, *The Origins of Modern European State System, 1494–1618* (London: Longman, 1998), 211; Peter Brightwell, "The Spanish System and the Twelve Years' Truce," *English Historical Review* 89 (April 1974): 273; Brightwell, "The Spanish Origins of the Thirty Years' War," *European Studies Review* 9 (October 1979): 410; C. V. Wedgwood, *The Thirty Years War* (New York: Anchor, 1961), 26–27; and S. H. Steinberg, *The Thirty Years' War* (New York: Norton, 1966), 8.

35. N. M. Sutherland, "The Origins of the Thirty Years War and the Structure of European Politics," *English Historical Review* 106 (July 1992): 615–16; J. V. Polišenský, *War and Society in Europe, 1618–1648* (Cambridge: Cambridge University Press, 1978), 58–60; Kenneth M. Selton, *Venice, Austria, and the Turks in the Seventeenth Century* (Philadelphia: American Philosophical Society, 1991), 35.

36. Brightwell, "Twelve Years' Truce."

37. Those seeing the war as part of the long-standing French-Hapsburg conflict include Sutherland, "Origins," 588–59; Wedgwood, *Thirty Years War*, 27; Steinberg, *Thirty Years' War*, 1–2; and Jonathan I. Israel, *Conflicts of Empires* (London: Hambledon, 1997), 64.

38. David Buisseret, *Henry IV* (London: Routledge, 1989), 178–79; Geoffrey Parker, *Europe in Crisis, 1598–1648* (Glasgow: Fontana, 1979), chap 4.

39. Parker, *Europe in Crisis*, 119.

40. J. P. Cooper, "General Introduction," in Cooper, ed., *The New Cambridge Modern History*, vol. 4 (Cambridge: Cambridge University Press, 1970), 14. By 1700, France's population would reach 19–20 million, while Spain's would fall to 6 million: Carl J. Friedrich, *The Age of Baroque, 1610–1660* (New York: Harper and Row, 1952), 5.

41. See Carlo M. Cipolla, *Before the Industrial Revolution*, 2d ed. (London: Methuen, 1981), chap. 10, and pp. 249, 261; Cooper, "General Introduction," 62–65; Niels Steensgaard, "The Seventeenth-Century Crisis," in Geoffrey Parker and Lesley M. Smith, eds., *The General Crisis of the Seventeenth Century* (London: Routledge, 1978), and Ivo Schöffer, "Did Holland's Golden Age Coincide with a Period of Crisis?" in ibid., 93–100.

42. See J. H. Elliott, *Spain and Its World* (New Haven: Yale University Press, 1989), esp. chaps. 6, 10, and 11.

43. Austria was already in financial trouble due to the accumulated debt from the 1593–1606 Austro-Turkish war. In fact, much of the religious conflict in Germany had a straightforward monetary root: many German princes did not want to pay the taxes resulting from such wars and other imperial expenditures. Geoffrey Parker, ed., *The Thirty Years' War*, 2d ed. (London: Routledge, 1997), 15; Parker, *Europe in Crisis*, 83; Sheilagh Ogilvie, "Germany and the Seventeenth Century," in Parker and Lesley M. Smith, eds., *The General Crisis of the Seventeenth Century*, 2d ed. (London: Routledge, 1997), 67–69.

44. Brightwell, "Spanish Origins"; Brightwell, "Twelve Years Truce"; Brightwell, "Spain, Bohemia, and Europe, 1619–21," *European Studies Review* 12 (October 1982): 371–99; Brightwell, "Spain and Bohemia: The Decision to Intervene," *European Studies Review* 12 (April 1982): 117–41.

45. The same month Spain occupied the strategic Valtelline passes through Switzerland.

46. Polišenský, *War*, 79–82.

47. Israel, *Conflicts*, chaps. 2–3.

48. Brightwell, "Spanish Origins," 426.

49. Quoted in Brightwell, "Twelve Years' Truce," 289.

50. Quoted in Brightwell, "Spain, Bohemia, and Europe," 386, 395.

51. Fernand Braudel, *The Wheels of Commerce* (New York: Harper and Row, 1982), 174; John Lynch, *Spain under the Habsburgs*, 2 vols. (New York: Oxford University Press, 1969), 2:74.

52. Quoted in Elliott, *Spain and Its World*, 253–54.

53. Ibid., chap. 11.

54. Ibid., 126; R. A. Stradling, *Spain's Struggle for Europe, 1598–1668* (London: Hambledon, 1994), 113.

55. Sweden's move was a defensive response to Olivares's plan, accepted by Austria in 1628, to build a Hapsburg fleet to challenge Dutch and Swedish control of Baltic trade. Parker, *Thirty Years War*, 94–95, 109.

56. Stradling, *Spain's Struggle*, 97–115; David Parrott, "The Causes of the Franco-Spanish War of 1635–59," in Jeremy Black, ed., *The Origins of War in Early Modern Europe* (Edinburgh: Donald, 1987), 92–103.

57. Parrott, "Causes of the Franco-Spanish War," 96.

58. Stradling, *Spain's Struggle*, 117 (Stradling borrows the phrase "master plan" from Elliott).

59. Quoted in ibid., 109.

60. Ibid., 116.

61. Parrott, "Causes of the Franco-Spanish War," 103–5; Ronald G. Asch, *The Thirty Years War* (New York: St. Martin's, 1997), 119–21.

62. Stradling, *Spain's Struggle*, 118. See also Olivares's argument in 1633 that France was plotting to destroy Hapsburg power: J. H. Elliott, *Richelieu and Olivares* (Cambridge: Cambridge University Press, 1984), 119.

63. J. H. Elliott, "The Decline of Spain," in Trevor Aston, ed., *Crisis in Europe, 1560–1660* (New York: Basic Books, 1965), 192.

64. Louis's legendary desire for *gloire* cannot be discounted completely as a cause of war, but two facts suggest that it was not determinative. First, French decision-making was collective: Louis led, but he relied heavily on the advice of ministers; John B. Wolf, *Louis XIV* (New York: Norton, 1968), passim. Second, when Louis invaded the eastern Rhineland in 1688–89, he immediately implemented a brutal scorched-earth policy. This action indicates that he hardly initiated war to promote his historical reputation; geopolitical concerns were dominant.

65. Quoted in Andrew Lossky, *Louis XIV and the French Monarchy* (New Brunswick: Rutgers University Press, 1994), 123.

66. Quoted in ibid., 129.

67. Ibid., 142–48; Paul Sonnino, "Louis XIV and the Dutch War," in Ragnhild Hatton, ed., *Louis XIV and Europe* (Columbus: Ohio State University Press, 1976); Wolf, *Louis*, 214–19; Peter Robert Campbell, *Louis XIV* (London: Longman, 1993), 63.

68. The war was not a major war by this book's definition. Like the Crimean War two centuries later, it was a limited conflict to maintain the regional territorial status quo, rather than a war of elimination involving all of the great powers at full mobilization.

69. Wolf, *Louis*, 194, 403–4; Campbell, *Louis*, 58–59; Lossky, *Louis*, 160.

70. J. S. Bromley, "Introduction," in Bromley, ed., *The New Cambridge Modern History*, vol. 6 (Cambridge: Cambridge University Press, 1971), 26; Jean Meuvret, "The Condition of France, 1688–1715," in ibid., 320; James B. Collins, *The State in Early Modern France* (Cambridge: Cambridge University Press, 1995), 122–23; Campbell, *Louis*, 5–6, 64; Pierre Goubert, *Louis XIV and Twenty Million Frenchmen* (New York: Vintage, 1966), 125, 148, 179–80; Lossky, *Louis*, 246; Geoffrey Symcox, "Louis XIV and the Outbreak of the Nine Years Wars," in Hatton, ed., *Louis XIV*, 179, 184; Wolf, *Louis*, 427.

71. Charles Woolsey Cole, *Colbert and a Century of French Mercantilism*, 2 vols. (New York: Columbia University Press, 1939); Inès Murat, *Colbert* (Charlottesville: University Press of Virginia, 1984), 236–41, 271–75; Glenn Ames, *Colbert, Mercantilism, and the French Quest for Asian Trade* (DeKalb: Northern Illinois University Press, 1996), 189; Goubert, *Louis*, 31.

72. Goubert, *Louis*, 180; Steensgaard, "Seventeenth-Century Crisis," 29.

73. Symcox, "Louis XIV," 185.

74. Statistics are problematic, but Paul Kennedy shows that, in 1689–90, France had

a significantly larger army than any other state and also the biggest navy: *The Rise and Fall of the Great Powers* (New York: Random House, 1987), 99. This would explain its ability to fight the system almost singlehandedly for twenty-five years. On French military superiority, see Campbell, *Louis*, 57; George Clark, "The Nine Years War, 1688–1697," in Bromley, ed., *New Cambridge Modern History*, 224–31; and Collins, *State in Early Modern France*, 123.

75. Symcox, "Louis XIV," 179; see also Wolf, *Louis*, 427.

76. Symcox, "Louis XIV," 183–88; John B. Wolf, *The Emergence of the Great Powers, 1685–1715* (New York: Harper and Row, 1951), 127–32.

77. Wolf, *Louis*, chap. 26; Lossky, *Louis*, 230.

78. Quoted in Lossky, *Louis*, 179.

79. Ibid., 176–81, 220–38; Wolf, *Emergence*, 35.

80. Quoted in Symcox, "Louis XIV," 187.

81. Quoted in ibid., 194.

82. Ibid., 196–98; Lossky, *Louis*, 230–31.

83. Quoted in Wolf, *Louis*, 650.

84. Quoted in ibid., 649.

85. See ibid., 427–44; Symcox, "Louis XIV"; Lossky, *Louis*, 230–31; Paul Sonnino, "The Origins of Louis XIV's Wars," in Black, ed., *Origins*, 123–25; Selton, *Austria*, 389–91; and Collins, *State in Early Modern Europe*, 122–27.

86. Quoted in Wolf, *Emergence*, 34.

87. George Clark, "From the Nine Years War to the War of the Spanish Succession," in Bromley, ed., *New Cambridge Modern History*, 396.

88. See ibid., 384–403; Lossky, *Louis*, chap. 11; Sonnino, "Origins of Louis XIV's Wars," 127–29; and Wolf, *Louis*, chap. 29. On France's long-standing interest in capturing Spanish and Mediterranean trade, see Goubert, *Louis*, 100, 185, 224–29; Charles Woolsey Cole, *French Mercantilism, 1683–1700* (New York: Columbia University Press, 1943), 22–32 and passim; Cole, *Colbert*, 1:383–415; Ames, *Colbert, Mercantilism*, 187–89; and Lossky, *Louis*, 104, 246–52.

89. Wolf, *Louis*, 231.

90. The War of Polish Succession (1733–35) and the War of Austrian Succession (1740–48) were not major wars by my definition. Both were wars of position driven largely by French efforts to compensate for Austrian territorial gains in the 1713 Treaty of Utrecht.

91. Walter L. Dorn, *Competition for Empire, 1740–1763* (New York: Harper and Row, 1963), 300.

92. Gordon A. Craig, *The Politics of the Prussian Army, 1640–1945* (London: Oxford University Press, 1955), chaps. 1–3.

93. Dennis Showalter, *The Wars of Frederick the Great* (London: Longman, 1996), 91.

94. Quoted in William J. McGill, "The Roots of Policy: Kaunitz in Vienna and Versailles, 1749–1753," *Journal of Modern History* 43 (June 1971): 232; see also Showalter, *Wars*, 91.

95. On Kaunitz's "grand design," see Dorn, *Competition*, 296–99; McGill, "Roots of Policy"; and Showalter, *Wars*, 90–93, 116–34.

96. Showalter, *Wars*, 131; Dorn, *Competition*, 308.

97. These figures are drawn from Herbert H. Kaplan, *Russia and the Outbreak of the Seven Years' War* (Berkeley: University of California Press, 1968), 85–92. On Russian fears of Prussia, see ibid., 32, 39; Dorn, *Competition*, 310; and Showalter, *Wars*, 130.

98. Karl Schweizer, "The Seven Years' War," in Black, ed., *Origins*, 252–53; G. P. Gooch, *Frederick the Great, the Ruler, the Writer, the Man* (Hamden, Conn.: Archon, 1947), 34–35; Showalter, *Wars*, 131–32; Herbert Butterfield, *The Reconstruction of a Historical Episode* (Glasgow: Jackson, 1951), 23.

99. See Kaplan, *Russia*, 80–82, 91–93, and Dorn, *Competition*, 316.

100. Kaplan's words, *Russia*, 92–93.

101. Frederick Le Grand, *Oeuvres de Frederick Le Grand*, vol. 26 (Berlin: Chez Rodolphe Decker, 1855), doc. 42, p. 115.

102. Dorn, *Competition*, 312–13.

103. Schweizer, "Origins of Seven Years' War," 245.

104. Showalter, *Wars*, 93–94.

105. This is a relaxation of the third parameter set out in chapter 2—the probability of the rising state attacking later—as a result of this state's unit-level characteristics.

106. Perhaps the closest is the formation of the German reich after victories in 1866 and 1870. This state's land mass, however, was many times that of Prussia's in 1756. Moreover, Bismarck's moderate peace terms made the other great powers at least somewhat uncertain about Germany's future intentions, and thus less able to overcome the fears of abandonment that naturally attend coalitional offensive-war preparations.

107. For analysis and references, see Stephen M. Walt, *Revolution and War* (Ithaca: Cornell University Press, 1996), chap. 3.

108. Paul Kennedy, *The Rise and Fall of British Naval Mastery* (London: Ashfield, 1976), 97–98, 106–7, 118–20; David S. Landes, *The Unbound Prometheus* (Cambridge: Cambridge University Press, 1969), 125; Georges Levebre, *Napoleon* (New York: Columbia University Press, 1969), 45–56; E. J. Hobsbawm, *Industry and Empire* (Harmondsworth: Penguin, 1968), 49–54.

109. Clive Trebilcock, *The Industrialization of the Continental Powers, 1780–1914* (London: Longman, 1981), chap. 3, esp. 114–33.

110. Kennedy, *Rise and Fall of the Great Powers*, 149.

111. Louis Bergeron, *France under Napoleon* (Princeton: Princeton University Press, 1981), 109–13; Kennedy, *Rise and Fall of Naval Mastery*, 117; Kennedy, *Rise and Fall of the Great Powers*, 99. By the 1890s, Britain's population would surpass France's (table A.2, appendix).

112. Olwen Hufton, *Europe: Privilege and Protest* (Ithaca: Cornell University Press, 1980), 126–29.

113. Steven T. Ross, *European Diplomatic History, 1789–1815* (Garden City, N.Y.: Anchor, 1969), chap. 5; R. M. Johnston, ed., *The Corsican: A Diary of Napoleon's Life in His Own Words* (Boston: Houghton, Mifflin, 1910), 75 (hereafter cited as *Diary*).

114. J. Christopher Herold, ed., *The Mind of Napoleon* (New York: Columbia University Press, 1955), 51–52.

115. Napoléon Bonaparte, *Correspondance de Napoléon 1er*, 32 vols. (Paris: Imprimerie Impériale, 1858–70), 3:392 (hereafter cited as *CN*); see also 376. In a conversation in 1798, Napoleon reportedly exclaimed: "If my voice has any influence, England will never have an hour's respite from us. . . . War to the death with England! Always—until she is destroyed!": Herold, *Mind of Napoleon*, 191.

116. *Diary*, 124.

117. J. M. Thompson, ed., *Napoleon's Letters* (London: Prion, 1998), 65. Eight months later, he wrote the czar to encourage him to challenge British economic domination (ibid., 67; see also his November 1805 letter to the Austrian emperor, ibid., 113).

118. Arnold Harvey, "The Continental Images of Britain," in Frank A. Kafker and James M. Laux, eds., *Napoleon and His Times* (Malabar: Krieger, 1989).

119. *CN*, 8:618–20; see also 616.

120. 28 October 1803, *Diary*, 163.

121. 12 November 1803, *CN*, 9:89.

122. See David Gates, *The Napoleonic Wars, 1803–1815* (London: Arnold, 1997), x; Fe-

lix Markham, *Napoleon and the Awakening of Europe* (New York: Collier, 1965), 70, 92–94; and Kennedy, *Rise and Fall of the Great Powers*, 99.

123. See his note, 19 February 1802, *CN*, 7:395.

124. See Ross, *Diplomatic History*, 241–42, and *CN*, 7: passim.

125. *CN*, 7:435–36.

126. See ibid., 395.

127. J. Christopher Herold, *The Age of Napoleon* (New York: American Heritage, 1963), 155.

128. P. Coquelle, *Napoleon and England, 1803–1813* (London: Bell, 1904), 39, 52.

129. *CN*, 8:326, 354–56; see also 288. In late 1802, he had already requested information on the state of British coastal defenses (*Diary*, 165).

130. Quoted in Desmond Seward, *Napoleon and Hitler* (New York: Touchstone, 1988), 166; Alan Schom, *Napoleon Bonaparte* (New York: Harper, 1997), 321–22.

131. Alistair Horne, *How Far From Austerlitz? Napoleon, 1805–1815* (New York: St. Martin's, 1996), 67.

132. *CN*, 11:87.

133. See *Diary*, 204; Albert Carr, ed., *Napoleon Speaks* (New York: Viking, 1941), 206–7; and Markham, *Napoleon*, 72.

134. In late August he stated that after finishing with Austria he would "get back to my original plans" of destroying England. Quoted in André Castelot, *Napoleon* (New York: Harper and Row, 1971), 264.

135. Paul W. Schroeder, *The Transformation of European Politics, 1763–1848* (Oxford: Clarendon, 1994), 307–10; Markham, *Napoleon*, 93; Levebre, *Napoleon*, 194–98; Trebilcock, *Industrialization*, 129; Seward, *Napoleon*, 165, 173.

136. Mary Loyd, ed., *New Letters of Napoleon I* (New York: Appleton, 1897), 45–47; Schroeder, *Transformation*, 326.

137. Schroeder, *Transformation*, 419–21.

138. Ibid., 405, 416–21; Eugene Tarle, *Napoleon's Invasion of Russia, 1812* (New York: Oxford University Press, 1942), 5, 38–39; Schom, *Napoleon*, 583–84; Seward, *Napoleon*, 196–98.

139. *Diary*, 333. See also his letter to the czar in February 1811, ibid., 336, and his note to his foreign minister in March, in Loyd, *New Letters*, 227.

140. Markham, *Napoleon*, 109–10; Schom, *Napoleon*, chap. 33; Tarle, *Napoleon's Invasion*, 55. An additional incentive was Napoleon's fear that Russia would grow if not constrained by the Continental System and by a Polish buffer state. In retirement on St. Helena, Napoleon reportedly stated that he worried in 1811–12 that Russia, with its huge army, would push eastward with all its weight. A strong Poland would act as a barrier "against that formidable empire which threatened sooner or later to subjugate Europe." Quoted in Somerset de Clair, ed., *Napoleon on Napoleon* (London: Cassell, 1992), 219, 227. See also Herold, *Mind of Napoleon*, 195–98, 201–2.

9. THE IMPLICATIONS OF THE ARGUMENT

1. Imre Lakatos, "Falsification and the Methodology of Scientific Research Programmes," in Lakatos and Alan Musgrave, eds., *Criticism and the Growth of Knowledge* (Cambridge: Cambridge University Press, 1970).

2. Waltz, *Theory of International Politics* (New York: Random House, 1979), 69–71, 121–23.

3. This book focuses primarily on the behavior of strong and declining states. In other work, I offer more detail about the behavior of great powers that are lower-

ranked or rising in relative power. See Dale C. Copeland, "From Structural Realism to Dynamic Realism," paper delivered at the International Studies Association annual meeting, Toronto, March 1997; Copeland, "Deterrence, Reassurance, and Machiavellian Appeasement," paper presented at the conference "Deterrence in Enduring Rivalries," sponsored by *Security Studies*, Washington, D.C., March 1996.

4. Recall as well that hegemonic stability theory cannot explain why it was the declining state that provoked each of these conflicts.

5. See the methodological discussion of chapter 1.

6. This, very briefly, restates the normative and structural explanations for the democratic peace. See Bruce Russett, *Grasping the Democratic Peace* (Princeton: Princeton University Press, 1993); Michael E. Brown, Sean M. Lynn-Jones, and Steven E. Miller, eds., *Debating the Democratic Peace* (Cambridge: MIT Press, 1996); John M. Owen, *Liberal Peace, Liberal War* (Ithaca: Cornell University Press, 1998); Miriam Fendius Elman, ed., *Paths to Peace: Is Democracy the Answer?* (Cambridge: MIT Press, 1997); and Randall L. Schweller, "Domestic Structure and Preventive War," *World Politics* 44 (January 1992): 235–69.

7. This qualifies Jack Snyder and Edward Mansfield's argument that democratization increases the probability of war: "Democratization and the Danger of War," *International Security* 20 (summer 1995): 5–38. They argue that democratizing states start wars as a result of the diversionary motives arising from the democratizing process. My argument, focusing on the preventive motives of declining states, suggests that rising and democratizing states can help *reduce* the likelihood of war versus what it would be were unit-level factors not considered.

8. There is no proper test of this proposition, since there has not yet been a system of all democratic great powers. My argument is therefore a purely deductive one, but one that follows from the logic of democratic peace theory.

9. Other liberal and constructivist variables can also be important. International institutions, for example, can help build a level of trust even between nondemocracies. Between democracies, they can instantiate shared identities and security communities that mitigate the effects of rise and decline. Still, given the problem of future intentions, a declining state's sense of long-term security will be most dependent on the estimated stability of the other's regime-type. Institutions and security communities will therefore have perhaps their strongest effects if they are able to strengthen the democratic structures within each of the states. See Emanuel Adler and Michael Barnett, eds., *Security Communities* (Cambridge: Cambridge University Press, 1998).

10. See esp. John J. Mearsheimer, "Back to the Future," *International Security* 15 (summer 1990): 5–56, and Aaron L. Friedberg, "Ripe for Rivalry: Prospects for Peace in a Multipolar Asia," *International Security* 18 (winter 1993–94): 5–33.

11. See Copeland, "Neorealism and the Myth of Bipolar Stability," *Security Studies* 5 (spring 1996): 29–89.

12. Revelations in 1999 that China has used spying to improve its knowledge of modern nuclear weaponry have heightened U.S. anxiety. On the growth of China, see statistics in International Institute for Strategic Studies, *The Military Balance* (London: Oxford University Press, 1987–99); Gerald Segal, "East Asia and the 'Constrainment' of China," *International Security* 20 (spring 1996): 107–35; Richard Bernstein and Ross H. Munro, *The Coming Conflict with China* (New York: Knopf, 1997); Andrew J. Nathan and Robert S. Ross, *The Great Wall and the Empty Fortress* (New York: Norton, 1997); and William Overholt, *The Rise of China* (New York: Norton, 1993).

13. See Francis Fukuyama, *The End of History and the Last Man* (New York: Avon, 1992).

14. See n. 6.

15. For references, see Dale C. Copeland, "Economic Interdependence and War," *International Security* 20 (spring 1996): 5–41.

16. Robert O. Keohane and Lisa L. Martin, "The Promise of Institutionalist Theory," *International Security* 20 (summer 1995): 39–51; George W. Downs, ed., *Collective Security beyond the Cold War* (Ann Arbor: University of Michigan Press, 1994)

17. See Joseph S. Nye, *Bound to Lead* (New York: Basic Books, 1991).

18. See Copeland, "Realism and the Origins of Major War" (Ph.D. diss., University of Chicago, 1993), chaps. 5–6.

19. See Paul Krugman, "The Myth of Asia's Miracle," *Foreign Affairs* 73 (November–December 1994): 62–78.

20. By comparison, Japan's small size imposes severe limits on its resources and its counterforce capability.

21. My argument may seem to bear some resemblance to the hegemonic stability thesis. Note, however, that the basis for stability is not American hegemony per se but the fact that the United States, as the dominant state, is not declining deeply and inevitably. As figures 1 and 2 in chapter 1 show, any system where the power trends are flat should be stable. Conversely, when the dominant state foresees significant decline, marked preponderance makes this state *more* dangerous, since it stands more chance of winning any major war that occurs.

22. China's rising economic interdependence, tied to positive expectations for future trade, has helped to promote stability. But the liberal model, by focusing solely on levels of interdependence, ignores the potential for such interdependence to foster conflict as well as peace. See Copeland, "Economic Interdependence and War," and "Trade Expectations and the Future of U.S.-Chinese Relations," paper presented at conference "Emerging International Relations in the Asia-Pacific Region," Dartmouth College, October 1998.

23. I continue to focus on the U.S.-China dyad, but the logic would still apply (with caveats regarding domestic structure) to the rise of other great powers.

24. If China's economy goes into a severe downturn, however, Chinese policy should become more conflictual.

25. Since power is relative, the United States will decline even if its absolute growth rate is positive, as long as China's absolute rate remains even stronger.

26. In terms of the theory, this is a relaxation of the assumption of a neutral offense-defense balance.

27. That is, the severity of decline is an independent variable, not a dependent variable. Of course, the more inferior the dominant military state is in potential power, the more likely its decline will be deep and inevitable.

28. Most obviously, realists disagree as to whether balances of power are stabilizing (classical realists and neorealists) or destabilizing (hegemonic stability theorists).

Index

à quatre negotiations (1914), 92, 97, 100–101
accidental war, 44. *See also* inadvertent war
accidents, 45, 103, 182
accommodation. *See* conciliation; engagement
Acheson, Dean, 163, 166, 173, 195
Adenauer, Konrad, 183
Albertini, Luigi, 74, 79, 112, 278n113
alliances, 4, 6, 38, 40, 47, 50, 52, 261n55; bipolarity and, 11–12, 55, 261n57; chain-ganging, 12, 261n52; classical realism and, 11–12, 55, 238; collective action problem and, 16, 23–24, 51, 261nn52, 54, 57; flexibility in, 11; hegemonic stability theory and, 14; multipolarity and, 11, 16–17, 261n56; offensive, 24, 261nn56, 57; restructuring of, 11, 41, 47–48; sideline-sitting and, 5, 17, 23–24
Allied Control Council, 169–70
anarchy, 12, 23, 49
Arab-Israeli War of 1967, 45
armored warfare, 127–28, 136
arms racing, 4, 6, 10, 11–12, 37, 38; economic and potential power and, 20, 40–41; relative success in, 6, 47–48, 50, 51. *See also* oscillations in power
arms spending. *See* arms racing; military spending
Art, Robert, 261n49, 287n5
assumptions: of dynamic differentials theory, 15, 29–32, 37–38; implication of relaxation of, 29, 238–40
Athens, 2, 9, 12, 21, 22, 44, 49–50, 149, 210–11, 236, 303nn9, 14
atomic bomb, 163, 171–72; diplomacy and, 156–59; dropping of, 150, 156, 157–59, 167, 170; Interim Committee and, 152, 157; sharing of secrets regarding, 150, 152–64, 167–68. *See also* cold war; nuclear weapons
audience costs, 45, 46. *See also* game theory
Austria-Hungary: and blank check from Berlin, 82–83; desire of, to avoid war with Russia, 63, 80, 88, 100–101, 109; German concerns regarding will to fight of, 59, 63, 67, 71, 79, 80–81, 85–90, 97, 100–101, 104, 105–9, 113–14; ultimatum to Serbia by, 57, 84, 85–87, 90, 93

balance of power, 2, 7, 11–13, 35–36, 48, 55, 236, 238. *See also specific nations*
balancing. *See* alliances; arms racing
Balkans: crises in 1912–13 in, 56–59, 62, 65, 72–75, 82; First Balkan War and, 72–74; Second Balkan War and, 73–75
Ball, George, 202–3
Beck, Ludwig von, 125–28, 130–32, 138, 282n45, 283n76
beliefs, 25, 45–46; testing and, 31–33. *See also* costly signals; irrationality; misperceptions
Berchtold, Leopold von, 72–75, 86, 88, 99–102
Berghahn, Volker, 75, 78
Berlin crises (1948, 1958–61), 179–81, 181–86; East German economic decline and, 182–86; relation of, to Korean War, 179; risk of major war and, 182; Soviet fear of West Germany and, 179–80, 182–83; tank confrontation and, 182
Berlin Wall, 181–82, 185
Bernhardi, Friedrich von, 61, 67, 272n76